TRUMAN CAPOTE'S IN COLD BLOOD: A CRITICAL HANDBOOK

TRUMAN CAPOTE'S IN COLD BLOOD: A CRITICAL HANDBOOK

edited by

Irving Malin

City College of New York

Wadsworth Publishing Company, Inc.

Belmont, California

1968

L. C. Cat. Card No.: 68–11952

Printed in the United States of America by American Book–Stratford Press, Inc.

For Betty and Al Nack,
who took me places

PREFACE

Although *In Cold Blood* can be read as a "simple thriller," it can also be studied as a complex work dealing with the nature of "fact" and "fiction." Does it give us reality? Is it artificial? Can Capote be objective? Such questions, raised by many of the selections reprinted here, force the student to think more carefully about the writing process.

In Cold Blood deals with the violence of American life. By juxtaposing (very neatly?) good citizens and criminals, Capote captures those social tensions we often forget. I hope that the selections by Friedenberg, Baumbach, and others will help the student to confront the "public" ambiguities of *In Cold Blood* and American life in general.

I have arranged this handbook in a simple manner. Part 1 consists of various interviews and background materials; the "nonfiction novel" and the Clutter murders are viewed from strikingly different perspectives. Even Capote himself apparently "changes" as he discusses his work. Part 2 moves closer to *In Cold Blood* itself, but it avoids easy answers. The ten reviewers disagree about the form and quality of Capote's achievement

—some consider *In Cold Blood* a "lightweight" effort; others praise it as a "grave and reverend" book. In the attempt to choose sides the student may have to refer to *Other Voices, Other Rooms; A Tree of Night,* etc. Part 3, therefore, contains long essays on Capote's previous novels and stories, an early interview, and "A Tree of Night." What are the connections between Gothic fiction and *In Cold Blood*? Do these help us to see the new work as the culmination of Capote's literary career? Part 4 takes one theme of *In Cold Blood*—the violence of American life—and demonstrates how journalists and short-story writers have explored the theme. These selections don't evade the problem of "fact" and "fiction"—they suggest that *Time* and Flannery O'Connor, for example, describe murder and madness differently. At the end of this handbook I have posed questions for study, discussion, and writing in the belief that these will help the student to understand more thoroughly the twenty-seven selections in the handbook and the book *In Cold Blood* itself.

To facilitate use of the handbook for the controlled-research paper, the original pagination of articles and reviews is indicated by numbers in brackets. The bracketed number before the virgule (/) indicates the end of the original page; the number after it signals the beginning of a new page. Bracketed numbers are not used in the much-reprinted Capote, Poe, and O'Connor short stories or in the Galloway, Friedman, Morris, and Baumbach pieces, which have never appeared in print before.

CONTENTS

4
Murder in America: Fact and Fiction

5
Questions and Bibliography

TRUMAN CAPOTE'S IN COLD BLOOD: A CRITICAL HANDBOOK

1. BACKGROUND OF
IN COLD BLOOD

A Farmer Looks at Farming 1954

C. B. PALMER

INTO THE GREAT, WHITE, TOWERING CYLINDERS OF THE GRAIN ELEVATORS
—"the skyscrapers of the prairies"—there is now pouring a torrent of
grain. Truckloads, carloads, tons, bushels of the produce of the fertile
land flow steadily and relentlessly into storage. Of wheat alone, the
headlines in the Kansas papers say such things as: "Bins Spill Over"
and "Thousands of Box Cars Filled With Harvest Yield Jam Terminals
Here."

The Government alone now owns or has under pledge through its
price support program 906 million bushels of wheat. To this must be
added 222 million bushels privately owned on farms, in grain elevators
and mills. And to this must soon be added this year's wheat crop,
estimated at nearly a billion bushels.

In varying degrees, the story is the same in other commodities.
The Government owns: 810 million bushels of corn, 7.8 million bales
of cotton, 619 million pounds of tobacco, 100 million pounds of rice,
255 million pounds of peanuts, 364 million pounds of butter, 361
million pounds of cheese, 656 million pounds of dried milk. The value
placed on all these is more than $6 billion.

What are we going to do about it? For many years now, the
farmers have been geared to growing more and more food to help feed
the world. Now they are being required to cut back their plantings,
because the surpluses pile up here, because other countries are in a
position to export after being out of production during World War II,
because economic barriers prevent ready distribution of food to needy
areas.

While political leaders and economists discuss ways and means of
meeting the problem, it is worth while listening to a man who is in the
business of growing food, who has tied his fortunes to the vagaries of
weather and world trade. Here in western Kansas, not far from the
Colorado border, there is a wheat farmer who is in an unusual position

From *The New York Times Sunday Magazine*, August 1, 1954, pp. 8, 23, 24.
© 1954 by The New York Times Company. Reprinted by permission of The New
York Times Company and C. B. Palmer.

to talk about the problem. His name is Herbert W. Clutter and he runs a large and successful operation, somewhat diversified, but with wheat as his mainstay. His background is solidly agricultural. He was born on a farm near here, spent his youth a little farther east, took his degree in agronomy and economics at Kansas State College.

Now in his early forties, he is spare, quick and dynamic in appearance. And his experience is notably varied. He is a former president and now secretary of the National Wheat Growers Association; served on Secretary Benson's Wheat Advisory Committee last year; is on the U.S. Department of Agriculture's Grain Advisory Committee; is a director of the Farm Credit Administration for the district covering Kansas, New Mexico, Oklahoma and Colorado and is an officer or member of half a dozen other farm groups.

His farm undertakings are impressive. By ownership or rental he farms land representing an investment of nearly half a million dollars; he owns machinery valued at more than $45,000; his annual operating budget runs between $65,000 and $70,000 exclusive of his cattle, of which he feeds 500 head a year for a further commitment of about $50,000. He has six full-time employes, plus extras in busy seasons; with his own wife and four children this means that thirty-five people are dependent on his farm's success.

This part of Kansas is in what is known as a "high-risk" area because of its chancy rainfall, and Mr. Clutter's experience over recent years shows the term is well earned. Not since 1951 has this locality had rainfall that came up to normal. In 1952, thanks to the carryover of moisture in the ground from the previous year, Mr. Clutter harvested a very satisfactory 42,000 bushels of wheat (his best yield was 50,000 in 1947). Since then there has been a steady drop and his present harvest which he calls "practically a failure" will run about 13,000 bushels.

Yet this does not represent the disaster it might to another farmer. For Mr. Clutter is a meticulous planner and husbandman. He has managed to save from the good years for the lean ones and moreover his other crops provide a cushion against a poor wheat harvest. He farms both dry and irrigated land; he grows alfalfa, maize and barley; he grows grass not only for pasture but for certified seed which he sells. The cattle he fattens on the feed he grows are a cash crop. For every bit of land he cultivates he has a "cropping plan" looking ahead three years.

And for one final measure of the tidy economy he runs there is the example of his irrigation from deep wells. There is plenty of water under his land but normally it would be fairly costly to pump up. But a while ago Mr. Clutter leased drilling rights to a natural gas company. In exchange he was entitled to a one-eighth share of the profits. But he uses some of the gas himself to run a big pump. He is charged for this gas of course, but the cost runs slightly under his royalty receipts. So he is getting both gas and water for nothing.

For all this, his style of living is by no means lavish; he doesn't have a "Cadillac pick-up just to run errands" as some folks might think. His Dodge sedan is a couple of years old, and it is the only family car.

The home is quite new, of yellow brick and white clapboard, set down on a pleasant site which Mr. Clutter is trying to find time to landscape. The interior is clean and fresh, the living room being furnished in blond wood even to the spinet-sized piano. His farm lands are in various locations round-about, some of them nine miles to the north and one piece thirty miles to the east.

The whole layout is tidy, efficient and unpretentious. There is little evidence of the wealth this land produces. In fact, the teen-age daughters who are doing the housekeeping while the mother is away convalescing from a stay in the hospital complain about "that old refrigerator," which Mr. Clutter ruefully admits needs replacing.

At one end of the house is a full-fledged office, befitting the size and efficiency of Mr. Clutter's operations and complete with desk, filing cabinets where he keeps his elaborate records, and bookshelves of reference works.

Sitting here, he talked about the farm situation from both the personal and national viewpoints. He explained that he had [8/23] been a lifelong Republican and still was, but "on some things about farming I'm sort of a radical fellow." Certainly he spoke with warmth on some topics.

"For one thing," he said, "some people talk about farm surpluses as though there was something regrettable or shameful about them. I think we should be grateful that our country is fertile enough to produce surpluses. They are of great value in that they are part of our strength; where a people are sure of having enough to eat you have political stability.

"There's no doubt that we have faults in our distribution system, but"—and here he sighed—"I wish people would stop trying political solutions to an economic problem."

He is convinced that there is too little understanding of the farmer's place in our economy. They are asked to assure a steady flow of the essential foods, yet, he says, they are constantly being squeezed between nature on the one hand and the general economy on the other.

"Look at the natural hazards we face. Too little rain; high winds that not only dry out the land but can shred a crop standing in the fields. There are all the insects and fungus diseases which can wipe us out. A hailstorm can destroy a year's work."

It is a familiar saying that "all farmers are gamblers." But in Mr. Clutter's view a lot of the gamble is taken on behalf of other people— to keep the food flowing to market—and no adequate recompense is offered. Parity prices are set once a year, but prices of the things a

farmer has to buy can fluctuate before the next adjustment is made—
"and those prices don't come down." He also finds a certain inequity in
taxes: "A business man with an industrial plant is given a generous
allowance for depreciation, writing off the cost long before the plant is
worn out. I only wish a farmer could do that. My land deteriorates
unless I spend money to keep it replenished. Moreover, I'm supposed
to preserve my farm for future generations; they are going to need it. I
can't use it up and leave it.

"A lot of wage-earners now have contracts which adjust to the cost
of living—which is the same idea as parity prices for farmers. Many
businesses get subsidies directly or indirectly because they are considered essential to the national welfare. Yet the farmers, certainly a
mainstay of the nation, are criticized for wanting firm protection and
support. As a matter of philosophy, a farmer pays 100 per cent [23/24]
for what he buys, why shouldn't he get 100 per cent of parity, in
other words be sure of maintaining his standard of living?"

There are plenty, of course, who would argue with that, including
Secretary Benson. His proposal was that price supports be flexible,
ranging between 75 per cent and 90 per cent, depending on supplies
on hand or to be anticipated. This, coupled with sharp percentage
cutbacks in the acreage a farmer may put into wheat, was intended to
start reducing the surpluses, and developing new markets.

To this, Mr. Clutter says: "I can't see it working that way. Cutting
acreage doesn't necessarily cut bushels. And neither does cutting
prices. A man who is told to plant only a certain percentage of his
present acreage in wheat can simply—if he can swing it—take on more
acreage and get about the same net harvest. Any farmer anywhere can
operate an exempt fifteen acres, free of any regulation. If he puts that
into wheat in Ohio or Indiana he can get as much as fifty bushels an
acre, against fifteen bushels for a dry farmer in the West. If enough
farmers did that you could still end up with a big surplus—and the
dry farmer would probably be forced out of business.

"The same with cutting prices; a man simply puts in extra effort to
make up the difference. We had wheat selling at 25 cents a bushel in
the Thirties; every farmer who could simply grew more wheat to bring
up his income.

"And there is one more factor that I think gives a completely false
aspect to our price policy. Apparently it is not very well known in the
East that all wheat, of any quality from the highest to the lowest,
commands the same support price. In other words, the Government
pays as much for the cattle-feed grades as it does for the top bread
grades; and it happens that the lower grades predominate. So there
you have a completely false value for the Government's holdings, a
completely unrealistic expenditure of Government money. Can you
imagine an automobile dealer giving the same allowance on a low-
bracket 1940 car and a high-bracket 1952?"

Mr. Clutter is by no means opposed to all aspects of the farm program. He believes strongly in the soil-conservation projects, in the crop loan program, in rural electrification (he does not approve this year's cut in R. E. A. funds). He does not believe that the Government should do everything; he feels there is room for private enterprise.

But, he says, there are certain fundamentals in our policy that have been wrong for years and should be corrected.

First, "We must make a differentiation in values"; that is, wheat should be graded and supported in some relation to the market demand.

Second, "We must get away from the acreage concept in controlling crops," that is, be more realistic and selective.

Third, "The farmer must have some sort of guarantees, but he need not be completely underwritten." On this point Mr. Clutter describes a plan he says has much support among other farmers.

The plan is called "domestic parity." It calls for no Government funds but it might use Government machinery for its administration. Under this plan half the wheat crop, those 500 million bushels which are used for domestic, human consumption, would have 100 per cent parity value. It would be bought by the millers at whatever the going price, but when it was shipped to the bakers the difference between market and parity would be made up and the money put into a fund for distribution to the growers. The other half of the wheat crop would have no parity guarantees at all and would be sold in the free market.

Mr. Clutter says this would have the advantage of discouraging the planting of the lower grades, used mostly for feed (which would also please the corn growers, who don't like the competition in this line). Another advantage, he feels, is that the plan would take price setting out of national politics; the farmers themselves would determine policy, perhaps on a commodity-by-commodity basis rather than across the board.

The plan may be a long time coming, if it ever does. Farmers are classically independent, indeed mutually competitive, and they do not readily resort to common action. "But," says Mr. Clutter, "this is increasingly an organized world, and the farmers will have to organize to survive in it." [24]

Wealthy Farmer, Three of Family Slain

HOLCOMB, KAN., Nov. 15 (UPI)—A wealthy wheat farmer, his wife and their two young children were found shot to death today in their home. They had been killed by shotgun blasts at close range after being bound and gagged.

The father, 48-year-old Herbert W. Clutter, was found in the basement with his son, Kenyon, 15. His wife, Bonnie, 45, and a daughter, Nancy, 16, were in their beds.

There were no signs of a struggle, and nothing had been stolen. The telephone lines had been cut.

"This is apparently the case of a psychopathic killer," Sheriff Earl Robinson said.

Mr. Clutter was founder of the Kansas Wheat Growers Association. In 1954 President Eisenhower appointed him to the Federal Farm Credit Board, but he never lived in Washington.

The board represents the twelve farm credit districts in the country. Mr. Clutter served from December, 1953, until April, 1957. He declined a reappointment.

He was also a local member of the Agriculture Department's Price Stabilization Board and was active with the Great Plains Wheat Growers Association.

The Clutter farm and ranch cover almost 1,000 acres in one of the richest wheat areas.

Mr. Clutter, his wife and daughter were clad in pajamas. The boy was wearing blue jeans and a T-shirt.

The bodies were discovered by two of Nancy's classmates, Susan Kidwell and Nancy Ewalt.

Sheriff Robinson said the last reported communication with Mr. Clutter took place last night about 9:30 P.M., when the victim called Gerald Van Vleet, his business partner, who lives near by. Mr. Van Vleet said the conversation had concerned the farm and ranch.

Two daughters were away. They are Beverly, a student at Kansas University, and Mrs. Donald G. Jarchow of Mount Carroll, Ill. [39]

America's Worst Crime
in Twenty Years

RICHARD EUGENE HICKOCK *as told to* MACK NATIONS

This is a story of sheer depravity. It is so amoral that upon first recital I could not believe it in spite of 25 years spent viewing the worst people in my capacity as a working newspaper reporter.

It is the story of Richard Eugene "Dick" Hickock who at 29 years of age has been on Death Row at the State Penitentiary, Lansing, Kansas, for a year and four months. With average luck he will be there another 10 or 12 months before he is hanged.

Dick Hickock was the instigator of four of the most brutal murders ever committed in the modern history of this country. The slayings were carefully premeditated, intricately planned and mercilessly executed. Only a threat by his partner in the crime prevented Hickock from raping one of his victims—an attractive teen-age girl with whom he spent 30 minutes discussing her church and school activities—before blasting her and three members of her family into Eternity.

Every word of his story was written by Dick Hickock and his vivid description of the emotions he experienced in planning, executing and trying to escape the consequences of murder is without precedent. Following scores of visits with him in the Death House, as well as an exhausting six-month investigation, I am convinced he believes every word he wrote is true.

In this story, Dick Hickock reveals—without reservation—every thought, emotion, action and reaction he encountered during the plotting and execution of the murder of four members of a western Kansas family. The victims were 48-year-old Herbert Clutter, a moderately wealthy farmer and cattleman; his 45-year-old wife, Mrs. Bonnie Clutter; and his two children, Nancy, 16, and 15-year-old Kenyon. [31/76]

Shortly after midnight on November 15, 1959, these four were methodically and ruthlessly beheaded by a close-range shotgun blast while bound hand and foot in their farm home at the outskirts of Holcomb, Kansas. In addition the throat of Herbert Clutter was "sawed on" with a knife by both of his assailants prior to his being shot. The bodies were not discovered for some eight hours after commission of the murders.

Because of the unbelievably brutal method used in slaying the family,

From *Male*, XI (December 1961), 30–31, 76–83. Reprinted by permission of Magazine Management Company.

law enforcement officers assumed the murderer was a psychopathic killer who had quenched the thirst of a long-standing grudge against the Clutters. So convincing was this evidence that officers at first refused to believe the man who gave them the names and motives of the killers. The story came from a convict in the State Penitentiary who had at one time worked for Herbert Clutter. That man was also a former cellmate of Dick Hickock and was present when Hickock first conceived his plan for killing four persons he had never seen.

This story has been supplemented with considerable testimony from the trial of Dick Hickock and his partner, Perry Edward Smith, both of whom were convicted on four counts of first degree murder. The material from the trial was taken directly from the official trial transcript.

You will observe glaring discrepancies in the story of Dick Hickock and you will be shocked by his brilliant description of the ugly, brutal and stupid crimes he committed.

But in the end you will undoubtedly conclude, as I did, that Richard Hickock is a product of your society and mine. He is responsible for his deeds. We are responsible for understanding what he did and why he did it—in the hope that someday, we can help his kind to rid themselves of the black desires that torment them.

AS MY PARTNER AND I TURNED WEST INTO THE ROAD LEADING TO THE Clutter house I turned off the lights. I figured there was no need to announce our arrival if we didn't have to.

There was a bright moon that night and I could see the roadway well. The first building I saw was the Clutter house. It was a large two-story affair and it appeared to be fairly new. What next took my eye was a building some distance to the west of the main house. There was a light burning in the second building.

My buddy Perry said he didn't like the setup. I didn't either but we had gone too far to back out now. I knew from the diagram that the house with the light belonged to the hired man and his family. But it was closer to the Clutter house than it was supposed to be. I turned the car around and drove back down the roadway. I told Perry that this guy must really be loaded. He was supposed to be wealthy and from the looks of his place—the house, barns and such—I was certain that he was.

We drove back down the road and I asked Perry if he had the cord and tape ready. He said that he did. I had already loaded the shotgun, so we parked the car to see if the lights would be turned out. We couldn't see the light from where we were, which meant we would have to again run the risk of being spotted when we returned to the house. We didn't know if we had been seen the first time but it was a risk we had to face if we were going through with it. Perry told me he didn't want to go through with it and said we should leave. In fact he continued to be reluctant until we got into the house.

A few minutes later we returned to the vicinity of the house and the light was out. We decided to go on with it. I turned the car around in the driveway and backed it up beside the west entrance of the house. I drove as carefully as possible. I told Perry that I would check and see if the light in the hired man's house had been turned on again. We couldn't see it from where we were because a shed blocked our view.

I eased the car door open and slipped over to the shed. I worked my way to the corner where I could see and had my look. It was all clear. There was no light burning. I retraced my steps to the car where I told Smith it looked like clear sailing for us. As we sat in the car Perry again told me he thought we'd better get out of there. I told him that I had far too much at stake to back out now and I was going to do the job alone if necessary. With that I got back out of the car.

I closed the door of the car and moved as silently as possible toward the west door of the Clutter home. The moon was shining with great brilliance and illuminated the house in every detail.

I knew I would have to gain entrance to the house as quickly as possible because anyone looking out a window would certainly have no trouble seeing me.

As I approached the house a multitude of thoughts raced through my mind. I had a feeling of suspense, then fear. Most of all, though, the experience was a thrill. I had never done anything like this before and I wondered if I could carry it out. I reached the door and my heart was hammering with such intensity that it felt like it was going to burst. I made up my mind to one thing. When I got into that house I was going to show them who was boss. Although my partner had never said so I knew he was thinking I didn't have the guts to go through with it. But I would show him who had guts.

I pressed against the door and gently turned the knob. We were in luck! It was unlocked. I left the door standing ajar a couple of inches and retraced my steps to the car as quickly and quietly as possible. I reported my find to my partner and we quickly put our plan into action.

I armed myself with a long thin-bladed [76/77] hunting knife that had been used on my hunting trip the weekend before. It had been left in the car. I also took a flashlight which belonged to my partner. Perry took the shotgun and followed me back to the house.

As I felt the knife in my hand I felt excitement, a thrill. I was going to kill a person—maybe more than one. Could I do it? Maybe I'll back out, I thought. What if they are not home? I hope they're not, I thought, but if they are I can't back out. What would my partner think if I chickened out? These thoughts raced through my mind.

A slight breeze swept across my face and I thought, what am I worrying about? Things like this happen every day. Other guys do it, why can't I? Of course I can. All I've got to do is put my mind to it. Actually there is nothing to it. It'll only take a minute and then it will be all over. All over, God. I'll be glad when it's all over!

The door was still standing ajar and when I tried to see inside a breath of warm air hit me in the face. I couldn't suppress a shiver, though I tried. It left me with a feeling of weakness in my legs. I shoved the door slowly inward until I could slip through. The inside of the house was extremely dark. The only light was filtering in past the blinds on the windows. The November moon was really bright and there were no clouds to dull its brilliance. As my eyes became accustomed to the dark, different objects came into view.

As I began to recognize these objects I experienced the strangest feeling I've ever had. It seemed that everything that was happening was taking place regardless of whether I put forth any effort. It seemed to me that I was viewing a movie in which I appeared.

But that doesn't quite explain my feeling. It was more like an incident was taking place and all I needed to do to become part of it was sit back and wait. To some degree I've always had the feeling that things would happen no matter what I did or where I was. I knew I couldn't control them if I tried. And I never tried.

We had entered the room Clutter used as an office and I noticed a fairly large desk on my left. According to the information I had a safe was located directly behind it. I turned the flashlight toward the wall and flicked on the switch. In the beam of light I saw a panelled wall of some kind but no safe. I quickly switched off the light and was immediately sorry I had turned it on. What if the light had been seen, I thought. Boy, am I stupid! It was really dark then.

If the diagram a convict buddy had made for me was correct the bedroom of Mr. Clutter was on the left side of a hallway that ran to the left of the office which we were then in. As I started toward the inner doorway the floor gave some protesting sounds that sounded loud enough to wake the dead. Every step I took seemed louder than the one before! We moved forward as quickly as possible, but no matter how hard I tried, I couldn't stop the floor from squeaking.

They hear it, I thought, I know they do. I've got to hurry! I'll bet they're getting out of bed right now, I thought. But then another thought hit me. Maybe they aren't home. All of a sudden I wished with all my might that they were not at home. Suddenly I was convinced that there was no one home and I hurried—almost ran— toward the place where Clutter would be sleeping if he were there.

Just as the diagram showed, a hallway led to the left and on the left of this was the bedroom. I flashed the light on as I entered the bedroom and I could hardly believe it. They were home! A man sat up in bed and said, "Is that you, dear?" That made me mad because I had been so sure they were not there. Controlling myself as best I could I told him, "Just take it easy pop, don't do anything foolish and everything will be okay."

I was thinking about the way to handle this. I wanted to do it the way I had read about it being done. I wanted to handle it the way a real pro would. Like a torpedo from Detroit or some place. It was very important to me that I make a good impression on my partner. I also wanted Clutter to think that he was facing a hood who knew what was what. Maybe the most important thing to me at that time was that I suddenly felt like I really was a big shot. I remember thinking. I wish I had worn a trench coat. Sounds foolish, I know, but it was important enough to me at the time that I still remember it.

"Come on, get up," my partner said. "You got a safe?" I asked. I hadn't seen one when I had the light on in the west room. Of course I didn't look good. Clutter said he had no safe. When he got out of bed we escorted Clutter back into the office and I began to question him in regard to the safe. A warm comfortable feeling had come over me, once I got over the shock of finding him at home. It was a feeling of power, of being boss. How many times in my life I had wished to be boss! A dozen, a hundred! Always before somebody was giving me orders. But not now!

Clutter kept telling me there was no safe and turned on the light in the office to prove it. By this time I knew there wasn't any safe. But I didn't care. I had never experienced this feeling before and I wouldn't trade it for anything.

My thoughts were interrupted when my partner informed me that some one had come down the steps from upstairs. I didn't see anyone, but I knew we were in trouble if there was a phone up there. I asked Clutter, "Where are your phones?" He said that there was one in the kitchen and one in the room where we were. My partner handed me the shotgun while we went to the kitchen to take care of the telephone.

I leaned against the wall and thought about how simple it would be to blow Clutter's hair all over the wall. The power of life and death was in my hands. The blood was pounding in my ears to such an extent that I put my hand to the side of my head to see if any was running out. Then my stomach seemed to tie into a knot and I got the shakes. I noticed Clutter was staring at me with his mouth open. He didn't say anything, he just stared. I broke out in a sweat and yelled at Clutter to get back in his bedroom just as my partner started back in the kitchen. Thank God I at least had sense enough to get out of that lighted room before my partner saw me!

When we got back in the bedroom I told Clutter to give me his wallet, which he did. It contained about $30 and some travel checks. I left the wallet lying on the bed. My partner had found some binoculars and he took these to the car. While my partner [77/78] was gone I was told by Clutter that the rest of his family was sleeping upstairs. I knew that Clutter had a daughter and maybe two. I believe he said that only one girl was home and never did say that he had any other children. I wondered what his daughter would look like. Was she good looking? How old was she?

When my partner returned I left him to guard Clutter while I went back to the office to look again for the safe. While I was gone Mr. Clutter offered my partner a check for $200 if we would leave. Of course this was refused. When I couldn't find a safe I returned to Clutter's bedroom and we escorted Clutter upstairs.

We were going to have to do something about the rest of the family. If we were to cut Clutter's throat and leave him downstairs the family would come down as soon as we left and the heat would be on. We had to at least tie them up. But, I thought, they would see us and that wouldn't do. Oh well, I would cross that bridge when I came to it. Clutter lead [sic] the way upstairs and Perry took the shotgun and followed him. I suddenly felt weak again and climbed the stairs very slowly.

When I got to the top of the stairs in the Clutter house I heard Perry asking Clutter where the rest of the family was. Before he could answer my partner told him to get them up. Mrs. Clutter, who was a frail sort of woman—not so much in stature, but in the way she carried herself—got up first. We told her to go into the bathroom. Next to get up was the daughter. When I saw her I thought, not bad, not bad at all. She was not very tall and had dark hair and eyes. I found out later that she was 15. I told her to go in the bathroom, along with her dad, and my partner and I went into the boy, Kenyon's room to get him up.

At first the boy didn't want to get up. I guess he was scared but my partner hit him on the back with the flat of his hand, not hard, but enough to let him know we meant business. Kenyon said, "All right, I'm getting up." He was a strapping kid for no older than he was. When he got up he just had on his shorts and we put him in the bathroom that way. About 10 minutes later we let him go to his room to put on his trousers.

With the family in the bathroom we continued our search for the safe. I looked upstairs and my partner looked downstairs. The only thing we took of any value from the second floor was a portable radio from the boy's room.

While we were looking through the house I had considerable time to do some thinking. This was easy, I thought, but these people were being too meek. I didn't like it. I wanted to be able to show them who was boss but they were actually letting me do whatever I wanted. Here we were, picking them like chickens and they weren't even raising a beef of any kind. How could I be tough if there was no reason to be?

It was then that I started thinking about the girl again. She looked pretty nice. I wondered what she would be like in bed. I made up my mind to find out before I left. And then it started. The same old thing. I could picture myself in bed with her. Not doing what everybody else does, but different. I've got to be different, I thought. I'm going to be different. Everything I do has to be different. In my mind I could visualize each and every detail of the intimate relationship I was planning for that night. My thoughts were interrupted by the return of my partner upstairs.

It was almost 2:00 o'clock in the morning and we decided we had better discontinue our search. We decided to tie the family up with me standing guard at the bathroom door while Perry did the tying. I thought that was a good set-up because it fit right in with my plans. I told my partner I planned to rape Nancy and he threw a fit. He looked at me and said, "If you do you and I are going to have one helluva fight." I didn't say anything but I thought to myself, I could slap you down with one hand and you say you want to fight. It wouldn't be much of a fight! I was mad and I decided I'd do as I damned well pleased.

Prior to this time my partner and I had discussed what we should do with the family. We knew that if we killed the old man and left the rest of the family alive we were going to leave a bunch of witnesses. So we decided we would tie them in separate rooms and cut their throats. That way no member of the family would know what was going on until their throat was cut. That would avoid a ruckus. We knew we had to tie them up so that one of them didn't make it outdoors some way or another. We didn't want to shoot them because it would be too noisy with all the shooting and screaming going on.

By this time the Clutters seemed convinced that we were just robbing them and none of them put up any fight when we took them out of the bathroom one at a time. Little did they know what was in store for them! Mr. Clutter was the first to be tied. Just where this was I didn't know at the time. I stayed upstairs and looked through the rooms again.

I started thinking, I should have pulled this myself. It would have been impossible to do but at the time I reasoned that if I killed them I could have handled the job by myself. The more I thought of the idea the better I liked the thought of killing them. Now that is doing something, I thought. When you bump somebody off you are really in the big time.

It happens every day and I don't know why I thought it would amount to so much. There really is nothing to killing a person. It's easy to do. A lot easier than committing [78/79] a burglary or cashing checks or stealing a car. At the time, though, I thought a person could get a lot of glory out of a killing. The word "glory" seemed to keep going through my mind.

All my life I had been told that nothing I would ever do would amount to anything. Well, this is my chance, I thought. I'm going to do it. Then nobody will be able to say Dick Hickock didn't do anything worth while. I'll have to tell them I did it, I thought, or how else will they know it was me? But that will take the fun out of it. No really big time operator would do that. No, I decided, I'll wait until they catch me—if they do—and then I can tell them. But what if nobody cares who did it? What then? That's ridiculous, I thought. Naturally they will care who did it. But that's in the future. What I care about is now.

The boy was next to be tied. Perry was taking the men downstairs so I supposed it was in the cellar. I supposed right. While the boy was being tied I told the girl to come out of the bathroom to answer some questions about money. When she came into the hall I lost all desire to do anything to her at all. I don't know why. I could feel the blood rush to my head when she looked at me. It seemed she was reading my mind. All of a sudden I was ashamed of what I was thinking.

We went into the boy's bedroom which was directly across the upstairs hall from the bathroom. Nancy and I talked about various things such as why I did things like this, where I was from, if I had any parents or brothers and sisters. I tried being gruff when I talked to her but it didn't come out right. My voice sounded like my throat was full of water and it gurgled. I don't remember all the answers I gave her but I did tell her I was from Chicago. Why I told her this I'll never know. Maybe I was trying to impress her with the idea that I was a tough guy from the Windy City. But I was failing miserably and I knew it.

I asked her if there was any more money in the house and she said, no. I then told her I had no parents and that my brother was dead. I told her my sister lived with a man who was not her husband. I asked her about school, boy friends and some other things. She told me about her church activities and I got to thinking that she was a pretty good kid.

It was about this time that Mrs. Clutter opened the bathroom door and saw us talking. Nancy went over to her mother who said she was worried about what was going on. She also said she was tired. I asked her if she wanted to go and lie down and she refused. She said she was afraid that I was going to hurt someone. I told her I had never hurt anyone before and that I wasn't going to start then.

I wondered to myself if I was. I had just about given up the idea of trying to be tough. I remember that I thought I ought to be real proud of myself, wanting to be tough and impress some one when all I had to be tough with was an elderly woman and a young kid. A feeling of reproach came over me. Then I thought to myself, why lie about it? Am I the one who is boss or not?

It was at this time that my partner returned from downstairs. If he had been gone another 10 minutes Mrs. Clutter might have talked me into leaving right then. Of course I can't be sure about that but as I look back on it I know it wouldn't have taken much to have induced me to have walked out. I was getting pretty soft-hearted.

I went to the basement with my partner, where Clutter and the boy were tied. I thought to myself, the time is getting close. My heart was pounding and I broke out in a sweat. My hands were trembling with excitement. I was going to show them. I was going to show everybody. All my life I had heard I wasn't ever going to do anything that amounted to much. But wait until they find these people, I thought, and they will know!

After the family had been tied, but before Mr. Clutter and Kenyon were moved from their first position in the furnace room, I was looking around on the first floor of the house when I came across a purse that I learned belonged to Nancy. I discovered it lying on a shelf fairly close to the first floor entrance to the basement steps. It contained several dollars. As I was looking through it I heard Mr. Clutter talking to Kenyon.

Mr. Clutter asked his boy if he could hear us. His boy said no. Clutter said, "I wonder if they have left yet." Kenyon said he didn't think so. Clutter then muttered something I couldn't make out. I then went down the steps, leaving the girl's purse on the floor. I went down to look at the north wall of the recreation room to see if the safe was located down there. As I passed the furnace room door Mr. Clutter asked me if the women were all right. I told him that they were both in bed and all right. He then told me his wife was sick and had been taking treatments from a doctor in Garden City. He asked if I had found what I had been looking for. I told him, "Never mind," and went back upstairs.

Perry and I then went back to the cellar where I helped my partner move the kid into another room. I looked at him and thought, I'm doing you a favor kid if you only knew it. Just think, it won't be long and your troubles will be over. And I smiled to myself, and thought, I'll be famous! My only regret at the time was that I'd have to share my glory with my partner. But I didn't really mind because he was a good guy.

We tied the kid on a couch and put old man Clutter on a big cardboard box in the furnace room. My partner and I then discussed who was going to do it. At first I revolted. Then, I thought, it was my idea. I became infuriated—I think at myself for being weak. If it is going to be done, I thought, I want to do it. I want the glory. I want to get into the big time! I had given no thought of how I was going to do it. I guess I never really thought I would go through with it. It had just seemed like a good idea.

The boy must have heard us talking because he started struggling as if he was trying to get loose. I walked over to where he was, out of the furnace room, and flashed the light on him. He was still tied.

It was then that I heard it! It sounded like someone trying to scream with a mouth full of water, a gurgling half scream. I thought, he has done it!

At the time I was still carrying the shotgun that my partner had handed me when he was tying Clutter. With the flashlight in one hand

and the shotgun in the other I rushed into the furnace room. In the beam of the flashlight I saw my partner sawing on [79/80] Clutter's throat. Clutter had come out of his ropes and was fighting for his life.

My heart was ready to pound itself out of my chest, my body was ready to explode! This isn't the way I planned it, I thought. I felt like I was being cheated.

Clutter was kicking and screaming out through his throat. Blood was everywhere. Clutter was still fighting, even with his throat cut.

I dropped down and tried to hold him but he had the strength of 10 men. I'm a weight-lifter and definitely no weakling but I couldn't hold him. I was getting madder all the time and on top of that I was hurt. I was hurt to think that I had planned it all and now was being cheated out of what was really mine.

By this time my partner had quit sawing on Clutter's throat. He handed me the knife and picked up the shotgun. I was still trying to hold Clutter when Perry said, "Cut him, I can't keep hold of the knife."

At first I didn't pay any attention. I was heartbroken and infuriated because I wasn't the one to cut Clutter's throat. I believe I was actually on the verge of tears.

I laid the knife down and Smith handed it back to me and said, "Stick him. It'll make you feel better."

I don't remember whether I grabbed the knife in a rough manner or not but I think I did. I thought, there is no use of my doing anything to Clutter because Smith has already done it. I thought I should use the knife on Smith! But then Clutter almost jumped straight up. I raised the knife and plunged it into his throat. It went in real easy and it surprised me. I twisted it real good once then I pulled it back out. Clutter was still for a second and I thought, that did it.

But then he started kicking even harder than ever. I was furious! I dropped the knife and hit Clutter in the face as hard as I could with my fist. It made no difference. He kept right on fighting.

I jumped up and yelled to Smith, "Shoot him! I'll hold the light!" My partner stopped Clutter's kicking. He blew his head off!

Suddenly I laughed. It was funny, very funny! Clutter wasn't ever going to give anyone a hard time again!

Perry pumped the shotgun and told me to pick up the shell. I did. I thought, why can't it go the way I planned it? Why I kept thinking this I don't know because I hadn't made any actual plans for the killings. Or had I? At the time I am writing this I can't remember all my thoughts. But I do remember that I was disappointed, very disappointed.

The boy was next. And he was having a fit. I held the flashlight and watched the kid struggle to get loose. I'm sure he had heard everything that had happened. He got it right in the face. I thought at the time that my partner was a lousy shot. He just caused the undertaker a lot of unnecessary work. Now the kid would need a facial. But I would like to have seen the embalmer fill that hole!

I had seen a lot of embalmers work when I drove an ambulance in Kansas City and I knew how much work there was on a guy that a shotgun was used on. A 12-gauge shotgun is really nasty and all undertakers cuss and go on when they have to work on someone who has been hit with one. I knew we were causing somebody a lot of work and I still think it is funny.

Suddenly I thought that the hired hand had probably heard the shots and might foul things up. I made up my mind that if he tried it I would kill him too. As we left the basement and went up the stairs— after I had picked up the shells—I had three different emotions. I was mad, I felt cheated, and I thought the shootings were the funniest things I had ever seen.

We ran up the stairs and headed for the girl's room. She was tied in bed in her room at the top of the stairs on the second floor. My partner was ahead of me with the shotgun and I thought, there is a solid boy. Nerves of steel. I never gave any thought to what he was thinking but I imagine he was like me, having a swell time.

As I think about it now I realize it was fun. Nobody was telling us what to do. We were boss in that house. It felt good to be able to do as I damn well pleased. No orders, no bosses, no nothing. The thought went through my mind that it would really be fun to do this to my in-laws. I'd heard a lot of guys say they'd like to but they were cowards. It took guts to do what we were doing, but it was so simple I was really surprised.

The girl was next. She said something just before the shotgun went off. She was the only one that wasn't gagged. Whatever she was saying was cut off by the roar of the shotgun as Perry pulled the trigger. It hit her in the back of the head I think.

That just proves, I thought, that all women aren't hard-headed. Which made me laugh. But then I felt a little sick. I'd liked her. I'll say this for her, she knew how to die. She didn't even kick. She knew how to go. But it is possible she didn't know what was going on.

She had said something but I don't remember what it was. It might have been her prayers and she might not have finished. I worry about that. But I pray for her so she is okay.

But Mrs. Clutter knew what was going on. She was almost out of her ropes. She was really struggling—I think even harder than the old man before he was shot. But her struggles soon stopped. I don't know where she was shot. The side of the head I think. At any rate she quit kicking.

The only fear I had at this time was that the hired man had heard the shotgun going off. He is liable to come running in the front door at any time, I thought. It would have been too bad for him if he had.

I picked up the last of the shells and we ran down the steps **and** out to the car.

It was over. We had killed four people. I didn't time it but it couldn't have taken long. Everything happened in the space of about 10 minutes, or even less, from the time we killed the first one (Mr. Clutter) to the time of the last one (Mrs. Clutter).

Boy, that fresh air felt good when we got out of the Clutter house! My ears were ringing from the noise of the shotgun so that I could hardly hear. When we got in the car my partner asked me what I thought about the hired hand. I told him I didn't think he had seen anything. The light wasn't on so we drove on down the road.

I felt as if a big weight was off my shoulders. But I was disappointed. It didn't go like I expected it to at all. I couldn't help but feel cheated.

All at once I knew I was scared. Just [80/81] what I was scared of I don't know. I remember that I was breathing real hard and I had a tight feeling in my chest as if I had run a long distance. I was real nervous. I tried, did light a cigarette and I noticed that my hands were shaking. I know I thought at the time I didn't want my partner to see it. But above all else I was disappointed.

In fact it looks to me now as if I was just like a kid getting ready to throw a fit. I felt like I wanted something but had been denied it. I felt almost exactly as I used to feel when I had to give up something to my brother. I kept thinking, over and over, why did it happen this way? And for the life of me, even as I write this, I can't think of any other way I wanted it to happen.

After we drove several miles I said to my partner, "I guess you know we've stirred them up like a hornets' nest around here." I felt a little resentment toward my partner. But other than that I felt good. I felt like a big load had been lifted from my shoulders. For a while I enjoyed a feeling of exhilaration. But then I began getting tired and suddenly I was hungry. Boy, was I hungry!

Most of our conversation driving away concerned our going to Mexico the next weekend. We thought we'd stay there a couple of weeks then head on south, probably to Brazil. I told Perry I would write all the checks I could before we left Kansas City for Mexico. We planned for me to work the following week as if nothing had happened. We were to leave Kansas City the following Saturday. I told Perry it would be best if he went to Kansas City to stay and that we shouldn't be seen together around Olathe. I knew a lot of people around town and my parole officer also lived there.

We decided that when we got back to Olathe my partner would register in a hotel until Monday night when I would take him to Kansas City. Perry sort of thought we ought to head for Mexico right then but I told him, no, that might put the heat on us.

After I left Perry Smith off at the Olathe Hotel I happened to look at the floor of my car opposite the driver's seat and thought, good God! The floor had blood all over it. I hadn't noticed it before but I certainly did now! Smith must have stepped in the blood because it was all over the floor where his feet had been. I knew I had to clean it up but I didn't know where I could do it. I couldn't do it at home without the folks seeing me. Maybe I can do it after dark, I thought. So I decided that as soon as it was dark I would wash it off, or try to.

It was pretty close to 12:00 o'clock noon when I drove into the yard at the farm. As I parked the car I looked in the kitchen window and saw that my folks were eating dinner. I decided to leave the shotgun in the car until later when I would give it a good cleaning.

Mom asked me if I was hungry and I told her, yes. She set a place at the table for me and I found that I was real hungry. During dinner Dad and I talked about first one thing and then another—mostly about work that needed to be done around the farm. When we finished eating Dad asked me if I was going to watch the ball game on television with him. I told him I would a little later. There was no one at the farm except my parents and myself all that day.

I went to the car and got the shotgun and brought it in the kitchen to clean it. I knew the folks wouldn't give a thought to the gun because around our house a gun was common and I was always hunting. I never left a gun lying around without cleaning it from time to time. I wanted to make sure it didn't rust. Also, I never handled a gun without wiping it off with an oiled rag. So I knew my cleaning of the gun would cause no comment.

While cleaning the gun I noticed that there was blood along the ventilated rib and in the cracks around the trigger guard. It took me about 15 minutes to clean it. After putting the gun in its case I went into the living room to watch television with my Dad.

I don't remember who was playing but it was a professional football game. I lay on the couch and Dad asked me if I was tired. I told him I hadn't got much sleep the night before and was a little tired. I told Mom to be sure and wake me when supper was ready if I happened to fall asleep. I don't know how long I watched television but it was only a few minutes before I dropped off to sleep. It was Dad who awakened me and said supper would be ready in a few minutes.

I had just finished washing when I heard a newscast start. I didn't want to appear overly interested in it but I watched the whole broadcast. Nothing was mentioned about any killing and I wondered if I had only dreamed about the Clutters. Maybe, I thought, I hadn't been involved in killing anyone at all. Then, I thought, Maybe it won't even be on television. I had felt quite excited at the prospect of it being mentioned.

While I was eating supper I thought about the blood on the floor of my car. If I had dreamed about the Clutters there definitely wouldn't be any blood in my car. I wanted to hurry and finish eating so I could inspect the floor-boards of my car. I must have been eating real fast because my Dad asked me if I was going to a fire. I said, "No, why?" He said, "You're shoveling your food in as fast as you can work your elbow."

I thought, I better slow down, I don't want to do anything to make my folks think something is wrong. But I could hardly wait to get out to the car. Then I thought, I wonder if Dad has seen the blood. Surely he hasn't or he would want to know where it came from. Maybe there isn't any. I just couldn't wait to find out!

Finally supper was over and I told my folks I was going out to get some fresh air. I took a rag which I found on the back [18/82] porch. I wet it in the rain barrel. I had also taken a flashlight with me. I opened the car door on the side that my partner had sat. When the dome light came on I saw the blood. I got busy with the wet rag wiping Clutter's blood off as fast as I could. I wondered if they had been found yet. There was the possibility that no one had discovered the bodies.

After cleaning the knife and washing the floor mat as good as I could I shoved the rag down in some trash I knew would be burned in a couple of days. I put the knife in a green fishing tackle box and headed for the house. I made up my mind that the first thing I was going to do when I got to work the next morning was give the car a good bath—inside and out. . . .

I seriously thought about leaving Smith shortly after we returned to the States from Mexico. We crossed the border at Tia Juana on December 7, 1959. Prior to our leaving Mexico City we had a wild fling which included wine, women but no song. Even without the music our last two days in Mexico City were costly ones.

I found that my partner never had any respect for a dollar and he threw money around more than I did. When we arrived in California we had less than $100 between us. Our only hope for future resources lay in using pistols.

We finally ended up in Kansas City, my home town, and our only purpose for returning to the U.S. was to pull a score big enough to finance a trip to South America. Our proposed destination was Brazil where they couldn't extradite us back to the States if they ever caught onto who pulled the Clutter deal.

During our 2,004 mile bus trip back to the States we had agreed that we were not going to stay for any length of time. As quick as a score could be set up and pulled, we were heading back across the border.

I started on one of the most cautious check passing sprees that part of the country had ever seen. I couldn't be sure but I had an idea we were hotter than a pistol because of the checks we'd passed before. I found out later that we were also wanted for the Clutter case. Every law enforcement agency in 17 states was on the alert for us and there I was in Kansas City, my home town, hanging paper!

I cashed over $500 worth of checks. I got a set of tires, a wrist watch, two television sets and some other stuff. I also managed to get some cash. About everything we got with the checks was sold later in Florida for about a fourth of what I had paid for it.

How I ever managed to cash the checks without getting busted I can't imagine. But I guess I really didn't get away with it because it was the purchase of one of the television sets which led to our eventual arrest in Las Vegas.

I used my own name in cashing the checks and the owner of one of the places where I bought a television set took down the license number of the car I was driving. He wrote the number on the check I gave him. I didn't know about that at the time or I could have very easily switched plates. But Perry told me when we were in jail waiting trial for the Clutter case that he saw him do it, but didn't think about telling me about it. Can you imagine being so stupid? But that's just how much help he was to me all the way through. I not only had to do all the work, I also had to do all the thinking!

Anyway, after we were under arrest one of the policemen told me the reason we were picked up was that when the check for the television set bounced, the number of our license tag was circulated all over the country. That is why the Las Vegas police picked us up while we were sitting in a car.

Our trial was more like a circus than anything else. It took only one day to choose the jury. The way the feeling was running around town I figured it would take at least three or four days for this. But the whole trial didn't last much longer than that.

The courtroom overflowed with spectators and the halls were lined with photographers and newspaper reporters. Every exit was covered by a pair of highway patrolmen. Extra deputy sheriffs were brought in from neighboring counties. I couldn't tell whether this was done to prevent our escape or to protect us. It could have been both, or more likely it was just for show.

I never did think much of the Finney County Attorney and I sure liked him less after our first day in court. He kept pointing his finger at me and telling the jury how no good I was. I resented it. It wasn't so much what he was saying but how he was saying it and who he was saying it in front of.

I looked at my Mom and Dad and I saw my Mom was crying. It was worse on her, I think, than anybody. I didn't care what the rest of the people thought but I did my Mom and Dad. Also, my Aunt and Uncle were sitting there and some friends from Hutchinson, Kansas. One was an old girl friend of mine.

Every time the county attorney pointed his finger at me I wanted to hit him. He was making a lot of statements that were not true and I certainly didn't like it. Things were bad enough without him telling a lot of lies. When he first started waving his finger at me I saw red.

I looked at my Dad and he knew what I was thinking because he shook his head and motioned to me to keep my seat, so I did. But I'd really like to get a crack at that boy in the free world! [82/83]

I wasn't surprised when the State asked for the death penalty. I had been told by the County Attorney over a month before the trial that he was going to ask for it. I don't know how my buddy Smith felt about it because we were kept in separate cells and weren't allowed to talk until after the trial was over.

When the jury started to deliberate I was taken back to my cell on the top floor of the courthouse. Taking into consideration the type testimony that was given and the attitude of the court I knew that the State was going to get just what it asked for. My only hope, I figured, was with the Judge.

As these thoughts went through my mind I began to have hopes of getting a break from the Judge. I knew that I wouldn't be sentenced for three or four days and I was determined to find out just what kind of a Judge this one was. He looked to me to be the type that would turn down any request that a man made. I had heard he was a friend of the Clutters and he would probably have a personal interest in the case that would make him biased toward me.

I decided that I wouldn't ask for anything unless I had a 50-50 chance of getting what I wanted. I had asked a favor of the police and had been turned down so I knew it was no use to ask them. I decided that when they took me down for sentencing I would have my lawyer enter a plea for parole. I had so many other charges against me that I figured if I entered a plea of guilty to them the Judge might give me a parole on the Clutter deal.

I had tried to work a similar deal in Johnson County once before but the Judge wouldn't go for it. I knew I didn't have much hope of getting it here because the State was asking the death penalty and the people were really stirred up.

I only had one real good argument and that was the fact that this was the first time I had ever been involved in murder and first time offenders in a lot of cases get a parole or probation. I figured it was worth a try. I had nothing to lose. The law didn't have much to lose by going along with it. I had enough other stuff against me to do 50 years in the penitentiary.

There was another guy in jail and since he might know the Judge I thought I would ask him if he thought I might swing a parole. But then I got to thinking this guy might say something to the FBI and they would queer the deal because they sure didn't like me.

I knew the jury would bring in a verdict of guilty when I returned to the courtroom and I told the guy in jail so. He asked me if I thought they would give me the death sentence. I told him probably, but I didn't know if the Judge would go for it.

I asked him what kind of a guy the Judge was and if he knew him. He said he did and added, "He would send his own mother to the gallows. If that jury brings in a guilty verdict you are in a world of trouble." I said, "The Judge won't deal, huh?" And he said, "In your case? You nuts? Why the people would run him out of town on a rail."

I thought, just as I figured. He can go to and stay put for all I care. I'll never ask him for a favor. But if he doesn't give me a parole on his own hook I'll file to the Supreme Court on it. I was supposed to get another lawyer when I got to the penitentiary and I was determined to let him know all about it. He is one of the best lawyers in the state and I figured it would be no sweat for him to get me out.

It was about this time that I was taken down to the courtroom. The jury had only taken about 25 minutes to deliberate. But the Judge was out feeding his horses and we had to wait until he got back.

Every other time I was taken to the courtroom the handcuffs were taken off. But this time they stayed on and I was kept cuffed to the undersheriff. When the verdict was given and the jury said the punishment was to be death I wasn't surprised. I leaned over to the undersheriff and I couldn't help laughing when I told him it was what I expected.

When the Judge was telling the jury what a good job they had done I thought that these pompous old ginks were the lousiest looking specimens of manhood I had ever seen; old cronies that acted like they were God or somebody.

Right then I wished every one of them had been at the Clutter house that night and that included the Judge. I would have found out how much God they had in them! If they had been there and had any God in them I would have let it run out on the floor.

I thought, boy, I'd like to do it right here. Now there was something that would have really stirred them up!

When the jury filed out of the courtroom not one of them would look at me. I looked each one in the face and I kept thinking, Look at me, look at me, look at me!

But none of them would. [83]

The Story Behind
a Nonfiction Novel

GEORGE PLIMPTON

"In Cold Blood" is remarkable for its objectivity—nowhere, despite his involvement, does the author intrude. In the following interview, done a few weeks ago, Truman Capote presents his own views on the case, its principals, and in particular he discusses the new literary art form which he calls the nonfiction novel.

Why did you select the particular subject matter of murder; had you previously been interested in crime?

Not really, no. During the last years I've learned a good deal about crime, and the origins of the homicidal mentality. Still, it is a layman's knowledge and I don't pretend to anything deeper. The motivating factor in my choice of material—that is, choosing to write a true account of an actual murder case—was altogether literary. The decision was based on a theory I've harbored since I first began to write professionally, which is well over 20 years ago. It seemed to me that journalism, reportage, could be forced to yield a serious new art form: the "nonfiction novel," as I thought of it. Several admirable reporters— Rebecca West for one, and Joseph Mitchell and Lillian Ross—have shown the possibilities of narrative reportage; and Miss Ross, in her brilliant "Picture," achieved at least a nonfiction novella. Still, on the whole, journalism is the most underestimated, the least explored of literary mediums.

Why should that be so?

Because few first-class creative writers have ever bothered with journalism, except as a sideline, "hack-work," something to be done when the creative spirit is lacking, or as a means of making money quickly. Such writers say in effect: Why should we trouble with factual writing when we're able to invent our own stories, contrive our

From *The New York Times Book Review,* January 16, 1966, pp. 2–3, 38–43. © 1966 by The New York Times Company. Reprinted by permission of The New York Times Company.

own characters and themes?—journalism is only literary photography, and unbecoming to the serious writer's artistic dignity.

Another deterrent—and not the smallest—is that the reporter, unlike the fantasist, has to deal with actual people who have real names. If they feel maligned, or just contrary, or greedy, they enrich lawyers (though rarely themselves) by instigating libel actions. This last is certainly a factor to consider, a most oppressive and repressive one. Because it's indeed difficult to portray, in any meaningful depth, another being, his appearance, speech, mentality, without to some degree, and often for quite trifling cause, offending him. The truth seems to be that no one likes to see himself described as he is, or cares to see exactly set down what he said and did. Well, even I can understand that—because I don't like it myself when I am the sitter and not the portraitist: the frailty of egos!—and the more accurate the strokes, the greater the resentment.

When I first formed my theories concerning the nonfiction novel, many people with whom I discussed the matter were unsympathetic. They felt that what I proposed, a narrative form that employed all the techniques of fictional art but was nevertheless immaculately factual, was little more than a literary solution for fatigued novelists suffering from "failure of imagination." Personally, I felt that this attitude represented a "failure of imagination" on their part.

Of course a properly done piece of narrative reporting requires imagination!—and a good deal of special technical equipment that is usually beyond the resources—and I don't doubt the interests—of most fictional writers: an ability to transcribe verbatim long conversations, and to do so without taking notes or using tape-recordings. Also, it is necessary to have a 20/20 eye for visual detail—in this sense, it is quite true that one must be a "literary photographer," though an exceedingly selective one. But, above all, the reporter must be able to empathize with personalities outside his usual imaginative range, mentalities unlike his own, kinds of people he would never have written about had he not been forced to by encountering them inside the journalistic situation. This last is what first attracted me to the notion of narrative reportage.

It seems to me that most contemporary novelists, especially the Americans and the French, are too subjective, mesmerized by private demons; they're enraptured by their navels, and confined by a view that ends with their own toes. If I were naming names, I'd name myself among others. At any rate, I did at one time feel an artistic need to escape my self-created world. I wanted to exchange it, creatively speaking, for the everyday objective world we all inhabit. Not that I'd never written nonfiction before—I kept journals, and had published a small truthful book of travel impressions: "Local Color." But I had never attempted an ambitious piece of reportage until 1956, when I wrote "The Muses Are Heard," an account of the first theatrical cultural exchange between the U.S.A. and the U.S.S.R.—that is, the "Porgy and Bess" tour of Russia. It was published in The New Yorker, the only magazine I know of that encourages the serious practitioners of this art form. Later, I contributed a few other reportorial finger-exercises to the same magazine. Finally, I felt equipped and ready to undertake a full-scale narrative—in other words, a "nonfiction novel."

How does John Hersey's "Hiroshima" or Oscar Lewis's "Children of Sanchez" compare with "the nonfiction novel"?

The Oscar Lewis book is a documentary, a job of editing from tapes, and however skillful and moving, it is not creative writing. "Hiroshima" is creative—in the sense that Hersey isn't taking something off a tape-recorder and editing it—but it still hasn't got anything to do with what I'm talking about. "Hiroshima" is a strict classical journalistic piece. What is closer is what Lillian Ross did with "Picture." Or my own book, "The Muses are Heard"—which uses the techniques of the comic short novel.

It was natural that I should progress from that experiment, and get myself in much deeper water. I read in the paper the other day that I had been quoted as saying that reporting is now more interesting than fiction. Now that's *not* what I said, and it's important to me to get this straight. What I think is that reporting can be made *as* interesting as fiction, and done *as* artistically—underlining those two "as"es. I don't mean to say that one is a superior form to the other. I feel that creative reportage has been neglected and has great relevance to 20th-century writing. And while it can be an artistic outlet for the creative writer, it has never been particularly explored.

What is your opinion of the so-called New Journalism—as it is practiced particularly at The Herald Tribune?

If you mean James Breslin and Tom Wolfe, and that crowd, they have nothing to do with creative journalism—in the sense that I use the term—because neither of them, nor any of that school of reporting have the proper fictional technical equipment. It's useless for a writer whose talent is essentially journalistic to attempt creative reportage, because it simply won't work. A writer like Rebecca West—always a good reporter—has never really used the form of creative reportage because the form, by necessity, demands that the writer be completely in control of fictional techniques—which means that, to be a good creative reporter, you have to be a very good fiction writer. [2/3]

Would it be fair to say, then, since many reporters use nonfiction techniques—Meyer Levin in "Compulsion," Walter Lord in "A Night to Remember" and so forth—that the nonfiction novel can be defined by the degree of the fiction skills involved, and the extent of the author's absorption with his subject?

"Compulsion" is a fictional novel suggested by fact, but no way bound to it, I never read the other book. The nonfiction novel should not be confused with the documentary novel—a popular and interesting but impure genre, which allows all the latitude of the fiction writer, but usually contains neither the persuasiveness of fact nor the poetic altitude fiction is capable of reaching. The author lets his imagination run riot over the facts! If I sound querulous or arrogant about this, it's not only that I have to protect my child, but that I truly don't believe anything like it exists in the history of journalism.

What is the first step in producing a "nonfiction novel?"

The difficulty was to choose a promising subject. If you intend to spend three or four or five years with a book, as I planned to do, then you want to be reasonably certain that the material will not soon "date." The content of much journalism so swiftly does, which is another of the medium's deterrents. A number of ideas occurred, but one after the other, and for one reason or another, each was eventually discarded, often after I'd done considerable preliminary work. Then one morning in November 1959, while flicking through The New York Times, I encountered, on a deep-inside page, this headline: Wealthy Farmer, 3 of Family Slain.

The story was brief, just several paragraphs stating the facts: A Mr. Herbert W. Clutter, who had served on the Farm Credit Board during the Eisenhower Administration, his wife and two teen-aged children, had been brutally, entirely mysteriously, murdered on a lonely wheat and cattle ranch in a remote part of Kansas. There was nothing really exceptional about it; one reads items concerning multiple murders many times in the course of a year.

Then why did you decide it was the subject you had been looking for?

I didn't. Not immediately. But after reading the story it suddenly struck me that a crime, the study of one such, might provide the broad scope I needed to write the kind of book I wanted to write. Moreover, the human heart being what it is, murder was a theme not likely to darken and yellow with time.

I thought about it all that November day, and part of the next; and then I said to myself: Well, why not *this* crime? The Clutter case. Why not pack up and go to Kansas and see what happens? Of course it was a rather frightening thought!—to arrive alone in a small strange town, a town in the grip of an unsolved mass murder. Still, the circumstances of the place being altogether unfamiliar, geographically and atmospherically, made it that much more tempting. Everything would seem freshly minted—the people, their accents and attitudes, the landscape, its contours, the weather. All this, it seemed to me, could only sharpen my eye and quicken my ear.

In the end, I did not go alone. I went with a lifelong friend, Harper Lee. She is a gifted woman, courageous, and with a warmth that instantly kindles most people, however suspicious or dour. She had recently completed a first novel ("To Kill a Mockingbird"), and, feeling at loose ends, she said she would accompany me in the role of assistant researchist.

We traveled by train to St. Louis, changed trains and went to Manhattan, Kan., where we got off to consult Dr. James McClain, president of Mr. Clutter's alma mater, Kansas State University. Dr. McClain, a gracious man, seemed a little nonplussed by our interest in the case; but he gave us letters of introduction to several people in western Kansas. We rented a car and drove some 400 miles to Garden City. It was twilight when we arrived. I remember the car-radio was playing, and we heard: "Police authorities, continuing their investigation of the tragic Clutter slayings, have requested that anyone with pertinent information please contact the Sheriff's office. . . ."

If I had realized then what the future held, I never would have stopped in Garden City. I would have driven straight on. Like a bat out of hell.

What was Harper Lee's contribution to your work?

She kept me company when I was based out there. I suppose she was with me about two months altogether. She went on a number of interviews; she typed her own notes, and I had these and could refer to them. She was extremely helpful in the beginning, when we weren't making much headway with the town's people, by making friends with the wives of the people I wanted to meet. She became friendly with all the churchgoers. A Kansas paper said the other day that everyone out there was so wonderfully cooperative because I was a famous writer. The fact of the matter is that not one single person in the town had ever heard of me.

How long did it take for the town to thaw out enough so that you were accepted and you could get to your interviewing?

About a month. I think they finally just realized that we were there to stay—they'd have to make the best of it. Under the circumstances, they were suspicious. After all, there was an unsolved murder case, and the people in the town were tired of the thing, and frightened. But then after it all quieted down—after Perry and Dick were arrested—that was when we did most of the original interviews.

Some of them went on for three years—though not on the same subject, of course. I suppose if I used just 20 per cent of all the material I put together over those years of interviewing, I'd still have a book two thousand pages long!

How much research did you do other than through interviews with the principals in the case?

Oh, a great deal. I did months of comparative research on murder, murderers, the criminal mentality, and I interviewed quite a number of murderers—solely to give me perspective on these two boys. And then crime. I didn't know anything about crime or criminals when I began to do the book. I certainly do now! I'd say 80 per cent of the research I did I have never used. But it gave me such a grounding that I never had any hesitation in my consideration of the subject.

What was the most singular interview you conducted?

I suppose the most startled interviewee was Mr. Bell, the meat-packing executive from Omaha. He was the man who picked up Perry and Dick when they were hitchhiking across Nebraska. They planned to murder him and then make off with his car. Quite unaware of all this, Bell was saved, as you'll remember, just as Perry was going to smash in his head from the seat behind, because he slowed down to pick up another hitchhiker, a Negro. The boys told me this story, and they had this man's business card. I decided to interview him. I wrote him a letter, but got no answer. Then I wrote a letter to the personnel manager of the meat-packing company in Omaha, asking if they had a Mr. Bell in their employ. I told them I wanted to talk to him about a pair of hitchhikers he'd picked up four months previously. The manager wrote back and said that they *did* have a Mr. Bell on their staff, but it was surely the *wrong* Mr. Bell since it was against company policy for employees to take hitchhikers in their cars. So I telephoned Mr. Bell and when he got on the phone he was very brusque: he said I didn't know what I was talking about.

The only thing to do was to go to Omaha personally. I went up there and walked in on Mr. Bell and put two photographs down on his desk. I asked him [3/38] if he recognized the two men. He said, why? So I told him that the two were the hitchhikers he said he had never given a ride to, that they had planned to kill him and then bury him in the prairie—and how close they'd come to it. Well, he turned every conceivable kind of color. You can imagine. He recognized them all right. He was quite cooperative about telling me about the trip, but he asked me not to use his real name. There are only three people in the book whose names I've changed—his, the convict Perry admired so much (Willie-Jay he's called in the book), and also I changed Perry Smith's sister's name.

How long after you went to Kansas did you sense the form of the book? Were there many false starts?

I worked for a year on the notes before I ever wrote one line. And when I wrote the first word, I had done the entire book in outline, down to the finest detail. Except for the last part, the final dispensation of the case—that was an evolving matter. It began, of course, with interviews—with all the different characters of the book. Let me give you two examples of how I worked from these interviews. In the first part of the book—the part that's called "The Last to See Them Alive" —there's a long narration, word for word, given by the school teacher who went with the sheriff to the Clutter house and found the four bodies. Well, I simply set that into the book as a straight complete interview—though it was, in fact, done several times: each time there'd be some little thing which I'd add or change. But I hardly interfered at all. A slight editing job. The school teacher tells the whole story himself—exactly what happened from the moment they got to the house, and what they found there.

On the other hand, in that same first part, there's a scene between the postmistress and her mother when the mother reports that the ambulances have gone to the Clutter house. That's a straight dramatic scene—with quotes, dialogue, action, everything. But it evolved out of interviews just like the one with the school teacher. Except in this case I took what they had told me and transposed it into straight narrative terms. Of course, elsewhere in the book, very often it's direct observation, events I saw myself—the trial, the executions.

You never used a tape-recorder?

Twelve years ago I began to train myself, for the purpose of this sort of book, to transcribe conversation without using a tape-recorder. I did it by having a friend read passages from a book, and then later I'd write them down to see how close I could come to the original. I had a natural facility for it, but after doing these exercises for a year and a half, for a couple of hours a day, I could get within 95 per cent of absolute accuracy, which is as close as you need. I felt it was essential. Even note-taking artificializes the atmosphere of an interview, or a scene-in-progress; it interferes with the communication between author and subject—the latter is usually self-conscious, or an untrusting wariness is induced. Certainly, a tape-recorder does so. Not long ago a French literary critic turned up with a tape-recorder. I don't like them, as I say, but I agreed to its use. In the middle of the interview it broke down. The French literary critic was desperately unhappy. He didn't know what to do. I said, "Well, let's just go on as if nothing had happened." He said, "It's not the same. I'm not accustomed to listen to what you're saying."

*You've kept yourself out of the book entirely. Why was that—
considering your own involvement in the case?*

My feeling is that for the nonfiction-novel form to be entirely
successful, the author should not appear in the work. Ideally. Once the
narrator does appear, he has to appear throughout, all the way down
the line, and the I-I-I intrudes when it really shouldn't. I think the
single most difficult thing in my book, technically, was to write it
without ever appearing myself, and yet, at the same time, create total
credibility.

*Being removed from the book, that is to say, keeping yourself out
of it, do you find it difficult to present your own point of view? For
example, your own view as to why Perry Smith committed the
murders.*

Of course it's by the selection of what you choose to tell. I believe
Perry did what he did for the reasons he himself states—that his life
was a constant accumulation of disillusionments and reverses and he
suddenly found himself (in the Clutter house that night) in a psychological cul-de-sac. The Clutters were such a perfect set of symbols for
every frustration in his life. As Perry himself said, "I didn't have
anything against them, and they never did anything wrong to me—the
way other people have all my life. Maybe they're just the ones who
had to pay for it." Now in that particular section where Perry talks
about the reason for the murders, I could have included other views.
But Perry's happens to be the one I believe is the right one, and it's the
one that Dr. Satten at the Menninger Clinic arrived at quite indepen-
dently, never having done any interviews with Perry.

I could have added a lot of other opinions. But that would have
confused the issue, and indeed the book. I had to make up my mind,
and move towards that one view, always. You can say that the
reportage is incomplete. But then it has to be. It's a question of
selection, you wouldn't get anywhere if it wasn't for that. I've often
thought of the book as being like something reduced to a seed. Instead
of presenting the reader with a full plant, with all the foliage, a seed is
planted in the soil of his mind. I've often thought of the book in that
sense. I make my own comment by what I choose to tell and how I
choose to tell it. It is true that an author is more in control of fictional
characters because he can do anything he wants with them as long as
they stay credible. But in the nonfiction novel one can also manipulate:
if I put something in which I don't agree about I can always set it in a
context of qualification without having to step into the story myself to
set the reader straight.

When did you first see the murderers—Perry and Dick?

The first time I ever saw them was the day they were returned to Garden City. I had been waiting in the crowd in the square for nearly five hours, frozen to death. That was the first time. I tried to interview them the next day—both completely unsuccessful interviews. I saw Perry first, but he was so cornered and suspicious—and quite rightly so—and paranoid that he couldn't have been less communicative. It was always easier with Dick. He was like someone you meet on a train, immensely garrulous, who starts up a conversation and is only too obliged to tell you *everything*. Perry became easier after the third or fourth month, but it wasn't until the last five years of his life that he was totally and absolutely honest with me, and came to trust me. I came to have great rapport with him right up through his last day. For the first year and a half, though, he would come just so close, and then no closer. He'd retreat into the forest and leave me standing outside. I'd hear him laugh in the dark. Then gradually he would come back. In the end, he could not have been more complete and candid.

How did the two accept being used as subjects for a book?

They had no idea what I was going to do. Well, of course, at [38/39] the end they did. Perry was always asking me: Why are you writing this book? What is it supposed to mean? I don't understand why you're doing it. Tell me in one sentence why you want to do it. So I would say that it didn't have anything to do with changing the readers' opinion about anything, nor did I have any moral reasons worthy of calling them such—it was just that I had a strictly aesthetic theory about creating a book which could result in a work of art.

"That's really the truth, Perry," I'd tell him, and Perry would say, "A work of art, a work of art," and then he'd laugh and say, "What an irony, what an irony." I'd ask what he meant, and he'd tell me that all he ever wanted to do in his life was to produce a work of art. "That's all I ever wanted in my whole life," he said. "And now, what has happened? An incredible situation where I kill four people, and *you're* going to produce a work of art." Well, I'd have to agree with him. It was a pretty ironic situation.

Did you ever show sections of the book to witnesses as you went along?

I have done it, but I don't believe in it. It's a mistake because it's almost impossible to write about anybody objectively and have that person really like it. People simply do not like to see themselves put down on paper. They're like somebody who goes to see his portrait in a gallery. He doesn't like it unless it's overwhelmingly flattering—I mean the ordinary person, not someone with genuine creative perception. Showing the thing in progress usually frightens the person and there's nothing to be gained by it. I showed various sections to five people in the book, and without exception each of them found something that he desperately wanted to change. Of the whole bunch, I changed my text for one of them because, although it was a silly thing, the person genuinely believed his entire life was going to be ruined if I *didn't* make the change.

Did Dick and Perry see sections of the book?

They saw some sections of it. Perry wanted terribly much to see the book. I had to let him see it because it just would have been too unkind not to. Each only saw the manuscript in little pieces. Everything mailed to the prison went through the censor. I wasn't about to have my manuscript floating around between those censors—not with those Xerox machines going clickety-clack. So when I went to the prison to visit I would bring parts—some little thing for Perry to read. Perry's greatest objection was the title. He didn't like it because he said the crime wasn't committed in cold blood. I told him the title had a double meaning. What was the other meaning? he wanted to know. Well, that wasn't something I was going to tell him. Dick's reaction to the book was to start switching and changing his story, saying what I had written wasn't exactly true. He wasn't trying to flatter himself; he tried to change it to serve his purposes legally, to support the various appeals he was sending through the courts. He wanted the book to read as if it was a legal brief for presentation in his behalf before the Supreme Court. But you see I had a perfect control-agent—I could always tell when Dick or Perry wasn't telling the truth. During the first few months or so of interviewing them, they weren't allowed to speak to each other. They were in separate cells. So I would keep crossing their stories, and what correlated, what checked out identically, was the truth.

How did the two compare in their recounting of the events?

Dick had an absolutely fantastic memory—one of the greatest memories I have ever come across. The reason I know it's great is that I lived the entire trip the boys went on from the time of the murders up to the moment of their arrest in Las Vegas—thousands of miles, what the boys called "the long ride." I went everywhere the boys had gone, all the hotel rooms, every single place in the book, Mexico, Acapulco, all of it. In the hotel in Miami Beach I stayed for three days until the manager realized why I was there and asked me to leave, which I was only too glad to do. Well, Dick could give me the names and addresses of any hotel or place along the route where they'd spent maybe just half a night. He told me when I got to Miami to take a taxi to such-and-such a place and get out on the boardwalk and it would be southwest of there, number 232, and opposite I'd find two umbrellas in the sand which advertised "Tan with Coppertone." That was how exact he was. He was the one who remembered the little card in the Mexico City hotel room—in the corner of the mirror—that reads "Your day ends at 2 P.M." He was extraordinary. Perry, on the other hand, was very bad at details of that sort, though he was good at remembering conversations and moods. He was concerned altogether in the overtones of things. He was much better at describing a general sort of mood or atmosphere than Dick who, though very sensitive, was impervious to that sort of thing.

What turned them back to the Clutter house after they'd almost decided to give up on the job?

Oh, Dick was always quite frank about that. I mean after it was all over. When they set out for the house that night, Dick was determined, before he ever went, that if the girl, Nancy, was there he was going [39/40] to rape her. It wouldn't have been an act of the moment—he had been thinking about it for weeks. He told me that was one of the main reasons he was so determined to go back after they thought, you know for a moment, they wouldn't go. Because he'd been thinking about raping this girl for weeks and weeks. He had no idea what she looked like—after all, Floyd Wells, the man in prison who told them about the Clutters, hadn't seen the girl in 10 years: it had to do with the fact that she was 15 or 16. He liked young girls, much younger than Nancy Clutter actually.

What do you think would have happened if Perry had faltered and not begun the killings? Do you think Dick would have done it?

No. There is such a thing as the ability to kill. Perry's particular psychosis had produced this ability. Dick was merely ambitious—he could *plan* murder, but not commit it.

What was the boys' reaction to the killing?

They both finally decided that they had thoroughly enjoyed it. Once they started going, it became an immense emotional release. And they thought it was funny. With the criminal mind—and both boys had criminal minds, believe me—what seems most extreme to us is very often, if it's the most expedient thing to do, the *easiest* thing for a criminal to do. Perry and Dick both used to say (a memorable phrase) that it was much easier to kill somebody than it was to cash a bad check. Passing a bad check requires a great deal of artistry and style, whereas just going in and killing somebody requires only that you pull a trigger.

There are some instances of this that aren't in the book. At one point, in Mexico, Perry and Dick had a terrific falling-out, and Perry said he was going to kill Dick. He said that he'd already killed five people—he was lying, adding one more than he should have (that was the Negro he kept telling Dick he'd killed years before in Las Vegas) and that one more murder wouldn't matter. It was simple enough. Perry's cliché about it was that if you've killed one person you can kill anybody. He'd look at Dick, as they drove along together, and he'd say to himself, Well, I really ought to kill him, it's a question of expediency.

They had two other murders planned that aren't mentioned in the book. Neither of them came off. One "victim" was a man who ran a restaurant in Mexico City—a Swiss. They had become friendly with him eating in his restaurant and when they were out of money they evolved this whole plan about robbing and murdering him. They went to his apartment in Mexico City and waited for him all night long. He never showed up. The other "victim" was a man they never even knew—like the Clutters. He was a banker in a small Kansas town. Dick kept telling Perry that sure, they might have failed with the Clutter score, but this Kansas banker job was absolutely for certain. They were going to kidnap him and ask for ransom, though the plan was, as you might imagine, to murder him right away.

When they went back to Kansas completely broke, that was the main plot they had in mind. What saved the banker was the ride the two boys took with Mr. Bell, yet another "victim" who was spared, as you remember, when he slowed down the car to pick up the Negro hitchhiker. Mr. Bell offered Dick a job in his meat-packing company. Dick took him up on it and spent two days there on the pickle line— putting pickles in ham sandwiches, I think it was—before he and Perry went back on the road again.

Do you think Perry and Dick were surprised by what they were doing when they began the killings?

Perry never meant to kill the Clutters at all. He had a brain explosion. I don't think Dick was surprised, although later on he pretended he was. He knew, even if Perry didn't, that Perry would do it, and he was right. It showed an awfully shrewd instinct on Dick's part. Perry was bothered by it to a certain extent because he'd actually done it. He was always trying to find out in his own mind why he did it. He was amazed he'd done it. Dick on the other hand, *wasn't* amazed, *didn't* want to talk about it, and simply wanted to forget the whole thing: he wanted to get on with life.

Was there any sexual relationship, or such tendencies, between them?

No. None at all. Dick was aggressively heterosexual and had great success. Women liked him. As for Perry, his love for Willie-Jay in the State Prison was profound—and it was reciprocated, but never consummated physically, though there was the opportunity. The relationship between Perry and Dick was quite another matter. What is misleading, perhaps, is that in comparing himself with Dick, Perry used to say how totally "virile" Dick was. But he was referring, I think, to the practical and pragmatic sides of Dick—admiring them because as a dreamer he had none [40/41] of that toughness himself at all.

Perry's sexual interests were practically nil. When Dick went to the whorehouses, Perry sat in the cafes, waiting. There was only one occasion—that was their first night in Mexico when the two of them went to a bordello run by an "old queen," according to Dick. Ten dollars was the price—which they weren't *about* to pay, and they said so. Well, the old queen looked at them and said perhaps he could arrange something for less; he disappeared and came out with this female midget about 3 feet 2 inches tall. Dick was disgusted, but Perry was madly excited. That was the only instance. Perry was such a little moralist after all.

How long do you think the two would have stayed together had they not been picked up in Las Vegas? Was the odd bond that kept them together beginning to fray? One senses in the rashness of their acts and plans a subconscious urge to be captured.

Dick planned to ditch Perry in Las Vegas, and I think he would have done so. No, I certainly don't think this particular pair wanted to be caught—though this is a common criminal phenomenon.

How do you yourself equate the sort of petty punk that Detective Alvin Dewey feels Dick is with the extraordinary violence in him—to "see hair all over the walls"?

Dick's was definitely a small-scale criminal mind. These violent phrases were simply a form of bragging meant to impress Perry, who *was* impressed, for he liked to think of Dick as being "tough." Perry was too sensitive to be "tough." Sensitive. But himself able to kill.

Is it one of the artistic limitations of the nonfiction novel that the writer is placed at the whim of chance? Suppose, in the case of "In Cold Blood," clemency had been granted? Or the two boys had been less interesting? Wouldn't the artistry of the book have suffered? Isn't luck involved?

It is true that I was in the peculiar situation of being involved in a slowly developing situation. I never knew until the events were well along whether a book was going to be possible. There was always the choice, after all, of whether to stop or go on. The book could have ended with the trial, with just a coda at the end explaining what had finally happened. If the principals had been uninteresting or completely uncooperative, I could have stopped and looked elsewhere, perhaps not very far. A nonfiction novel could have been written about any of the other prisoners in Death Row—York and Latham, or especially Lee Andrews. Andrews was the most *subtly* crazy person you can imagine—I mean there was just one thing wrong with him. He was the most rational, calm, bright young boy you'd ever want to meet. I mean *really* bright—which is what made him a truly awesome kind of person. Because his one flaw was, it didn't bother him *at all* to kill. Which is quite a trait. The people who crossed his path, well, to his way of thinking, the best thing to do with them was just to put them in their graves.

What other than murder might be a subject suitable for the nonfiction novel?

The other day someone suggested that the break-up of a marriage would be an interesting topic for a nonfiction novel. I disagreed. First of all, you'd have to find two people who would be willing—who'd sign a release. Second, their respective views on the subject-matter would be incoherent. And third, any couple who'd subject themselves to the scrutiny demanded would quite likely be a pair of kooks. But it's amazing how many events *would* work with the theory of the nonfiction novel in mind—the Watts riots, for example. They would provide a subject that satisfied the first essential of the nonfiction novel—that there is a timeless quality about the cause and events. That's important. If its going to date, it can't be a work of art. The requisite would also be that you would have had to live through the riots, at least part of them, as a witness, so that a depth of perception could be acquired. That event, just three days. It would take years to do. You'd start with the family that instigated the riots without ever meaning to.

With the nonfiction novel I suppose the temptation to fictionalize events, or a line of dialogue, for example, must at times be over-whelming. With "In Cold Blood" was there any invention of this sort to speak of—I was thinking specifically of the dog you described trotting along the road at the end of a section on Perry and Dick, and then later you introduce the next section on the two with Dick swerving to hit the dog. Was there actually a dog at that exact point in the narrative, or were you using this habit of Dick's as a fiction device to bridge the two sections?

No. There was a dog, and it was precisely as described. One doesn't spend almost six years on a book, the point of which is factual accuracy, and then give way to minor distortions. People are so suspicious. They ask, "How can you reconstruct the conversation of a dead girl, Nancy Clutter, without fictionalizing?" If they read the book carefully, they can see readily [41/42] enough how it's done. It's a silly question. Each time Nancy appears in the narrative, there are witnesses to what she is saying and doing—phone calls, conversations, being overheard. When she walks the horse up from the river in the twilight, the hired man is a witness and talked to her then. The last time we see her, in her bedroom, Perry and Dick themselves were the witnesses, and told me what she had said. What is reported of her, even in the narrative form, is as accurate as many hours of questioning, over and over again, can make it. All of it is reconstructed from the evidence of witnesses—which is implicit in the title of the first section of the book—"The Last to See Them Alive."

How conscious were you of film techniques in planning the book?

Consciously, not at all. Subconsciously, who knows?

After their conviction, you spent years corresponding and visiting with the prisoners. What was the relationship between the two of them?

When they were taken to Death Row, they were right next door to each other. But they didn't talk much. Perry was intensely secretive and wouldn't ever talk because he didn't want the other prisoners— York, Latham, and particularly Andrews, whom he despised—to hear anything that he had to say. He would write Dick notes on "kites" as he called them. He would reach out his hand and zip the "kite" into Dick's cell. Dick didn't much enjoy receiving these communications because they were always one form or another of recrimination— nothing to do with the Clutter crime, but just general dissatisfaction with things there in prison and . . . the people, very often Dick himself. Perry'd send Dick a note: "If I hear you tell another of those filthy jokes again I'll kill you when we go to the shower!" He was quite a little moralist, Perry, as I've said.

It was over a moral question that he and I had a tremendous falling-out once. It lasted for about two months. I used to send them things to read—both books and magazines. Dick only wanted girlie magazines—either those or magazines that had to do with cars and motors. I sent them both whatever they wanted. Well, Perry said to me one time: "How could a person like you go on contributing to the degeneracy of Dick's mind by sending him all this 'degenerate filthy' literature?" Weren't they all sick enough without this further contribution towards their total moral decay? He'd got very grand talking in terms that way. I tried to explain to him that I was neither his judge nor Dick's—and if that was what Dick wanted to read, that was *his* business. Perry felt that was entirely wrong—that people had to fulfill an obligation towards moral leadership. Very grand. Well, I agree with him up to a point, but in the case of Dick's reading matter it was absurd, of course, and so we got into such a really serious argument about it that afterwards, for two months, he wouldn't speak or even write to me.

How often did the two correspond with you?

Except for those occasional fallings-out, they'd write twice a week. I wrote them both twice a week all those years. One letter to the both of them didn't work. I had to write them both, and I had to be careful not to be repetitious, because they were very jealous of each other. Or rather, Perry was terribly jealous of Dick, and if Dick got one more letter than he did, that would create a great crisis. I wrote them about what I was doing, and where I was living, describing everything in the most careful detail. Perry was interested in my dog, and I would always write about him, and send along pictures. I often wrote them about their legal problems.

Do you think if the social positions of the two boys had been different that their personalities would have been markedly different?

Of course there wasn't anything peculiar about Dick's social position. He was a very ordinary boy who simply couldn't sustain any kind of normal relationship with anybody. If he had been given $10,000, perhaps he might have settled into some small business. But I don't think so. He had a very natural criminal instinct towards everything. He was oriented towards stealing from the beginning. On the other hand, I think Perry could have been an entirely different person. I really do. His life had been so incredibly abysmal that I don't see what chance he had as a little child except to steal and run wild.

Of course, you could say that his brother, with exactly the same background, went ahead and became the head of his class. What does it matter that he later killed himself. No, it's there—it's the fact that the brother *did* kill himself, in spite of his success, that shows how really awry the background of the Smiths' lives were. Terrifying. Perry had extraordinary qualities, but they just weren't channeled properly—to put it mildly. He was really a talented boy in a limited way—he had a genuine sensitivity—and, as I've said, when he talked about himself as an artist, he wasn't really joking at all.

You once said that emotionality made you lose writing control —that you had to exhaust emotion before you could get to work. Was there a problem with "In Cold Blood," considering your involvement with the case and its principals?

Yes, it was a problem. Nevertheless, I felt in control throughout. However, I had great difficulty writing the last six or seven pages. This even took a physical form: hand paralysis. I finally used a typewriter— very awkward as I always write in longhand.

Your feeling about capital punishment is implicit in the title of the book. How do you feel the lot of Perry and Dick should have been resolved?

I feel that capital crimes should all be handled by Federal [42/43] Courts, and that those convicted should be imprisoned in a special Federal prison where, conceivably, a life-sentence could mean, as it does not in state courts, just that.

Did you see the prisoners on their final day? Perry wrote you a 100-page letter that you received after the execution. Did he mention that he had written it?

Yes, I was with them the last hour before the execution. No, Perry did not mention the letter. He only kissed me on the cheek, and said, "Adios, amigo."

What was the letter about?

It was a rambling letter, often intensely personal, often setting forth his various philosophies. He had been reading Santayana. Somewhere he had read "The Last Puritan," and had been very impressed by it. What I really think impressed him about me was that I had once visited Santayana at the Convent of the Blue Nuns in Rome. He always wanted me to go into great detail about that visit, what Santayana had looked like, and the nuns, and all the physical details. Also, he had been reading Thoreau. Narratives didn't interest him at all. So in his letter he would write: "As Santayana says—" and then there'd be five pages of what Santayana *did* say. Or he'd write: "I agree with Thoreau about this. Do you?"—then he'd write that he didn't *care* what I thought, and he'd add five or ten pages of what he agreed with Thoreau about.

The case must have left you with an extraordinary collection of memorabilia.

My files would almost fill a whole small room, right up to the ceiling. All my research. Hundreds of letters. Newspaper clippings. Court records—the court records almost fill two trunks. There were so many Federal hearings on the case. One Federal hearing was twice as long as the original court trial. A huge assemblage of stuff. I have some of the personal belongings—all of Perry's because he left me everything he owned; it was miserably little, his books, written in and annotated; the letters he received while in prison . . . not very many . . . his paintings and drawings. Rather a heart-breaking assemblage that arrived about a month after the execution. I simply couldn't bear to look at it for a long time. I finally sorted everything. Then, also, after the execution, that 100-page letter from Perry got to me. The last line of the letter—it's Thoreau, I think, a paraphrase, goes, "And suddenly I realize life is the father and death is the mother." The last line. Extraordinary.

What will you do with this collection?

I think I may burn it all. You think I'm kidding? I'm not. The book is what is important. It exists in its own right. The rest of the material is extraneous, and it's personal, what's more. I don't really want people poking around in the material of six years of work and research. The book is the end result of all that, and it's exactly what I wanted to do from it.

Detective Dewey told me that he felt the case and your stays in Garden City had changed you—even your style of dress . . . that you were more "conservative" now, and had given up detachable collars. . . .

Of course the case changed me! How could anyone live through such an experience without it profoundly affecting him? I've always been almost overly aware of the precipice we all walk along, the ridge and the abyss on either side; the last six years have increased this awareness to an almost all-pervading point. As for the rest—Mr. Dewey, a man for whom I have the utmost affection and respect, is perhaps confusing comparative youth (I was 35 when we first met) with the normal aging process. Six years ago I had four more teeth and considerably more hair than is now the case, and furthermore I lost 20 pounds. I dress to accommodate the physical situation. By the way, I have never worn a detachable collar.

What are you going to work on now?

Well, having talked at such length about the nonfiction novel, I must admit I'm going to go on to write a *novel*, a straight novel, one I've had in mind for about 15 years. But I will attempt the nonfiction form again—when the time comes and the subject appears and I recognize the possibilities. I have one very good idea for another one, but I'm going to let it simmer on the back of my head for awhile. It's quite a step—to undertake the nonfiction novel. Because the amount of work is enormous. The relationship between the author and all the people he must deal with if he does the job properly—well, it's a full 24-hour-a-day job. Even when I wasn't working on the book, I was somehow involved with all the characters in it—with their personal lives, writing six or seven letters a day, taken up with their problems, a complete involvement. It's extraordinarily difficult and consuming, but for a writer who tries, doing it all the way down the line, the result can be a unique and exciting form of writing.

What has been the response of readers of "In Cold Blood" to date?

I've been staggered by the letters I've received—their quality of sensibility, their articulateness, the compassion of their authors. The letters are not fan letters. They're from people deeply concerned about what it is I've written about. About 70 per cent of the letters think of the book as a reflection on American life—this collision between the desperate, ruthless, wandering, savage part of American life, and the other, which is insular and safe, more or less. It has struck them because there is something so awfully inevitable about what is going to happen: the people in the book are completely beyond their own control. For example, Perry wasn't an evil person. If he'd had any chance in life, things would have been different. But every illusion he'd ever had, well, they all evaporated, so that on that night he was so full of self-hatred and self-pity that I think he would have killed *some*body—perhaps not that night, or the next, or the next. You can't get through life without ever getting anything you want, ever.

At the very end of the book you give Alvin Dewey a scene in the country cemetery, a chance meeting with Sue Kidwell, which seems to synthesize the whole experience for him. Is there such a moment in your own case?

I'm still very much haunted by the whole thing. I have finished the book, but in a sense I *haven't* finished it: it keeps churning around in my head. It particularizes itself now and then, but not in the sense that it brings about a total conclusion. It's like the echo of E. M. Forster's Malabar Caves, the echo that's meaningless and yet it's there: one keeps hearing it all the time. [43]

In Cold Fact

PHILLIP K. TOMPKINS

As every literate American must know by now, *In Cold Blood* is the "true account of a multiple murder and its consequences." Late in 1959, four members of the Herbert W. Clutter family were bound and shot to death in Holcomb, Kansas, by Richard Eugene Hickock and Perry Edward Smith. Nearly five and a half years later, the killers were hanged; this execution allowed Truman Capote to complete the last chapter of what came to be called the literary sensation of the year. *In Cold Blood* is organized into four main parts and eighty-six unnumbered chapters which generally alternate between events in Kansas and the travels of the killers. Actually the chapters are more like short stories; many of them could stand by themselves with little or no additional context. All together they constitute the substance of Capote's claim that he has established a new literary form: the "nonfiction novel."

How does one evaluate a new literary form? Does it require a new method of criticism? Obviously one must begin by asking after the author's purpose. If the novel is defined as a "fictional prose narrative of substantial length," Capote's new form must be a self-contradiction: nonfiction fiction. He cannot have it both ways; and he seems not to want it both ways. For example, Capote told the *Saturday Review,* "And then I got this idea of doing a really serious big work—it would be precisely like a novel, with a single difference: every word of it would be true from beginning to end." Each installment in *The New Yorker* began with this claim from the Editor: "All quotations in this article are taken either from official records or from conversations, transcribed verbatim, between the author and the principals." Capote's strongest statement on the authenticity of his book was made in *The New York Times Book Review:* "One doesn't spend almost six years on a book, the point of which is factual accuracy, and then give way to minor distortions." Mr. Capote asks us to believe his book is true, is without even "minor distortions."

It seems apparent that the criteria of conventional novelistic criti-

From *Esquire,* LXV (June 1966), pp. 125, 127, 166–171. © 1966 by Esquire, Inc. Reprinted by permission of Esquire Magazine.

cism cannot be brought to bear fully on this work. How can one be critical of the plot probabilities of true events? The only relevant criteria would seem to be those normally applied to journalism and history. In other words, is the work good reportage? If facts are basis for the plot, and if the artistic success of such a work must rest upon their accuracy, is the author's account of the events, by objective standards, true?

Kansas is my home state. I grew up in Wichita and passed through Garden City and Holcomb many times on my way to and from college in Colorado. I taught for two years at the University of Kansas where a minor character in Capote's book, Lowell Lee Andrews, was enrolled in one of my courses.

On February 4, 1966, a cold and snowy morning in Detroit, I left on a nine-day trip to Kansas to look for external evidence. My methods were those of conventional journalism: interviews with principals and a search for documentary confirmation. I had been anticipated in my search by another reporter with the same interests. In a lengthy Kansas City *Times* article of January 27, with numerous photographs, Robert Pearman suggested the possibility of several minor inaccuracies in the book by interviewing some of the principals in Garden City and Holcomb.

Bobby Rupp, the last person (other than the killers) to see the Clutters alive, told Pearman: "He [Capote] put things in there that to other people make good reading but the people who were actually involved know that he exaggerated [125/127] a little bit. . . . He makes me out to be some kind of great athletic star and really I was just an average small-town basketball player." (This is not false modesty on Rupp's part; I talked to several people who had seen him play.) "And he has me always running back and forth to the Clutter place. I didn't do that."

And the conclusion of Pearman's article:

There is one character in the book that Capote was dead wrong about—Nancy Clutter's riding horse Babe. Capote has the horse sold to a Mennonite farmer for a plow horse for $75.

(Capote wrote: " 'I hear fifty . . . sixty-five . . . seventy . . .' the bidding was laggardly, nobody seemed really to want Babe, and the man who got her, a Mennonite farmer who said he might use her for plowing, paid seventy-five dollars. As he led her out of the corral, Sue Kidwell ran forward; she raised her hand as though to wave good-bye, but instead clasped it over her mouth.")

"Hell, I couldn't even get a bid in until the mare got to $100," says Seth Earnest, father of the postmaster, the man who actually bought Babe. Mr. Earnest is neither Mennonite by religion nor farmer by occupation.

"I gave $182.50 for Babe," he said. "I wanted her for a couple of reasons. One was sentimental and the other was that she was in foal to a registered quarter horse, Aggie Twist, and I wanted the colt."

Earnest's prudent judgment would pay later rewards. He sold the colt as a two-year-old for $250 and she has raised two more.

In the summertime Babe is used by the Y.M.C.A. to train children to ride.

To Earnest it is a much happier end for Nancy Clutter's horse than the fate to which Capote resigned her, and it is one to which Nancy, who loved the horse dearly, would have surely subscribed.

The significant point about this rather minor interpolation is that it provides the flourish Capote needed to complete short story number seventy.

If the discrepancies in Capote's account were all as minor as these, one might easily dismiss them as quibbles. They lead, however, into questions of greater import—questions of how much license a purportedly objective reporter can be permitted in selecting and interpreting one set of facts as opposed to another equally or even more convincing set of facts. In life, truth is complicated and often ambiguous. The same is true of art. But the artist, to make his point, can eliminate certain awkward complications the better to suggest a larger truth. Because Capote has not chosen to make his stand in *In Cold Blood* on artistry alone, but claims literal truth, an awareness of Capote's method in rendering the climax of *In Cold Blood* is enlightening and disturbing. The climax is literally and ironically the moment of truth in the book; until that point the reader is unsure of just how, and by whom, the Clutter murders were committed. In the sixty-first chapter we learn that, although Hickock has made a statement in the Las Vegas City Jail blaming Smith for all four killings, Smith has admitted only the falsity of his alibi—nothing more. Capote wrote: "And though even [K.B.I. agent] Duntz had forfeited his composure— had shed, along with his tie and coat, his enigmatic drowsy dignity —the suspect seemed content and serene; he refused to budge. He'd never heard of the Clutters or Holcomb, or even Garden City."

In the sixty-third chapter (the intervening one is a flashback to Hartman's Café in Holcomb), K.B.I. agents Dewey and Duntz, along with Smith, are in the first of a two-car caravan headed for Garden City. Smith has still not budged. The agents try to goad Smith into confessing by repeating parts of Hickock's confession—with no success. Agent Dewey, without anticipating any unusual response from the accused, mentions an incident in which Smith had supposedly beaten a Negro to death some years earlier.

To Dewey's surprise, the prisoner gasps. He twists around in his seat until he can see, through the rear window, the motorcade's second car, see inside it: "The tough boy!" Turning back, he stares at the dark streak of desert highway. "I thought it was a stunt. I didn't believe you. That Dick let fly. The tough boy! Oh, a real brass boy. Wouldn't harm the fleas on a dog. Just run over the dog." He spits. "I never killed any nigger. But *he* thought so. I always knew if we ever got caught, if Dick ever really let fly, dropped his guts all over the goddam floor—I knew he'd tell about the nigger." He spits again. "So Dick was afraid of me? That's amusing. I'm very amused. What he don't know is, I almost did shoot him."

Dewey lights two cigarettes, one for himself, one for the prisoner. "Tell us about it, Perry."

And Perry Smith tells.

An alternative version exists in the office of the Clerk of the Supreme Court of Kansas, where there is on file the official transcript of case number 2322, District Court of Finney County, Kansas: "THE STATE OF KANSAS, Plaintiff, vs. RICHARD EUGENE HICKOCK and PERRY EDWARD SMITH, Defendants." It is a document of 515 pages, the last one of which is signed by Lillian C. Valenzuela, Certified Shorthand Reporter, Garden City, Kansas. The following exchange, between Logan Green (assistant to the County Attorney) and K.B.I. agent Dewey, is taken verbatim from pages 231–233. Dewey is testifying as to the first time that Smith made a remark implicating himself in the crime.

Q: Where was that?
A: That was at the Police Department at Las Vegas.
Q: Did he give you any information concerning the crimes?
A: He did. I told Perry Smith that Hickock had given the other agents a statement and that Hickock had said that they had sold the radio, the portable radio, that they had taken from Kenyon Clutter's room, that they had sold it in Mexico City. I told Smith that we were going to send an agent down there to get the radio and that before we sent this agent I wanted to know for sure that where Hickock said that radio was, that it was there. Present when I was talking to Perry Smith on this occasion was Mr. Duntz and Mr. Nye of the Kansas Bureau of Investigation. Mr. Nye told Perry Smith where Hickock had said that he sold the portable radio, and Smith said that was right.
Q: Did he give you any further information in connection with the crimes at that time?
A: No, sir.
Q: Subsequent to that did you have any other conversation with him?
A: Yes. I talked to Perry Smith later that same day, which was on the 4th of January, 1960. At that time I talked to him when we were in the car en route back to Garden City.
Q: Who was with you on that trip back to Garden City?
A: Smith and Mr. Duntz and myself were in one car. Sheriff Robinson and Mr. Church, of the Kansas Bureau of Investigation, and Hickock were in the other car.
Q: On the way back you say he gave you some additional information?
A: He did.
Q: I will ask you to tell the Court and jury what he said to you.
A: As we were leaving Las Vegas, before we were out of the city limits—Sheriff Robinson, Hickock and Mr. Church were in the lead car. Myself, Perry and Mr. Duntz were following, and Perry could see in the car ahead and Hickock was talking, and Perry said to us, he says, "Isn't he a

tough guy?" meaning Hickock. He says, "Look at him talk." He said, "Hickock had told me that if we were ever caught that we weren't going to say a word but there he is, just talking his head off." He then asked me what Hickock said in regard to the killing of the Clutter family, who killed them. I told Perry that Hickock says that he killed all of the family. Perry told me that wasn't correct, but he said, "I killed two of them and Hickock killed two of them."

Several inferences can be drawn from this testimony. First, contrary to Capote's account, Perry had begun to crack in the Las Vegas City Jail. His remarks about Kenyon Clutter's radio implicated him in the crime. Second, contrary to Capote's account, Dewey, Duntz and Smith were not in the lead car; Smith would have seen nothing but a dark streak of desert highway had he turned around to see out the rear window at that moment. Third, contrary to Capote's account, Sheriff Robinson was in the lead car (Capote neither has Robinson on the trip to Las Vegas nor the return to Garden City). Indeed, it was Robinson's car in the lead; the Garden City *Telegram's* account of the trip chronicled a small crisis when Robinson's car suffered a burned-out wheel bearing in Lamar, Colorado, and Hickock had to be transferred twice to get him to Garden City. Fourth, contrary to Capote's account, it was not the "nigger" incident that precipitated the sudden confession from Smith. Rather, it was simply Smith's observation of Hickock's loquaciousness in the lead car.

At this point I began to wonder about the "nigger" incident. Had Dewey simply forgotten that by relating this story he had forced Smith to gasp and confess? The answer came later, in Duntz's testimony of the same events (pages 276 to 282 of the transcript). After establishing that he, Duntz, had first become acquainted with Smith in the "forepart of March, 1956" (a coincidence unmentioned in the book), Duntz went on to mention the first time Smith had implicated himself [127 /166] in the Clutter case. The direct examination is by County Attorney Duane West:

A: That was also at Police Headquarters and we were just making arrangements to leave and Agent Nye was making preparation to go to look for the radio that we had information had been taken. Perry was asked by Mr. Dewey if he cared to tell us where that was.

Q: Did he do so?

A: Yes, he did.

Q: What did he tell you at that time?

A: As I recall, he stated that it was sold in Mexico City to the same person who had bought Richard Hickock's car.

Q: Mr. Duntz, what further conversation did you have with the defendant, if any?

A: Very little. I can't recall any there at Police Headquarters after that.

Q: Did you have conversation with the defendant after you left Las Vegas?

A: Yes.

Q: Would you relate to the jury where this conversation was and when it was?

A: It was soon after we had left Las Vegas en route back to Kansas.

Q: Would you tell the jury just exactly what happened, as you recall it?

A: Perry Smith asked—do you mind if I clarify myself how we were riding?

Q: Go ahead.

A: I was riding in the car with Mr. Dewey and Perry Smith. They were riding in the front seat. I was in the back seat. The conversation was had between Perry Smith and Mr. Dewey. Perry asked Mr. Dewey if he could tell him what Dick had said about the murder and Mr. Dewey answered, "Yes, Dick said that you tied and killed all of them," and Perry said, "That isn't right." He said, "He killed two and I killed two."

Q: Was there any further conversation at that time, Mr. Duntz?

A: Well, at that time I told Perry of a conversation that I had had with Richard Hickock at Las Vegas, and that was Richard had told me soon after he had signed the statement that if I would tell Perry about a killing that Perry had told him about, and that pertained to an incident that was supposed to have happened previous to the time that Perry got in trouble—pardon me, in 1955—and Richard Hickock told me if I would tell Perry Smith that Perry had told him that previous to that time he had killed a nigger by clubbing him to death, then Perry would know that he, Richard Hickock, had been talking to us and giving us a statement.

Several inferences can also be drawn from this testimony. First, it corroborates Dewey's testimony—establishing that Smith had begun to crack in the Las Vegas City Jail, establishing also that it was Dewey's answer to a question from Smith that preceded the confession. Second, contrary to Capote's account, the "nigger" incident was related by the agents to Smith *after* he admitted two of the slayings. Third, contrary to Capote's account, it was Duntz, not Dewey, who repeated the fictitious story to Smith.

We now have the word, given under oath, of two of the three principals to the climax of the story. We can presume that this pair of professionals did not perjure themselves; can we be so sure of what Smith may have told Capote? And if Capote favors Smith's version over the one given by Dewey and Duntz, is he not discrediting Dewey as a source? How then should we evaluate the remaining portions of the book in which we see events through Dewey's eyes?

So much for the manner of the confession. What of its contents? During the trial, Dewey was forced to testify as to the substance of Smith's confession because the statement was never signed by the defendant. Newspaper reports of Dewey's testimony at the trial (in the Garden City *Telegram* and the Hutchinson *News*—the latter gave the case the most extensive coverage in the state) do not conform with Capote's version of the contents of the confession. Nevertheless, one

might raise the possibility that Capote—by means of his intimacy with
the principals—had been able to do a better job of reporting than
these Kansas newspapermen who had to get their stories in the
courtroom and hurriedly write copy for deadlines.

Here is Capote's account of Smith's confession to the murder of
Mr. Clutter, the first victim:

"Wait. I'm not telling it the way it was." Perry scowls. He rubs his legs;
the handcuffs rattle. "After, see after we'd taped them, Dick and I went off
in a corner. To talk it over. Remember, now, there were hard feelings
between us. Just then it made my stomach turn to think I'd ever admired
him, lapped up all that brag. I said, 'Well, Dick. Any qualms?' He didn't
answer me. I said, 'Leave them alive, and this won't be any small rap. Ten
years the very least.' He still didn't say anything. He was holding the knife.
I asked him for it, and he gave it to me, and I said, 'All right, Dick. Here
goes.' But I didn't mean it. I meant to call his bluff, make him argue me out
of it, make him admit he was a phony and a coward. See, it was something
between me and Dick. I knelt down beside Mr. Clutter, and the pain of
kneeling—I thought of that goddam dollar. Silver dollar. The shame. Disgust. And *they'd* told me never to come back to Kansas. But I didn't realize
what I'd done till I heard the sound. Like somebody drowning. Screaming
under water. I handed the knife to Dick. I said, 'Finish him. You'll feel
better.' Dick tried—or pretended to. But the man had the strength of ten
men—he was half out of his ropes, his hands were free. Dick panicked. Dick
wanted to get the hell out of there. But I wouldn't let him go. The man
would have died anyway, I know that, but I couldn't leave him like he was.
I told Dick to hold the flashlight, focus it. Then I aimed the gun. The room
just exploded. Went blue. Just blazed up. Jesus, I'll never understand why
they didn't hear the noise twenty miles around."

In contrast to this account, Dewey's testimony was as follows:

. . . So they debated who was going to do what and who was going to
start it, and finally Smith said, "Well," he says, "I'll do it," so he said
Hickock had the shotgun and the flashlight at this time and that he, Smith,
had the knife and he said he put this knife in his hand with the blade up
along his arm so that Mr. Clutter couldn't see it and he walked over to
where Mr. Clutter was laying on this mattress cover and he told him that he
was going to tighten the cords on his hand, and he said he made a pretense
to do that and then he cut Mr. Clutter's throat. Smith said that after doing
that he got up and Hickock said to him, "Give me the knife," and [166/167]
he said about that time they heard a gurgling sound coming from Mr.
Clutter and Smith said that Hickock walked over to where Mr. Clutter was
just as Smith was walking off of this cardboard box, and he said he turned
for just a second and then Dick plunged this—Hickock plunged this knife
into Mr. Clutter's throat, either once or twice. He said he couldn't tell
which, but he heard the slap of the knife go in, and he said that he thought
it went in full length because he heard a sound that went something—as he
described to me, something like this (indicating). He said that after
Hickock stepped away from Mr. Clutter that Mr. Clutter jerked one arm
loose, his left arm, I believe, and he put it to his throat to try to stop the

bleeding, and he said after that Hickock ran over to where he was and he said, "Let's get the hell out of here," and Smith said that he could see that Mr. Clutter was suffering and told Hickock that that was a hell of a way to leave a guy, because he felt he was going to die anyway, so Smith said he said to Hickock, "Shall I shoot him?" and Hickock said, "Yes, go ahead," so Smith said that he shot Mr. Clutter in the head while Hickock held the flashlight. . . .

The two versions differ in many small details, but the most serious discrepancy concerns the mental state of Smith at the moment of the murder. Capote has Smith say, "But I didn't mean it." And, "But I didn't realize what I'd done till I heard the sound." (In The New York Times interview, Capote referred to Smith's mental state at that moment as a "brain explosion.") Dewey, on the other hand, has Smith committing the murder with *full consciousness and intent*. On Dewey's word, the act was premeditated to the degree that Smith announced his intention, took pains to conceal the knife from the victim and deceived Mr. Clutter into thinking he was going to tighten his bonds. He made that pretense—and then cut Mr. Clutter's throat. The two versions suggest different mental states.

I see three possible explanations that Capote might offer for these discrepancies: first, that the oral confession given during the automobile trip from Las Vegas was different from the statement Smith made upon arriving in Garden City (it was about the latter that Dewey was testifying); second, that Smith later told Capote of details that he did not reveal while confessing to Dewey; and third, that Smith's later recollections of the confession (as told to Capote) were more accurate than Dewey's recollections (as told to the Court).

We can dismiss the first explanation, that the confession in the car was different from the one dictated in the Sheriff's private office in Garden City. Capote describes, on page 255, the second confession by saying it "recounted admissions already made to Alvin Dewey and Clarence Duntz." Furthermore, there is no indication in either the book or the transcript that the two confessions differed in any way.

The second possible explanation, that Smith told Capote details he had not revealed to Dewey, is undoubtedly true; Capote claims to have had more than two hundred interviews with the killers. But to include these remarks is not to report the confession as it took place. And I doubt, for reasons to be discussed later, that Smith could have truthfully given such radically different versions of the confession. (Wendle Meier, former Undersheriff of Finney County, told me that he had visited Smith at Lansing; that Smith told him that there would be inaccuracies in the book; that when he Meier, asked what these would be, Smith would only say: Read it and see for yourself.)

The third possible explanation, that Smith's later recollections of the confession (as told to Capote) were more accurate than Dewey's testimony, is not difficult to refute. Duntz's testimony in the transcript

corroborates Dewey's testimony in every way. [167/168] More con-
clusive is the fact that Dewey gave an extremely accurate account of
the contents of the confession. I know because I have examined it. It is
now in the possession of former County Attorney West; like the
transcript of the trial, it was taken down in shorthand and transcribed
by Mrs. Valenzuela. This sample is relevant to the point at issue.

. . . I think we was debating who was going to do what and who was
going to start it, so I told him, "Well," I says, "I'll do it," so I walked over
to Mr. Clutter and he couldn't hear us talk from where we was over at the
door. We was kind of talking in a whisper. I walked over to Mr. Clutter and
Dick come over close. He had the flashlight and had the shotgun in his
hand and I would say he was standing, oh, about at Mr. Clutter's feet, and
Mr. Clutter didn't see the knife. I had it with the handle in my hand and
the blade up like this (indicating) and down about my side. I went up toward Mr. Clutter's head and I told him I was going to tie his hands a little
tighter and he was laying on his right side and he was taped then. He didn't
say anything or he didn't mumble and, well, as I made a pretense to tie his
hands again I cut Mr. Clutter's throat. That's when I cut Mr. Clutter's
throat, and he started to struggle and I got up right away and Dick says,
"Give me that knife." I could see he was nervous and that's when the
gurgling sound of Mr. Clutter was noticed. . . .

Here we have Smith's own words, taken verbatim from official
records. There is hardly an implication of either "brain explosion," or
"mental eclipse," or "schizophrenic darkness" at this critical moment.

After Hickock and Smith were returned to Garden City, they were
housed in the County Jail. To separate them, Smith was kept in an
isolated unit inside the Sheriff's residence; occupying the residence at
that time were Undersheriff Meier and his wife. Smith's cell adjoined
Mrs. Meier's kitchen; it is from her point of view that we learn of
Smith's stay there. For example, the final paragraph of the sixty-fifth
chapter is narrated by her; she is describing a discussion she and her
husband had in bed shortly after Smith had been jailed. She remarks
that Smith was not the worst young man she had met. Mr. Meier
reprimands her for such thoughts.

While in Garden City, I talked to Mr. Meier about the incident;
he was adamant that it had not taken place. On February 26, 1966, I
placed a long-distance telephone call to Mrs. Meier (she had been out
of town while I was in Garden City). She also insisted that this
incident had never taken place—and that she had not told Capote any
such thing. She explained that her husband—as did all the officers
involved—worked day and night on the case. She rarely saw him
during that period. When he did get a chance to get some sleep, the
last thing he wanted to talk about was the case. In short, the only two
principals to this event insist that it did not take place—and that they
did not tell Capote any such story.

The finishing touch of the seventy-seventh chapter evokes considerable sympathy for Perry Smith. Mrs. Meier is quoted as saying: "I heard him crying. I turned on the radio. Not to hear him. But I could. Crying like a child. He'd never broke down before, shown any sign of it. Well, I went to him. The door of his cell. He reached out his hand. He wanted me to hold his hand, and I did, I held his hand, and all he said was, 'I'm embraced by shame.' "

During our telephone conversation, Mrs. Meier repeatedly told me that she *never* heard Perry cry; that on the day in question she was in her bedroom, not the kitchen; that she did not turn on the radio to drown out the sound of crying; that she did not hold Perry's hand; that she did not hear Perry say, "I'm embraced by shame." And finally— that she had never told such things to Capote. Mrs. Meier told me repeatedly and firmly, in her gentle way, that these things were not true.

Mrs. Meier said that she actually saw very little of Perry Smith. She had only occasional conversations with him while working in the kitchen. She said that she saw him the day after he received the death penalty and that he was rather bitter. But again, she never heard him cry. Perhaps Smith told Capote of these things, but it is inaccurate to put these words in Mrs. Meier's mouth—and even more inaccurate to have her participate in events that did not take place.

Now let us turn to another significant part of the book—the conclusion. In the final chapter of *In Cold Blood* we see the execution of the killers. Hickock was hanged first. Smith was brought into the warehouse and asked whether or not he wished to make a statement. Those last words as quoted by Capote, are: " 'I think,' he said, 'it's a helluva thing to take a life in this manner. I don't believe in capital punishment, morally or legally. Maybe I had something to contribute, something—' His assurance faltered; shyness blurred his voice, lowered it to a just audible level. 'It would be meaningless to apologize for what I did. Even inappropriate. But I do. I apologize.' "

Bill Brown, editor of the Garden City *Telegram,* represented the Kansas newspapers as a witness of the execution. He stood four feet from Smith when these words were spoken (Capote was unable to watch; he walked away, out of earshot). Brown took notes. He immediately compared his notes with those of the wire-service representatives standing on either side of him—they were identical. Here are Smith's last words as recorded and reported by Brown in the *Telegram* of April 14, 1965:

Asked if he had anything to say before mounting the gallows, Smith stated, "Yes, I would like to say a word or two.

"I think it is a hell of a thing that a life has to be taken in this manner.

"Any apology for what I have done would be meaningless at this time. I say this especially because there's a great deal I could have offered society. I certainly think capital punishment is legally and morally wrong.

I don't have any animosities toward anyone involved in this matter. I think that is all."

Brown is today convinced that Smith did not apologize.

Tony Jewell of Garden City's radio station KIUL was the first radio newcaster to be invited to witness an execution in Kansas. Immediately after the execution, Jewell and Brown telephoned their reports from the prison to the radio station in Garden City; the remarks were recorded for later broadcasts. I have a tape recording of that broadcast; again, there was no apology from Smith. Furthermore, there is no indication of an apology in the Associated Press story filed that day.

Finally, in a telephone conversation [168/170] with Alvin A. Dewey on February 5, I asked him how Capote had obtained Smith's last words (in the book it is through Dewey's eyes and ears that we see and hear these events). Mr. Dewey did not know. "Perhaps he overheard me talking about it later," he suggested. Had Perry apologized? Mr. Dewey could not recall Perry's exact words, but thought they were "something along that line." What is certain is that Capote did not hear Perry's words at firsthand. Dewey, the narrator of the event in the book, is now unsure of the words spoken by Smith and also unsure of how Capote gathered the information. Capote's reconstruction, then, conflicts with the report by two newsmen who made their notes on the spot—not sometime later, which is the method of recording Capote tells us he used. The best evidence supports the conclusion that Perry Smith did not apologize.

In addition to searching for documentation while in Kansas, I was curious about the legal question raised by Rebecca West in her *Harper's* review of *In Cold Blood:* "Hickock was hanged for murder which he had not committed, when he should have been sentenced to a term of imprisonment as an accessory, but this was his own fault. The truth could only be established if both he and Perry chose to give evidence, but this, for a reason Mr. Capote does not explain, they did not do."

Who would know the answer?

The newspaper files show that former County Attorney Duane West played a significant, if not the most significant, role in the case. He was on the scene of the crime the day the bodies were discovered; he was involved in the investigation from beginning to end; he held daily press conferences; he prepared the brief and the trial outline for the case; he asked the County Commissioners for permission to hire an assistant—Logan Green; he gave the opening remarks for the prosecution; he handled much of the examination of witnesses; he gave a forty-five-minute closing argument for the prosecution; he represented the County and State in the appeal before the Supreme Court of Kansas. (In the book, however, West is made to appear somewhat lower in rank than a law clerk.)

Legally, as Attorney West told the jury (and me), it made no difference whether Hickock killed any or all of the Clutters. Under the Felony Murder Rule, which applies in Kansas and many other states, any party to a felony in which a life is taken can be prosecuted for murder. "If you and I conspired to rob a store," West explained, "and I killed someone while robbing it—you could be tried for murder."

West had decided to try Smith and Hickock together; when it became known that they might request separate trials, West moved to have their names added to the list of witnesses (which he could not do if they were to be tried together). "Our feeling was that Perry would testify against Dick. He was willing to take the blame for all four killings to make it easier for Hickock's mother, but he was not willing to take the blame for the idea and the plan."

West told me on two occasions that he believed Smith's confession to be true—that Hickock killed the two Clutter women. Another man intimate with the case from beginning to end, Bill Brown, agrees that Hickock did two of the killings. And so, apparently, did Alvin A. Dewey. When asked, during the trial, why he would not allow Smith to change his confession (to take the blame for all four murders), Dewey explained that Smith and Hickock had been able to shout back and forth from their respective cells and negotiate the changes. They knew that, regardless of the details of the confessions, they would both "swing." Smith was willing to make the changes to spare Hickock's family that much pain. The clear implication of the testimony is that Dewey did not believe Smith. The most we can say for Capote on this point is that it was poor reporting to lead such a careful reader as Rebecca West to the confident conclusion that Smith had committed all the Clutter murders while the principals were less than unanimous.

Before offering my hypothesis for these discrepancies, let me state that Capote's awareness of the errors is not an issue. It is conceivable that they are completely unintentional. As Capote told Jane Howard of *Life* within three hours of each interview he retreated to his motel, wrote up his notes and filed them. "Funnily enough," he said, "I seldom had to look at my notes after that: I had it all in my head." The transformation of facts may well have resulted from his failure to consult his notes more closely.

Capote himself has given us a broad, general hypothesis to explain the discrepancies. A nonfiction novel is more difficult than a conventional novel, he said to *Life*, because "you have to get away from your own particular vision of the world." But possibly Capote did not succeed in doing so; he presumably still needed that very conventional element of the novel as he knows it—a dramatic climax, a moment of truth. Thus, there followed a subtle but significant alteration of the facts to fit a preconception of the novelistic, transforming an unexciting confession into a theatrical catharsis.

But the occasion for transformation demands a more extended

explanation, a closer inspection of the characterization of Perry Smith. Capote was drawn to him more than to Hickock. It is Perry Smith— not the victims, the investigators, the lawyers, not even the pair of killers—who dominates this book. When Smith stood up, wrote Capote, "he was no taller than a twelve-year-old child." The Avedon photographs of the two standing together reveal that Capote, if anything, is a "slippery spray" of hair shorter than Smith. Furthermore, Smith had a miserable childhood. Harper Lee, who has known Capote long and well, told *Newsweek*, "I think every time Truman looked at Perry he saw his own childhood."

But there the similarities—which may have attracted Capote to Smith—would appear to end. Smith, after all, lived in a world very different from Capote's, a world of violence. A measure of the emotional and cultural gap between them is that Perry invented a tale in which he had beaten a Negro to death. It was a boast, calculated to increase the esteem in which his friend Dick held him. Capote, on the other hand, told the *Saturday Review:* "I am not interested in crime per se; I hate violence."

In his vision of the world, Capote found it difficult, if not impossible, to understand how a man could kill, and do so without feeling. He could understand, however, that an outcast and accursed poet might kill while under a "mental eclipse," while [170/171] deep inside a "schizophrenic darkness"—a "brain explosion" if you will—and thus avenge the wrongs "they" had done him.

And so were the facts transformed. Perry Smith, who could hardly utter a grammatical sentence while dictating his confession, becomes *le poète maudit*, corrects the grammar in newspaper articles about him. To judge from his confession, Perry Smith was an obscene, semiliterate and cold-blooded killer. But, as Yuric correctly guessed in the *Nation*, we cannot rest with the Perry Smiths as they are: "Before we kill them we make sure they negate themselves by turning into literate, psychopathic heroes."

By having Smith say, "I didn't realize what I'd done," Capote projected his own vision of the world onto Smith at that moment. In so doing he created a hybrid of Capote-Smith predispositions and the real Smith becomes even less understandable. Should we believe he suffered a "brain explosion" when he poised the rock to open the head of the Omaha salesman? And again when he wished out loud that he could have killed his sister along with the Clutters? And when he planned with Hickock two other murders which Capote told the *Times* he chose to omit from the book? Capote appears to have fallen into the trap of believing that operational definition of insanity one frequently hears: "Anyone who can kill *has* to be insane."

Perry's values toward human life derived from a world in which men expect to kill and be killed. He explained these values quite succinctly (and demonstrated just how much shame he felt) to his friend, Donald Cullivan, on page 291 of the book. Perry insisted that he was not sorry for what he had done; he was only sorry that he could not walk out of the cell with his visitor. Cullivan, like Capote, could scarcely believe that Perry was so devoid of conscience and compassion.

Perry said, "Why? Soldiers don't lose much sleep. They murder, and get medals for doing it. The good people of Kansas want to murder me—and some hangman will be glad to get the work. It's easy to kill—a lot easier than passing a bad check."

For premeditated murder performed in cold blood, Capote substituted unpremeditated murder performed in a fit of insanity. Art triumphs over reality, fiction over nonfiction. By imparting conscience and compassion to Perry, Capote was able to convey qualities of inner sensitivity, poetry and a final posture of contrition in his hero. The killer cries. He asks to have his hand held. He says, "I'm embraced by shame." He apologizes. It is a moving portrait but not, I submit, of the man who actually was Perry Smith—the man who, in real life, told his friend Cullivan he was *not* sorry, the same man who would not play the hypocrite with Cullivan or his old friend Willie-Jay.

In describing Perry, Capote wrote: "His own face enthralled him. Each angle of it induced a different impression. It was a changeling's face." In *Newsweek* Capote described himself: "If you looked at my face from both sides you'd see they were completely different. It's sort of a changeling face." And when Jane Howard of *Life* asked him whether or not he liked Perry and Dick, he said, "That's like saying, 'Do you like yourself?' " Capote's characterization of Smith clearly tells us more about the former than the latter.

As for Capote's unwillingness to deal completely with the question of Hickock's involvement in the actual killings, one plausible explanation is that it makes for a more simplified narrative in an already complex book to let readers assume that there was unanimity among the principals on the point. But, in addition, Capote's conception of the novel places high value on irony. His choice of title, for example, can only be read as irony; he wants us to believe the murders were emotional, spontaneous acts. (After examining the evidence, the title becomes a double irony.) And how much more ironic to present the true, the only, killer in the case as the more appealing figure of the two.

By applying his great artistry to the facts of the Clutter case, Capote has found the inspiration for a multitude of short, internal dramas with effective final curtains. He has achieved a theatrical climax in his confession scene. He has created a heroic, poetic villain—a villain capable of evoking considerable sympathy (as Hollywood was quick to realize). Perhaps we should not have expected anything different from Capote. His good friend, Harper Lee, told *Newsweek:*

"He knows what he wants and he keeps himself straight. And if it's not the way he likes it, he'll arrange it so it is."

Capote has, in short, achieved a work of art. He has told exceedingly well a tale of high terror in his own way. But, despite the brilliance of his self-publicizing efforts, he has made both a tactical and a moral error that will hurt him in the short run. By insisting that "every word" of his book is true he has made himself vulnerable to those readers who are prepared to examine seriously such a sweeping claim. In the long run, however, Capote's presumption will be forgotten. The living people who were involved in the case will no longer testify to another version of the story. The documents will have been pushed to the back of the files by other, more urgent, matters and crimes. Future literary historians and scholars will undoubtedly place Capote's discrepancies of fact as well as his pretensions and rationalizations in perspective, and they will join with the present and future public in enjoying the work for its own sake. "Time . . ." as Auden wrote, "worships language and forgives Everyone by whom it lives. . . ." [171]

2. REVIEWS OF
IN COLD BLOOD

Capote in Kansas

STANLEY KAUFFMANN

Capote's life centered around character

HERE IS A READABLE, GENERALLY INTERESTING BOOK ABOUT FOUR MURDERS in Kansas in 1959. If the author were John Doe, literary consideration could well end there. One might perhaps add that some of the writing is overripe, much of the detail is extraneous "color," some of the handling of material injudicious, and that a 343-page true-crime chronicle which does little more than recount a crime is inflated. Beyond that, however, the treatment, the style, the result would preclude extensive criticism.

Only good point in favor

But extension is inevitable here because of Truman Capote's reputation, the bruited years of preparation, the advance publicity (the book was praised three years before completion by Mark Schorer in his introduction to a volume of Capote's selected writings).

It is not flogging of the author with the publisher's blurb to quote: "*In Cold Blood* . . . represents the culmination of [Capote's] long-standing desire to make a contribution toward the establishment of a serious new literary form: the Non-fiction Novel." This view has been vociferously put forward by the author himself in an interview in *Life*, January 7, 1966 (of which more later). The stated aim is worth discussion, but that Capote has accomplished it is untrue. When I reviewed his selected writings in this journal (February 23, 1963), I noted that he seemed to me an author in search of a character, that his affinity with non-fiction was evident, that his forthcoming book might provide the role as writer for which he has observably, if not consciously, been looking during all his professional life. *In Cold Blood* is not a happy conclusion to that search, if it is a conclusion. The role in which it puts Capote is less than one could have hoped for. The book has been executed without the finese of which, at his best, he has been capable, and it is residually shallow.

It tells the story of the murders of a Kansas farmer named Herbert Clutter, his wife, his teen-age son and daughter by two men

From *The New Republic*, CLIV (January 22, 1966), pp. 19–21, 23. © 1966 Harrison-Blaine of New Jersey, Inc. Reprinted by permission of The New Republic.

named Hickock and Smith: of the criminals' detection, trial, eventual execution. The men had never previously seen any of the Clutters and had never been in the west Kansas town of Holcomb. They were ex-convicts who had been tipped off by a fellow-prisoner to what was thought to be a rich haul from a wealthy farmer. In fact, the killers took "between forty and fifty dollars" in return for four corpses.

Capote's structural method can be called cinematic: he uses intercutting of different story strands, intense closeups, flashbacks, traveling shots, background detail, all as if he were fleshing out a scenario. There is nothing intrinsically defective in the method (although it seems the most obvious choice); but its mechanisms creak here because the hand of the maker is always felt, pushing and pulling and arranging. The chief defect, or imbalance, in the structure is that by page 74 we know that four people have been butchered by two degenerates and we wonder what in the world is going to occupy the remaining 269 pages. Just a detective story? Some psychoanalytical delving? The account of the trial and appeals and execution? All of these are included, of course, but none of them is sufficiently interesting to justify the length accorded them. All of them are overdone, except the psychological inquiry, which is insufficient.

There are attractions in the book. The narrative has impetus, although it is diluted in the latter sections. Western Kansas—wide, flat, almost a separate sovereignty—is well established, a notch all its own in the Bible Belt. Some of the characters are vivid, such as Nancy Clutter, the cheerful, scrubbed, healthy daughter. There are snatches of simon-pure flavorful dialogue. A lunchroom owner (a woman): "Some people say I'm a tough old bird, but the Clutter business sure took the fly out of me." Holcomb's 75-year-old mail messenger (also a woman): "Lots of boys would like to be mail messengers, yes-sir. But I don't know how much they'd like it when the snow's high as old Mr. Primo Carnera, and the wind's blowing blue-hard, and those sacks come sailing—Ugh! Wham!" One of the quotations is unforgettable. In his confession Smith said of Clutter: "I didn't want to harm the man. I thought he was a very [19/20] nice gentleman. Soft-spoken. I thought so right up to the moment I cut his throat."

But it is ridiculous in judgment and debasing of all of us to call this book literature. Are we so bankrupt, so avid for novelty that, merely because a famous writer produces an amplified magazine crime-feature, the result is automatically elevated to serious literature just as Andy Warhol, by painting a soup-carton, has allegedly elevated it to art? (Already I regret writing that; some Capote partisan may take it as the book's pop *raison d'être*, if this has not already been done.) Look first at the writing. Capote demonstrates on almost every page that he is the most outrageously overrated stylist of our time. There is congenital inability to write straightforward English. The mail messenger seems "younger than her years, which amount to seventy-five."

Bernard McCabe noticed the same

Why not "seems younger than her seventy-five years"? Another woman is "sparsely fleshed." Why not "gaunt" or "spare" or "thin"? There is continual strain for the unusual word, a sure sign of insecurity. "His apartment was not the ideal lair for a would-be author." Does Capote know what "lair" means? If so, will he explain why would-be authors need a different kind from other authors? There is much of the clumsy, crammed, *New Yorker*-type sentence: "Though as yet unpublished, young Hendricks, a he-mannish [*sic*] ex-sailor from Oklahoma who smokes a pipe and has a mustache and a crop of untamed black hair, at least looks literary. . . ." There is, inevitably, much "fine" writing: "Though mud abounded underfoot, the sun, so long shrouded by snow and cloud, seemed an object freshly made, and the trees . . . were lightly veiled in a haze of virginal green." Or the very last line: "Then, starting home, he walked toward the trees, and under them, leaving behind him the big sky, the whisper of wind voices in the wind-bent wheat." (Presumably he decided not to take the sky and the wind voices with him.) This is Reddiwhip writing—goo that gushes out under the force of compressed air and that, unless one puts it to the test of taste, looks like the real thing. Capote has also made sure to include what is probably the oldest solecism in English: " . . . an old man who hissed at him: 'Killer! Killer!' "

Sometimes poor writing is separable [20/21] from illumination. In non-fiction, particularly, the distinction between style and content is easier to make than in fiction and is more relevant. But Capote's illumination goes little further than supplying us with facts—and he has vastly oversupplied facts. Condensation by about a third would have improved the book threefold. He suffers from the current craze for fact-gathering and the inability to "waste" material once he has gathered it. On a television panel a few years ago he made the truthful comment about the Kerouac school of fiction: "That isn't writing, it's typing." One can say of this book—with sufficient truth to make it worth saying: "This isn't writing, it's research."

Thus we get: three pages about the brief friendship after the crime between the dead girl's boy friend and her close girl friend; five pages of biography about a man who merely happens to be a fellow-prisoner of Hickock and Smith in Death Row; extensive cute details of the home life of the detective who solved the case; and much, much more superfluous material. We do get fairly clear pictures of the two murderers, but this is surely minimal in so long a book; and the portraits, though extended, are not deep. Some of the more penetrating comment comes from biographical statements that the two men prepared and from a long letter written to Smith by his married sister when he was in prison a year before the murders—this letter is the most interesting document in the book. Statements like these, from people not customarily given to writing, are often phrased pungently and contain perceptions that, probably snobbishly, we would not expect.

There seems to be an impulse to biography, towards preservation of self on paper, which is buried in the normally unliterate and which is released by an occasion that forces them to write.

Nevertheless we do not know enough about these two men at the close to justify the time we have spent with them. It is possibly unjust to ask Capote to solve the mystery of criminal behavior when psychologists, penologists, sociologists are baffled, but if some reasonably satisfactory attempt is not made in this direction, then what *is* the justification for such a book? Mere accretion of grisly fact and the thrills therefrom? *not enough time with killers*

Even the deployment of fact, as such, is wobbly. For example, a major point about Hickock—his sexual predilection for little girls—is not even mentioned until Page 201. Again, there is no comment on the odd relationship between the two criminals. Nothing homosexual occurs overtly, but Hickock constantly calls the other man "honey," there were strange feminine jealousies between them, and Smith was sometimes in the same room while Hickock had intercourse with a girl. No Freudian sage is needed to reveal the girl as a surrogate. Capote leaves unexplored this whole area of latent homosexuality.

In the *Life* interview about this book Capote says:

My theory, you see, is that you can take *any* subject and make it into a nonfiction novel. By that I don't mean a historical or documentary novel— those are popular and interesting but impure genres, with neither the persuasiveness of fact nor the poetic altitude of fiction. . . . What I've done is much harder than a conventional novel. You have to get away from your own particular vision of the novel.

In itself the statement is ludicrous. (Presumably their "own particular vision" is what hamstrung Flaubert, Proust, and Joyce.) What it all amounts to is the puffery of an artistically unsuccessful writer of fiction pursuing his love of the Gothic (which he established in his first novel and his short stories) into life. Why poetize about mules hanging by their necks from balcony railings (as in *Other Voices, Other Rooms*), which is only manufactured grotesquerie, when you can write fancily about real events leading up to and including two real hangings of men? (I do not suggest that crime should not be chronicled. For comparison with Capote, let me recommend John Bartlow Martin's *Why Did They Kill?*, an account of the impromptu murder of a woman by three teen-agers in Ann Arbor in 1951, which Martain published some years before he left first-class journalism for diplomacy. His 131-page book is superior to Capote's in almost every way, makes some attempt to answer the question in its title, and is devoid of any suspicion of conscious [21/23] self-gratifying aggrandizement into Literature.)

But what lies under Capote's statement and the rest of the interview is the question currently much debated—the present pertinence of fiction; whether the writing of factual books is not more appropriate than fiction to talented writers today, whether the functions of the novel have been historically concluded, whether the context for fiction—social structure, community ideals, accepted cosmology—is lacking. It is my view that, in both old and new modes of fiction, much interesting work is being done today; but the question is valid, and anyone who predicted that the status and health of the novel will be no worse a century from now would be, to say the least, sanguine.

In Capote's book, however, there is no kind of answer to the question. There is little fusion of the insights of art with the powers of fact—not as much use of the novelist's eye as there was, for instance, in *The Muses Are Heard*. We have seen in non-fiction, from Lytton Strachey to Barbara Tuchman, how subjective literary values can enrich the retailing of fact. The Non-fiction Novel is a term that, as such, may stand with "hard-top convertible" and "fresh-frozen food," but it is possibly a worthy ideal, an avenue for writers who feel that the anatomization and re-synthesis of experience is a doubtful process in a society without implicit guidelines. However, there is little in Capote's book to help clear that avenue. He says:

I don't think that crime is all that interesting a subject. What could be more cut and dried, really, than two ex-convicts who set out to rob a family and end up killing them? The important thing is the depth you can plunge to and height you can reach.

Agreed. The depth in this book is no deeper than its mine-shaft of factual detail; its height is rarely higher than that of good journalism and often falls below it.

The *Life* article settles one other point. While I was reading the book, I wondered at the absence of photographs. *Life* includes a number of photographs of the victims, the killers, some of the other principal persons and places, and indirectly explains why Capote was wise to leave them out. Any one of the pictures is worth several thousand of his words. [23]

No one can sustain critical scrutiny that
C. is the "master" of the art of fiction.
Early works writer with gift for surfaces

Real Gardens with Real Toads ✗

HILTON KRAMER

THE BELIEF, APPARENTLY WIDELY HELD, THAT TRUMAN CAPOTE IS A "master" of the art of fiction is not one that critical scrutiny can sustain. His early books were the work of a writer with a gift for surfaces—of language, of feeling, of life itself. To penetrate those carefully wrought surfaces was to find oneself, not in a credible world of the author's creation but in a very stylish void. Capote's sense of evil, so extravagantly praised, turned out to be mainly a sense of interior decoration. All those exquisite symbolic situations resembled nothing so much as beautifully decorated, elaborately wrapped boxes gotten up for display: Upon examination, they proved to be perfectly empty.

No, the author of *Other Voices, Other Rooms* and *A Tree of Night* was no master. But he was an interesting literary and publishing phenomenon. At a time when news of Faulkner and Henry James was just beginning to get through to a larger reading audience, he brought enough syntactical glitter, Gothic distortion, and simulated intellectual density to his work to make it seem somehow related to the accomplishments of these newly discovered figures. At the same time, Capote was careful not to tax his readers with anything like Faulkner's or James' moral complexities. His fiction gave one the sensation of reading something serious and artful while exacting very little in the way of cerebration or even involvement. But slight as it was, Capote's fiction enjoyed a considerable vogue. Its acclaim prompted a succession of imitations. For a time, the atmosphere was quite thick with a kind of literary wisteria, behind which one could just barely discern some evidence of the real world—mainly pederasty in various forms of decorative disguise. Capote's fiction was never as meretricious as Tennessee Williams', but, like Williams', its interest lay primarily in its being an episode in the history of taste.

If one feels compelled to underscore this point now, it is because the press campaign surrounding the publication of Capote's extraordinary new book, *In Cold Blood* (Random House, 343 pp., $5.95), is

Reprinted with permission from *The New Leader* of January 31, 1966, pp. 18–19. Copyright 1966 by The American Labor Conference on International Affairs, Inc.

like Stanley Kauffmann

so patently designed to suggest that a major novelist has succeeded in turning some kind of literary handspring. Through the miracle of modern publicity, we are invited to take a job of inspired reportage as a new and superior form of fiction. What nonsense! It is not enough, apparently, for this book to be very good; it must be thought great. It is not enough that it has something to tell us about our own time, but must be promoted as if it were a work for all time. As Capote's whole career has been, to a large extent, a product of the publishing industry's public relations machine, it would have been expecting too much to think his best book—actually rather modest in design, but powerful in its detail—could be launched with anything less than a campaign that might have been a little overdone for the emergence of a new political personality. Still, it is worth insisting that both Capote's real accomplishment in *In Cold Blood* and its limitations do not exactly correspond to the transcendent object described by this army of heady publicists for whom Capote himself, tirelessly granting interviews, issuing directives, and otherwise overstating his case *ad nauseum,* has served as both field commander and chief strategist.

The narrative is already too familiar to bear retelling here. The murder of the Clutter family by Dick Hickock and Perry Smith had about it more than the requisite horror for holding our interest—and not for holding it only, but for exciting and aggravating it, like an exposed nerve stretched taut. The crime itself had an almost folk-tale simplicity in its moral counterpoint. Capote exploits this counterpoint —first of all, between the enormity of the act and its meager reward, but even more, between the uprightness of the murdered and the lowdownness of the murderers—for all it is [18/19] worth; and he shows it to be worth, in terms of its power to haunt our minds, a great deal. We are made to feel that, not only in the case of Nancy, the teen-age daughter of the house, but with the entire Clutter household, it was a case of virgin blood being ruthlessly and senselessly shed: a slaughter of the innocents, American-style. Much of Capote's skill has gone into rendering this moral contrast of the victims and their executioners with exceptional pictorial vividness. Here is the world of a Norman Rockwell Thanksgiving Day poster invaded by two evil spirits out of Dostoevsky by way of Sherwood Anderson—the homely odor of clean linen and the savory smells of the country kitchen overcome by the stink of the lower depths.

Reading the story in installments in the *New Yorker,* alternately impressed and aghast, and certainly too pained and absorbed to question the subtleties and deceptions of craft involved, one accepted the awful tale on its own terms—or what then seemed, in the magazine, to be its own terms—and accepted them completely. The vignettes of minor characters were sharp and memorable, yet even their humor and surpassing corniness served to distend still further the shock one felt on first reading the bloody details. The reader's initial

people on edge

well abiding people get slaughtered

stunned response was kept raw and unresolved by its reflection and extension in the "real" response registered by these minor figures, whose actual lives—one had to remind oneself—had been so exacerbated by the real villainy.

There was shock of an altogether different, more delightful, more sheerly literary kind, too, in the wonderful talk of these figures—that living mid-Western American speech for which our writers of the '20s, so many of them mid-Westerners themselves, had an expert and sympathetic ear, and which they coaxed so successfully into forming a new fictional instrument. Capote has filled his book with this talk—has, one may say, cut and pasted his book out of that living speech—and not the least of one's pleasure in reading his dreadful narrative was the sense it gave one of what, after all the calculated artifice of recent fiction, that speech could mean again for the art of the novel.

Still, Capote has not written a novel, and it remains to be seen whether his brilliant journalistic use of this virtually rediscovered language will lead to anything significant in the fiction of the future. Capote himself, though he now writes a markedly less florid prose than formerly (the beneficent influence of the *New Yorker* perhaps?), still reaches for something fancy and elevated wherever circumstance permits—and succeeds, too, I think, in effecting a beautiful prose rhythm in this orchestration of plain and fancy styles. But it is, all the same, the prose rhythm of a superior reporter; it is not what the language of fiction, the medium of a significant art, always is: the refraction of a serious moral imagination.

Rereading the story now in book form, it is this last deficiency that stands out on every page, that not only renders Capote's claim to have created a new form of the novel mere highfalutin, but clarifies something central to his whole sensibility. It is not, of course, that one believes fiction alone to have the requisite moral specifications. A work like Henry James' *The American Scene* or, at a somewhat lower altitude, the reportage of Rebecca West or the essays of James Baldwin—these shed, not only on the subjects at hand but on experience at large, precisely the kind of light one finds missing from Capote's painstaking journalistic reconstruction. Such works have, first of all, a voice that never feigns innocence, that refuses to separate itself from the events passing before us, that openly acknowledges its own stake in the issues under scrutiny. And to the extent that the writer feels himself implicated, not as a mere observer but as a moral agent, so the reader too feels himself drawn into the moral vortex of the experience being portrayed.

Capote's craft is designed to have quite the opposite effect. It leaves one removed, distant, even a little cynical. Its detailed accounts of the lives of the murderers—the only lives we are given in any depth—are explanations in a void. The irony on which the book closes—the hapless murderers themselves murdered by judicial decree

—is too pat, too easy, too abstract. So successful has the author been in keeping himself "out" of the tale that one closes the book mentally searching him out, suspecting at last that there is a far more revealing story to be told in his own involvement with the characters and events whose fate is so icily recounted. And until *that* story is revealed—a real novelist would, of course, have found in that connection his moral crux—everything else remains only brilliantly delineated evidence placed before a jury disabused of its pieties.

Admittedly, there is something ungrateful about these strictures. They are the observations of a reader who has been through the story twice. The first time around one was perfectly pleased to have the author out of sight; one gave oneself up to his shattering tale, and waited impatiently, week by week, for more. And from this particular author, the work seemed a miracle of specification about an area of American life no longer written about with much literary intensity, or even with much accurate observation. A writer whose imaginary garden—to borrow a term from Marianne Moore—had never contained a toad one could believe in was, astonishingly, giving us a real garden with toads all too real. Or so it seemed. I had never before appreciated the forces of Miss I. Compton-Burnett's remark that "Real life seems to have no plots"; rereading *In Cold Blood*, the remark cuts deeper, for Capote has written a book that puts that observation to a crucial test, and ends by confirming its wisdom. [19]

Truman Capote's Score

F. W. DUPEE

POOR DEAD BONNIE CLUTTER APPEARED TO A FRIEND IN A DREAM. "To be murdered," she wept. "No. No. There's nothing worse. Nothing worse than that. Nothing." *In Cold Blood* is strewn with snatches of pregnant speech, with glimpses of things that grow and grow in the eye of memory. None of these particulars surpasses the grimly clinching effect of Mrs. Clutter's dream speech.

For the still living Mrs. Clutter, moreover, the horror of being murdered herself had been triply compounded. Roped to her bed, her

From *The New York Review of Books,* VI (February 3, 1966), 3–5. Copyright © 1966 The New York Review. Reprinted by permission of *The New York Review of Books* and F. W. Dupee.

lips sealed with adhesive tape, she was the last of four members of her family to be despatched by two youthful intruders, entire strangers to the family, in the Clutters' roomy farmhouse on the plains of western Kansas one moonlit night in November of 1959. At intervals she heard the gunshots—in a single instance possibly the gaspings of a slit throat as well—that announced the deaths, one by one, of her husband, her fifteen-year-old son, Kenyon, and her sixteen-year-old daughter, Nancy. For some reason Nancy Clutter's lips had been left untaped. Her head turned to the wall and away from the flashlight beamed on it, the shotgun levelled at it, she was able to plead briefly with her killer, again possibly within hearing of her mother across the hall: "Oh, no! Oh, please don't! No! No! No! No! Don't! Oh, please don't! Please!" Mrs. Clutter's turn to be flashlighted and blasted at close range came next. Was her death a deliverance that she welcomed? Among her pitying, grieving, haunted friends in the small town of Holcomb, some hoped that it was. A dim comfort glimmered in the thought.

No other comfort was at first to be found in any aspect of the seemingly inexplicable massacre of this respected, in part beloved, family. Even those natives of the place who resorted to fanciful theorizing and secret finger pointing seem to have done so out of pure fear—a fear too burdensome to find support in religious patience or rational wait-and-see. Here and there, speculation survived the very capture and conviction of the criminals. It was suggested that still darker forces and larger figures hovered in the infinitely contorted and receding backgrounds of an occurrence so monstrous itself, so unprecedented in local history, as the Clutter murder was. Up to then, Holcomb and its environs had made up a somewhat "backward" community. A degree of frontier austerity, religious and moral, persisted in those hinterland fastnesses despite all the well-filled grain elevators, the ranch-type houses, the television sets, the outdoor movies, the teen-age dating. Overnight, as it were, Holcomb had joined the mid-twentieth century. The ages, alike of faith and of rational doubt, had been quickly passed. Our time of suspicion, this sinister synthesis of faith and doubt, of fierce conviction and mad ratiocination, had been reached.

Thus is Holcomb's brutal coming of age pictured in Truman Capote's *In Cold Blood*. The picture, if I have it right, provides one of the numerous "angles" that exercise the mind as well as chilling the blood while one follows Mr. Capote's intricately circumstantial account of the Clutter murder, its causes and aftermath. There is of course a considerable public, generally indulgent, often profitable, for books that reconstruct, whether in a wholly journalistic or a partly "fictionalized" form, one or another of the more significant criminal episodes of the recent or distant past. To the perennial, the probably aboriginal, appeal of crimes and criminals there is sometimes added a sentimental, even an ironically patriotic, motive when the given epi-

sode has occurred in the United States. From Jesse James to Loeb and
Leopold, from the perpetrators of the Saint Valentine Day's Massacre
to the Lindbergh kidnapper and beyond, our celebrated delinquents
have become a part of the national heritage. They figure in a sort of
musée imaginaire, half Madame Tussaud's, half Smithsonian, of
American crime.

In Cold Blood is the best documentary account of an American
crime ever written, partly because the crime here in question is not yet
a part of the heritage. Only in the region where it took place was the
Clutter murder large-scale news. Generally ignored elsewhere (there
have since been so many other virtually gratuitous rampages of blood
and sex), the Clutter affair has been spared the attentions of the
memorialists. Its horrors, its meanings, its supposed relation to the
Zeitgeist have gone unexplored. For Mr. Capote the incident is pristine
material; and the book he has written about it is appropriately and
impressively fresh.

But if *In Cold Blood* deserves highest marks among American
crime histories, it also raises certain questions. What, more or less, is
the narrative intended to be; and in what spirit are we supposed to
take it? While the book "reads" like excellent fiction, it purports to be
strictly factual and thoroughly documented. But the documentation is,
for the most part, suppressed in the text—presumably in order to
supply the narrative with a surface of persuasive immediacy and
impenetrable omniscience. Nor are the author's claims to veracity set
forth in any detail elsewhere in the volume. They are merely asserted
in a brief introductory paragraph wherein his indebtedness to several
authorities ranging from the Kansas police to William Shawn, editor of
The New Yorker, is acknowledged. With all respect to the author, how
can anyone be sure that the book's numerous angles, including Mrs.
Clutter's dream speech and the social portrait of Holcomb, are in any
reasonable degree authentic? To ask such questions of a book that is
otherwise so praiseworthy may be captious; but to praise without
asking is foolish. For these are years not only of neurotic suspicious-
ness but of much that is really, and grossly, suspect, in art as in
politics. As the present writer has at times felt obliged to remark in
print, a lot of what passes for sociological observation is only private
fantasy, the pulse not of the patient but of the hypochondriac healer
at the bedside. "Parajournalism" is Dwight Macdonald's perhaps too
glamorous-sounding term for this "creative" reportage or social criticism. And parajournalism is detestable because, to the many real crises
that now lurk and loom, it adds another and quite unnecessary one, a
crisis of literary truthfulness.

I am myself convinced that *In Cold Blood* is not parajournalism.
Its general authenticity is established, for me, by what I hope to show
is a species of internal evidence. I do nevertheless wish that Mr.
Capote had gone to the trouble of taking us into his confidence—

perhaps by way of an appendix explaining his procedures—instead of covering his tracks as an interviewer and researcher, and of generally seeming to declaim, with Walt Whitman in one of his seizures of mystical clairvoyance, "I am there . . . I witness the corpse with its dabbled hair, I note where the pistol has fallen." A journalist turned poet; Whitman went on to write what was unmistakably poetry, so far, at least, as its frankly visionary immersion in man's total experience was concerned. At present, all reportorial writing aspires to the condition of poetry, or of myth or—in the still more abused word—of "story." *In Cold Blood*'s similar aspirations are, as I say, largely justified by its unique excellence. Meanwhile, the questions have proliferated, mostly in conversation, since last autumn, when the work appeared serially in *The New Yorker*.

Some of these questions had to do with documentation. Others were more intangible, "personal," and, as I now think, impertinent. Given, for example, the preoccupations of Capote's early fiction, its nostalgia for states of innocence together with its fascination with deformed or precocious or odd-ball types of human creepiness (that Miss Bobbitt in "Children on Their Birthdays"! That New York City dream collector in "Master Miscry"!)—given, in short, Capote's repertory of fictional themes, to what extent did he impose it upon the actualities of the Clutter case, "identifying" with one or another of the figures in the case and distorting this or that situation? In their original form such speculations have, as I say, proved to be mostly irrelevant. But they were not without justification if one considers Capote's seeming possessiveness towards his subject, his determination to make the subject his *very* own, to the point of refusing to share with the public the means by which he has done so.

Perhaps his reportorial activities, which I understand were arduous and prolonged, are another story, to be made public later, like Gide's *Journal of "The Counterfeiters."* Meanwhile Mr. Capote, interviewed by a New York *Times* reporter, has suggested further reasons for his suppressing documentation. The book, he says, is an attempt at what is in effect a new genre, the "non-fiction novel." To this claim the only possible retort is a disbelieving grin. The book chills the blood and exercises the intelligence just because it reports, without much novelistic comment or simplification, what one is persuaded really and horribly *happened*. Nor do "genres" as such really matter; certain of anyone's favorite books—*A Sentimental Journey, Walden*—are *sui generis*. If anything, Capote has perfected an old form of journalism and done so by virtue of qualities peculiar to his subject and to himself. Not the book's admirable essence but its glittering aureole of fame achieved and money made in heaps is what is likely to attract imitators.

Whatever its "genre," *In Cold Blood* is admirable: as harrowing as

it is, ultimately, though implicitly, reflective in temper. Capote's possessiveness towards his subject is understandable in terms of the industry,
intelligence, and passion he has brought to the book's making. One's
belief in its merits deepens on re-reading *In Cold Blood* [314] in its
present form as a volume. Indeed the book has the special merit of
requiring, and repaying, thoughtful attention even while it tempts one
to devour its contents with uninterrupted excitement. Many of the
original questions are effectively answered, and the speculations
silenced, by re-reading the work in all its astonishing abundance of
provocative detail.

This abundance flows chiefly from two circumstances: the character of the two criminals and the nature of Capote's participation in the
proceedings. To speak first of the criminals: one of them, Richard
Hickock, combined a high IQ and a gift of almost total recall with a
marked deficiency of imagination and feeling. The other, Perry Smith,
had imagination and feeling in fearful and wonderful plenitude. Smith
was a disappointed *poète maudit.* Repeatedly he dreamed or day-
dreamed of vague paradises, of great winged creatures that did injury
to others in return for the injuries done to him. He cherished writing of
any kind, his own or that of others, so long as it applied directly or
indirectly to himself. To his partner's annoyance he packed almost
everywhere with them his boxes of old letters and other documents. In
effect this bulky, messy, assorted archive was at once an apologia and
a guarantee of identity for this man who in his thirty fugitive years had
led several rather different lives and been as many varying selves. So
the archive, or some part of it, went with them to Miami, to Mexico,
across the deserts of the American West, into the bars or motels where
the two men took shelter, into a car which, as hitchhikers, they
planned (and failed) to make off with after doing in the driver. In the
end, of course, this background material, together with the foreground
material supplied by their confessions, formed part of the court record
and hence came to Mr. Capote's knowledge.

Factually speaking, what Smith remembered about the crime
itself and about their subsequent wanderings was less extensive than
Hickock's memories. But the recollections of both were in substantial
agreement. Naturally Smith's memories included things that escaped
Hickock's less impressionable mind or that didn't concern him. Among
them were the brutality and neglect to which Smith had been subjected as a child, the suicides of a sister, a brother, and the brother's
wife. Among his memories, too, was the far-off presence of a second
sister, Bobo, and her success, thus far, in eluding the family curse.
Bobo had acquired a respectable husband, three children, a house and
home. This good fortune on her part seems to have made Perry despise
Bobo in proportion as he envied her. It made him express a strange
wish concerning her, express it repeatedly and almost to the end—he
and Hickock remained quite unrepentant during their trial and the

long years they spent in the death house of the Kansas State Penitentiary until, in April of last year, their original sentence of death by hanging was finally carried out—Smith wished that his sister Bobo had been present that night in the Clutters' house. In his mind, obviously, her precarious respectability got connected with the manifest respectability of the Clutters. On first seeing their large farmhouse and extensive grounds by moonlight, he thought them "sort of *too* impressive"; and he almost succeeded in convincing Hickock and himself to abandon the "score," as Hickock called the felonious job they had undertaken.

No doubt Smith's voluble confessions to the police and, one gathers, his conversations with Capote, contributed much to the abundance of circumstantiality that characterizes *In Cold Blood*. Inevitably they also awoke in Capote, as surely they must in almost any reader, a kind of sick compassion and wonder. That so much suffering could be taken and given by a single youthful human creature is a fact that unsettles the intelligence and works with desperate confusion upon the emotions, especially when one comes to know the creature as intimately as one does Perry Smith in the pages of *In Cold Blood*. A half-breed and, virtually, an orphan like the fictional Joe Christmas of Faulkner's *Light in August*, Perry Smith has exactly what Faulkner's killer lacks, a personality.

Does, then, the author seem to identify himself with *this* particular specimen of human oddness, who is even short-legged like several of Capote's early characters? Beyond a point, definitely not. Any such sentimental conjunction of egos or alter-egos is precluded by what is gradually revealed about Perry Smith in and between the lines of the book. Smith's excess of imagination and feeling was his undoing and that of the Clutters. It was his blandishments, as contrasted with Dick's bullying, that reassured the Clutters as to the probable intentions of the two intruders, and caused the Clutters to go to their deaths without resistance, perilous as resistance must have been in any case. Perry's will to deceive—perhaps to deceive himself—was matched by the Clutters' will to believe, which in turn sprang from simple shock and fear. Moreover, it was Perry who, after thwarting Hickock's intention of raping Nancy, sat down at her bedside for a pleasant chat about horses, which she loved, and other innocent things. It was Perry who thought Mr. Clutter a nice gentleman at the very moment that he put the knife to Mr. Clutter's throat. Finally, it was Perry who pillowed his victims, tucked them in their beds, or otherwise made them as comfortable as possible, considering that he had also used his ex-seaman's skill to tie them up and that he was soon to slaughter them, one by one. That Pal Perry is no Pal Joey, and thus a projection of the author's fears or desires concerning himself, becomes certain, if only because the *facts,* again, make it impossible. Perry Smith is a heel to end all the heels in modern American fiction.

Not that the slaughter itself was a foregone conclusion. True, "no witnesses" had been Hickock's slogan from the start. But during their four-hundred mile drive to Holcomb, Smith had thought of avoiding detection by masking their faces with women's stockings—black ones. Their attempts to secure these unfashionable articles failed, and the whole stocking-hunt forms one of the more grotesque elements in the wonderful configuration of choices and chances, identities within differences, appearances and realities, which shows everywhere in Capote's narrative.

Between Hickock and Smith, tensions developed during their lengthy occupation of the Clutters' house. Besides keeping Hickock away from Nancy, Smith annoyed him by crediting Mr. Clutter's insistence that there really was no safe in the house. Dick, on the other hand, kept searching for the safe, his whole "score," and the self-esteem that went with it, being at stake for him. Except for these tensions, they might have left the Clutters tied up and unharmed, making their escape with the small portable radio, the pair of binoculars, and the fifty-odd dollars in cash they did find and take. But something, or everything together, awoke in Perry Smith an hallucinated state of mind. He took leave, not merely of his senses, but of his very self, amorphous as it was at best. He was suddenly someone else, the observer of a scene in which his other self was fated to act out its essential impulses. The cutting of Mr. Clutter's throat confirmed Perry's sense of his doubleness. By this act of gratuitous violence, this former petty thief, and, like Dick, parolee from the state prison, became what he had earlier dreamed about and bragged about being, a killer, the avenging bird.

Here, then, is some of the internal evidence (or my version of it) that persuades me *In Cold Blood* is to be read as *fact*, its author's claims to the contrary. Even the propriety of his including Bonnie Clutter's dream speech is thus established, apart from its great dramatic value. He got it, directly or indirectly, from the dreamer herself, an acquaintance of Mrs. Clutter's and the wife of the local police investigator whose involvement in the case was urgent throughout. Similarly with the portrait of Holcomb and its environs. This is as convincing as any such sociological panorama is ever likely to be, especially because of the presence in it of other, somewhat more worldly, "enclaves" beyond the Clutter circle, which is strictly Methodist, Republican, temperance, and 4-H Club. Within and roundabout the Clutter group itself there are also significant differences, despite the seeming harmony. Unlike the others, Bonnie Clutter is a "mental," a partial recluse, subject to bad "spells," convinced that she is unneeded in her generally extroverted family, and given to guilt-stricken gestures and monologues. Then there is Bobby Rupp, the neighbor boy whose teen-age romance with Nancy Clutter has been firmly discouraged by her father because the Rupps are Catholic. Indeed, suspicion fixes, unofficially and briefly, on Bonnie Clutter herself; while Rupp is promptly submitted by the police to the formalities of an interrogation. Thus do those grotesquely opposite numbers, the stranger and the friend, the normal and abnormal, the killer and the killed, shade into one another.

As for Capote's part in the proceedings, these consisted in his making himself so thoroughly familiar with the circumstances and the surviving people involved that he was able to feel himself almost a participant and to make the reader feel a participant also. Thus the various possible clues and suspects are introduced, not with the mechanical trickery of a detective story, but as they might have been dreamed up by the natives or pursued by the police from day to day on the spot. Meanwhile, in alternating chapters, we are made aware of Hickock and Smith, parolees on the loose, meeting at distant Olathe, Kansas, consuming their root beers and aspirins, or vodka orange blossoms, planning the job in their shrewd but half-baked way, and starting on the long drive to the isolated farmhouse which neither of them has ever seen, which only Hickock has heard about, from a former cellmate who, several years earlier, had been one of Mr. Clutter's field workers, and whose account of the Clutter setup included a money-filled safe which isn't, and never was, there.

In short, Capote has it both ways, the mystification and the clarification. And the narrative evolves through a succession of firmly written scenes—scenes that are occasionally, I think, *too* slickly executed and that end with too obtrusive "curtains." These, unfortunately, embrace a concluding graveyard scene where the weather and the sentiment—Life Goes On—are unmitigated Hollywood.

But no known film maker could easily convey in his medium that elusive interplay of the gratuitous and the determinate which makes *In Cold Blood* at its best both artful and lifelike. True, Perry Smith, although thoroughly individualized, is also a clinically perfect type of the misfit turned psychopath and the psychopath turned killer. But his partner? Nothing in Hickock's antecedents accounts for his becoming a criminal on this scale of brutal inconsequence. In so far as the crime has a definable and possibly remedial cause, it lies in the nature of prisons, the kind of mentalities and associations apt to be fostered by prisons. For the rest the cause is something in the relationship of Smith and Hickock, a relationship so involuted and internal that it can be made believable, as Capote does make it, not through any of the usual formulas of partnership or palship, but solely in the shifting minutiae of their behavior from incident to incident. How, moreover, to represent in any medium less flexible than Capote's, other significant relationships? For example, that of Mrs. Clutter and her daughter, the mother who feels herself displaced and the daughter who, in all apparent humility and sweetness, has filled her place? Or that of the two principal fathers, Nancy Clutter's and Perry Smith's, who never of course meet but who are, each in his own place, Kansas and Alaska, and in his own way, embodiments of free enterprise and the pioneering spirit?

Until now, Truman Capote's literary record has been somewhat uneven. A series of well-written, never quite negligible, passes at literature has made it up. At last, in a small Kansas town disrupted by a peculiarly horrible and bewildering crime, he seems to have found, for a time, a sort of spiritual home, complete with a lovable police force. At least he discovered there a subject equal to his abilities. These appear to have required that he profess, and no doubt sincerely believe, that he was composing a non-fiction *novel*. In a way, Capote's claim is the more believable because it perpetuates, by inversion, an ancient literary impulse: the impulse of romancers to create a fiction within a fiction. The tale twice told of Cervantes or of Hawthorne, the story shaped within the consciousness of some imaginary observer (Henry James and others), are of this tradition. [4/5] Capote's inversion of the tradition is itself a striking response to the present-day world and to the tendency noted earlier in this review: the tendency among writers to resort to subjective sociology, on the one hand, or to super-creative reportage, on the other. As Lionel Trilling once observed, it is no longer poetry but history, preposterous current history, which beggars the literary imagination and requires us to attempt a "willing suspension of disbelief." But it is surely to Capote's credit that one cannot quite suspend one's disbelief that *In Cold Blood* is a novel. [5]

Sob-Sister Gothic

SOL YURICK

WRITERS WILL HAVE MUCH TO THANK TRUMAN CAPOTE FOR. LEADING celebrants of the "subjective" life, such as Selby, Pynchon and Heller, have been shown the way. Legions of poets will scan newspapers instead of lines, seeking the coordinates of truth!

Actually, taken by itself (aside from a still uncured tendency to rodomontade), *In Cold Blood* is not a bad book. It is better than the usual police reportage, fast moving, melodramatic, suspenseful in the

From *The Nation*, CCII (February 7, 1966), 158–160. © 1966 by *The Nation*. Reprinted by permission of *The Nation*.

way of its genre, even a little artful. But it is impossible to dissociate *In Cold Blood* from the claims its author and publisher are making for it: that it is a new art form and, as such, represents a higher objectivity. Capote's establishment of the new art form reminds one of those special 3-pound weight classes which are staked out in boxing from time to time to fatten the take: junior lightweight; senior bantam-weight. Capote's first defense of his new title is successful: we are told Oscar Lewis has written a documentary, ". . . an *impure* form . . ." (italics added); poor Lillian Ross only managed to write a novella; Daniel Defoe's *Journal of The Plague Year* certainly wasn't poetic enough; Meyer Levin wrote a novel "suggested" by fact; and as for those thirty or more a year case studies in the annals of aberrant crime, forget it; the Dreisers, the Farrells, the Algrens—they are not in it at all. The *minnesinger* of engineer reality wins in a stylish walk.

And it turns out that what we are really witnessing is a kind of morality play: the conversion of Truman Capote who, turning away from the sinful, the decadent, the tumid prose pathologic, comes into the clear and healthful air of the world of objectivity and, at the same time, throws open new markets of opportunity by the example of his redemption. He also manages to save the moribund novel which has priced itself out of the market with too much exotic experimentation.

As for the higher objectivity—we are to be persuaded that it is reportage shotgun-wed to poetics. How beguiled we are by the thought of the lived or witnessed experience; what paeans our dust jackets sing to that author who has lived the rich, full life as ritually exemplified by homage to the *Dictionary of Occupational Titles*. But the critics are demonstrating a deplorable lack of homework in the history of litera-ture and psychology when they respond enthusiastically to this book: we should expect as much from fans of the *Reader's Digest*. The dramatic distillation of this vast assemblage of data (trunks full, we are assured) follows the paths of mythic selection dictated by the stylebook of *New Yorker* fact pieces. And Capote's choice of detail is more influenced by *The Folk-Motif Index*, or amateur readings in Jung's moonshine of the racial unconscious than by any disinterested resolution of social forces. If you accuse Capote of distortion, he can plead the novelist's license; if you point out that Perry Smiths' dreams of a poisonous diamond tree defended by a snake is lifted out of mythology and worse, parlor Freud—or that the godlike giant parrot is cribbed from Flaubert's *A Simple Heart*—his defense will be re-portage: *the man said it.*

Capote's first section, "The last to see them alive," shows how, that dramatic night, the Clutters' destiny intersected with the destiny of the killers, Perry Smith and Richard Hickock. It is done in the best tradition of newspaper sob sisterism wedded to Southern Gothic prose. Each section ends on a doom-note hooker as he switches back and forth from the innocent family going about its business to the ap-

proaching killers. "Then, touching the brim of his cap, he headed for
home and the day's work, unaware that it would be his last." "A
bookmark lay between its pages, a stiff piece of watered silk upon
which an admonition had been embroidered: 'Take ye heed, watch
and pray: for you know not when the time is.' " "I can't imagine you
afraid. No matter what would happen, you'd talk your way out of it."
⚹ Why go on? Objective? It is "little-did-they-think" writing, fat with
portent. Possibly the enthusiastic response is due to years of conditioning by newspaper reportage: At last! a recognizable form; you don't
have to work to recognize reality—it's like you see in the newspapers
all the time. And like the newspaper approach, the poverty of Capote's
"new" art form is appalling, the shallowness stupefying. This is a man
who gives us the stunning psychological metaphor, ". . . the criminal
mind. . . ." As they say on the radio: "Make this simple test." Read
any newspaper or magazine account of Capote's *In Cold Blood*, then
read the book: you will not learn one new thing; you will even have
been given all the worth-while lines. A work of art should, presumably,
⚹ continue to shape our easy acceptance of the world, make us see in
new ways, create new metaphors with which to view the world: new
art should go beyond engineer reality.

This higher objectivity consists of such factual sentences as
". . . the left eye being truly serpentine, with a venomous, sickly-blue
squint that although it was involuntarily acquired, seemed nevertheless to warn of bitter sediment at the bottom of his nature." How
wonderful that any accident should adapt itself to the eternal verity of
a thing, how right for the world is that "nevertheless." ". . . from first
footfall to final silence, flawlessly devised," a fine formation of a florid
phrase! One compares it with Lillian Ross's masterly understatement,
or with Hubert Selby's restrained catalogue of horrors, the very
impersonality of which raises any "truly serpentine eye" from a prosaic
given to a poetic fact.

How Capote excels at the list! He enumerates, piling up detail,
taking care to shed the aura of doom on artifact so that each item
acquires enormous pathos and drips sentimentality. This kind of
emotion amplification serves to make one weep over crumpled tissues;
pie baking becomes a footnote to the short life of man, what a weak
vessel is he; tears are baked in with the cherries. To be sure, after the
first section, Capote's prose lavenders more lightly; itinerary, document, presumable interview are more in evidence; but he reprises at
the end with an underplayed crescendo of tear-jerking effects, giving
us a sheriff's elegy in a country graveyard where the Clutters are
buried. Naturalism decays into case history. Case [158/159] history's
half-life becomes decadence, a concern with the emotional charging of
literary ornaments, not substance: the sought after effect is the vicarious charge, the tear. This is where we came in: it is still that unrecon-
structed devil, Capote, not too far off from his earliest ventures. We

are still in the presence of Huysmans, not Huntley-Brinkley. The
implications for American Fiction are bad because it argues, more and
more, a turning away from the recognizably fictional modes not
because they are presumably less true but less marketable, less emotion provoking. Capote is in the forefront fleeing the subjective life.
But is he?

"*In Cold Blood* is remarkable for its objectivity—nowhere, despite
his involvement, does the author intrude," Mr. Plimpton informs us in
The New York Times. Nonsense. One of the most studied *omissions* of
the history is the role Capote played in the life of the killers. He tells
us with pride that he disdains mechanical recording instruments
because they cause a distortion of the interview—that he has trained
himself to have 95 per cent memory retention. I won't doubt his word
at all. I will suspend belief and accept that the killers said what
Capote remembers they said. But how much of their words were,
nevertheless, Capote's art and none of their own? Any interviewer has
an effect on the interviewed; there is always a subconscious effort to
please the questioner, to give him what he wants. Guidance comes in
the form of subliminal hints: facial gestures, hand movements denot-
ing approval or disapproval, the very diction of questioning conditions
and cues. The interrogatory moral-seeking words of one reporter are
useful as response to the next breathless inside-story seeker. Here is
Heisenberg's uncertainty principle in action; observation alters the
observed. Hitherto illiterate prisoners respond in categories of humility, piety, absurdity, and begin to sound like Dostoevskian heroes on
the verge of an epiphany. Prisoners learn their literary style on the
edge of the gallows.

And where there has been, admittedly, as in Capote's case,
excessive involvement, preoccupation, breathless obsession—a whole
vicarious involvement is hinted at—what room and time there was for
a leisurely programing of the prisoners in the use of ironic moral
overtones, reportorial portentousness: remember, Capote was in touch
with them, personally and by mail, for years: he was present at their
execution. Capote didn't have to be afraid of tape recorders after all;
the prisoners buried the evidence of what they were and forgot about
it. Why does Capote leave himself out of it? He is one of the prime
actors. Lillian Ross wasn't afraid to include herself in *Picture* and
made a much better book for it. And who's not to say that the
polishing of a crude phrase—merely editorship, of course—might not
lead to a statement like: "And it wasn't because of anything the
Clutters did. They never hurt me. Like other people. Like people have
all my life. Maybe it's just that the Clutters were the ones who had to
pay for it." How neat. Could Joe Mankiewicz have said it better?

Even the title irritates. Not only is it in the best tradition of
sensational headline mongering but it represents the standard incanta-
tion used by prosecuting attorneys in asking for the extreme penalty.

But the description of the killing indicates that it was done not "in cold blood" but in the grip of obsession, almost sexual passion, bringing a release that was almost as intense as any orgasm or mystical experience. "In cold blood" argues logic, reason, planning, cause-effect thinking, personal responsibility, above and beyond any social conditioning, in the committing of a crime: the phrase is the Establishment invocation of sanity. And Capote's use of the title argues his tacit approval of the system.

It is the middle class which is responsive to and outraged by that violent dislocation, by that apparent unmotivation of certain acts which it is stylish to call irrationality or absurdity in literature. The very words argue the exception that tests a pervasive condition, an everyday state of being. And, after all, it is the middle class which has created a social medium whose very nature is shored up by an ideology that stresses personal volition, cause-effect, reason, logic, historicism. Anything that appears to violate this order is shattering, outrageous, deserving of the death penalty; the very presentation, the very special pleading, of *In Cold Blood* implies the *unusualness* of the murderer's act and so becomes diversion, entertainment in case history, and tries to persuade us that what are in fact common patterns of behavior are aberrations. But the poor, for instance, live in a world of violent and "criminal" dislocations, casual unmotivated brutality which no police force tries seriously to stop, so long as it doesn't spill over; it is a world whose inhabitants are not too strongly programed in the ethics of cause-effect, and kill without much feeling, who do not find such behavior absurd, but expected. How few Capotes put their [159/160] obsessed talents to dramatizing such worlds. Selby convinces us, for instance, that the world of taken-for-granted violence and brutality interpenetrates our world. And since they are of these related worlds, we cannot rest with the Perry Smiths and the Richard Hickocks as they are; before we kill them we make sure they negate themselves by turning into literate, psychopathic heroes. We make sure that it is understood that the relationship of the killers to the Clutters is considered aberrant by treating it as a one-of-a-kind case history. Possibly it would have made more sense if Perry Smith's statement read: "And it was everything the Clutters did. They always hurt me. Like other people. Like people have all my life. It's the Clutters who are the ones who should pay for it." They did: and not for the cheap, shallow, sentimental reasons Capote gives us.

The higher objectivity? We are still waiting for it. [160]

Crime and Punishment in Kansas:
Truman Capote's *In Cold Blood*

GEORGE GARRETT

> *The book will be a classic.* Truman Capote, quoted in *Life*.

MAYBE IT WILL BE. ONE THING FOR SURE, IT'S BOUND TO BE A FORMIDABLE success. This book makes its appearance with all the rockets, whistles, and fireboat fanfare usually reserved for the welcome of a brand new ocean liner on its maiden voyage. Publicity, Promotion, Advertising and the Sales Campaign are as massive and impressive as the Front Four of the Green Bay Packers. *In Cold Blood* has already been successfully and expensively serialized in *The New Yorker*. It is a Book-of-the Month Club [1/2] Selection. Paperback rights and, apparently, movie rights are cut and dried and extravagant. It is already what they call a Big Package Deal. None of this, however, can in any way influence or affect the author's characteristic and disarmingly direct claim for his work. Nor should it influence any critic's judgment of it. It would be easy to leap to the occasion and go off barking down the wrong trail, to ridicule the crude claims and clumsy commerce of the publishing world. And that would be wrong and a waste of time. Publishers are not interested in "classics." Except, of course, in the extremely profitable enterprise of publishing editions and reprints of long-since accepted, tried and true works by decently dead authors. No, from the publishing point of view *In Cold Blood* is a "major" book. As such it is receiving the firstclass major book treatment. One cannot ignore this entirely, for it is not intended to be overlooked. One purpose, though not the most important by any means, of the major book treatment is to overawe the reviewers and critics who are susceptible to demonstrations of affluence and, if possible, to spike the guns of those who can recognize real power when they see it. It is a waste of time both ways, however; for *In Cold Blood* is an excellent book and will no doubt be treated as such by even the most rebellious reviewers. All the to-do is irrelevant. Nor, for that matter, can Truman Capote's separate but equal career history as a "living legend," a type of celebrity, be permitted to add or detract from anything. Except insofar as his

From *The Hollins Critic*, III (February 1966), 1–12. © 1966 Hollins College, Virginia. Reprinted by permission of *The Hollins Critic*.

notoriety and station may seem to be to the point, as, for example, as measurement of his veracity as a reporter or validity as a witness.

It has been a good twenty years since Truman Capote's first novel, *Other Voices, Other Rooms,* established him simultaneously and with wit and grace as a gifted writer, a successful one, and a colorful enough personality to merit the attentions of celebrity. The remarkable thing is that he has kept his gift demonstrably alive and kicking. Although he could not by any standards be called a prolific writer, he has continued to create, the steady and regular production of a good professional. From the first his work has received and continues to receive considerable critical attention, most of it favorable. As a writer he has continued to grow, change, and develop without the vice of obvious repetition; and at the same time he has managed to preserve and consolidate his place in the literary establishment. This is no mean feat in recent American literary history. (Whatever happened to Speed Lamkin anyway?) The distinction of his efforts is solidly attested to by his most recent book—*Selected Writings.* Excluding the poets, this is a rare thing, the kind of thing reserved [2/3] for those writers whose reputation is firmly established in the literary sense and secure enough commercially to merit a publisher's interest in things literary.

All of which leads to a genuinely praiseworthy fact about *In Cold Blood.* The book is, flatly and without question, his biggest, boldest, most serious, most difficult and best written work. Which is saying a great deal. In many ways it is his most vital and interesting work, and certainly it is the most ambitious and risky. It is more, then, than a good book by a good writer. It is more than a demonstration of growth, power, and promise for the future. It is a frank bid for greatness. A great many of our serious writers would and indeed *have* settled for a good deal less than what Capote has already done and earned for himself—a long season of honorable and sustained creativity blessed with the fortunate comforts of recognition and an assured place as a good writer. Capote deserves great praise for doing this book. His action is exemplary.

Starting with a frankly brutal and sordid subject, one which could just as easily have languished in the pages of *True Detective* and *Police Action,* he has brought together his gifts and powers, already demonstrated separately, as a storyteller and as a reporter, to tell "A True Account of a Multiple Murder and Its Consequences." Using his gifts for a controlled and charged language and a beautiful style to advantage, he has arranged the telling, the sequence of related events, in such a way that the reader is compelled to share the whole urgent experience. Building around a conventional, four-part classical structure, he manages to keep suspense at a very high level throughout. The first three sections race along, breathlessly yet easily, moving back and forth between murderers and victims and, later, the hunters and the hunted, without strain, always allowing for great freedom of time and space, for the metaphorically relevant digression, the superb use of the tricky flashback, permitting profoundly realized and dimensional characterization, and, not least, a cumulative, haunting evocation of place. In the final section, with the killers at last caught, devoted to their trial and punishment, we see the work of a virtuoso. For at this point the *original* suspense has been dissipated and the conclusion is obligatory. As Capote's artful arrangement of the story proves, he could easily have avoided this challenge had he wished to. For there is no such thing as inevitability in the structure of a story. It is the sign of a real storyteller that he makes his arrangement *seem* inevitable. Capote not only performs this magic trick, but also he manages to reach his own chosen and obligatory conclusion without a weakening of either intensity or interest. I can think of very few writers, living or dead, who could have done this.

These qualities and others in *In Cold Blood* may seem even more remarkable to readers who have followed Capote's earlier work. He has always been known as a distinguished stylist and as an imaginative storyteller, but he has not previously shown a great deal of interest in the possibilities of innovative arrangement. He has not been a technical experimenter. In the past, he has been conservative technically. And though he has created a rich gallery of interesting and memorable characters in his fiction, he has never until now displayed such ability to handle a large number of characters, all of whose lives and fortunes are intricately and subtly inter-related, and to treat them with depth and understanding. There are true moments of unveiling, of startling revelation. Before this he had seemed content to offer a kind of fan dance, showing only glimpses and then chiefly by the allusive method of signs, clues, hints and symbols. Here the chief characters are stripped. If what is exposed is yet another veiled mystery, that is itself a profound revelation. It is exactly the kind of thing he seemed to be sidestepping in his other work. And, no getting around [3/4] it, *In Cold Blood* is fundamentally a blood and guts story. Truman Capote's previous accomplishments have a great many virtues, and they have been acknowledged and praised: but nobody has ever accused him of being a blood and guts writer.

The fact is that he has been most frequently and conveniently labelled as a writer of romances, of the school of Poe and Hawthorne, a fabulist. There is a certain accuracy in this label. In *Radical Innocence* Ihab Hassan sums up the general consensus this way: "The idea of romance, informed by the modern techniques of dream symbolism and analysis, suggests the general quality of Capote's work." Hardly a recommendation for a job of police reporting. Not a hint of the author's ability to deal honestly and powerfully with the brutal murder of a Kansas farm family. Certainly no indication that he could be trusted to report such an event. Yet he has done it and done it brilliantly.

In Cold Blood is classic in the sense that it is an addition to the ancient and immemorial *genre* of the tale of crime and punishment which has fascinated writers and readers for as long as there have been any. In that sense it stands as an important book. It is as "major" as any publisher or critic could ask. Whether or not, it will end up as *a* classic, only time and the wheel of fortune will tell. However, by all rights it demands to be judged and must be judged by the highest standards. When this happens, the standards of "good writing" are vestigial, assumed but irrelevant.

> *It's what I really think about America. Desperate, savage, violent America in collision with sane, safe, insular even smug America—people who have every chance against people who have none.* Truman Capote, quoted in *McCall's.*

No matter how different superficially *In Cold Blood* may seem to be from Capote's earlier work, both fiction and non-fiction, it is rooted in that work. It exists as part of the context of all his work. Never mind for the moment that it is billed as an adventure in "a serious new literary form; the Non-fiction Novel." No one except the people directly concerned, those who are still alive, is competent to pass judgment on its final validity as *reportage.* That, too, is a false scent, a wrong trail. It must be seen always as a story, though always as a true one.

The marked difference between his fiction and *In Cold Blood* ironically works to make the relationship between them more evident. In his three novels and his short stories, whether written in his "nocturnal" or "daylight" manner (as critics have seen fit to classify his work), Capote has, indeed, written a certain kind of romance or fable. For all their truth and decorative detail, both *Other Voices, Other Rooms* and *The Grass Harp* take place in a never-never land, a kind of no-man's land deliberately isolated from at least the world of "realistic" fiction, and even if the New York of *Breakfast At Tiffany's* is a real place, the central character, the marvelous Miss Holiday Golightly, is as extraordinary and magical as, say, Bellow's Henderson in *Henderson, The Rain King.* Moreover, she, unlike Henderson, is seen at one remove, filtered through the consciousness of a writer-narrator. One of the characteristics of the story which does not depend on apparent surface credibility or verisimilitude, whether it is fable pure and simple or romance, is that it has always been pre-eminently a *moral* tale, from Aesop until now. This is inevitable, since attention is by rhetorical consent and agreement diverted from what happened to what [4/5] is being said. Classical and medieval rhetoricians, too, often ignored at present, dealt with this kind of writing in all its possible forms in great detail. It was recognized as more directly *allegorical,* in the widest and deepest sense of that word, than work with what we might think of as realistic surface. On the simplest level this merely means that though foxes, jackasses and lions don't really talk to each other, what they have to say to each other in a fable and what they do may have truth and meaning. In a romance like *Other Voices, Other Rooms* it means that nightmarish, grotesque and surrealistic things may happen and be meaningful, that Joel Knox, Zoo, Randolph, Jesus Fever, Miss Wisteria and all the others suffer wounds, but the wounds are not real. Collin Fenwick, Dolly, Catherine, Judge Cool and the others in *The Grass Harp* are more obviously involved in a social world. The world comes up against them where they sit, happy outcasts in a tree house; but again their triumphs and their suffering are seen at the little distance of romance. The effect is, by definition, allegorical and moral. Holly Golightly seems to be vaguely conscious of her own allegorical function when she defines it: "Good? Honest is more what I mean. Not low-type honest—I'd rob a grave, I'd steal two-bits off a dead man's eyes if I thought it would contribute to the day's enjoyment—but unto-thyself-type honest. Be anything but a coward, a pretender, an emotional crook, a whore: I'd rather have cancer than a dishonest heart." So, while apparently asserting a position beyond ordinary *morals,* she defines as honestly her own morality, her own clear sense of good and evil.

Even though each of these works is quite different, all have the outlines of a fairly clear, consistent, and conventional moral framework. Conventional in the literary sense. Which is to say unconventional only if measured against what are, again conventionally, [5/6] thought to be the basic accepted standards of American middleclass morality. In each of the books it is the outsiders and the outcasts who are, by virtue of their disengagement from worldly values, the examples of goodness. Those who seem to get along well in the "real" world, that is the world of practical affairs, are exposed as either deceitful or self-deceived. It is they who work mischief and cause trouble, usually invoking the name of conventional morality; and in the end, thanks to the operation of a whimsical kind of poetic justice, they usually get what's coming to them. "Safe, sane, insular" . . . , long before that knockout punch "smug" comes along, these adjectives glisten like black hats on horseopera bad guys to anyone who has ever read Truman Capote.

From the first, then, we shiver for the Clutters, fearing their fate, because they are such natural victims. You just *know* about Mr. Clutter when he is first described: "Though he wore rimless glasses and was of but average height, standing just under five feet ten, Mr. Clutter cut a man's-man figure. His shoulders were broad, his hair had held its dark color, his square-jawed, confident face retained a healthy-hued youthfulness, and his teeth, unstained and strong enough to shatter walnuts, were still intact." There's more, but anybody familiar with the World of Truman Capote's fiction has already reacted with the stark simplicity of the movie audience of *Shane* when Jack Palance rode into town, head to toe in black and scaring even the dogs with his shadow. Each of the Clutters, in the terms of his fiction, manages to include all the "bad" characteristics. In fiction, of course, neither the inverted morality nor the signs and symbols thereof are new. These are working conventions, bordering on pure cliché in modern fiction. Certainly in romance and even in more "realistic" fiction [6/7] these conventions are accepted. Perfectly [ironically] *respectable*. But here we are up against a real and different problem. The Clutters were real people, not symbols of anything, and their murder was a matter of brutal fact. At least at the outset, then, the effect is ambiguous. We find ourselves asking, no doubt as the author intended, is Capote still following the Old Law or will his work be a new dispensation? The larger audience reading Capote for the first time won't have that problem. Maybe that is just as well.

When we get to the killers we begin to get answers. They come on as clearly labelled as the pilgrims in the Prologue to *The Canterbury Tales*. Both are hurt because of accidents; both are tattooed; but there is a difference. Dick Hickock's tattoos are crude, cheap, conventional. Perry Smith's are "more elaborate—not the self-inflicted work of an amateur but epics of the art contrived by Honolulu and Yokohama masters." There is an explicit archetypal malevolence about Dick, with his head "halved like an apple, then put together a fraction off center." With his "left eye being truly serpentine, with a venomous, sickly-blue squint that although it was involuntarily acquired, seemed nevertheless to warn of bitter sediment at the bottom of his nature." We get our first description of the remarkable Perry Smith. All Capote heroes have been cheerful narcissists, this in turn a symbol for richness of imagination and the interior life. Or as Capote carefully explains it:

Time rarely weighed upon him, for he had many methods of passing it—among them, mirror gazing. Dick had once observed, "Every time you see a mirror you go into a trance, like. Like you was looking at some [7/8] gorgeous piece of butt, I mean, my God, don't you ever get tired?" Far from it; his own face enthralled him. Each angle of it induced a different impression. It was a changeling's face, and mirror-guided experiments had taught him how to ring the changes, how to look now ominous, now impish, now soulful; a tilt of the head, a twist of the lips, and the corrupt gypsy became the gentle romantic.

Much, much later the Detective Nye, seeing him for the first time, while Smith is being questioned, is struck by the "pert, impish features" which remind him of the suspect's pretty sister, "the nice Mrs. Johnson."

In short Perry Smith is perfectly, patly, and in almost every detail a spooky embodiment of Capote's earlier fiction. He has all the right characteristics: a rich and childish imagination, his dreams including one marvelous recurring dream which is mystical in beauty and implication, his physical deformity, his sensitivity, even his background. What could be more perfect than to be the child of "a lean Cherokee girl [who] rode a wild horse, a 'bucking bronc,' and her loosened hair whipped back and forth, flew about like a flamenco dancer's"? Her name was Flo Buckskin and her husband was a "homely-handsome Irish cowboy" named Tex John Smith.

It is probably the amazing fact that a real human being could accidentally have all the characteristics of his typical fictional protagonists which permitted Capote to give us through his study of Perry Smith a fascinating look at the curious workings of a murderer's *psyche*. By the same token, however, for or maybe because of all his natural sympathy and compassion for Perry Smith, Capote clearly sets him in sharp contrast to the other killer, Hickock. Hickock is intelligent, but not nearly so interesting. The result is that he receives fairly short shrift in comparison to Smith. And much about him is given pejoratively. He likes to run over stray dogs; he pursues little girls; he asserts his dubious masculinity by making love in the presence of Perry, etc. All these things, by the way, must come to us through *Perry*, but in context are treated like facts. There is, of course, a real and neat narrative value to be derived from this contrast of the two. Since we never really know Hickock the way we do Smith and since we are never invited to squander much sympathy on him, he can serve beautifully as a conventional "heavy." It is quite necessary to engage as much of the reader's sympathy as possible for Perry. So there has to be a foil, a sacrificial victim served up to ease the reader's reluctant conscience and to appease, like patent medicine, the reader's taste for conventional morality. In the making of fiction this method is honorable and traditional, and it works well here. So well that we are thoroughly engaged in the pathos of Perry Smith, and his final words from the gallows are deeply moving, come close to real tragic utterance, leave Perry at the end as a kind of inverted, mid-century Billy Budd. But when one realizes *how* this has been achieved, by the trick of fiction, that author and reader have conspired to make Hickock expendable, catharsis is dissipated by ambiguous feelings.

Again the problem is that we are dealing with a real murder and a real hanging. The author goes to great pains to emphasize the *reality* of the story. (And for an epigraph he has invoked Villon's *"Ballade des pendus,"* which is for *all* the hanged.) That we do not get the same kind of involvement with Hickock as we do with Smith is a failure in this book. A wise failure, though. Perhaps even a shrewd one. For the whole truth and nothing but the truth of this event, even if it were possible to articulate, would not likely be acceptable to the general audience. Better half a loaf . . . Except that in one sense the trick of heaping the burden of evil on the head of Hickock is what is sometimes called cheating. [8/9] ere are so many superbly realized things, large and small, in ook that one can be easily diverted and almost distracted from laws. Almost, but not quite. The two chief and central actions of ook are the murder and the hanging. Although we are given plenty of the painful details of both actions, neither scene is presented as directly as other scenes. In each case, a little differently, Capote has chosen to shy away from the heart of these scenes, to "write around" them.

There is good narrative justification for holding back on the naked brutality of the murder scene until late. What happened is essential to the suspense of the story in Capote's arrangement, and so we do not really know and do not see the event happen until the killers have been caught and confess. Meanwhile, in the interim, something else happens. By then we have been led into deep involvement with the killers. The account of the murder, though horrifying, is by then curiously remote and comes too late to damage the other rhetorical purpose. By putting the account of the murder exactly in the language of the confessions, gaining the virtues of documentation of course, Capote gains another more subtle effect. That language simply cannot compete with the author's. Possibly there is the horror of understatement by comparison, but the effect is to soften the event of the murder. It can be reasonably argued that Capote gives his reader a gracious plenty of detail from which to shape a completely *imagined* scene and that this, another time-honored device of fiction, is often much more powerful than a headon and direct encounter with the scene. Nevertheless there is a very real and nagging question as to whether or not the [9/10] author wanted to give us that scene fully. Had he ever done so, early or late, he could probably never again have engaged the reader's sympathy for Perry Smith. And had he chosen to do so he would have risked appealing to and arousing some very deep, atavistic human feelings that are more powerful than poetic. And had he done so he might also have weakened the satirical effect of the fear and corruption which beset the little town. Still, it might have been more honest.

In a somewhat more subtle and complex way, Capote has managed to "write around" the hanging. The most shocking elements of a hanging occur not at the hanging itself but in a nightmare of Perry's. But that is not precisely the problem. It is not a question of gruesome or explicit details. One of the most memorable hangings in fiction is Faulkner's disposal of Popeye in *Sanctuary* in a very few lines. In this case it is a question of the right details, of something being missing. Within the exclusive context of the book it is very hard to say what may be missing, just that as a scene this does not somehow measure up to many other less important scenes. The *Life* magazine article and interview, however, has come along with a kind of an answer. He was there. His own personal involvement and the scene he witnessed are described, and significant details are given which do not appear in the book. They are powerful and deeply moving things which had to be sacrificed, evidently, because of the author's decision to keep himself out of the story.

That decision was his and his alone to make, but it is a fair subject for consideration. In telling the story with a novelistic arrangement and the seeming objectivity of the novelist, Capote has had to exclude, except by implication, his own story, the entire story of his engagement and involvement. It is simply not in the book. But we know through the widespread publicity if no other way that he was very much involved. And not just reporting. He was witness to important parts of the story, and it is precisely his involvement and nobody else's which has shaped the whole story and its arrangement. What a story that might be! All that he has given us in the book together with the true account of a highly sophisticated, civilized, sensitive and successful man of letters who is suddenly fascinated by a newspaper story, captured and obsessed by the mystery to the extent of going to the scene of the crime. With a doggedness and persistence matching that of the police he pursues *his* quarry (in this case the "story") to its bitter end. It would have an essentially nightmarish quality as bit by bit and piece by piece the abstract event became concrete and then real. With the odd logic of a dream, patterns began to emerge, patterns of fate, fortune and behavior which had always intrigued him as a writer of fiction but which he could not have dreamed existed until in this wild dream of discovery, there they were. Much as if he had been dreaming toward this for twenty years and waked to find his dream was real. Where you end the story depends on who is writing it. It could be tragic. It could be bitter and grotesque comedy if, for example, the author should find . . . himself! . . . and then vault to fame and honor, using six corpses for leverage. Perhaps, with a grand irony, you could have a story in which the author, starting from abstract fascination, digging up the facts, coming at last face to face in a dark mirror with the ineradicable horror at the heart of things, should then in the very act of writing and publishing his story purge himself of both the facts and the vision and come out untouched like a child, smelling like a rose.

I am not being facetious. A very large and important part of this story is at least concealed, if suppressed isn't a better word. Here I am not playing any innuendo game. What I mean is that while this deliberate suppression of self does give the narrative a fairly straight line and a great deal of strength, it also appears to be the [10/11] cause of certain weaknesses. Some sign of final commitment is missing. Of course the author is already there, carefully arranging the order and sequence of events, moving his characters on and off stage etc. If the truth about the "consequences" is really his concern, why doesn't he really appear? Curiously enough, the weakest parts of the book are precisely where the author had the most firsthand knowledge, the most direct encounter with the experience. *And he himself was very much part of the experience of many of the characters.* His presence, his actions, his questions must have affected them, just as, now, the finished book is bound to have an effect on them too. If he has removed himself from the experience, we are entitled to ask what else he may have chosen to remove or suppress. A reporter need not necessarily deal with this question. A valid witness cannot ignore it and be really believed.

There is something missing, then, in this story which Capote says is what he really thinks about America. Of course, there is nothing new or shocking or even unfashionable in what he appears to think. We have been told by all kinds of people, some of them good men and many of them not artists at all, that unless we do something (nobody quite knows what) about all that's "desperate, savage, violent" we are going to suffer the consequences and they will be very bad. Capote's tale, as it stands, reflects this profound concern with accuracy. Somehow, though, the Clutters were not representative abstractions, and neither were Dick and Perry. They did not live or die to prove any point or to illustrate what anyone may or may not think about "America." In spite of the local dismay and shock, the brutal and terrible death of the Clutters proves nothing about the nature of God or the universe one way or the other. The deaths of Dick Hickock and Perry Smith tell us nothing about justice. With enormous skill, skill and art beyond the means and reach of most of his rivals and contemporaries, Capote has managed to give some pattern and meaning to a brutal, stupid, pointless, senseless murder and some of its consequences. He has been able to arouse compassion and to evoke pity and terror. In all fairness, nobody is really [11/12] treated like an abstraction. But somehow, in some almost indefinable way, the romancer has overcome the reporter and the final effect is one of "nocturnal" romance. Which, of course, is a false rendering.

There remains one more question. What about the "new" form? There is nothing whatever new about the use of the devices of fiction for "non fiction." A very long list could be made of such works and it would include some very distinguished books, past and present. In recent times one would not want to forget such classic examples as Cummings' *The Enormous Room* or Hemingway's *The Green Hills of Africa, Death In The Afternoon,* and *A Moveable Feast,* each experiments, and so labelled, in the *genre* Capote is credited with inventing. Certainly you would have to include some of Wright Morris' experiments. And what would you do with the use of real events and characters in something like Robert Penn Warren's *Brother To* ̄he examples are multitudinous. And one would have to f all the books and the non-books done in the manner of

Walter Lord's *A Night To Remember*. In what way does *In Cold Blood* really differ from these? There are some which can match it in distinction.

The claim of inventing a new form may be blamed on the publisher and dismissed as a device. About on the level of the "new, improved ingredients" that show up with depressing regularity in advertisements for toothpaste, detergents, deodorants, etc.

The question of form, however, remains a challenge, unresolved and probably unanswerable. One would have to begin by saying that a very great number of writers, past and present, have in the form of fiction, in stories of crime and punishment, achieved as much as *In Cold Blood*. But it is not fiction. Aside from the simple and statistical fact that many more people prefer to read "true" stories than fiction, the principal gain of calling the book a "Non-fiction Novel" would seem to be to call attention to the literary excellency of the reporting job. But what are we invited to compare this job with? *True Detective?* Newspaper and magazine stories? Conventional popular non-fiction? Obviously not.

In Cold Blood is a work of art, the work of an artist. There is much truth in it, though whether or not it is "true" is at least debatable. Whether or not it turns out to be a classic, it is an important and provocative book, one which is bound to generate the kind of deep interest, intense discussion, re-reading and scrutiny which only a very few really excellent books deserve to enjoy. [12]

A Grave and Reverend Book

REBECCA WEST

IT IS TO MR. CAPOTE'S DISADVANTAGE THAT EVERY BOOK HE WRITES TURNS into what our great grandmothers used to call "a pretty book." He knows that ours is a bloodstained planet but he knows also that it turns on its axis and moves round the sun with a dancer's grace, and his style defines the dancer as ballet-trained. For this reason Mr. Capote is often not taken as seriously as he should be, and it is possible that his new book, *In Cold Blood,* may be regarded simply as a literary

From *Harper's*, CCXXXII (February 1966), 108, 110, 112–114. Copyright © 1966, by Harper's Magazine, Inc. Reprinted from the February 1966 issue of Harper's Magazine by permission of A. D. Peters & Co.

tour de force instead of the formidable statement about reality which it is.

In six long years Mr. Capote crawled like an ant of genius over the landscape where, on a November night in 1959, a prosperous Kansas farmer, his wife, his daughter of sixteen, and his son of fifteen, were murdered by two ex-convicts, who gained only forty or fifty dollars by the slaughter. That Mr. Capote has invented nothing and recorded with a true ear and utter honesty is proved by the conversations in the book. The inhabitants of Holcomb, Kansas, do not on any page engage in the subtle and economical dialogue Mr. Capote ascribes to the characters in his novels. They speak the words which reporters hear when they interview the participants in prodigious events, and listen to with embarrassed ears. The stuff is corny, yet not just corny. The corn is celestial. Even the cleverest writer who tries to invent it achieves an obvious fakery, which is quite absent from this book.

If there be one point in this book more admirable than another, it is its treatment of a certain technical difficulty. Some years ago I wrote for *The New Yorker* an account of a peculiarly sordid murder in which a man dropped a dismembered corpse from a plane onto a sea marsh, where it was discovered by a fisherman. When I went to see the fisherman, I found that he and his family were people of acute intelligence, so acute that they could, had they chosen, have been as aggressive and complicated and self-seeking as the worst of us. But they had made another choice. They did one a great kindness by talking to one, they gave one a share in a strong, unpriggish, gracious sort of peace they had made for themselves. I could not get these people down on paper as I got the man who had thrown the corpse out of the plane. I perceived that for me, at any rate, it was not so easy to write about the dynamically good as about the dynamically bad. Immodestly, I did not leave it there. Thinking it over, I reflected that the schizophrenic character of "Paradise Lost," its fundamental unease, is due to Milton's surprise at finding that throughout his epic Satan kept on coming up as more interesting than God. As Milton was 90 per cent pure writer and a raging egotist he imagined that this aesthetic situation had moral implications. I also reflected that since Bach's "Sheep May Safely Graze" hardly anybody has written music so serene without toppling over into *schmaltz*. I thought I had discovered a limitation likely to apply to the writers of our time.

But Mr. Capote represents the victims of the murder as brilliant, powerful, and important in their goodness. Mr. Clutter was a gifted and able man, an expert in the elaborate techniques of modern farming, his vision of the material world so clear and his mastery over it so assured that it might well have been his sole interest. But he was a just man, who knew that the only true justice is mercy, and a kind, unstinting man, to whom giving people a fair chance was a quiet kind of pleasure. True, he had his chilling aspects. His contracts with his employees were voidable if they were "harboring alcohol," as one might say "harboring vermin" or "harboring diseases." But Mr. Capote convinces us that the dead man's puritanism was a long-term scheme for enjoyment. If he kept a rein on his daughter Nancy, it was only because he wanted a future for her which would match her perfection.

As for Nancy, it took great courage on the part of Mr. Capote to set down the fact of her angelic radiance. Deliciously pretty, she was president of her class and a leader of the 4-H program, she won prizes at the county fair for pastry and preserves and needlework, and in the last hours of her life she taught little Jolene how to make cherry pie in her incomparable way, coached little Roxie Lee on [108/110] her trumpet solo for the school concert, got on with her bridesmaids' dresses for her absent sister's approaching wedding, and, as always, got on with the family chores. Worse still, for the playroom she shared with her brother she embroidered cushions with the legends "Happy?" and "You Don't Have To Be Crazy To Live Here But It Helps." She did not cross herself and murmur the words, "Pop Art," before committing this dreadful act. She did it cold.

Nevertheless, when the community lost the Clutters it was as if there had suddenly vanished from the district some natural feature which also served a practical purpose, say a mountain lake which had also provided a water supply. Yet the family labored under a handicap. Mrs. Clutter was a melancholic, a weeping wraith, given to periods of inassuageable grief and delusions of intense cold which persisted throughout sweltering summers. Mr. Clutter and his daughter and his son were joined together to protect the poor woman from her misery, to protect each other from this invasion of the abnormal, and to go on giving the community what it needed from them, in spite of this drain on their resources. All this Mr. Capote does not merely tell the reader, he proves it, and without a shade of *schmaltz*.

The two murderers were drawn to the Clutters' home because its beneficence had so impressed the twilit mind of a convict that he made a symbol for it in a wholly imaginary safe stuffed with dollars. He had babbled of this to Richard Hickock, whom he had known in prison, the younger of the two murderers, and the simpler character. Hickock had only two serious cases against life. First, he had been born into the grinding poverty of a poor farm; but his parents were affectionate and agreeable, and he had ample intelligence to work himself up to a good level of living. Second, at nineteen an automobile accident had spoiled what had been considerable good looks. But there was an abnormality in him which predated his accident. When he was a boy a neighbor's son had come back from a holiday on the Gulf Coast with a collection of shells. These he had stolen, and hammered one by one into dust. "Envy," writes Mr. Capote, "was constantly with him; the Enemy was anyone who was someone he wanted to be or who had anything he wanted to have." As he appears in *In Cold Blood* he is the most complete study I can remember of the spite which makes a certain sort of criminal, such as the men whose entries in the card index of burglars of Scotland Yard are of a special color, because they make a practice, when they have neatly packed up their loot, of defecating on the best carpet on the premises.

The other murderer, Perry Smith, was worse because he was better. He was a physical oddity, with the torso of an athlete and stunted legs, so that he stood no taller than a twelve-year-old child. He had a hideous life, being born into a family disrupted by misfortune, and subjected during his childhood to institutional experiences which, whether they were as he recalled them, filled him with resentment. He spent some time in the merchant marine, and went with the Army to Korea and Japan, where he piled up a crime sheet, returned to the United States, and was injured in an automobile accident far worse than Hickock's, which seven years after left him with agonizing pains in his legs and made him an aspirin addict. He drifted into crime, and was soon in a penitentiary. There was a strain in him which made him bear unhappiness badly. His only brother and one of his two sisters committed suicide.

He was half-Cherokee and had a dark charm; he was literate, read verse, was musical, loved his guitar, cultivated his sensitiveness, and bore himself according to the rumor of the romantic tradition which had reached him from far-off. And his woe was real. He had, Mr. Capote tells us, "the aura of an exiled animal, a creative walking wounded." He excites pity as Hickock does not. Yet he was far more dreadful, as Mr. Capote admits with heroically honest detachment. If one asks why he was so dreadful, the answer seems to be that he was guilty of a sin which is the spiritual equivalent of usury. He exploited all his misfortunes to the full; he laid them out with cool prudence to bring in the heaviest possible yield of pity; he came to love pity too much. He coveted the precious substance more and more, he could not bear anyone else to get any, he wanted all there was in the world. He became infinitely cruel, as was shown in his relations with his father. [110/112]

That poor wretch had had as sad a life as his son. He was a rodeo performer who had married a Cherokee bronco rider in the same show. They were both cut down by illness when the family were still little children, and both had to leave the show. Smith had nothing to fall back on in the waning West during the Depression but such obsolete arts as bear skinning; and at the same time his wife had become a drunkard, a prostitute, a maniac, and died a disgusting death. He loved his children and was horrified when two of them committed suicide, and he finally became eccentric. Perry could not forgive him. It was his father's duty to be happy, so that he could provide his son with happiness.

Perry's inhumanity was exhibited also in his relations with his one surviving sister, Barbara, who had burrowed her way out of the family hell and made a good life out of a modest marriage. She understood her brother well, and uttered a very competent analysis of one of his characteristics, the generalized sensitiveness of the romantic:

He can seem so warmhearted and sympathetic. Gentle. He cries so easily. Sometimes music sets him off and when he was a little boy he used to cry because he thought a sunset was beautiful. Or the moon. Oh, he can fool you. He can make you feel so sorry for him.

She might have said worse, for he had committed a considerable offense against her. He had sent her a young girl, with a letter saying that this was his twenty-year-old wife, and asking that she be looked after as he was in trouble. After a day or two the girl (who was in fact fourteen and nobody's wife) departed with her hosts' suitcases, crammed with their clothes, their silver, and the kitchen clock. Nevertheless when Perry was in prison Barbara wrote him a long, clumsy, touching, unhappy, loving letter, asking him not to blame his father for his misfortunes and to get on with his life. He kept it only because of the "very sensitive" commentary on it which was written in pidgin psychologese by a fellow prisoner, an Irish tenor who had spent twenty years in prison for dismal little thefts, and thought nothing of Barbara. Perry loved jargon; he kept a little notebook, full of rare words, such as "thanatoid" and "amerce." Also he loved contempt. He was an inveterate moralizer. Almost any act committed by any person other than himself provoked him to sneering condemnation on high ethical grounds.

Perry was to exhibit the holier-than-thou attitude very strangely in the death house. To an Army buddy, a saintly young man, who visited him out of Christian charity, he explained he felt no remorse for murdering the Clutters:

It's easy to kill—a lot easier than passing a bad check. Just remember, I only knew the Clutters maybe an hour. If I'd really known them, I guess I'd feel different. I don't think I could live with myself. But the way it was, it was like picking off targets in a shooting gallery.

But he had prefaced these blank and icy words by a brief exercise of his talent for moralizing on a subject which never ceased to shock him.

Soldiers don't lose much sleep. They murder, and get medals for doing it. The good people of Kansas want to murder me—and some hangman will be glad to get the work.

He could not get over the disgusting barbarism which made the inhabitants of the State of Kansas retain capital punishment on their statute book and voluntarily incur the blood guilt of hanging him. Yet it was he who had killed all four Clutters. Hickock had conspired with him to kill them, but Perry confessed that it was he who had cut Mr. Clutter's throat and shot the others. Before Perry got to the death house he had reason to know that he had not been attacked by a unique and unrepeated impulse. Twice after the murder he and Hickock had stood in the highway and thumbed a lift from prosperous drivers, meaning to rob and murder them. The first stopped, gave them a look over, did not like what he saw, and drove on. The second, when the rock was already neatly packed in the handkerchief to crash down on his skull, was saved by his own good nature. With two hitchhikers in his automobile, he suddenly stopped for a third, a Negro soldier. Yet to the end Perry looked down on the citizens of Kansas because they found themselves [112/113] capable of killing him. "I don't believe in capital punishment, morally or legally," he said on the gallows. What bourgeois today could achieve such a fine flower of hypocrisy? Tartuffe still lives, but has changed his address.

In Cold Blood leaves us asking whether the waste of these six lives could have been avoided by a society which had the wits and was willing to take the pains. Some elements in the tragedy are beyond our control. Nothing in Hickock's origin or upbringing explains his spite, and Perry Smith's situation explains his all too well. It is one of the few notable omissions in the book that Mr. Capote does not tell us if he found any material in the California child-welfare files, to throw any light on the degree to which Perry was helped or abandoned in his childhood. One can imagine that he would have been as hard to help as a trapped animal. For the rest, the trial of the two was consonant with the law. Hickock was hanged for murder which he had not committed, when he should have been sentenced to a term of imprisonment as an accessory, but this was his own fault. The truth could only be established if both he and Perry chose to give evidence, but this, for a reason Mr. Capote does not explain, they did not do. This curious abstinence is a proof of the irrelevance of capital punishment. The prospect of hanging could never have acted as a deterrent to these two men who were, to use a word from Perry Smith's little book, obstinately thanatoid. They were obsessed with death.

Yet society has its blame to carry. As companions in the death house Hickock and Perry had two very handsome boys, one eighteen, one nineteen, one with a background like Perry's, the other from a home in every way fortunate. They had gone on a ten days' murder jag round the South, killing four men and three women, one a little motel waitress of eighteen. None of these people had done anything against them, one man had stopped to ask if their automobile had broken down and if he could help them; the little girl had let them sleep with her. When the boys were asked why they had butchered these people, they explained the world was rotten and to kill people was to do [113/114] them a favor. "We hate the world," they smiled from the local television screen. One is aware of a process which Mr. Capote has constantly demonstrated during his superb exposition of the doom shared by Hickock and Perry Smith: the seeping of a certain literary tradition through society from the top to the bottom.

It is within the knowledge of all of us that life is often hard to bear. But it has oddly happened that our society which is, if not perfect, at least more generally comfortable than any society has succeeded in being before, has produced a literature quite often taking as its basis the pretense that life is quite unbearable. This pretense is behind some good plays and novels and some bad ones. A work of art does not have to be completely valid either in its facts or in its philosophy, so it may share imperfection with books and plays which cannot be classed as works of art at all. This pretense that life is unbearable is not accepted as literally true by any but a minute number of readers or writers; very few people commit suicide. But it is widely adopted as an intellectual counter, not an opinion which one sincerely holds and would act upon, but which one uses as a substitute for opinion when talking or writing, like the chips one uses when gambling at casinos. It then passes into general currency, in films, on television, in chatter, and so it happens that one day a naïve person with stronger dramatic instincts than most, and less sense of self-preservation, comes to believe that sophisticated people believe life to be unbearable, and therefore it is not terrible to carry the belief to its logical conclusion and to deprive his fellowmen of their lives. When society shows its horror the murderer feels himself lifted into the distinction so difficult to attain in our vast societies: he is one of the few strong and logical people in a community of weaklings afraid to act up to their beliefs.

What air do these people breathe not permeated with the culture we have made? Where else could they have caught this infection but from us? There is a hateful continuity between the world of literature and the world of Mr. Capote's criminals. Hickock bought an expensive gun on credit from the store beside his parents' home, took it with him to the Clutters' house, where it did its work, took it back to his parents' home, and abandoned it there. They, thinking he had used it only once on a pheasant shoot, tried to get the storekeeper to take it back, but he refused, and they had to pay for it. At all times they were poverty-stricken and his father was dying of cancer. It is depressing to recognize how easily this episode would find a home in fiction. It would work in nicely to a certain kind of Roman Catholic novel, in which God would find the ripe sinnerhood of Hickock far preferable to the insipid Pelagian virtue of his parents. It would be warmly welcomed in a violence cult novel, which would maintain that the murder of the Clutters would extend the experience of the murderers so far beyond ordinary limits, that they would rank as supermen, and the parents could be regarded as serfs justly paying tribute to their lords. It would also find a place in the physical-horror type of novel, which would

revel in Hickock's father's cancer and Perry's habit of bed-wetting.
Literature must go its own way, sometimes a blessing to its age, sometimes a curse; for no soothsayer can ever predict when it is going to be
the one or the other. All the same there are occasions when it is
comprehensible why Plato felt fear lest the poets corrupt the minds of
the people. But at any rate nothing but blessing can flow from Mr.
Capote's grave and reverend book. [114]

Death in Kansas

TONY TANNER

'AFTER ALL, EVERY SORT OF SHOUTING IS A TRANSITORY THING. IT IS THE
grim silence of facts that remains' (Conrad). On November 15, 1959, in
Holcomb, Kansas, Richard Hickock and Perry Smith shot the four
members of the Clutter family for no apparent motive, purpose or
profit. Brute fact. And starting from the meaningless horror of that
night, Capote has gathered together groups and clusters of related
facts so that the sudden bout of blood-spilling is retrieved from its
status as an isolated fact and provided with a complex context in which
it becomes the focal point of converging narratives. Capote works on
the valid assumption that a fact is simply a moment in an on-going
sequence, that it ramifies in all directions, and that to appreciate something of the full import of any incident you must see as much of the
sequence and as many of the ramifications as possible. He has done
this for the Clutter murders and now presents his version of the revealing sequence.

Thoreau wrote: 'I would so state facts that they shall be significant, shall be myths or mythologic' and Capote is continuing an old
American tradition when he tries to get at the 'mythic' significance of
the facts by simply stating them. It is a tradition based on the belief
that 'if men would steadily observe realities only' they would discover
that 'reality is fabulous' (again the words are Thoreau's); a tradition
which reaches back to Emerson and encompasses writers like Hemingway, Sherwood Anderson, and William Carlos Williams. Capote's contribution to this tradition, judging by the tremendous popularity of

From *The Spectator* CCVIII (March 18, 1966), 331–332. © 1966 by *The
Spectator*. Reprinted by permission of *The Spectator*, London, and Tony Tanner.

this book in America, seems to have been to extract a black fable from contemporary reality which has a peculiar relevance for his society.

By juxtaposing and dovetailing the lives and values of the Clutters and those of the killers, Capote produces a stark image of the deep doubleness in American life. For here is a 'true' parable of the outlaw against the community; the roving life of random impulse cutting across the stable respectability of continuous ambition; the gangster versus the family man. It is many other things as well. Dangerous footloose dreamers intruding on sober industrious farmers; the maimed and lethal throw-outs of society pouncing, as from a black nowhere, on to the prosperous pillars of the community; the terrible meeting of the cursed and the blessed of America.

Perhaps most graphically it is a collision between the visible rewards and the suppressed horrors of American life which resulted in four people splattered all over their imposing 'lovely home' and two more hanging from the gallows. It is the American dream turning into an American nightmare. Clearly this feeling of the frightening double life of America goes very deep. Norman Mailer wrote in one of *The Presidential Papers:* 'Since the First World War Americans have been leading a double life, and our history has moved on two rivers, one visible, the other underground.' On one level is the life of the ordinary, respectable, money-making community—'concrete, factual, practical and unbelievably dull'; 'and there is a subterranean river of untapped, ferocious, lonely and romantic desires, that concentration of ecstasy and violence which is the dream life of the nation.' Capote's story corroborates this vision of the two rivers of American life.

Thus by constructing the last day in the life of the Clutters, Capote gives us a sort of shorthand summary of the respectable surface of American life in its most extreme form. Mr. Clutter ('eminent Republican and church leader'), rigidly abstemious and harshly intolerant of all users of tobacco and alcohol, surveys his land, helps a neighbour, takes out an insurance policy. Nancy, his pretty, popular daughter, having acted in *Tom Sawyer* the night before, teaches another girl to make cherry-pie, works on bridesmaids' dresses for her sister's wedding, does errands, has her boy friend round to watch television. Her brother Kenyon messes around in his carpentry den and does some gardening. Life for them all is 'organised,' just as their surroundings are 'so tended and cared for.' Yet even here, perhaps all is not well within the citadel of respectability. Mrs. Clutter has nervous attacks and sleeps apart from her husband; there is a hint that Mr. Clutter has taken to the solace of secret cigarettes—while Nancy is a compulsive nail-biter. Their dog is a coward. Still, as Capote fills in the details of the town and community around them, we get a sense of a life which is worthy and decent enough, even if somewhat desolate, self-righteous and dull.

The killers, by contrast, inhabit a different world even if it is on

the same continent. A world, for a start, of endless travel and movement (they have both been smashed up in serious road accidents). We
first see Perry Smith ('an incessant conceiver of voyages') hunched
over a well-used map, and we follow both of them into Kansas, down
to Mexico, out to California, back to Florida, on to Kansas where,
incredibly, they returned, thence to Las Vegas where they were
caught. It is a world also of wild private dreams, particularly for Perry
who dreams of becoming a night-club singer, and of diving for buried
treasure (he has already bought the maps), although with his crippled
legs he cannot even swim. It is a world where violence is accepted
with a casual indifference which covers God knows what sort of
suppressed hysteria (they roared with laughter as they drove away
from the Clutter household, their clothes dripping blood). A world of
scavenging, stolen cars, dirty flophouses; of rough temporary loyalties,
bitter loneliness, and futile rancour. And also the dangerous unreason
of the beaten-down, the left-behind. Hickock and Smith are not
unique, as is revealed by the number of other horrendous mass
murders Capote has occasion to mention. They are part of what
society is producing at the same time as it is producing the Clutters.
And by marshalling the facts of their lives, Capote takes us a bit nearer
to the abysmal mystery of that moment when, not in greed and not in
anger, indeed almost as a 'dare,' Perry Smith slipped his knife into Mr.
Clutter's throat.

Perry is the most interesting character in the book. Capote of
course has always had a feeling for the loner, the lost one, the unloved,
the fatherless, and in Perry Smith he found someone with a life which
made his powers of invention redundant (although his romantic
feeling for the type emerges in the imagery he provides for Perry; in
the court 'he looked as lonely and inappropriate as a seagull in a
wheatfield'). He was a half-breed and was pushed around through a
life of much misery and no love (a brother and sister committed
suicide), a life mainly of blows received (in an orphanage the nuns
punished him for bedwetting by beating him with a flashlight, immers-
ing him in freezing water, and putting stinging ointment on his penis).
The blows were stored up—bound to erupt in some wild act of
irrational violence at a later date. Thus, chillingly, he had absolutely
no feelings against the Clutters at all, and chatted kindly to them
before he shot them. ('They never hurt me. Like other people. Like
people have all my life. Maybe it's just that the Clutters were the ones
who had to pay for it.') But Perry was also sensitive and had artistic
inclinations. Most touching is his personal treasure trove, his box of
memorabilia which he carts around wherever he goes. It held not only
his Korean War medal, but lyrics and songs, notebooks containing lists
of 'beautiful' or 'useful' words, and a diary full of interesting facts and
quotations. Sad tokens of hopeless, inchoate literary ambitions. His last
words on the gallows apparently were: "Maybe I had something to

contribute, something . . .' He emerges as not only a pathetic, but a sympathetic figure, an unwanted crippled dreamer whose moment of appalling violence was somehow not of his own making. One might compare one's feelings in reading the factual report on Lee Oswald, another messed-up failure lashing out at the supreme symbol of American success. Horror, certainly—but also a sort of stunned compassion.

There is no doubt that Capote has written a remarkable book, a book which, casting its net wide, does draw together some terribly revealing facts about America. But a word about his technique is in order. He claims to have written a 'Non-Fiction Novel,' to have assembled only facts derived from observation, official records, and interviews. He does not comment, he presents; he does not analyse, he arranges. This means, for one thing, that he cannot approach the profound inquiring insights into the significance of the psychopath offered by, for example, Musil in his analytic study of Moosbrugger. However, since his material is 'true,' it has its own kind of powerful impact: the illusion is of art laying down its tools as helpless and irrelevant in front of the horrors and mysteries of life itself. But I find something just a shade suspicious in this maintained illusion of objective factual presentation. Certainly it is in the American grain—'pleads for itself the fact,' said Emerson. But facts do *not* 'sing themselves,' as Emerson maintained. Facts are silent, as Conrad said, and any singing they do depends on their orchestration by a human arranger.

As Goethe insisted, there is no such thing as pure objectivity. 'Looking at a thing gradually merges into contemplation, contemplation into thinking, thinking is establishing connections and thus it is possible to say that every attentive glance which we cast on the world is an act of theorising.' The way Capote 'establishes connections' reveals his subjective feeling about the world he presents, and this should not be overlooked. It is, for instance, Capote who manipulates some of the very melodramatic contrasts and ironies by his selective juxtapositions (e.g., from seeing Perry hunched up with pain in a toilet, we cut straight to Nancy Clutter's bedroom and a prominent pink Teddy-bear). It is Capote who provides some of the atmospheric [331/332] detail. Thus when the police open up Perry's case: 'A cockroach emerged, and the landlady stepped on it, squashing it under the heel of her gold leather sandal.' It did? I wonder. Isn't it rather that behind the mask of the dispassionate reporter we can begin to make out the excited stare of the southern-gothic novelist with his febrile delight in weird settings and lurid details (the red ball bouncing down the stairs in *Other Voices, Other Rooms*)? There are other such details, not the least dubious being the 'reminiscence' accredited to Detective Dewey as he watches Perry hang. This ends the book and, if this were a plain novel, it would be regarded as pretty cheap and sentimental. 'If' is, of course, the point. Because 'if' this were a novel one might be more liable to notice the lapses into bad and clichéd writing ('The detective's trained eye roamed the scrubbed and humble room') and a marked penchant, not wholly pleasing, for just that arrangement or schematisation of details which will make life appear at its most queasily macabre.

I am not saying that Capote has twisted the facts so that life appears as a Capote novel. But tampering there has been, and a subtle exploitation or highlighting of ghastly or pathetic effects which leaves me feeling a little uneasy about the enormous appeal of this book (rather as I am made uneasy by those 'art' films about concentration camps). Say what he will, Capote *has* manipulated the facts to produce a particular kind of *frisson*. The great novels about a criminal act—by Dostoievsky, Stendhal, etc.—may be initially provoked by an actual reported crime. But by making their works frankly 'fictions' they tacitly assumed that to explore the latent significance of the grim, silent facts, the most valuable aid is the human imagination. I cannot see that Capote goes anywhere near to proving them wrong. [332]

But Is It Good for Literature?

WILLIAM PHILLIPS

TRUMAN CAPOTE'S *In Cold Blood* IS A CROSS BETWEEN A DETECTIVE story and a crime documentary. It cannot be considered in any meaningful sense a novel, though it invites criticism as a novel by pretending somehow to be one and by using the machinery of fiction. (On most bestseller lists, *In Cold Blood* is listed as non-fiction, though of course newspapers do not recognize any ultra-modern category between fiction and non-fiction.) Perhaps I can best sum up my response to the book by saying that when I finished it I thought it was good in its own way, but that the question remained—as in the old Jewish joke—whether *In Cold Blood* was good for literature. By this I do not mean that the book does not measure up to some fancy or sacred or strict notion of literature or of the novel. Nor am I denying its qualities: qualities that are appropriate to its own genre, such as the fact that it is a good story, competently though too mechanically told, its smooth,

From *Commentary*, XLI (May 1966), 77–80. Copyright © 1966 by the American Jewish Committee. Reprinted by permission of *Commentary* and William Phillips.

standardized prose and somewhat contrived shifting of scenes giving off an aura of fictional skill and urbanity and imaginative re-creation. *In Cold Blood* reads like high-class journalism, the kind of journalism one expects of a novelist.

Some people have been spreading the notion, promoted by Capote himself, that *In Cold Blood* represents a new literary genre, the non-fiction novel. Now the idea of a non- or anti-fiction novel is quite chic and fits in with fashionable attitudes about modern forms, and with attitudes about novelty in general. Capote's book, however, has nothing to do with these catchy—and saleable—hints of a literary breakthrough. It is almost reassuringly old-fashioned in its straightforward rendition of a "true story." For the use of real events is as old as fiction or story-telling itself. And if we are looking for more immediate examples, there is of course *An American Tragedy*, based largely on actual happenings, or works like *The Possessed*, or *Sons and Lovers*, or Proust's great novel, all of which took off from occurrences either in or outside the lives of the authors. But even the most naturalistic works were not chained to the facts; in all of them, the art of the novel was to transform the original experience. In Truman Capote's book, what stands out is not Capote's inventiveness but his fidelity to the "facts." The emphasis is on the fact, not on the fiction, on re-creation, not creation. Capote's aim seemed to be to preserve the picture of the place and of the events before, during, and after the murder, in the way it appeared to everyone involved or as it might appear to an all-seeing, objective observer—like God, who is clearly not a novelist.

There is no need to retell the story, since so many reviewers have showed off their narrative gifts in stylish summaries of the action, with a few side-effects and fringe insights thrown in. But one is struck by the fact that many of the reviewers as well as the author himself (particularly when he was interviewed in the New York *Times*) put so much emphasis on the importance of the plot. No doubt the appearance of a good, juicy, easily readable tale that lent itself to a kind of instant, home-made symbolism was bound to be welcomed by readers and reviewers fed up with the more complex forms of modern writing in which the so-called story is only an aspect, and a highly stylized one, of the total vision of the novel. Here in this seemingly normal chronicle was the answer to all the distorted and morbid and tortured re-creations of experience, going by the name of modernism, that simply do not look like what is commonly assumed to be the shape of experience. The standardized notions of experience are of course themselves fabrications, but they are soothing ones, deriving from popular myths and outworn beliefs, perpetuated by journalism and by the mass media, particularly by television and Broadway. (Though, recently, shocking and outrageous things have been passed off as original.) In self-defense, modern literature—like modern art—had to free itself of the cliches of naturalism in popular story-telling, where the orderly plot reduces everything to a consensus of feelings about life, and affirms an orderly view of existence.

In Cold Blood does involve some such consensus of feeling. No doubt Capote was originally drawn to the murder, despite his statements expressing a purely professional interest in the story, because it touched something very personal inside himself. But except for some hints and echoes, In Cold Blood sounds as though it need not have been written by Capote. The popular strains of Americana, the mystique of Kansas and the Midwest, the folksy philosophy and style of most of the characters, the attempt to understand but not to forgive the murderers in the best tradition of benevolent psychiatry and criminology—those things which give the book its wholesomeness are not attitudes or views normally associated with Capote. The impression one gets from this book is that of a clever synthesis of American prejudices and American wisdom. It is almost as though everything were seen through the eyes of the mythic American: the fabled kind and strong man of the midland who knows nothing and understands everything. All the [77/78] characters, including the murderers, are conceived of as generalizations of themselves. And the murdered family, as so many reviewers proudly observed, represented a composite of everything decent and ordinary in American life—the very combination of these elements being a triumph of the American character. Also the moral symbolism, which seemed to delight most of the reviewers, is actually a moral resumé, a rehash of all the lessons we have ever been taught. The good guys, who include everyone except the murderers, illustrate the enlightened idea that man is a mixture of good and evil, say about 60–40 in favor of good, while the bad guys, the murderers, simply reverse the proportion. And in the last analysis, everyone is a victim of circumstance, thus preserving the faith, the hope, and the belief in social sanity that our ideals of advancement depend on. As everyone has said, the crime itself is so awful it is painful to think about. Yet the book as a whole is made palatable by the fact that its horrrors are part of the order of things and are soluble in criminology, psychology, sociology—the disciplines which stabilize the meaning of crime and punishment.

A kind of catharsis might be said to be effected by the typicality of the people and events of the book. The judge, the cops, the Clutter family, the murderers, are so thoroughly stereotyped that their motives and their behavior scarcely belong to them. They belong to all of us, and since they are so broad and so general they sweep up our free-floating feelings of guilt and terror and desire—which, I suppose, is the secret of the detective story's success. Who are the leading characters? Herbert Clutter is the legendary rugged individualist, the American Gothic who inevitably is conjured up when you try to picture the average middle-class citizen, the man whose life and opinions explain why the country thinks and acts as it does at any given time. Mrs. Clutter is faded, depressed, but a good woman, the soft underbelly of the American dream. Their children, Nancy and Kenyon, round out the family: Nancy is the embodiment [78/79] of every father's fantasy; Kenyon, that dreamy combination of shyness and strength, is nothing less than American youth. And so on: Judge Tate mixes his prejudices and his duties in the austere tradition of frontier justice; the jailers are simple and warmhearted; the detectives are plain and self-righteous, doing a job that fortunately puts them on the side of right against wrong.

The killers, Perry Smith and Dick Hickock, are more complex and more interesting. And in conceiving them, Capote almost achieves the true novelist's lack of objectivity. For one thing, Capote spends much more time digging into the characters of the killers. Obviously he was strongly drawn to them, and not only because the narrative required that he focus on them. His re-creation of their lives suggests more than the standard liberal conception of their pathology. It suggests a feeling, not entirely detached, for that pathology, particularly for Perry Smith, the more twisted of the two. Hence Capote does succeed in giving a sense of the psychopathic haze in which the impulses outlawed by society are mixed up with so-called normal—or conventional —thinking. Clinically, the distorting factors are thought to be some lack of guilt, weak superego, and affectlessness; and Capote does suggest some such psychological picture. But these are only medical categories, and whatever power is generated in portraying the killers comes from Capote's need to humanize the criminal mind, to connect it with the most ordinary, often legitimate, sometimes appealing acts and feelings. If Smith and Hickock come alive at all, it is because Capote has tried to see them as whole men, so that their sexual habits, their feeling toward their friends and families, their sense of themselves—all appear to be of a piece. Sometimes it almost seems as though Capote identifies himself with the killers, particularly when he makes their most perverse desires look plausible and ordinary, the way we like to think of our own desires.

Usually, though, Capote hangs back from putting himself into the [79/80] killers or—what amounts to the same thing—putting the killers into himself. Instead, he generalizes them, blowing them up into case histories which, as we know, are interchangeable, equally morbid, seductive, meaningful.

Only in the portrait of Perry Smith does Capote come close to drawing a truly novelistic figure, someone who is more than a composite of everything we know about him. Stunted, childish, and savage, like an underdeveloped pirate, Perry Smith lives constantly on the edge of frenzy. But there is very little difference between his "normal" way of thinking and the state he is in when he is about to steal something from a supermarket or cut someone's throat. In this respect he is, by the norms of our imagination, a monster. (One is reminded of Eichmann, whose normalities and abnormalities were often indistinguishable, though in Nazi Germany his behavior was more socially acceptable.) And to re-create Smith as a monster, Capote would have had to stretch him out of shape—a shape people find disturbing but still comfortably familiar—to push to the extreme some of his traits instead of underplaying them. Thus, Perry would have had to become possible rather than just reasonable. But to effect this, Capote would have had to stock Perry with some of his own obsessions. As for Dick Hickock, he is less of a monster, more of a typical con man. But to be realized, he, too, would have had to be carried away by some morbid idea, superimposed on him by Capote; and such a fusion of the author with his character would have endowed Hickock with a novelistic personality.

Perhaps the key to Capote's failure is his muting of the homosexual theme. I don't mean to suggest that he should have made overt the homosexuality constantly hinted at in each of the killers and in their quibbling, jealous, dependent relationship, like that of a very old or very young couple. That would have been even more banal, just another psychological package. But Capote could have exploited the homosexual theme by transposing it or connecting it with other life styles, as, for example, Proust and Genet have done, and thus might have been able to lift the killers out of the pettiness of their lives and their crimes. If their crimes are to be seen as extensions of their lives, their lives must be seen in more monstrous and more seductive—really in more absolute, terms.

A comparison with writers like Gide and Camus, who found the proper means for handling similar themes, is not unfair if we take seriously the claims for *In Cold Blood*. Gide's and Camus's ideas invaded their characters, and each character enacts the meaning, not just the events, of his life. Gide's immoralists act out their own moral logic, and their seemingly unmotivated acts exemplify the illogic of existence. And Camus's Meursault is an ordinary man, a nobody, who becomes a killer because one thing leads to another. But in refusing to connect himself with his crime, Meursault holds on till the very end to his idea of himself, and in so doing exemplifies Camus's idea that moral will is the content of freedom. Capote's murderers, on the other hand, are simply reconstituted.

Literary questions of the kind raised by Capote's new book often appear more sharply in a generational form. And, in fact, *In Cold Blood* seems to have very little appeal for younger people. I do not think that one is necessarily joining the youth brigade in suggesting that younger people, brought up on more adventurous kinds of writing, do not take to a fairly conventional, almost sentimental, portrait of the psychopath as a little man. Still, one need not be under thirty to tell the difference between a fictionalized crime story and a new kind of fiction. [80]

Capote's Crime and Punishment

DIANA TRILLING

ONE CAN DISPOSE QUICKLY ENOUGH OF THE ISSUE TRUMAN CAPOTE HAS
himself made salient in discussion of his book—*In Cold Blood* is not
a novel, as Mr. Capote would have us think; it is "only" a book, a work
of journalism of an exceptionally compelling kind. Whatever else it
may or may not be, the novel is a literary form in which the writer is
free to make any use he wishes of material drawn from real life. It was
Mr. Capote's decision to stay wholly with the facts of the Clutter murders; in their presentation he employs various strategies learned in his
practice of fiction. This does not mean he has discovered a new fiction
form nor—for that matter—a new form of nonfiction. Works of autobiography such as Isak Dinesen's *Out of Africa*, works of history such as
Cecil Woodham Smith's *The Reason Why*, works of journalism like
James Agee's *Let Us Now Praise Famous Men* are all at least as close
to, or far from, proposing a new nonfiction form as Mr. Capote's *In
Cold Blood*.

Indeed, a comparison of Truman Capote's report on the Clutter
murders with James Agee's report on the condition of the sharecroppers during the Depression is useful in demonstrating some of the
accomplishments, but more of the shortcomings, of *In Cold Blood*
even as a work of nonfiction. That Mr. Capote's prose is flaccid, often
downright inept, and that his narrative is overmanipulated in order to
keep things at a constant high pitch of suspense: these are defects
apparent without reference to Agee's uncommon talent. But it is in the
difference in their approaches to the journalistic enterprise that comparison makes its sharp—but not simple—point.

Let Us Now Praise Famous Men was conceived not in loyalty to
fact but in its author's loyalty to himself as an artist; which is to say, in
the interplay between the actuality on which Agee had undertaken
[252/253] to report and his own sensibility. Just as Mr. Capote went
West for *The New Yorker*, Agee had gone South on commission from
Fortune magazine. But Agee's "assignment" had at once yielded in
importance (perhaps perversely, but this is of only tangential, chiefly

From *Partisan Review*, XXXIII (Spring 1966), 252–259. © 1966 by *Partisan
Review*. Reprinted by permission of *Partisan Review* and Diana Trilling.

biographical, interest) before the imaginative possibilities of the material which presented itself to him. He comprehended only subjectively
the world he had set out to describe—in splendid lyrical bursts, he
castigated, and eventually celebrated, himself for being a well-fed
man, a middle-class man, a writer (of all improbable human appari-
tions!) daring to spy upon lives this remote from his own. It turned
out that this subjectivity was so intense that it largely dominated the
object under investigation; *Let Us Now Praise Famous Men* implicates
us much more with its author than with the sharecroppers. Its bias also
distorted the social actuality on which Agee was supposed to be
reporting—surely people are not, as *Let Us Now Praise Famous Men*
would have it, innocent in proportion as they are miserable and poor,
nor can one readily suppose that sharecroppers are the superlative
instance of humankind that Agee, in his impulse to self-abasement
before suffering, makes them out to be. Nevertheless, by licensing his
consciousness to prevail over external fact, Agee was able to create an
artistic reality, that of his own felt experience. His book intensified our
capacity to feel acutely about something, if not about sharecroppers.

Truman Capote's method is exactly the opposite. It was Mr.
Capote's decision to report the Clutter case wholly objectively, in as
much as possible of its manifest social and personal complication, and
to give us both the Clutter family and their murderers without
permitting himself any partisanship to either of the extreme opposi-
tions embodied in the two sets of characters. Now on first glance this
seems an acceptable enough intention. But, not too surprisingly, it
develops that in his submission to actuality, or factuality, and his
abrogation of the artist's right to emphasize or even to suppress or
distort reality for his own purposes, Mr. Capote prepared for himself
an almost inevitable artistic defeat. The neutrality of his posture
announces itself even in his prose, whose indistinctiveness is of a sort
with which we are familiar in popular writing, where communication
is believed to be impeded rather than created by an author's presence
on his page. The social object of Mr. Capote's investigation remains
intact. And the dramatic impact of his story is not diminished by the
impersonality of his approach. On the contrary, it is reinforced, but
this only makes for a sensationalism proportionate to the horror of the
actual events which are being described. The overtones of *In Cold
Blood*—if, in a book so lacking in literary [253/254] resonance, we can
call them that—are those of a socially-well-documented story of crime
and detection, not of a work of the imagination.

Still, even as we admit the inadequacy of *In Cold Blood* as a work
of literary art, it is hard for us to suppose that this alone would
account for the large, odd, often unformulable, reservations which so
many different kinds of readers have about it. These seem to me to be
reservations of a moral, or "human," more than of an esthetic nature,
and they derive, I think, from Mr. Capote's stance as the wholly

neutral reporter of facts-from-life which, while themselves so highly charged, are presented to us by a mind which refuses to be adequate to their tortuous meanings or appropriate to their terror. By his unwillingness to be implicated in his story, whether by the way he disposes his emotions between the murderers and their victims or by the way he invests his narrative with the intensity and anxiety proper to an unresolvable moral dilemma, Mr. Capote is employing objectivity as a shield for evasion. This is what is resented.

Certain of Mr. Capote's readers would wish he had thrown his weight to the Smith-Hickock side of the moral equation; these, of course, are the readers who believe that psychopaths and criminals, because they live outside the social order, have a special call on our tenderness. There are other readers who, though immune to the particular appeal of psychopaths and criminals, feel that in his unquestioning acceptance of Kansas farmers, members of 4-H Clubs, even KBI agents, Mr. Capote by strong implication gives his assent to American society in terms long outmoded in serious writing. Still others accuse Mr. Capote of having been seduced by personal acquaintance with Smith and Hickock, of having let himself forget the hideousness of their crime and of portraying them *too* sympathetically. If this diversity of negative response requires some common denominator of disappointment, it must be found in the sense shared in some dim way by virtually all of Mr. Capote's audience of having been unfairly used in being made to take on the burden of personal involvement pridefully put aside by Mr. Capote himself. An unpleasant critical charge leveled against *In Cold Blood* is that it is itself written in cold blood, exploiting tragedy for personal gain. One does not have to concur in this harsh opinion (I do not); one can even recognize that if anyone is misused by Mr. Capote it is not the Clutters or their murderers but we, the public, and still understand what inspires the charge of exploitation and, however imprecisely, warrants it.

And yet Mr. Capote's book has virtues which are perhaps not to be detached from the objectivity of his method. It is full of well-reported social detail: here at least Mr. Capote handsomely takes over what was once, in a less subjective day, an important function of the novelist. [254/255] And his book speaks to us with disquieting force on psychiatry and the law—Mr. Capote may not tell us to what end he delved so deep into the Clutter killings, but he thoroughly impresses upon us the small progress our society has made in solving the legal problems posed by criminals like Smith and Hickock. And certainly *In Cold Blood* has a healthily unsettling effect on some of our easier assumptions about social and human causality.

What—Mr. Capote asks us—are we to do about our psychopathic murderers: kill them; put them in prison; put them in hospitals? Although little approval is now given to capital punishment for any class of criminal, it still exists in the majority of American states. But let us suppose—hopefully—that soon this form of punishment will everywhere be abolished (and the movement for its abolition can only be forwarded by Mr. Capote's harrowing description of a hanging: it took twenty minutes for Hickock to be legally strangled), what then do we do with our Smiths and Hickocks? Obviously they cannot be let free in society. Shall it then be prison or hospitalization? If prison, rehabilitation is hopeless. But so too, in the case of murderers like Smith and Hickock, is psychiatric cure virtually hopeless in our present state of therapeutic knowledge. What distinguishes these cold-blooded killers, Smith, Hickock, the young Andrews who was with them in the death row, from at least some persons who commit crimes of passion is their incapacity to feel remorse for their crimes. Where there is no guilt for a murder, there is nothing to stop further killings—psychiatry as yet knows no way to inculcate the capacity for remorse, of sufficient strength to be counted on as a restraint of action, in someone lacking this human dimension. It may scarcely seem practical to commit incurable criminals to hospitals for the rest of their lives; but this is what we do with incurable noncriminals who cannot live in society, and to make a distinction between the two categories, criminal and noncriminal, could only mean that it is punishment and not protection of others which guides our conduct.

But there are even knottier problems than this which Mr. Capote's book brings out of the professional parish where they usually stay hidden from general view. Not only has the law not discovered a proper disposition of the incurable criminal, it has not yet devised a reliable method for separating out the offender who is susceptible of cure from incurables like Smith and Hickock. The legal sanity of these two men was tested by the M'Naghten Rule which still obtains in most states, not only in Kansas. In accordance with this Rule, which asks but a single question, whether the defendant was able to distinguish right from wrong at the time of the crime, Smith and Hickock were clearly able [255/256] to stand trial for the Clutter murders. True, they had been "driven" to commit these terrible killings by forces beyond their control, and they had none of the emotions appropriate to wrongdoing. Under psychiatric examination they exhibited a wide range of symptoms of severe mental disorder. But there is no doubt that they were intellectually capable of telling right from wrong, and knew they had done wrong in killing the Clutter family; the awareness of wrongdoing may in fact have given added zest to their criminal acts. None of this complicated pathology could of course be introduced into a court which abides by the M'Naghten Rule, or certainly not without clinical evasion or imprecision.

Nor is the Bazelon Rule, which substitutes for the M'Naghten Rule in the District of Columbia, a useful advance on the older test for criminal insanity. According to the Bazelon Rule, a criminal need not stand trial if he can be proved to be mentally ill. But at least one wing of psychiatric opinion holds it as self-evident that the mere commission of a crime is indicative of mental illness. The Bazelon Rule, no less than the M'Naghten Rule, fails adequately to meet the central question of criminal responsibility—to trace, that is, if only for legal purposes, the chain of causality in the life of the individual in order to discover in what sense he can be said to be responsible for the way he is and acts.

By his equal emphasis upon the life stories of Smith and Hickock and of the family they killed, so that it is in the glaring immediate light of the *outcome* of the pathologies of the two murderers that we examine their personal histories, Mr. Capote gives an unusual stringency to the enterprise of socio-psychological understanding. The presence of the Clutters within the same pages as the men who so vagrantly murdered them denies us, or should, recourse to sentimentality; it restrains us, or should, from sliding too smoothly into the grooves prepared for us by our present-day preference for the deterministic view of society. Perry Smith, to be sure, has a life story so casebook as to be a cliché of the environmental explanation of mental disease and crime. So awful were the circumstances of his early life—a brutish incompetent father, a raging alcoholic promiscuous Cherokee mother, a vicious Catholic orphanage, ignorance, poverty, degradation —that the question in our minds is not how did this man come to be as he was but, rather, how did his sister manage to salvage herself, if we can think it salvation, for her life of tortured respectability? But the Hickock story is different; Hickock is not at all the social victim, or at least not in the sense of being a product of gross want, mistreatment and neglect. While he was disadvantaged economically, it was in circumstances which according to old-time fable are supposed to make for the peculiar American heroism of [256/257] success. His parents were industrious, honest, clean-living, loyal and loving. Even after their son had been caught in his crime, they never deserted him. A picture like this controverts our readiest notions about the genesis of the psychopathic criminal—until we look more closely and see that, shamed and anguished though they were by what their son had done, Hickock's parents felt no more actual revulsion (however mitigated by love) from their son's crime than the son did himself. The peculiarly awful nature of the Clutter killings reached them only as an idea—a social idea, so to speak—without an emotional affect appropriate to the act itself. One is led to conclude that well before Hickock had arrived on the family scene, the tragic outcome of his life had already been made emotionally possible for him.

Nor is this the only element in the Smith-Hickock story to upset our too-mechanical psychological assumptions. If the two men were unable to experience guilt for taking human life, this does not mean, as we might expect, that they were simply lacking in conscience, any kind of conscience. What someone else might feel about committing murder, Smith and Hickock would seem to have felt about being physically dirty: washing, shaving, showering, caring for their nails was a major occupation of their nonviolent hours. Even more demanding was their concern with language. For Smith, the more literate of the pair, it constituted a measurable and well-exercised superiority to Hickock that he could correct his friend's errors or infelicities of speech, and offer so many more and better words for communicating the complex life of feeling. Everywhere on his travels, as far as his last jail, Smith took with him lists of "beautiful" and "useful" words, obscure bits of information, poems and literary quotations he had anthologized in substitute for the education he had missed. He thought of himself as someone who might have been, who should have been, an artist, and it was from his sense of himself as an artist that he plumbed the depths of his "sensitivity" and nourished his spirit in self-pity. This was met, on Hickock's side, by a highly ambivalent respect for so gifted a friend, an envious admiration which could not but encourage at least his half of their (concealed) homosexual attachment. If we are to say of Smith and Hickock that they were emotionally incapable of our usual old-established moral valuations, we must in accuracy add that they were not without other valuations of a sort to which we are accustomed to give moral weight.

But it is not alone Smith and Hickock but the Clutters too, who, especially as we are shown them confronting their murderers, reveal a far more complicated personal and social principle than we are in the habit of ascribing to virtuous, substantial, Republican, churchgoing, civicminded citizens of the Middle West. At the head of the family [257/258] stands Mr. Clutter—and was anyone ever more the head of his family, more the whole source and apex of its authority? Certainly there was never such a man of policy, in formulated control of every minute and act of his life, even—or so he would have hoped—of every secret terror. He not only took no stimulants himself, not even tea or coffee, but contracted his employees to total abstinence. He disbursed money only by check, so that every penny could be accounted for to whatever still higher authority might probe his affairs. He permitted himself no rage, even kept a dog that was gun-shy. He was a pillar of his community, himself so fashioned for respect that he could even depend upon it for his "nervous" wife, who, after the birth of each of her children, had wandered always further into sadness and uncertainty. But this pillar of strength was a murderer—or so at least I read the story.

From Mr. Capote's detailed reconstruction of the night of the murders, Mr. Clutter was not only himself unable to meet the aggression directed against him by this invasion of his home, he would seem to have incapacitated his grown son and daughter for any self-defense, even by effective guile. Smith and Hickock were of course armed. But it was an hour between the time they arrived in the Clutter farmhouse and the killings. In this period, which included an interval when the family was locked, untied, in a bathroom and several intervals when the two intruders were separated from each other in different parts of the house, no one screamed, no one fought, no one tried to drop out of the bathroom window to run for help. It was apparently inconceivable to Mr. Clutter, and therefore to his obedient son and daughter, that the two men might do worse than rob them, harm them. Only the poor neurotic Mrs. Clutter was available to this kind of imagination. Her "fantasy" was quickly countered by Mr. Clutter's "realism"—it would, one can suppose, have been a familiar situation as between this husband and wife.

Indeed, for me, by far the most interesting aspect of Mr. Capote's book as an American story lies not in the gratuitous violence of the crime it describes—this is not an American invention, though it is as ready to hand for us as if it were—nor in the dreary circumstances of the lives of Smith and Hickock—of this we already have some knowledge—but in the curiously ambiguous personality of Mr. Clutter. If Mr. Capote is at all a novelist in this book, it is, paradoxically enough, as an accident of his entirely literal reporting of this highly "masculine" character undone by his passivity and by—if you will—his lack of actual identity. One is reluctant (it seems like chic) to draw so exemplary a citizen, a successful teetotaling Republican devout progressive farmer, into the circle of self-alienated Americans. Yet manifestly this was a man without connection [258/259] with his inner self, living by forced intention, by conscious design, programmatically, rather than by any happy disposition of natural impulse. His response to anger could not have been more contemporary in its "enlightened" propitiatoriness and in its lack of instinctual manliness. Otherwise, would it not have allowed for something other than the guilt-ridden reaction—if these people less fortunate than himself wanted his money, he must give it to them—which was his only reaction to an invasion of his home? Mr. Clutter was a towering figure in his community. One of the last things said to him on the day of his death was said by a neighbor: "Can't imagine you afraid. No matter what happened, you'd talk your way out of it." This sounds like a compliment to courage. But then one thinks of what is actually implied in the idea that we now can define fearlessness as the ability "to talk your way out of" danger: is there nothing beyond the reach of reasonable persuasion? Certainly Mr. Clutter was a talker—not a conversationalist—and this is an American and contemporary thing to be. But according to most folk wisdom, it is also not a very masculine thing to be; it is not supposed to go along with power, force or any other older principle of manliness. In men who had come to his home "to splatter hair on the walls," Mr. Clutter confronted a spirit which he was unprepared to meet and before which he was fatally disarmed. [259]

Capote's Nonfiction Novel

ROBERT LANGBAUM

NO ONE AT THIS LATE DATE HAS TO BE TOLD THAT THIS SPECTACULARLY best-selling account of the murder of the Clutter family in Holcomb, Kansas, on November 14, 1959, makes good reading, that it is not only the sort of thriller you "can't put down" but the sort that the most sophisticated people can thrill to. The question I want to take up arises from Mr. Capote's claim, made in an inconspicuous note at the end, that this, his "ninth published book, represents the culmination of his long-standing desire to [570] make a contribution toward the establishment of a serious new literary form: the Nonfiction Novel." The claim was elaborated in the long interview that appeared in the *New York Times Book Review* of January 16, behind the front-page review of *In Cold Blood*. Mr. Capote described in the interview his five years of research, from the time the murder was committed to the day, April 14, 1965, when the criminals, Richard Hickock and Perry Smith, were finally hanged.

Most reviewers extolled the book, but pooh-poohed the idea of a nonfiction novel as too patently absurd to be worth discussing. I would like to give the claim serious consideration, because the tie between journalism and the novel is an old and perplexing one, going back to Defoe. As Ortega y Gasset has observed, the novel is the only literary form that does not want to look like a literary form—that wants to look like a bundle of letters, a journal, an autobiography, like life itself. We know how many novels are really autobiographies or accounts of true crimes—but disguised, with perhaps some loss from the disguise. Why not, therefore, substantiate the novel's claim to truthfulness by being truthful?

Besides, Mr. Capote has pinpointed with his phrase, "nonfiction novel," a series of questions that have been going the rounds in literary discussions since World War II. With the decline of the novel since the war, critical and discursive writing has so often seemed bolder and

From *The American Scholar*, XXXV (Summer 1966), 570–580. Copyright © 1966 by the United Chapters of Phi Beta Kappa. Reprinted by permission of the publishers and Robert Langbaum.

more imaginative then fiction as to make us feel that the line between so-called creative and noncreative writing is not so easily discernible as we used to think. The New Critics have also taught us since the war to give more weight to the actual structure of a work than to the circumstances that brought it into being. Once we look at structure, we find many nonfiction works as artful and sometimes more artful than many novels. Northrop Frye has, in his influential *Anatomy of Criticism*, gone so far as to apply the word *fiction* to any "work of art in prose."

Mr. Capote wanted primarily, I believe, to call attention to the artfulness of his book. For many people think, when they [572/573] hear a book is "true," that the facts wrote it and that anyone given the same facts would come up with the same book. He wanted also to tell us that the book is no digression from his career as a fiction writer, but a "culmination"—that all his experience writing stories went into it. By taking him at his word and comparing his book to a novel, we can both appreciate his achievement and see its limits. For its best effects are novelistic and it falls short just where it is not novelistic enough.

Mr. Capote tells a mainly chronological narrative with himself as omniscient and invisible author. He might have enhanced the reportorial quality and given us a more intricate novelistic structure had he made us aware of his evidence, of how he came to know the facts. Instead the book itself, without the *Times* interview, requires the same confidence we give a novelist before we can get on with the story. Mr. Capote gains the advantages of any writer who uses a historical or allegedly historical subject—public significance, and an effect of fatefulness that comes of our knowing in advance how the story must come out. Mr. Capote achieves a hallucinated fatefulness through repeated references to the black Chevrolet that carries the murderers inexorably to their victims—although the murderers start hundreds of miles from their victims and with no apparent connection to them. There is the same hallucinated fatefulness in the return of the murderers from Mexico to Las Vegas, where they are arrested just after they have withdrawn from the post office the boots that match the footprints found in the Clutter house.

De Quincey long ago pointed out, in discussing *Macbeth*, that the writer turns crime stories into high literature by throwing "the interest on the murderer: our sympathy must be with *him*," our "sympathy of comprehension," not "approbation." Mr. Capote manages to do this, with really reprehensible murderers; but he also writes a detective story, in which our interest is in seeing the criminals caught. In the same way, he writes a tragedy of fate; but he also writes a suspense story, by deliberately withholding [573/574] information—we do not learn until midway in the book how the criminals so much as know of the existence of their victims. It is because Mr. Capote has combined literary levels and captured all possible audiences that his book is selling so well.

When he tells us in the *Times* interview what a tiny account of the information he gathered has actually gone into the book, we realize that the process of selection was a creative act. And assuming that his informants could remember the elaborate dialogue and intimate trains of thought given us, and that Mr. Capote, who used no tape recorder, remembered the interviews correctly, it is still the author who creates meaning through the placing of details and the repetitions. Mrs. Clutter, for example, the mother in the prosperous farm family who are to be murdered that night, shows a young girl her collection of miniature objects and comes to a little paper fan that "only cost a penny." " 'Little things really belong to you,' she said, folding the fan. 'They don't have to be left behind. You can carry them in a shoebox.' " The author then tells us that Bonnie Clutter went away some years earlier for mental treatment, and the information operates as though it were part of the dialogue. That is why Bonnie's repetition, as she presses the fan into the hand of the departing girl, rounds out the scene so perfectly: "It's only a penny thing—but it's pretty."

One feels the author's hand there. And indeed, when the virginal genteel Mrs. Clutter, who has mental troubles and sleeps apart from her husband, displays a collection of miniature objects, we are reminded of Tennessee Williams' *Glass Menagerie* and feel we are being prepared for one of those stories the Southern writers do so well, in which brutal sexuality breaks in on sex-starved respectability to the secret satisfaction of both parties. Mr. Capote expends art to sound ominous notes of imminent disorder beneath the apparently placid surface of the Clutters' life. Mr. Clutter's militant teetotalism, his intolerance even of smoking and of tea and coffee, are described in such a way as to suggest emotional inadequacy; and life even hands [574/575] Mr. Capote a coincidence no novelist would dare invent— Mr. Clutter takes out double-indemnity life insurance the day of the murder. These adumbrations make fascinating reading, but lead us up a false trail.

For the point Mr. Capote really wants to make is that the Clutters, far from reaching out for their destiny, were "of all people in the world . . . the least likely to be murdered." They were like you and me, the sort to whom the inconceivable does not happen. That is why Mr. Clutter, when he was awakened that night, spoke gently to the murderers, led them to the rest of his family and allowed them to tie him up and tape his mouth—because, conceiving only rational motivation, he assumed they were only after money. When Perry Smith cut his throat, he screamed out beneath the tape his supernatural surprise. His son, daughter and wife experienced nightmare come true as, after his murder, they waited bound and taped to be shot one by one. But until that point, the Clutters were not equipped to conceive of—*evil*, we are tempted to say; for the parallel with Dostoevski suggests itself when we deal with gratuitous crime. But Mr. Capote is, by implication at least, more nihilistic than Dostoevski. For what the Clutters could not conceive of was sheer screwiness.

The case is like that of Oswald, when we thought there must be an organization behind him because nothing so catastrophic as President Kennedy's assassination could have occurred for no reason at all. Because of the human need to rationalize experience, the citizens of Holcomb, Kansas, assumed the murderers must have come from their own limited circle, must have been connected to the victims. The chief detective, Dewey, when he finally got confessions from Smith and Hickock, felt disappointment; for "the confessions . . . failed to satisfy his sense of meaningful design. The crime was a psychological accident, virtually an impersonal act; the victims might as well have been killed by lightning."

That, at least potentially, is Mr. Capote's vision of American life—an apparently placid surface shot through by sporadic eruptions of violence. To show the Clutter [575/576] case is not unique, he describes other multiple murders, all zany, all with an aura of sexuality about them. The sexual aura would seem to be *de rigueur* for murder stories nowadays; and it is not crimes of passion that interest us, but rather murder as a substitute for sexual expression, as stemming from sexual and emotional deficiency. Mr. Capote depicts his murderers, with exquisite precision, as deformed and stunted.

The half-breed Cherokee, Perry, a bed-wetter with no settled character to his face, had legs too short for his torso: "when he stood up he was no taller than a twelve-year-old child." Dick, patched up after an auto accident, "had a face which seemed composed of mismatching parts." Although he boasted of being "a normal," Dick raped little girls. Perry was moralistically, fastidiously hostile to sex. It is a nice touch that Perry, the more attractive one, actually committed the murders; Dick, who planned them, hadn't the stomach for murder —he was a rapist and passer of bad checks, a punk. The relation between the pair is described as latently homosexual; Perry committed murders for Dick because he was under the spell of Dick's masculinity. But they did not understand the force that moved them. They themselves thought their aim in the Clutter house was burglary, although they went on with the carnage after they discovered there were only some forty dollars to be stolen. Perry did not know he was going to murder until Mr. Clutter's scream made him aware he was cutting the man's throat.

It is the nullity of all this that fascinates us, bringing our advanced ideas into play. Yet (to answer Kenneth Tynan's obtuse comments in the London *Observer*) these criminals are not insane in any simple technical sense, or there would have been no story worth telling. Mr. Capote, supported by the ambiguous psychiatric evidence, artistically blurs the distinction between sanity and insanity, as it is blurred in so many criminals of literature—in a motiveless malignity

like that of Iago, or in Raskolnikov. As against the criminals of nineteenth-century literature, who had more positive [576/577] qualities
than the rest of us, more energy and moral complexity, the frantic
gestures of Mr. Capote's criminals point only to the void at their
center. Does this make them different from us, or have they hit the
zero we all approach?

This is a question Mr. Capote has not resolved—the question of
how seriously we are to take the shallow lives of his respectable people,
the sort of life represented by the Clutter daughter, leader of the 4-H
Club and champion baker of cherry pies. Mr. Capote no doubt wanted
to admire these good people so much at the center of American life.
But they did not really interest him, and they come out therefore
rather like soap-opera characters. His depiction of them is not, like his
depiction of the criminals, penetrated by his intelligence. He fails, in
other words, to fill out his vision of American life, because he fails to
be sufficiently ironical—if for the sake of journalistic impartiality, then
✕ journalism has here interfered with comprehensiveness.

Another such failure of irony is in the fact that the psychiatrist's
report at the trial is given as entirely adequate to the case, whereas in
✕ any good novel, there ought to be an ironic disparity between such an
analysis and the living mystery of the characters. Perry Smith is finally
enigmatic. Yet Mr. Capote announces without reservation that the
report confirms Perry's own analysis of his motives—an analysis showing only that Perry was intelligent enough to have picked up the
sociopsychological point of view. The Clutters "never hurt me. Like
other people," he said. "Like people have all my life. Maybe it's just
that the Clutters were the ones who had to pay for it."

The scene in which Perry says this is conspicuously artful. Playwrights and novelists often introduce a new, somewhat mysterious
character near the end; and sure enough, a man whom Perry hardly
remembers from the army writes him in prison, saying he is a devout
Catholic and wants to help him. The holy stranger visits Perry during
the trial; but the scene, set for moral and religious discussion, comes to
nothing [577/578] because Perry is precisely not sorry. "I don't feel
anything about it. I wish I did. . . . It's easy to kill—a lot easier than
passing a bad check."

Even more ironic and profound is the scene where Perry, when he
returns to his cell after the death sentence, shows quite another side of
his nature. The undersheriff's wife, who had been taking care of Perry
and had come to like him, heard him crying like a child and went to
his cell. "He reached out his hand. He wanted me to hold his hand,
and I did, I held his hand, and all he said was, 'I'm embraced by
shame.'" Just that night, unfortunately, when Perry reached out for
human contact, she and her husband, who seldom went out, had an
engagement. Perry had reached out that way before in his life and
been rebuffed—most notably when he followed his father to Alaska

and the relation he had banked on so much ended with a tremendous
scene, epic in its emotional range, in which they almost killed each
other.

In Mr. Capote's short story "The Headless Hawk," the hero recalls
his childhood attraction to carnival freaks and realizes "that about
those whom he'd loved there was always a little something wrong,
broken." It is that sensibility in the author that makes the characterization of Perry the triumph of this book. For Perry is irresistibly attractive, with his talent for music and drawing, his fine feeling for words,
his gentleness—he prevented Dick from raping the Clutter daughter
and made the Clutters as comfortable as he could after he tied them
up. Yet he is not sentimentalized; for the gentleness makes the
murderousness all the zanier. We are never allowed to forget that he is
a child-man, a freak.

Mr. Capote said in the *Times* interview that he wanted to achieve
with nonfiction "the poetic altitude fiction is capable of reaching." He
achieves such altitude in the characterization of Bonnie—the one
Clutter who is "broken"—as a ghost. In life, she was always cold and
she feared her children would remember her "as a kind of ghost." After
her death, the detective's wife saw her in a dream, crying, "To be
murdered. No. No. There's nothing worse. Nothing [578/579] worse
than that. Nothing." Real speech is made to yield that much poetry
because it has been prepared for by a carefully arranged pattern of
imagery. Mr. Capote works like those *avant-garde* moviemakers who
turn real-life shots into art in the cutting room.

The highest altitude is reached in Perry's dream in the death
house. All his life Perry had dreamed of a snake that would fall upon
him out of a diamond-laden but foul-smelling jungle tree, and of a
towering yellow, a sunlike, parrot that would wing him to paradise.
Once in the death house he woke up shouting, "The bird is Jesus." And
then, in his climatic dream, he sees himself in his favorite guise as the
entertainer Perry O'Parsons, tap-dancing up a short flight of gold-
painted prop steps. But when he takes his bow at the top, the strange
audience, mostly men and Negroes, do not applaud.

Staring at them, the perspiring entertainer at last understood their silence,
for suddenly he knew that these were phantoms, the ghosts of the legally
annihilated, the hanged, the gassed, the electrocuted—and in the same
instant he realized that he was there to join them, that the gold-painted
steps had led to a scaffold, that the platform on which he stood was opening
beneath him. His top hat tumbled; urinating, defecating, Perry O'Parsons
entered eternity.

Here, through a powerfully ironic comprehension of the whole of
Perry's psychic life, Mr. Capote has achieved a genuinely literary
moment. One is reminded of the end of Browning's dream poem
"Childe Roland," and of Bloom's dream apotheosis in *Ulysses*.

And yet the penetration here is at odds with the flatness of the other characters. The insight into Perry does not contribute to any general vision; and the book rather loses literary magic and turns into journalism after the hallucinated events leading up to the murder and the capture of the criminals. Here, as in his symbolist fiction, Mr. Capote fails to understand all the implications of the imagery he sets in motion (his best stories are the sentimental comedies, [579/580] like *House of Flowers* and *Breakfast at Tiffany's,* which stick frankly to the surface). This limitation makes him a lightweight, although a sophisticated craftsman, a "pro" in the best sense of the word. The implications of *In Cold Blood* are so frightening that more rigor would undoubtedly have made the book less entertaining. As it stands, *In Cold Blood* is first-rate entertainment that at moments gives illusory promise of being something more than that. [580]

3. THE WORLDS OF TRUMAN CAPOTE

A Tree of Night

TRUMAN CAPOTE

IT WAS WINTER. A STRING OF NAKED LIGHT BULBS, FROM WHICH IT SEEMED all warmth had been drained, illuminated the little depot's cold, windy platform. Earlier in the evening it had rained, and now icicles hung along the station-house eaves like some crystal monster's vicious teeth. Except for a girl, young and rather tall, the platform was deserted. The girl wore a gray flannel suit, a raincoat, and a plaid scarf. Her hair, parted in the middle and rolled up neatly on the sides, was rich blondish-brown; and, while her face tended to be too thin and narrow, she was, though not extraordinarily so, attractive. In addition to an assortment of magazines and a gray suede purse on which elaborate brass letters spelled Kay, she carried conspicuously a green Western guitar.

When the train, spouting steam and glaring with light, came out of the darkness and rumbled to a halt, Kay assembled her paraphernalia and climbed up into the last coach.

The coach was a relic with a decaying interior of ancient red-plush seats, bald in spots, and peeling iodine-colored woodwork. An old-time copper lamp, attached to the ceiling, looked romantic and out of place. Gloomy dead smoke sailed the air; and the car's heated closeness accentuated the stale odor of discarded sandwiches, apple cores, and orange hulls: this garbage, including Lily cups, soda-pop bottles, and mangled newspapers, littered the long aisle. From a water cooler, embedded in the wall, a steady stream trickled to the floor. The passengers, who glanced up wearily when Kay entered, were not, it seemed, at all conscious of any discomfort.

Kay resisted a temptation to hold her nose and threaded her way carefully down the aisle, tripping once, without disaster, over a dozing fat man's protruding leg. Two nondescript men turned an interested eye as she passed; and a kid stood up in his seat squalling, "Hey,

Mama, look at de banjo! Hey, lady, lemme play ya banjo!" till a slap from Mama quelled him.

There was only one empty place. She found it at the end of the car in an isolated alcove occupied already by a man and woman who were sitting with their feet settled lazily on the vacant seat opposite. Kay hesitated a second then said, "Would you mind if I sat here?"

The woman's head snapped up as if she had not been asked a simple question, but stabbed with a needle, too. Nevertheless, she managed a smile. "Can't say as I see what's to stop you, honey," she said, taking her feet down and also, with a curious impersonality, removing the feet of the man who was staring out the window, paying no attention whatsoever.

Thanking the woman, Kay took off her coat, sat down, and arranged herself with purse and guitar at her side, magazines in her lap: comfortable enough, though she wished she had a pillow for her back.

The train lurched; a ghost of steam hissed against the window; slowly the dingy lights of the lonesome depot faded past.

"Boy, what a jerkwater dump," said the woman. "No town, no nothin'."

Kay said, "The town's a few miles away."

"That so? Live there?"

No. Kay explained she had been at the funeral of an uncle. An uncle who, though she did not of course mention it, had left her nothing in his will but the green guitar. Where was she going? Oh, back to college.

After mulling this over, the woman concluded, "What'll you ever learn in a place like that? Let me tell you, honey, I'm plenty educated and I never saw the inside of no college."

"You didn't?" murmured Kay politely and dismissed the matter by opening one of her magazines. The light was dim for reading and none of the stories looked in the least compelling. However, not wanting to become involved in a conversational marathon, she continued gazing at it stupidly till she felt a furtive tap on her knee.

"Don't read," said the woman. "I need somebody to talk to. Naturally, it's no fun talking to *him*." She jerked a thumb toward the silent man. "He's afflicted: deaf and dumb, know what I mean?"

Kay closed the magazine and looked at her more or less for the first time. She was short; her feet barely scraped the floor. And like many undersized people she had a freak of structure, in her case an enormous, really huge head. Rouge so brightened her sagging, flesh-featured face it was difficult even to guess at her age: perhaps fifty, fifty-five. Her big sheep eyes squinted, as if distrustful of what they saw. Her hair was an obviously dyed red, and twisted into parched, fat corkscrew curls. A once-elegant lavender hat of impressive size flopped crazily on the side of her head, and she was kept busy brushing back a drooping cluster of celluloid cherries sewed to the brim. She wore a plain, somewhat shabby blue dress. Her breath had a vividly sweetish gin smell.

"You do wanna talk to me, don't you honey?"

"Sure," said Kay, moderately amused.

"Course you do. You bet you do. That's what I like about a train. Bus people are a close-mouthed buncha dopes. But a train's the place for putting your cards on the table, that's what I always say." Her voice was cheerful and booming, husky as a man's. "But on accounta *him*, I always try to get us this here seat; it's more private, like a swell compartment, see?"

"It's very pleasant," Kay agreed. "Thanks for letting me join you."

"Only too glad to. We don't have much company; it makes some folks nervous to be around him."

As if to deny it, the man made a queer, furry sound deep in his throat and plucked the woman's sleeve. "Leave me alone, dear-heart," she said, as if she were talking to an inattentive child. "I'm O.K. We're just having us a nice little ol' talk. Now behave yourself or this pretty girl will go away. She's very rich; she goes to college." And winking, she added, "He thinks I'm drunk."

The man slumped in the seat, swung his head sideways, and studied Kay intently from the corners of his eyes. These eyes, like a pair of clouded milky-blue marbles, were thickly lashed and oddly beautiful. Now, except for a certain remoteness, his wide, hairless face had no real expression. It was as if he were incapable of experiencing or reflecting the slightest emotion. His gray hair was clipped close and combed forward into uneven bangs. He looked like a child aged abruptly by some uncanny method. He wore a frayed blue serge suit, and he had anointed himself with a cheap, vile perfume. Around his wrist was strapped a Mickey Mouse watch.

"He thinks I'm drunk," the woman repeated. "And the real funny part is, I am. Oh shoot—you gotta do something, ain't that right?" She bent closer. "Say, ain't it?"

Kay was still gawking at the man; the way he was looking at her made her squeamish, but she could not take her eyes off him. "I guess so," she said.

"Then let's us have us a drink," suggested the woman. She plunged her hand into an oilcloth satchel and pulled out a partially filled gin bottle. She began to unscrew the cap, but, seeming to think better of this, handed the bottle to Kay. "Gee, I forgot about you being company," she said. "I'll go get us some nice paper cups."

So, before Kay could protest that she did not want a drink, the woman had risen and started none too steadily down the aisle toward the water cooler.

Kay yawned and rested her forehead against the window-pane, her fingers idly strumming the guitar: the strings sang a hollow, lulling tune, as monotonously soothing as the Southern landscape, smudged in darkness, flowing past the window. An icy winter moon rolled above the train across the night sky like a thin white wheel.

And then, without warning, a strange thing happened: the man reached out and gently stroked Kay's cheek. Despite the breathtaking delicacy of this movement, it was such a bold gesture Kay was at first too startled to know what to make of it: her thoughts shot in three or four fantastic directions. He leaned forward till his queer eyes were very near her own; the reek of his perfume was sickening. The guitar was silent while they exchanged a searching gaze. Suddenly, from some spring of compassion, she felt for him a keen sense of pity; but also, and this she could not suppress, an overpowering disgust, an absolute loathing: something about him, an elusive quality she could not quite put a finger on, reminded her of—of what?

After a little, he lowered his hand solemnly and sank back in the seat, an asinine grin transfiguring his face, as if he had performed a clever stunt for which he wished applause.

"Giddyup! Giddup! my little bucker-ROOS . . ." shouted the woman. And she sat down, loudly proclaiming to be, "Dizzy as a witch! Dog tired! Whew!" From a handful of Lily cups she separated two and casually thrust the rest down her blouse. "Keep 'em safe and dry, ha ha ha. . . ." A coughing spasm seized her, but when it was over she appeared calmer. "Has my boy friend been entertaining?" she asked, patting her bosom reverently. "Ah, he's so sweet." She looked as if she might pass out. Kay rather wished she would.

"I don't want a drink," Kay said, returning the bottle. "I never drink: I hate the taste."

"Mustn't be a kill-joy," said the woman firmly. "Here now, hold your cup like a good girl."

"No, please . . ."

"Formercysake, hold it still. Imagine, nerves at your age! Me, I can shake like a leaf, I've got reasons. Oh, Lordy, have I got 'em."

"But . . ."

A dangerous smile tipped the woman's face hideously awry. "What's the matter? Don't you think I'm good enough to drink with?"

"Please, don't misunderstand," said Kay, a tremor in her voice. "It's just that I don't like being forced to do something I don't want to. So look, couldn't I give this to the gentleman?"

"Him? No sirree: he needs what little sense he's got. Come on, honey, down the hatch."

Kay, seeing it was useless, decided to succumb and avoid a possible scene. She sipped and shuddered. It was terrible gin. It burned her throat till her eyes watered. Quickly, when the woman was not watching, she emptied the cup out into the sound hole of the guitar. It happened, however, that the man saw; and Kay, realizing it, recklessly signaled to him with her eyes a plea not to give her away.

But she could not tell from his clear-blank expression how much he understood.

"Where you from, kid?" resumed the woman presently.

For a bewildered moment, Kay was unable to provide an answer. The names of several cities came to her all at once. Finally, from this confusion, she extracted: "New Orleans. My home is in New Orleans."

The woman beamed. "N.O.'s where I wanna go when I kick off. One time, oh, say 1923, I ran me a sweet little fortune-teller parlor there. Let's see, that was on St. Peter Street." Pausing, she stooped and set the empty gin bottle on the floor. It rolled into the aisle and rocked back and forth with a drowsy sound. "I was raised in Texas—on a big ranch—my papa was rich. Us kids always had the best; even Paris, France, clothes. I'll bet you've got a big swell house, too. Do you have a garden? Do you grow flowers?"

"Just lilacs."

A conductor entered the coach, preceded by a cold gust of wind that rattled the trash in the aisle and briefly livened the dull air. He lumbered along, stopping now and then to punch a ticket or talk with a passenger. It was after midnight. Someone was expertly playing a harmonica. Someone else was arguing the merits of a certain politician. A child cried out in his sleep.

"Maybe you wouldn't be so snotty if you knew who we was," said the woman, bobbing her tremendous head. "We ain't nobodies, not by a long shot."

Embarrassed, Kay nervously opened a pack of cigarettes and lighted one. She wondered if there might not be a seat in a car up ahead. She could not bear the woman, or, for that matter, the man, another minute. But she had never before been in a remotely comparable situation. "If you'll excuse me now," she said, "I have to be leaving. It's been very pleasant, but I promised to meet a friend on the train. . . ."

With almost invisible swiftness the woman grasped the girl's wrist. "Didn't your mama ever tell you it was sinful to lie?" she stage-whispered. The lavender hat tumbled off her head but she made no effort to retrieve it. Her tongue flicked out and wetted her lips. And, as Kay stood up, she increased the pressure of her grip. "Sit down, dear . . . there ain't any friend . . . Why, we're your only friends and we wouldn't have you leave us for the world."

"Honestly, I wouldn't lie."

"Sit down, dear."

Kay dropped her cigarette and the man picked it up. He slouched in the corner and became absorbed in blowing a chain of lush smoke rings that mounted upward like hollow eyes and expanded into nothing.

"Why, you wouldn't want to hurt his feelings by leaving us, now, would you, dear?" crooned the woman softly. "Sit down—down—now, that's a good girl. My, what a pretty guitar. What a pretty, pretty guitar . . ." Her voice faded before the sudden whooshing, static noise of a second train. And for an instant the lights in the coach went off; in the darkness the passing train's golden windows winked black-yellow-black-yellow-black-yellow. The man's cigarette pulsed like the glow of a firefly, and his smoke rings continued rising tranquilly. Outside, a bell pealed wildly.

When the lights came on again, Kay was massaging her wrist where the woman's strong fingers had left a painful bracelet mark. She was more puzzled than angry. She determined to ask the conductor if he would find her a different seat. But when he arrived to take her ticket, the request stuttered on her lips incoherently.

"Yes, miss?"

"Nothing," she said.

And he was gone.

The trio in the alcove regarded one another in mysterious silence till the woman said, "I've got something here I wanna show you, honey." She rummaged once more in the oilcloth satchel. "You won't be so snotty after you get a gander at this."

What she passed to Kay was a handbill, published on such yellowed, antique paper it looked as if it must be centuries old. In fragile, overly fancy lettering, it read:

LAZARUS

The Man Who Is Buried Alive
A MIRACLE
SEE FOR YOURSELF

Adults, 25c—Children, 10c

"I always sing a hymn and read a sermon," said the woman. "It's awful sad: some folks cry, especially the old ones. And I've got me a perfectly elegant costume: a black veil and a black dress, oh, very becoming. *He* wears a gorgeous made-to-order bridegroom suit and a turban and lotsa talcum on his face. See, we try to make it as much like a bonafide funeral as we can. But shoot, nowadays you're likely to get just a buncha smart alecks come for laughs—so sometimes I'm real glad he's afflicted like he is on accounta otherwise his feelings would be hurt, maybe."

Kay said, "You mean you're with a circus or a side-show or something like that?"

"Nope, us alone," said the woman as she reclaimed the fallen hat. "We've been doing it for years and years—played every tank town in the South: Singasong, Mississippi—Spunky, Louisiana—Eureka, Alabama . . ." these and other names rolled off her tongue musically, running together like rain. "After the hymn, after the sermon, we bury him."

"In a coffin?"

"Sort of. It's gorgeous, it's got silver stars painted all over the lid."

"I should think he would suffocate," said Kay, amazed. "How long does he stay buried?"

"All told it takes maybe an hour—course that's not counting the lure."

"The lure?"

"Uh huh. It's what we do the night before the show. See, we hunt up a store, any ol' store with a big glass window'll do, and get the owner to let *him* sit inside this window, and, well, hypnotize himself. Stays there all night stiff as a poker and people come and look: scares the livin' hell out of 'em. . . ." While she talked she jiggled a finger in her ear, withdrawing it occasionally to examine her find. "And one time this ol' bindlestiff Mississippi sheriff tried to . . ."

The tale that followed was baffling and pointless: Kay did not bother to listen. Nevertheless, what she had heard already inspired a reverie, a vague recapitulation of her uncle's funeral; an event which, to tell the truth, had not much affected her since she had scarcely known him. And so, while gazing abstractedly at the man, an image of her uncle's face, white next the pale silk casket pillow, appeared in her mind's eye. Observing their faces simultaneously, both the man's and uncle's, as it were, she thought she recognized an odd parallel: there was about the man's face the same kind of shocking, embalmed, secret stillness, as though, in a sense, he were truly an exhibit in a glass cage, complacent to be seen, uninterested in seeing.

"I'm sorry, what did you say?"

"I said: I sure wish they'd lend us the use of a regular cemetery. Like it is now we have to put on the show wherever we can . . . mostly in empty lots that are nine times outa ten smack up against some smelly fillin' station, which ain't exactly a big help. But like I say, we got us a swell act, the best. You oughta come see it if you get a chance."

"Oh, I should love to," Kay said absently.

"Oh, I should love to," mimicked the woman. "Well, who asked you? Anybody ask you?" She hoisted up her skirt and enthusiastically blew her nose on the ragged hem of a petticoat. "Bu-leeve me, it's a hard way to turn a dollar. Know what our take was last month? Fifty-three bucks! Honey, you try living on that sometime." She sniffed and rearranged her skirt with considerable primness. "Well, one of these days my sweet boy's sure enough going to die down there; and even then somebody'll say it was a gyp."

At this point the man took from his pocket what seemed to be a finely shellacked peach seed and balanced it on the palm of his hand.

He looked across at Kay and, certain of her attention, opened his eyelids wide and began to squeeze and caress the seed in an undefinably obscene manner.

Kay frowned. "What does he want?"

"He wants you to buy it."

"But what is it?"

"A charm," said the woman. "A love charm."

Whoever was playing the harmonica stopped. Other sounds, less unique, became at once prominent: someone snoring, the gin bottle seesaw rolling, voices in sleepy argument, the train wheels' distant hum.

"Where could you get love cheaper, honey?"

"It's nice. I mean it's cute. . . ." Kay said, stalling for time. The man rubbed and polished the seed on his trouser leg. His head was lowered at a supplicating, mournful angle, and presently he stuck the seed between his teeth and bit it, as if it were a suspicious piece of silver. "Charms always bring me bad luck. And besides . . . please, can't you make him stop acting that way?"

"Don't look so scared," said the woman, more flat-voiced than ever. "He ain't gonna hurt you."

"Make him stop, damn it!"

"What can I do?" asked the woman, shrugging her shoulders. "You're the one that's got money. You're rich. All he wants is a dollar, one dollar."

Kay tucked her purse under her arm. "I have just enough to get back to school," she lied, quickly rising and stepping out into the aisle. She stood there a moment, expecting trouble. But nothing happened.

The woman, with rather deliberate indifference, heaved a sigh and closed her eyes; gradually the man subsided and stuck the charm back in his pocket. Then his hand crawled across the seat to join the woman's in a lax embrace.

Kay shut the door and moved to the front of the observation platform. It was bitterly cold in the open air, and she had left her raincoat in the alcove. She loosened her scarf and draped it over her head.

Although she had never made this trip before, the train was traveling through an area strangely familiar: tall trees, misty, painted pale by malicious moonshine, towered steep on either side without a break or clearing. Above, the sky was a stark, unexplorable blue thronged with stars that faded here and there. She could see streamers of smoke trailing from the train's engine like long clouds of ectoplasm. In one corner of the platform a red kerosene lantern cast a colorful shadow.

She found a cigarette and tried to light it: the wind snuffed match after match till only one was left. She walked to the corner where the lantern burned and cupped her hands to protect the last match: the flame caught, sputtered, died. Angrily she tossed away the cigarette and empty folder; all the tension in her tightened to an exasperating pitch and she slammed the wall with her fist and began to whimper softly, like an irritable child.

The intense cold made her head ache, and she longed to go back inside the warm coach and fall asleep. But she couldn't, at least not yet; and there was no sense in wondering why, for she knew the answer very well. Aloud, partly to keep her teeth from chattering and partly because she needed the reassurance of her own voice, she said: "We're in Alabama now, I think, and tomorrow we'll be in Atlanta and I'm nineteen and I'll be twenty in August and I'm a sophomore. . . ." She glanced around at the darkness, hoping to see a sign of dawn, and finding the same endless wall of trees, the same frosty moon. "I hate him, he's horrible and I hate him. . . ." She stopped, ashamed of her foolishness and too tired to evade the truth: she was afraid.

Suddenly she felt an eerie compulsion to kneel down and touch the lantern. Its graceful glass funnel was warm, and the red glow seeped through her hands, making them luminous. The heat thawed her fingers and tingled along her arms.

She was so preoccupied she did not hear the door open. The train wheels roaring clickety-clack-clackety-click hushed the sound of the man's footsteps.

It was a subtle zero sensation that warned her finally; but some seconds passed before she dared look behind.

He was standing there with mute detachment, his head tilted, his arms dangling at his sides. Staring up into his harmless, vapid face, flushed brilliant by the lantern light, Kay knew of what she was afraid: it was a memory, a childish memory of terrors that once, long ago, had hovered above her like haunted limbs on a tree of night. Aunts, cooks, strangers—each eager to spin a tale or teach a rhyme of spooks and death, omens, spirits, demons. And always there had been the unfailing threat of the wizard man: stay close to the house, child, else a wizard man'll snatch you and eat you alive! He lived everywhere, the wizard man, and everywhere was danger. At night, in bed, hear him tapping at the window? Listen!

Holding onto the railing, she inched upward till she was standing erect. The man nodded and waved his hand toward the door. Kay took a deep breath and stepped forward. Together they went inside.

The air in the coach was numb with sleep: a solitary light now illuminated the car, creating a kind of artificial dusk. There was no motion but the train's sluggish sway, and the stealthy rattle of discarded newspapers.

The woman alone was wide awake. You could see she was greatly excited: she fidgeted with her curls and celluloid cherries, and her plump little legs, crossed at the ankles, swung agitatedly back and forth. She paid no attention when Kay sat down. The man settled in the seat with one leg tucked beneath him and his arms folded across his chest.

In an effort to be casual, Kay picked up a magazine. She realized the man was watching her, not removing his gaze an instant: she knew this though she was afraid to confirm it, and she wanted to cry out and waken everyone in the coach. But suppose they did not hear? What if they were not really *asleep?* Tears started in her eyes, magnifying and distorting the print on a page till it became a hazy blur. She shut the magazine with fierce abruptness and looked at the woman.

"I'll buy it," she said. "The charm, I mean. I'll buy it, if that's all—just all you want."

The woman made no response. She smiled apathetically as she turned toward the man.

As Kay watched, the man's face seemed to change form and recede before her like a moon-shaped rock sliding downward under a surface of water. A warm laziness relaxed her. She was dimly conscious of it when the woman took away her purse, and when she gently pulled the raincoat like a shroud above her head.

Truman Capote Interview

PATI HILL

Truman Capote lives in a big yellow house in Brooklyn Heights, which he has recently restored with the taste and elegance that is generally characteristic of his undertakings. As I entered he was head and shoulders inside a newly arrived crate containing a wooden lion.

"There!" he cried as he tugged it out to a fine birth amid a welter of sawdust and shavings. "Did you ever see anything so splendid? Well, that's that. I saw him and I bought him. Now he's all mine."

"He's large," I said. "Where are you going to put him?"

"Why, in the fireplace, of course," said Capote. "Now come along into the parlor while I get someone to clear away this mess."

The parlor is Victorian in character and contains Capote's most intimate collection of art objects and personal treasures, which, [285/286] for all their orderly arrangement on polished tables and bamboo bookcases, somehow remind you of the contents of a very astute little boy's pockets. There is, for instance, a golden Easter egg brought back from Russia, an iron

dog, somewhat the worse for wear, a Fabergé pillbox, some marbles, blue
ceramic fruit, paperweights, Battersea boxes, picture postcards, and old
photographs. In short everything that might seem useful or handy in a day's
adventuring around the world.

Capote himself fits in very well with this impression at first glance. He
is small and blond, with a forelock that persists in falling down into his eyes,
and his smile is sudden and sunny. His approach to anyone new is one of
open curiosity and friendliness. He might be taken in by anything and, in
fact, seems only too ready to be. There is something about him, though, that
makes you feel that for all his willingness it would be hard to pull any wool
over his eyes and maybe it is better not to try.

There was a sound of scuffling in the hall and Capote came in, preceded by a large bulldog with a white face.

"This is Bunky," he said.

Bunky sniffed me over and we sat down.

INTERVIEWER: When did you first start writing?

CAPOTE: When I was a child of about ten or eleven and lived near
Mobile.

I had to go into town on Saturdays to the dentist and I joined the
Sunshine Club that was organized by the Mobile Press Register. There
was a children's page with contests for writing and for coloring pictures, and then every Saturday afternoon they had a party with free
Nehi and Coca-Cola. The prize for the short-story writing contest was
either a pony or a dog, I've forgotten which, but I wanted it badly. I
had been noticing the activities of some neighbors who were up to no
good, so I wrote a kind of *roman à clef* called "Old Mr. Busybody" and
entered it in a contest. The first installment appeared one Sunday,
under my real name of Truman Streckfus Persons. Only somebody
suddenly realized that [286/287] I was serving up a local scandal as
fiction, and the second installment never appeared. Naturally, I didn't
win a thing.

INTERVIEWER: Were you sure then that you wanted to be a writer?

CAPOTE: I realized that I *wanted* to be a writer. But I wasn't sure
I *would* be until I was fifteen or so. At that time I had immodestly
started sending stories to magazines and literary quarterlies. Of course
no writer ever forgets his first acccptance; but one fine day when I was
seventeen, I had my first, second, and third, all in the same morning's
mail. Oh, I'm here to tell you, dizzy with excitement is no mere phrase!

INTERVIEWER: What did you first write?

CAPOTE: Short stories. And my more unswerving ambitions still
revolve around this form. When seriously explored, the short story
seems to me the most difficult and disciplining form of prose writing
extant. Whatever control and technique I may have I owe entirely to
my training in this medium.

INTERVIEWER: What do you mean exactly by "control"?

CAPOTE: I mean maintaining a stylistic and emotional upper hand over your material. Call it precious and go to hell, but I believe a story can be wrecked by a faulty rhythm in a sentence—especially if it occurs toward the end—or a mistake in paragraphing, even punctuation. Henry James is the maestro of the semi-colon. Hemingway is a first-rate paragrapher. From the point of view of ear, Virginia Woolf never wrote a bad sentence. I don't mean to imply that I successfully practice what I preach. I try, that's all.

INTERVIEWER: How does one arrive at short-story technique?

CAPOTE: Since each story presents its own technical problems, obviously one can't generalize about them on a two-times-two-equals-four basis. Finding the right form for your story is simply to realize the most *natural* way of telling the story. The test of whether or not a writer has divined the natural shape of his story is just this: after reading it, can you imagine it differently, or does it silence your imagination and seem to you absolute and final? [287/288] As an orange is final. As an orange is something nature has made just right.

INTERVIEWER: Are there devices one can use in improving one's technique?

CAPOTE: Work is the only device I know of. Writing has laws of perspective, of light and shade, just as painting does, or music. If you are born knowing them, fine. If not, learn them. Then rearrange the rules to suit yourself. Even Joyce, our most extreme disregarder, was a superb craftsman; he could write *Ulysses because* he could write *Dubliners.* Too many writers seem to consider the writing of short stories as a kind of finger exercise. Well, in such cases, it is certainly only their fingers they are exercising.

INTERVIEWER: Did you have much encouragement in those early days, and if so, by whom?

CAPOTE. Good Lord! I'm afraid you've let yourself in for quite a saga. The answer is a snake's nest of no's and a few yes's. You see, not altogether but by and large, my childhood was spent in parts of the country and among people unprovided with any semblance of a cultural attitude. Which was probably not a bad thing, in the long view. It toughened me rather too soon to swim against the current—indeed, in some areas I developed the muscles of a veritable barracuda, especially in the art of dealing with one's enemies, an art no less necessary than knowing how to appreciate one's friends.

But to go back. Naturally, in the milieu aforesaid, I was thought somewhat *eccentric,* which was fair enough, and *stupid,* which I suitably resented. Still, I despised school—or schools, for I was always changing from one to another—and year after year failed the simplest subjects out of loathing and boredom. I played hooky at least twice a week and was always running away from home. Once I ran away with a friend who lived across the street—a girl much older than myself who in later life achieved a certain fame. Because she murdered a half-dozen people and was electrocuted at Sing Sing. Someone wrote a book about her. They called her the Lonely Hearts Killer. But there, I'm wandering again. Well, [288/289] finally, I guess I was around twelve, the principal at the school I was attending paid a call on my family, and told them that in his opinion, and in the opinion of the faculty, I was "subnormal." He thought it would be sensible, the humane action, to send me to some special school equipped to handle backward brats. Whatever they may have privately felt, my family as a whole took official umbrage, and in an effort to prove I wasn't subnormal, pronto packed me off to a psychiatric study clinic at a university in the East where I had my I.Q. inspected. I enjoyed it thoroughly and—guess what?—came home a genius, so proclaimed by science. I don't know who was the more appalled: my former teachers, who refused to believe it, or my family, who didn't want to believe it—they'd just hoped to be told I was a nice normal boy. Ha ha! But as for me, I was exceedingly pleased—went around staring at myself in mirrors and sucking in my cheeks and thinking over in my mind, my lad, you and Flaubert—or Maupassant or Mansfield or Proust or Chekhov or Wolfe, whoever was the idol of the moment.

I began writing in fearful earnest—my mind zoomed all night every night, and I don't think I really slept for several years. Not until I discovered that whisky could relax me. I was too young, fifteen, to buy it myself, but I had a few older friends who were most obliging in this respect and I soon accumulated a suitcase full of bottles, everything from blackberry brandy to bourbon. I kept the suitcase hidden in a closet. Most of my drinking was done in the late afternoon; then I'd chew a handful of Sen Sen and go down to dinner, where my behavior, my glazed silences, gradually grew into a source of general consternation. One of my relatives used to say, "Really, if I didn't know better, I'd swear he was dead drunk." Well, of course, this little comedy, if such it was, ended in discovery and some disaster, and it was many a moon before I touched another drop. But I seem to be off the track again. You asked about encouragement. The first person who ever really helped me was, strangely, a teacher. An English teacher I had in high school, Catherine Wood, who backed my ambitions in every way, and to whom I shall always be grateful. Later on, from the [289/290] time I first began to publish, I had all the encouragement anyone could ever want, notably from Margarita Smith, fiction editor of *Mademoiselle*, Mary Louise Aswell of *Harper's Bazaar*, and Robert Linscott of Random House. You would have to be a glutton indeed to ask for more good luck and fortune than I had at the beginning of my career.

INTERVIEWER: Did the three editors you mention encourage you simply by buying your work, or did they offer criticism, too?

CAPOTE: Well, I can't imagine anything *more* encouraging than having someone buy your work. I never write—indeed, am physically incapable of writing—anything that I don't think will be paid for. But, as a matter of fact, the persons mentioned, and some others as well, were all very generous with advice.

INTERVIEWER: Do you like anything you wrote long ago as well as what you write now?

CAPOTE: Yes. For instance, last summer I read my novel *Other Voices, Other Rooms* for the first time since it was published eight years ago, and it was quite as though I were reading something by a stranger. The truth is, I am a stranger to that book; the person who wrote it seems to have so little in common with my present self. Our mentalities, our interior temperatures are entirely different. Despite awkwardness, it has an amazing intensity, a real voltage. I am very pleased I was able to write the book when I did, otherwise it would never have been written. I like *The Grass Harp* too, and several of my short stories, though not "Miriam," which is a good stunt but nothing more. No, I prefer "Children on Their Birthdays" and "Shut a Final Door," and oh, some others, especially a story not too many people seemed to care for, "Master Misery," which was in my collection *A Tree of Night.*

INTERVIEWER: You recently published a book about the *Porgy and Bess* trip to Russia. One of the most interesting things about the style was its unusual detachment, even by comparison to the reporting of journalists who have spent many years recording events in an impartial way. One had the impression that this version must have been as close to the truth as it is possible to [290/291] get through another person's eyes, which is surprising when you consider that most of your work has been characterized by its very personal quality.

CAPOTE: Actually, I don't consider the style of this book, *The Muses Are Heard,* as markedly different from my fictional style. Perhaps the content, the fact that it is about real events, makes it seem so. After all, *Muses* is straight reporting, and in reporting one is occupied with literalness and surfaces, with implication without comment—one can't achieve immediate depths the way one may in fiction. However, one of the reasons I've wanted to do reportage was to prove that I could apply my style to the realities of journalism. But I believe my fictional method is equally detached—emotionality makes me lose writing control: I have to exhaust the emotion before I feel clinical enough to analyze and project it, and as far as I'm concerned that's one of the laws of achieving true technique. If my fiction seems more personal it is because it depends on the artist's most personal and revealing area: his imagination.

INTERVIEWER: How do you exhaust the emotion? Is it only a matter of thinking about the story over a certain length of time, or are there other considerations?

CAPOTE: No, I don't think it is merely a matter of time. Suppose you ate nothing but apples for a week. Unquestionably you would exhaust your appetite for apples and most certainly know what they taste like. By the time I write a story I may no longer have any hunger for it, but I feel that I thoroughly know its flavor. The *Porgy and Bess* articles are not relevant to this issue. That was reporting, and "emotions" were not much involved—at least not the difficult and personal territories of feeling that I mean. I seem to remember reading that Dickens, as he wrote, choked with laughter over his own humor and dripped tears all over the page when one of his characters died. My own theory is that the writer should have considered his wit and dried his tears long, long before setting out to evoke similar reactions in a reader. In other words, I believe the greatest intensity in art in all its [291/292] shapes is achieved with a deliberate, hard, and cool head. For example, Flaubert's *A Simple Heart*. A warm story, warmly written; but it could only be the work of an artist muchly aware of true techniques, i.e., necessities. I'm sure, at some point, Flaubert must have felt the story very deeply—but *not* when he wrote it. Or, for a more contemporary example, take that marvelous short novel of Katherine Anne Porter's, *Noon Wine*. It has such intensity, such a sense of happening-now, yet the writing is so controlled, the inner rhythms of the story so immaculate, that I feel fairly certain Miss Porter was at some distance *from* her material.

INTERVIEWER: Have your best stories or books been written at a comparatively tranquil moment in your life or do you work better because, or in spite, of emotional stress?

CAPOTE: I feel slightly as though I've never lived a tranquil moment, unless you count what an occasional Nembutal induces. Though, come to think of it, I spent two years in a very romantic house on top of a mountain in Sicily, and I guess this period could be called tranquil. God knows, it was quiet. That's where I wrote *The Grass Harp*. But I must say an iota of stress, striving toward deadlines, does me good.

INTERVIEWER: You have lived abroad for the last eight years. Why did you decide to return to America?

CAPOTE: Because I'm an American, and never could be, and have no desire to be, anything else. Besides, I like cities, and New York is the only real city-city. Except for a two-year stretch, I came back to America every one of those eight years, and I never entertained expatriate notions. For me, Europe was a method of acquiring perspective and an education, a stepping stone toward maturity. But there is the law of diminishing returns, and about two years ago it began to set in: Europe had given me an enormous lot, but suddenly I felt as though the process were reversing itself—there seemed to be a taking away. So I came home, feeling quite grown up and able to settle down where I belong—which doesn't mean I've bought a rocking chair and turned to stone. [292/293] No indeed. I intend to have footloose escapades as long as frontiers stay open.

INTERVIEWER: Do you read a great deal?

CAPOTE: Too much. And anything, including labels and recipes and advertisements. I have a passion for newspapers—read all the New York dailies every day, and the Sunday editions, and several foreign magazines too. The ones I don't buy I read standing at news stands. I average about five books a week—the normal-length novel takes me about two hours. I enjoy thrillers and would like someday to write one. Though I prefer first-rate fiction, for the last few years my reading seems to have been concentrated on letters and journals and biographies. It doesn't bother me to read while I am writing—I mean, I don't suddenly find another writer's style seeping out of my pen. Though once, during a lengthy spell of James, my own sentences *did* get awfully long.

INTERVIEWER: What writers have influenced you the most?

CAPOTE: So far as I consciously know, I've never been aware of direct literary influence, though several critics have informed me that my early works owe a debt to Faulkner and Welty and McCullers. Possibly. I'm a great admirer of all three; and Katherine Anne Porter, too. Though I don't think, when really examined, that they have much in common with each other, or me, except that we were all born in the South. Between thirteen and sixteen are the ideal if not the only ages for succumbing to Thomas Wolfe—he seemed to be a great genius then, and still does, though I can't read a line of it now. Just as other youthful flames have guttered: Poe, Dickens, Stevenson. I love them in memory, but find them unreadable. These are the enthusiasms that remain constant: Flaubert, Turgenev, Chekhov, Jane Austen, James, E. M. Forster, Maupassant, Rilke, Proust, Shaw, Willa Cather—oh the list is too long, so I'll end with James Agee, a beautiful writer whose death over two years ago was a real loss. Agee's work, by the way, was much influenced by the films. I think most of the younger writers have learned and borrowed from the visual, structural side of movie technique. I have. [293/294]

INTERVIEWER: You've written for the films, haven't you? What was that like?

CAPOTE: A lark. At least the one picture I wrote, *Beat the Devil*, was tremendous fun. I worked on it with John Huston while the picture was actually being made on location in Italy. Sometimes scenes that were just about to be shot were written right on the set. The cast were completely bewildered—sometimes even Huston didn't seem to know what was going on. Naturally the scenes had to be written out of a sequence, and there were peculiar moments when I was carrying around in my head the only real outline of the so-called plot. You never saw it? Oh, you should. It's a marvelous joke. Though I'm afraid the producer didn't laugh. The hell with them. Whenever there's a revival I go to see it and have a fine time.

Seriously, though, I don't think a writer stands much chance of imposing himself on a film unless he works in the warmest rapport with the director or is himself the director. It's so much a director's medium that the movies have developed only one writer who, working exclusively as a scenarist, could be called a film genius. I mean that shy, delightful little peasant, Zavattini. What a visual sense! Eighty per cent of the good Italian movies were made from Zavattini scripts— all of the De Sica pictures, for instance. De Sica is a charming man, a gifted and deeply sophisticated person; nevertheless he's mostly a megaphone for Zavattini, his pictures are absolutely Zavattini's creations: every nuance, mood, every bit of business is clearly indicated in Zavattini's scripts.

INTERVIEWER: What are some of your writing habits? Do you use a desk? Do you write on a machine?

CAPOTE: I am a completely horizontal author. I can't think unless I'm lying down, either in bed or stretched on a couch and with a cigarette and coffee handy. I've got to be puffing and sipping. As the afternoon wears on, I shift from coffee to mint tea to sherry to martinis. No, I don't use a typewriter. Not in the beginning. I write my first version in longhand (pencil). Then I [294/295] do a complete revision, also in longhand. Essentially I think of myself as a stylist, and stylists can become notoriously obsessed with the placing of a comma, the weight of a semicolon. Obsessions of this sort, and the time I take over them, irritate me beyond endurance.

INTERVIEWER: You seem to make a distinction between writers who are stylists and writers who aren't. Which writers would you call stylists and which not?

CAPOTE: What is style? And "what" as the Zen Koan asks, "is the sound of one hand?" No one really *knows;* yet either you *know* or you don't. For myself, if you will excuse a rather cheap little image, I suppose style is the mirror of an artist's sensibility—more so than the *content* of his work. To some degree all writers have style—Ronald Firbank, bless his heart, had little else, and thank God he realized it. But the possession of style, *a* style, is often a hindrance, a negative force, not as it should be, and as it is—with, say, E. M. Forster and Colette and Flaubert and Mark Twain and Hemingway and Isak Dinesen—a reinforcement. Dreiser, for instance, has *a* style—but oh, *Dio buono!* And Eugene O'Neill. And Faulkner, brilliant as he is. They all seem to me triumphs over strong but negative styles, styles that do not really add to the communication between writer and reader. Then there is the styleless stylist—which is very difficult, very admirable, and *always* very popular: Graham Greene, Maugham, Thornton Wilder, John Hersey, Willa Cather, Thurber, Sartre (remember, we're *not* discussing content), J. P. Marquand, and so on. But yes, there *is* such an animal as a nonstylist. Only they're not writers; they're typists. Sweaty typists blacking up pounds of bond paper with formless, eyeless, earless messages. Well, who are some of the younger writers who seem to know that style exists? P. ·H. Newby, Françoise Sagan, somewhat. Bill Styron, Flannery O'Connor—she has some fine moments, that girl. James Merrill. William Goyen—if he'd stop being hysterical. J. D. Salinger—especially in the colloquial tradition. Colin Wilson? Another typist.

INTERVIEWER: You say that Ronald Firbank had little else but [295/296] style. Do you think that style alone can make a writer a great one?

CAPOTE: No, I don't think so—though, it could be argued, what happens to Proust if you separate him from his style? Style has never been a strong point with American writers. This though some of the best have been Americans. Hawthorne got us off to a fine start. For the past thirty years Hemingway, stylistically speaking, has influenced more writers on a world scale than anyone else. At the moment, I think our own Miss Porter knows as well as anyone what it's all about.

INTERVIEWER: Can a writer learn style?

CAPOTE: No, I don't think that style is consciously arrived at, any more than one arrives at the color of one's eyes. After all, your style *is* you. At the end the personality of a writer has so much to do with the work. The personality has to be humanly there. Personality is a debased word, I know, but it's what I mean. The writer's individual humanity, his word or gesture toward the world, has to appear almost like a character that makes contact with the reader. If the personality is vague or confused or merely literary, *ça ne vas pas*. Faulkner, McCullers—they project their personality at once.

INTERVIEWER: It is interesting that your work has been so widely appreciated in France. Do you think style can be translated?

CAPOTE: Why not? Provided the author and the translator are artistic twins.

INTERVIEWER: Well, I'm afraid I interrupted you with your short story still in penciled manuscript. What happens next?

CAPOTE: Let's see, that was second draft. Then I type a third draft on yellow paper, a very special certain kind of yellow paper. No, I don't get out of bed to do this. I balance the machine on my knees. Sure, it works fine; I can manage a hundred words a minute. Well, when the yellow draft is finished, I put the manuscript away for a while, a week, a month, sometimes longer. When I take it out again, I read it as coldly as possible, then read it aloud to a friend or two, and decide what changes I want to make and [296/297] whether or not I want to publish it. I've thrown away rather a few short stories, an entire novel, and half of another. But if all goes well, I type the final version on white paper and that's that.

INTERVIEWER: Is the book organized completely in your head before you begin it or does it unfold, surprising you as you go along?

CAPOTE: Both. I invariably have the illusion that the whole play of a story, its start and middle and finish, occur in my mind simultaneously—that I'm seeing it in one flash. But in the working-out, the writing-out, infinite surprises happen. Thank God, because the surprise, the twist, the phrase that comes at the right moment out of nowhere, is the unexpected dividend, that joyful little push that keeps a writer going.

At one time I used to keep notebooks with outlines for stories. But I found doing this somehow deadened the idea in my imagination. If the notion is good enough, if it truly belongs to *you*, then you can't forget it—it will haunt you till it's written.

INTERVIEWER: How much of your work is autobiographical?

CAPOTE: Very little, really. A little is *suggested* by real incidents or personages, although everything a writer writes is in some way autobiographical. *The Grass Harp* is the only true thing I ever wrote, and naturally everybody thought it all invented, and imagined *Other Voices, Other Rooms* to be autobiographical.

INTERVIEWER: Do you have any definite ideas or projects for the future?

CAPOTE: (*meditatively*): Well, yes, I believe so. I have always written what was easiest for me until now: I want to try something else, a kind of controlled extravagance. I want to use my mind more, use many more colors. Hemingway once said anybody can write a novel in the first person. I know now exactly what he means.

INTERVIEWER: Were you ever tempted by any of the other arts?

CAPOTE: I don't know if it's art, but I was stage-struck for years and more than anything I wanted to be a tap-dancer. I used to [297/298] practice my buck-and-wing until everybody in the house was ready to kill me. Later on, I longed to play the guitar and sing in night clubs. So I saved up for a guitar and took lessons for one whole winter, but in the end the only tune I could really play was a beginner's thing called "I Wish I Were Single Again." I got so tired of it that one day I just gave the guitar to a stranger in a bus station. I was also interested in painting, and studied for three years, but I'm afraid the fervor, *la vrai chose*, wasn't there.

INTERVIEWER: Do you think criticism helps any?

CAPOTE: Before publication, and if provided by persons whose judgment you trust, yes, of course criticism helps. But after something is published, all I want to read or hear is praise. Anything less is a bore, and I'll give you fifty dollars if you produced a writer who can honestly say he was ever helped by the prissy carpings and condescensions of reviewers. I don't mean to say that none of the professional critics are worth paying attention to—but few of the good ones review on a regular basis. Most of all, I believe in hardening yourself against opinion. I've had, and continue to receive, my full share of abuse, some of it extremely personal, but it doesn't faze me any more. I can read the most outrageous libel about myself and never skip a pulsebeat. And in this connection there is one piece of advice I strongly urge:

never demean yourself by talking back to a critic, never. Write those letters to the editor in your head, but don't put them on paper.

INTERVIEWER: What are some of your personal quirks?

CAPOTE: I suppose my superstitiousness could be termed a quirk. I have to add up all numbers: there are some people I never telephone because their number adds up to an unlucky figure. Or I won't accept a hotel room for the same reason. I will not tolerate the presence of yellow roses—which is sad because they're my favorite flower. I can't allow three cigarette butts in the same ashtray. Won't travel on a plane with two nuns. Won't begin or end anything on a Friday. It's endless, the things I can't and won't. But I derive some curious comfort from obeying these primitive concepts. [298/299]

INTERVIEWER: You have been quoted as saying your preferred pastimes are "conversation, reading, travel, and writing, in that order." Do you mean that literally?

CAPOTE: I think so. At least I'm pretty sure conversation will always come first with me. I like to listen, and I like to talk. Heavens, girl, can't you *see* I like to talk? [299]

Truman Capote: The Revelation
of the Broken Image

PAUL LEVINE

THE INCLUSION OF TRUMAN CAPOTE IN ANY DISCUSSION THAT PRETENDS to be at most scholarly and at least literary is usually frowned upon by the more stern-faced of our critics. The mention of his name conjures up images of a wispish, effete soul languishing on an ornate couch, emitting an ether of preciousness and very little else. The reaction to the amazing success of his early books, *Other Voices, Other Rooms* and *A Tree of Night*, has relegated Capote to the position of a clever, cute, coy, commercial, and definitely minor figure in contemporary literature, whose reputation has been built less on a facility of style than on an excellent advertising campaign. Even an earnest supporter would have to admit that Capote's stories tiptoe the tenuous line between the precious and the serious.

Yet the attacks on Capote seem more personal than literary.

From the *Virginia Quarterly Review*, XXXIV (Autumn 1958), 600–617, by permission of the author and the editors.

Critics like John Aldridge—whose essay appears in *After the Lost Generation,* a book that generally has little good to say about anyone (except Mr. Aldridge)—have blatantly confused the author's private life with his literary ability. The notion—as fantastic as any of Capote's stories—that Capote's style comes too easily is an excellent example. Not only is the banner of the tortured writer rather tattered by now but in Capote's case the charge of a "natural style" is false. His first stories—"These Walls Are Cold" and "The Shape of Things"—are written in the painfully realistic prose associated with those young writers in transition from the *Saturday Evening Post* to the *New Yorker.* Moreover, Capote is really no more precocious than a number of our outstanding writers. J. D. Salinger published his first [600/601] story at twenty-one and Carson McCullers had written two novels before she was twenty-four. As with the legend surrounding Fitzgerald, critics have a difficult time discerning Capote from his work, a slight not only to the author but to the critic. Mr. Capote is no more an *enfant terrible* than Mr. Aldridge is.

Perhaps the most frequent criticism leveled at Capote's work is that he is limited in scope and remote from life. While it is true that Capote writes fantastic and grotesque stories, it is not necessarily true that these stories, because of their genre, must be remote from life. In many ways, Capote has chosen the most universal medium in which to present his thematic material, because the genre of the fantasy, evolving from the day dream, the fairy tale, and the tall tale, is among the oldest and most elemental of fictional forms.

While we must acknowledge Capote's admission that "style is the mirror of an artist's sensibility—more so than the *content* of his work," we must also recognize that there is no dearth of content in his work. To understand that content fully we must first posit some very elemental points, because Capote is to a great extent an erudite writer about primal things. At the heart of his writing is the dichotomy in the world between good and evil, the daylight and the nocturnal, man and nature, and between the internal and external manifestation of things. As Harry Levin has pointed out in a different context:

This takes us back to the very beginning of things, the primal darkness, the void that God shaped by creating light and dividing night from day. That division underlies the imagery of the Bible from Genesis to the Apocalypse, and from the word of life to the shadow of death. It is what differentiates the children of light from the children of darkness in the Dead Sea Scrolls. . . . But all religions, in accounting for the relation of the earth to the sun and for the diurnal and seasonal cycles, seem to posit some dichotomy, such as the Yin and the Yang of the Orient or the twin paths of the Bhagavad-Gita. [601/602]

The dichotomy of good and evil exists in each Capote character just as the dichotomy of daylight and nighttime exists in the aggregate of his stories. We might almost say that Capote's stories inhabit two worlds—that of the realistic, colloquial, often humorous daytime and that of the dreamlike, detached, and inverted nocturnal world. This double identity must be viewed with a double vision because Capote stories can be interpreted either psychologically or as an expression of a spiritual or moral problem. In either case, whether the story be realistic or fantastic, the central focus is on the moment of initiation and the central character is either adolescent or innocent.

One way to distinguish the daylight from the nocturnal tales is to note the hero's position in relation to his private world and the public world. In the daylight stories the movement is out towards the world while in the darker tales the hero tends to move away from the world and in towards his inner Id or soul or imagination. In the daylight variety, there is a tension between the hero and his society which resolves itself often in a humorous and always in a creative or imaginative way. All these stories are told in the first person but none of them tries to move into the character's psyche or soul. The focus, instead, is on the surfaces, the interest and humor deriving from the situation and the action.

The realism in these daylight stories seems to evolve from Capote's early pieces, printed in *Decade Magazine*. But the warmth, humor, and ease of style lacking in these surface stories is picked up in "My Side of the Matter," which closely resembles Eudora Welty's "Why I Live at the P. O." in its colloquial use of language. This slim tale of a minor skirmish between a young, beleaguered hero and his querulous in-laws is slight in comparison to the later "Jug of Silver" and "Children on Their Birthdays." Both of these stories are markedly similar in that they are concerned with extraordinary, almost supernatural children. The hero of the first story, Appleseed, is blessed with a kind of extrasensory power for determining [602/603] the amount of money in a jar filled with silver: a power acquired from being born with a caul over his head.

Similarly, the heroine of Capote's most perfect story in the daylight genre, "Children on Their Birthdays," is a precocious child with an uncanny power. Like Cousin Lymon in Carson McCullers' *Ballad of the Sad Cafe*, Miss Bobbit comes to a new town and disrupts its whole pattern of living with her awesome brand of animal magnetism. From her first appearance, grotesquely made up like an adult and sporting a parasol, Miss Bobbit impresses as a fantastic mixture of innocence and experience, morality and pragmatism. She sings like Sophie Tucker, dances like Gypsy Rose Lee, and possesses the business acumen of a Polly Adler. Miss Bobbit doesn't go to church because she finds the odor there offensive but she adds:

I don't want you to think I'm a heathen, Mr. C; I've had enough experience to know that there is a God and that there is a Devil. But the way to tame the Devil is not to go down there to church and listen to what a sinful mean fool he is. No, love the Devil like you do Jesus: because he is a powerful man, and will do you a good turn if he knows you trust him. He has frequently done me good turns, like at dancing school in Memphis. . . . I always called in the Devil to help me get the biggest part in our annual show. That is common sense; you see, I knew Jesus wouldn't have any truck with dancing. Now, as a matter of fact, I have called in the Devil just recently. He is the only one who can help me get out of this town. Not that I live here, not exactly. I think always about somewhere else, somewhere else where everything is dancing, like people dancing in the streets, and everything is pretty, like children on their birthdays. My precious papa said I live in the sky, but if he'd lived more in the sky he'd be rich like he wanted to be. The trouble with my papa was he did not love the Devil, he let the Devil love him. But I am very smart in that respect; I know the next best thing is very often the best.

It is necessary to distinguish here between the hero in the two worlds of day and night. Notice that the *mana*-laden [603/604] child is the hero in the stories discussed so far, while this same figure becomes the shadowy antagonist in Capote's nocturnal stories. Instead, the protagonist becomes an impotent Prufrock, a character to whom things happen. Yet the relationship between the antagonist and the protagonist is ambiguous: one seems the alter ego of the other. The uncanny power in the daylight hero is a creative force—the manifestation of the imagination. In the nocturnal stories the hero is forced to come to grips with the destructive element—the power of blackness which resides in each of us. The confrontation of the psyche leads to the exposure of the constructive and destructive elements: the wish for death and the wish for life.

In Capote's nocturnal stories the movement out into the world becomes simultaneously the movement into the self. John Aldridge has compared Capote's novel *Other Voices, Other Rooms* unfavorably to Joseph Conrad's *Victory*. The comparison between the two writers is a just, almost obvious one when used in a different context. If we juxtapose Conrad's "Heart of Darkness" with any Capote twilight story, it becomes immediately apparent that the structures are the same. In Conrad's story, Marlowe moves into the heart of the dark continent at the same time he moves into the heart of his own subconscious or soul. In reality, the two movements are the same. The same idea occurs in Paul Bowles' *The Sheltering Sky,* in which two Americans move into the primitive Arab world and the primal inner world simultaneously. Similarly, each Capote nocturnal hero must face a fiendish form of *mana,* an external force, and his inner guilt. The relationship in all cases is the same: there is an inescapable fascination with the outer and inner faces of evil. The moment of initiation, the shock of recognition, comes when the hero discovers that the two are the same: the *mana* which confronted him was an external manifestation of his inner identity. The dichotomy then is not only between the two worlds but between the two faces of each world: the constructive and the destructive. [604/605]

The story of initiation is the search for identity. For instance, in "Master Misery," one of Capote's favorites by his own admission, his heroine, Sylvia, is caught between the outside world represented by her insensitive girlhood friend, Estelle, and the impersonal, mechanical Santa Clauses in store windows, and the personal world of her own dreams. In an attempt to escape the outside world, Sylvia sells her dreams to the anonymous Master Misery, only to discover that she has not escaped the outer world but only lost the inner.

Sylvia is befriended by Oreilly, a used-up clown with no more dreams to sell, who squints one eye and says: "I don't believe in Jesus Christ, but I do believe in people's souls; and I figure it this way, baby; dreams are the mind of the soul and the secret truth about us." When Oreilly leaves her with a smile to go "travelling in the blue" where *the best old pie is whiskeyberry pie"* and not *"loveberry pie,"* Sylvia is left completely alone, having lost her dreams and her friend:

I do not know what I want, and perhaps I shall never know, but my only wish from every star will always be another star; and truly I am not afraid, she thought. Two boys came out of a bar and stared at her; in some park some long time ago she'd seen two boys and they might be the same. Truly I am not afraid, she thought, hearing their snowy footsteps following after her: and anyway, there was nothing left to steal.

In no other nocturnal story is the reader as conscious of the tension between the individual and society. Sylvia, in attempting to escape from society, discovers that the destructive element comes from within. Master Misery is himself a bogey man that "all mothers tell their kids about": a force outside the self and yet an extension of the self. Sylvia's surrender at the end of the story is not to society but to the dark side of her soul, the destructive element which dominates when the creative imagination is exhausted. In this lies the idea that the creative imagination of the dream world is [605/606] the one *thing* by which the individual is identified; the surrender of identity and of the creative force is the acquiescence to the death wish.

The differences between the lighter and darker sides of Capote's writing come out more clearly in one of his most famous stories, "Miriam." In it, an old woman, Mrs. Miller, is haunted by a striking and uncanny child who is her namesake—Miriam. The story shows how Miriam moves in and takes over Mrs. Miller's home, person, and life. The plot is similar to "Children on Their Birthdays" and "Jug of Silver": an uncanny child upsets the equilibrium of the drab routine of living. Miriam is in many ways similar to Miss Bobbit and we may almost think of her as that remarkable child's darker sister. But in "Miriam" there are some significant differences from the daylight stories, most important of which is the withdrawal from the outside world, a movement from the relationship of self to society to a confrontation of the self by the self in which Miriam becomes an uncanny device—a result of *mana* and projection. In fact, Miriam stands as the primal alter ego to Mrs. Miller: an extension of her destructive, unconscious instinct. The withdrawal from the outer world is accompanied by a complementary shift in style; the clarity and realism of "Children" is replaced by a filmy and surreal style in which Miriam's fingers "made cobweb movements over the plate, gathering the crumbs."

The hero's encounter with, and surrender to, *mana* is perhaps most richly stated in the inverted story, "The Headless Hawk," in which an extraordinary young girl, half child, half adult, innocent, experienced, demented, homocidal, naïve, and primitive, invades the sterile life of a young failure on the fringes of the art world. Vincent is "a poet who had never written poetry, a painter who had never painted, a lover who had never loved (absolutely)—someone, in short, without direction and quite headless. Oh, it wasn't that he hadn't tried—good beginnings, always, bad endings, always . . . a man in the sea, fifty miles from shore; a victim, born to be [606/607] murdered, either by himself or another; an actor unemployed." Vincent falls under the spell of a demented young girl, D. J., whose painting of a headless hawk hovering over a headless body—a vivid symbol of his own disconnectedness—forces on Vincent "a note of inward recognition." Vincent takes the girl as his mistress because she recalls from his past his incurable fascination with carnival freaks and because "it was true that about those he loved there was always a little something wrong, broken." D. J. thus becomes a mirror of his own disconnected self into which he can retreat. He shuns all his old friends because he does not know how to explain his relationship with the grotesque young girl.

However, Vincent's immersion in D. J. takes a sharp turn when he discovers her obsession with a Mr. Destronelli, a shadowy figure out of her past who she is sure will kill her. When Vincent discovers her dementia he knows he must betray her in favor of his old life, just as he had betrayed his other lovers, just as "he'd betrayed himself with talents unexploited, voyages never taken, promises unfulfilled . . . why in his lovers must he always find the broken image of himself?" He soon turns her out of the house and on the same day symbolically stabs the headless hawk in her painting as he is trying to catch a butterfly. But, of course, he has not escaped her. D. J. haunts him night and day, convinced that he is Destronelli. Vincent, returned to his old world which he now finds "sterile and spurious," discovers that he is held by "a nameless disorder . . . a paralysis of time and identity." Vincent's fascination with D. J. is the fatal confrontation with Mr. Destronelli—the executioner in each of us: he sees in D. J. the grotesque reflection of his own broken image.

The heart of the matter—the heart of darkness—is revealed significantly enough in a dream that Vincent has on the night of D. J.'s eighteenth birthday. He is at a huge party with "an old man with yellow-dyed hair, powdered cheeks, kewpie-doll lips: Vincent recognizes Vincent." The old man is on Vincent's back and Vincent feels out of place until he [607/608] notices that he is not alone. "He notices then that many are also saddled with malevolent semblances of themselves, outward embodiments of inner decay." The host has a headless hawk attached to his wrist drawing blood with its talons. Suddenly the host announces in a soprano voice: "Attention! The dancing will commence." Vincent finds himself dancing with a succession of old lovers.

Again, a new partner. It is D.J., and she too has a figure barnacled to her back, an enchanting auburn-haired child; like an emblem of innocence, the child cuddles to her chest a snowball kitten. "I am heavier than I look," says the child, and the terrible voice retorts, "But I am heaviest of all." The instant their hands meet he begins to feel the weight upon him diminish; the old Vincent is fading. His feet lift off the floor, he floats upward from her embrace. The victrola grinds away loud as ever, but he is rising high, and the white receding faces gleam below like mushrooms on a dark meadow.
The host releases his hawk, sends it soaring. Vincent thinks, no matter, it is a blind thing, and the wicked are safe among the blind. But the hawk wheels above him, swoops down, claws foremost; at last he knows there is to be no freedom.

The confrontation of the inner world becomes the confrontation of man's innate guilt. The dark side of the subconscious reflects not only the death instinct but the Christian sense of man's depravity. The burden that each carries becomes more than the darker alter ego: it is also the sense of original sin which each of us carries like a cross. Thus even the child is heavier than she looks; and thus Vincent cannot transcend his wickedness, even among the blind, even through love. Truly, there is to be no freedom from original sin.
The ingredients in all of Capote's nocturnal stories are present in their most striking expression, "A Tree of Night." Kay, a young college girl on her way back to her insulated environment from her uncle's funeral, is intimidated by two grotesque carnival performers: a deaf mute who plays Lazarus by being buried alive in tank towns and his one connection with the outside world, a woman made freakish [608/609] by her huge head. Much against her will, Kay is coerced, almost mesmerized, into buying a worthless charm which she had previously refused to buy. Like Capote's other heroes, Kay finds herself acquiescing to an uncanny power.

As Kay watched, the man's face seemed to change form and recede before her like a moon-shaped rock sliding downward under a surface of water. A warm laziness relaxed her. She was dimly conscious of it when the woman took away her purse, and when she gently pulled the raincoat like a shroud above her head.

On the one level the story may be read as a tawdry and ironic parable of Lazarus—

"I am Lazarus come from the dead,
Come back to tell you all, I shall tell you all"—
If one, settling a pillow by her head,
    Should say: "That is not what I meant at all;
    That is not it, at all."

—just as Carson McCullers' novel, *The Heart Is a Lonely Hunter,* can be read as an ironic parable of Christ. But perhaps the religious significance is being overemphasized:

(Confronted by the afflicted mute) Kay knew of what she was afraid: it was a memory, a childish memory of terrors that once, long ago, had hovered above her like haunted limbs on a tree of night. Aunts, cooks, strangers—each eager to spin a tale or teach a rhyme of spooks and death, omens, spirits, demons. And always there had been the unfailing threat of the wizard man: stay close to the house, child, else the wizard man'll snatch and eat you alive! He lived everywhere, the wizard man, and everywhere was danger. At night, in bed, hear him tapping at the window? Listen!

Fear seems the motivating emotion in these stories just as love is the motivating force in McCullers' novels. "*All our acts are acts of fear,*" remembered Walter Ranney, the hero of "Shut a Final Door," and perhaps he was right. For the wizard men and the Master Miseries are all personifications of some form of *mana,* formalized by superstition—that primitive and perhaps honest type of religious observance. At the same time, the Master Miseries and the Destronellis are not the products of our creative imagination but the very heart of darkness, the black, destructive, guilt-ridden side of our subconscious and soul. In each of these nocturnal stories, a seemingly normal but creatively bankrupt person encounters a destructive force at once outside himself and within his depths, which is so dreadful that he is utterly vanquished by fear and surrenders his very essence—his identity. The hero is drawn towards the source of power—the primal heart of darkness—and in doing so removes himself from the public world. Like Narcissus watching his reflection, Capote's hero becomes fascinated and mesmerized by his own evil alter ego. Like Jacob wrestling with the dark angel, the hero in these stories is wrestling not only with the outside world of reality but with his own personal world, losing the former while winning the latter. For the [609/610] moment of defeat, of despair, of unconditional surrender, is also the moment of revelation.

What we have discovered about the two worlds of Truman Capote's short stories is equally true in his two novels. Conveniently, one novel describes each world: *The Grass Harp* seems the daylight metaphor of *Other Voices, Other Rooms*. And yet both novels exhibit a deepening of perception, a widening of scope, and an enrichening of the dense thematic material found in the stories. On the other hand, neither novel is entirely successful, whereas some of his stories—notably "Children on Their Birthdays" and "A Tree of Night"—are striking examples of their medium. Even Capote admits he is most at home in the short story.

Still, no piece of Capote's fiction has elicited as much comment, criticism, and bewilderment as the gothic and complex first novel, *Other Voices, Other Rooms*. Indeed, the dust jacket picture of the sensitive reclining face staring out from beneath boyish bangs was perhaps as great a cause for [610/611] the excited confusion as anything in the book. But the difficult and fantastic remoteness of the book has been exaggerated by the mistaken identification of the hero with his exotic and precocious creator. Basically, *Other Voices* resembles Capote's twilight stories in that it concerns an adolescent's initiation into the private and inverted adult world, full of danger and evil. John Aldridge has called it essentially a search for the father and Carvel Collins has likened it to the quest for the Holy Grail: both are right. Yet Joel Knox's search for his father, which leads him from the realistic daylight of New Orleans to the fantastic twilight of Skully's Landing, can be considered as a search for identity. Joel moves from the outside world towards the personal, just as he moves from the bright afternoon heat of Noon City to the dream-like darkness of his new home—Skully's Landing.

John Aldridge has accused Capote of being metaphorical and remote, but his symbolic treatment of thematic material seems clear enough if examined in the same manner as we have examined his other stories. Like his other work, *Other Voices* can be read from either a psychological or a moral, perhaps Christian, viewpoint. Basically, Joel "was trying to locate his father, that was the long and short of it," for the discovery of his father's identity would cast some light on his own essence. But when Joel discovers the terrible truth that his father is a helpless, paralyzed invalid, he must look elsewhere for help in his search for identity. Joel stands as a stranger at Skully's Landing, poised between going further into the private world with his fascinating, witty, cynical, and homosexual cousin, Randolph, and moving out into the real world with the adolescent tomboy, Idabel. Joel's initiation can be seen as a straight-line development from the outside world of Noon City through the decadent limbo of Skully's Landing to the private, dreamlike ruins of the Cloud Hotel—and back again.

In order to tell his story, Capote has expanded the technique of metaphorical use of characterization seen [611/612] in "Miriam" and "The Headless Hawk." Each character in *Other Voices* is a metaphor or alter ego of another. The tomboy, Idabel, has a twin sister, Florabel, because, as Florabel says, "the Lord always sends something bad with the good." Similarly, the dwarfish Miss Wisteria, "weeping because little boys must grow tall," is a grotesque reflection of Randolph's hopeless, homosexual quest for completion. Little Sunshine, the hermit who inhabits his own private world at the Cloud Hotel, mirrors the old Negro servant, Jesus Fever. And, finally, Joel himself is reflected in Jesus Fever's daughter, Zoo: both must reject their fathers in an effort to escape from the Landing.

Joel's first test comes when he is not allowed to meet his father. In his mind the illusions he had built around his father are confused with the reality of his father's absence. "He couldn't believe in the way things were turning out: the difference between this happening and what he'd expected was too great." With the confrontation of his father's impotence, Joel must look elsewhere for the key to his identity. Randolph offers him one possibility: the narcissistic immersion in the self.

They can romanticize us so, mirrors, and that is their secret: what a subtle torture it would be to destroy all the mirrors in the world: where then could we look for reassurance of our identities? I tell you, my dear, Narcissus was no egotist . . . he was merely another of us who, in our unshatterable isolation, recognized, on seeing his reflection, the one beautiful comrade, the only inseparable love. . . . Poor Narcissus, possibly the only human who was ever honest on this point.

But even in the personal world Randolph cannot escape his own guilt, for "it is easy to escape daylight, but night is inevitable, and dreams are the giant cage." Like Vincent, in "The Headless Hawk," Randolph is "a victim born to be murdered, either by himself or another." He remains a broken figure hopelessly committed to, and castrated by, the destructive side of his personal vision. [612/613]

Caught between a loyalty to his father and a need to escape his stultifying influence, Joel at first rejects his father for Idabel, with whom he plans to run away. But the final act of initiation—the revelation of his own guilt that smashes the tinted glasses of childhood—renders Joel powerless to escape. In leaving his father, Joel, like Zoo, is judged guilty by his father and must act as his own executioner. Both he and Zoo can never really leave the Landing; their dreams of escape from limbo are shattered. When Randolph takes Joel to the Cloud Hotel—the private world which Randolph never left—a revelation of identity comes to Joel in a flash of insight:

(He looked into the fire, longing to see their faces as well, and the flames erupted an embryo: a veined, vacillating shape, its features formed slowly, and even when complete stayed veiled in dazzle; his eyes burned tar-hot as he brought them nearer: tell me, tell me, who are you? are you someone I know? are you dead? are you my friend? do you love me? But the painted disembodied head remained unborn beyond its mark, and gave no clue. Are you someone I am looking for? he asked, not knowing whom he meant, but certain that for him there must be such a person, just as there was for everybody else: Randolph with his almanac, Miss Wisteria and her search by flashlight, Little Sunshine remembering other voices, other rooms, all of them remembering, or never having known. And Joel drew back. If he recognized the figure in the fire, then what ever would he find to take its place? It was easier not to know, better holding heaven in your hand like a butterfly that is not there at all.)

Unable to live in either the private or the real world, Joel makes the compromise of the artist: finding his identity by walking the tenuous line between the illusory and the tangible, between the imaginative and the real:

"I am me," Joel whooped. "I am Joel, we are the same people" . . .
And Joel realized then the truth; he saw how helpless Randolph was: more paralyzed than Mr. Sansom, more childlike than Miss Wisteria, what else could he do, once outside and alone, but describe a circle, the zero of his nothingness? Joel [613/614] slipped down from the tree; he had not made the top, but it did not matter, for he knew who he was, he knew that he was strong.

Yet Joel's search for his identity contains another and perhaps more significant level of meaning. At the very beginning of the book, while riding to Skully's Landing, Joel passes a sign—a sign for him and for the reader: "The Lord Jesus is Coming! Are you ready?" But the Christ figure we meet is one we are not prepared for: the paralytic father, Mr. Sansom, who drops red tennis balls like drops of blood, an ironic, afflicted Christ similar to the deaf-mute, Singer, in Carson McCullers' *The Heart Is a Lonely Hunter*. Joel's search for his father leads to the confrontation of his innate guilt—guilt symbolized in the desertion of his father and manifested in his sudden awareness of the disparity between illusion and reality and his perception of the impossibility of escape from the Landing. His situation is mirrored by Zoo, who leaves her father's grave to escape the Landing only to find that she has taken "the wrong road" to salvation. She is crucified by assaulters just as Joel, like Christ, is condemned and abandoned by his father and crucified by surrendering to Randolph. But in the act of the crucifixion are the seeds of redemption: Joel is crucified a boy and resurrected a man.

Every Capote character is scarred permanently just as Zoo bears the marks of a razor slashing on her neck. They are all marked men, marked perhaps by original sin. Even the artist—like Joel—is afflicted: "the feeble-minded, the neurotic, the criminal, perhaps, also, the artist, have unpredictability and perverted innocence in common." But Capote's nocturnal hero remains essentially the failure. And in Randolph he has created his most fascinating and grotesque failure, who speaks for Vincent and Sylvia, Mrs. Miller and Walter Ranney, when he says:

But we are alone, darling child, terribly, isolated each from the other; so fierce is the world's ridicule we cannot speak or show our tenderness; for us, death is stronger than life, it pulls [614/615] like a wind through the dark, all our cries burlesqued in joyless laughter; and with the garbage of loneliness stuffed down us until our guts burst bleeding green, we go screaming round the world, dying in our rented rooms, nightmare hotels, eternal homes of the transient heart.

In *The Grass Harp,* Capote again moves to the daylight style. Essentially, it is the story of a group of innocents, alienated from society because of their innocence, who move into a tree house to escape the world and discover their true selves. The theme is again the search for *true* identity. For the tree dissolves all of society's restrictions and replaces them with a beatific feeling of freedom; it is a realm where wish becomes fulfillment. The tree becomes the refuge for the outcasts from society: the saintly Dolly, the most innocent of all, who, like J. D. Salinger's misfit hero, Seymour Glass, loves people so much she hides in corners for fear of scaring them with her love. With Dolly is her constant companion, Catherine, a zany mixture of Negro and Indian, harshness and loyalty, who brings to the tree house a sense of hard-headed reality, and Collin Fenwick, the adolescent narrator, who lives with Dolly and her brutish sister, Verena. These three have left home after a quarrel over Dolly's home-remedy dropsy cure: Verena wants to mass produce it and Dolly refuses to commercialize it. They are soon joined by a retired judge, Judge Cool, whose sons feel he has outgrown his usefulness. "I sometimes imagine," he says, "all those whom I've called guilty have passed the real guilt on to me: it's partly that that makes me want once before I die to be right on the right side." The fifth party is a "tense, trigger-tempered," directionless youth, Riley Henderson, who also happens to be Collin's idol.

Like Salinger's Holden Caulfield, these five stage a "quixotic" battle against hypocrisy, materialism, and anything that takes beauty away from the world. The small revolt from society forces them to move towards the inner world of the imagination. Judge Cool sums up the whole idea nicely: [615/616]

"But ah, the energy we spend hiding from one another, afraid as we are of being identified. But here we are, identified: five fools in a tree. A great piece of luck provided we know how to use it: no longer any need to worry about the picture we present—free to find out who we truly are. If we know that, no one can dislodge us; it's the uncertainty concerning themselves that makes our friends conspire to deny the differences. By scrapes and bits I've in the past surrendered myself to strangers—men who disappeared down the gangplank, got off at the next station: put together, maybe they would've made the one person in the world—but there he is with a dozen different faces moving down a hundred separate streets. This is my chance to find that man—you are him, Miss Dolly, Riley, all of you."

But this leafy retreat seems hardly the place for soul-searching; Verena soon has the authorities there to demand that they return to their homes. A pitched battle occurs between the rebels and the authorities, which, with the help of the right of creative imagination and the might of an ingenious family of gypsies, is decided in favor of the rebels. However, they do leave the tree house when Verena returns broken by the swindler of her heart and money—the bogus doctor who was to bottle the dropsy cure. Dolly returns to Verena because she is needed and the magic of the "dissolving" chinaberry tree is gone.

In the story the end of innocence is two-fold. For Collin, it is an elegiac remembrance of things past, a vicarious initiation at Dolly's own loss of innocence, and his real initiation at Dolly's death. But for Collin the act of initiation brings the discovery of love and the redemption of the identity. It now becomes clear that for Capote love is the redeeming element in life. Echoing the judge's words in an earlier part of the book, Dolly tells Collin just before her death:

Charlie said that love is a chain of love. I hope you listened and understood him. Because when you can love one thing . . . you can love another, and that is owning, that is something to live with. You can forgive everything. [616/617]

Like Carson McCullers in her story, "A Tree, A Rock, A Cloud," Capote here shows "that life is a chain of love, as nature is a chain of life." Arching over the story of Dolly and Collin and the chinaberry tree is the grass harp, a symbol of the immutable moral order, an order of the good and the imaginative which always tells a story of the lives of the people, good and bad, with and without identity, who have lived and died there. And so the search for identity comes to rest in the shock of recognition—recognition of the primacy of the natural order of the creative instinct—of love and imagination over the death wish. Both Joel and his daylight brother, Collin, have learned the same thing: the search inward for identity must eventually turn outward if it is to reflect anything but the broken image of the grotesque self.

The world was a frightening place, yes, he knew: unlasting, what could be forever? or only what it seemed? rock corrodes, rivers freeze, fruit rots; stabbed, blood of black and white bleeds alike; trained parrots tell more truth than most, and who is lonelier: the hawk or the worm? every flowering heart shrivels dry and pitted as the herb from which it bloomed, and while the old man grows spinsterish, his wife assumes a mustache; moment to moment, changing, changing, like the cars on the ferris-wheel. Grass and love are always greener; but remember Little Three Eyes? show her love and apples ripen gold, love vanquishes the Snow Queen, its presence finds the name, be it Rumpelstiltskin or merely Joel Knox: that is constant. [617]

Why the Chickens Came Home
to Roost in Holcomb, Kansas:
Truman Capote's *In Cold Blood*

DAVID GALLOWAY

In America violence is idiomatic. Read our newspapers. To make the first
page a murderer has to use his imagination, he has to use a particularly
hideous instrument. Take this morning's paper: FATHER CUTS SON'S
THROAT IN BASEBALL ARGUMENT. It appears on an inside page. To
make the first page, he should have killed three sons with a baseball bat
instead of a knife. Only liberality and symmetry could have made this daily
occurrence interesting.

WITH THESE WORDS AMERICAN NOVELIST NATHANAEL WEST BEGAN AN
essay on violence published in the little magazine which he and William
Carlos Williams edited for a time during the 1930's. Many of his contemporaries—including John Steinbeck, James T. Farrell, and Sinclair
Lewis—shared West's concern with the anarchic forces which continuously threatened to erupt (and frequently did) during the Great
Depression, but no other novelist devoted himself so consistently to a
study of the sources and the ultimate potential of that violence. From
the surrealistic *Dream Life of Balso Snell*, through the crucified *Miss
Lonelyhearts*, and the brutal picaresque, *A Cool Million*, West pared
away at the dreams, the myths, the illusions of American life, to reveal
the distortions and frustrations which they masked. As the manager of a
New York hotel he had watched the lobby fill with shabby, unwanted
men and women who fed themselves on the narcotic daydreams of
glossy magazines and the vicarious thrills provided by the tabloids.
It was a natural response to their own frustration, as West himself
realized: "Men have always fought their misery with dreams," but he
added the important and sinister qualification that "Although dreams
were once powerful, they have been made puerile by the movies, radio,
and newspaper." It was inevitable that West should turn his satirical
vision on Hollywood, the dream capital of the world, and not surprising
that his most successful (and final) novel, *The Day of the Locust*,
was originally entitled *The Cheated*. In the Hollywood phantasmagoria

West was able to picture the American masquerade in all its grotesqueness; it was from the frustration of man's terror-filled craving for ever more resplendent dreams that West saw the ultimate potential for violence in America.

It was an unpleasant message, and one which most Americans were eager to disregard—especially when its ultimate indictment, as West made clear in *A Cool Million,* was of the American Dream itself. Revered by a small in-group, West was otherwise forgotten during the quarter-century that followed his death in 1940. As a stylist he was well in advance of his time, and as a social commentator he has proved to have more to say to members of the Great Society than he did to the malcontents of the Great Depression—or so his continuing rehabilitation would suggest. His work represented only one stage in the denunciation of the American Dream, but West went beyond denunciation (and hence considerably beyond the scope of a work like Norman Mailer's *American Dream*) in the ardor with which he attempted to assess the failure of a national myth which had played such a central role in political, economic, and social life in the United States.

Even in this age of relative plenty, violence seems as idiomatic in America as it did when West wrote his article for *Contempo;* as a theme it continues to occupy the attention of novelists and playwrights, but no single writer of the post-war era has viewed that savage potential with so much insight or compassion as Truman Capote: *In Cold Blood* is a parable for our times—one whose social significance we cannot afford to overlook, and whose literary merits demand serious discussion in their own right. There are, to be sure, interesting peripheral questions—of Capote's own personal relationship to the killers of the Clutter family, and of the impulses which led him so far beyond the outlines of the original *New Yorker* assignment in which this book originated. Questions of the author's "motivation" and of his personal responsibility will eventually be the province of Capote's biographers, but for the moment they must not be allowed to obscure the compelling manner and substance of the work itself: *In Cold Blood* is a literary fact which both calls for and rewards an intense analysis.

Perhaps the first question which the critic rightly asks is the degree to which this "True Account of a Multiple Murder" is not only "non-fiction" but also a novel, as Capote maintains. Such labelling is in some respects irrelevant, but it is worth observing that while *In Cold Blood* is certainly not a work of "fiction," neither is it a "documentary" in the conventional sense of that word. The 284 published pages of this work do not represent a simple condensation or summary of the thousands of pages of notes and transcripts which rest behind its composition: it is a careful and artful selection of details, calculated to evoke a variety of moods, to establish character, to produce suspense, and to convey a number of intricately related themes. It is in the selection of such details and in their arrangement that the technique of the novelist is vividly apparent; and there are gaps in the narrative which have clearly been filled out of the writer's own imagination—but filled (despite the occasional moment of self-indulgent prose) in such a way as to grow organically out of the facts themselves, or to give at least the crucial *appearance* of doing so. Perhaps the sense of immediacy and involvement which the book produces should be pre-requisites of the documentary, but they are qualities all too rarely found there. And as the action shifts from the Clutter family to their killers, to narrative flashbacks and vivid descriptions of the varied landscapes through which the major characters move, we recognize the shaping intelligence of a sensitive and experienced novelist. (The reader who has any doubts in this regard need only compare *In Cold Blood* with the intelligent, well documented, but *detached* manner of the summary volume of *The Warren Commission Report*.) And it is easy to see why Capote felt no necessity to "fictionalize" this story, for in it there were qualities which so transcended the particular as to render the conflict of fiction and non-fiction almost meaningless. But perhaps only a novelist would have seen the events in this manner and have succeeded in presenting them in a fashion which at once documents and transcends the documentary.

The shotgun murder of four members of the Clutter family in Holcomb, Kansas, on November 15, 1959, possessed the "liberality and symmetry" which Nathanael West claimed as a necessary ingredient for making an act of violence "interesting": father, mother, teenage son and daughter, trussed up in identical, elaborate knots, arranged in comfortable positions by their murderers, and shot once, "neatly," through the head; only the fact that Mr. Clutter's throat had also been cut seemed to deny the symmetry. But what accorded the Clutter murder its publicity in a country where mass murders are not uncommon news was not its symmetry, or even liberality, but its apparent pointlessness. Robbery seemed an inadequate motive, since Mr. Clutter was widely known to conduct all business by checks; a grudge killing seemed unlikely; and none of the victims had been sexually abused. Furthermore, outside of a single bloody footprint, there were no clues. Both the savageness and the senselessness of these murders claimed a brief flurry of attention in the national press and left far more permanent marks on the residents of a small Kansas town.

Capote's choice of the "non-fictional" mode in this case may well have been stimulated by a realization that the "facts" of this bizarre case themselves possessed a universal quality—even those facts least subject to the writer's own imaginative arrangements. There are numerous antecedents to this discovery of a sort of "instant symbolism," but in American literature there are two which stand out with particular significance—Melville's adaptation of a portion of Captain Amasa

Delano's *Journal* for his novella *Benito Cereno,* and Dreiser's treatment of the Gillette-Brown murder case in *An American Tragedy.* In
both instances there was more rearrangement of the actual facts than
there is in Capote's work, but Melville and Dreiser both concluded
their accounts with almost literal transcriptions of the murderers' trials.
In Delano's turgid account of the rebellion of a group of African
slaves, with its elaborate scheme of disguise and deception, Melville
found an immediate imaginative source for his own ambiguous vision
of freedom and responsibility; so too, in the Grace Brown murder,
Dreiser found a factual anagram for his disillusionment with the American Dream, for his growing belief that the individual was a victim
both of his own heredity and of the environment which played so
remorselessly on his weaknesses. Capote shares with Melville and
Dreiser in the discovery of an intense and compelling episode in real
life whose implications are so sweeping and suggestive as to take hold
of the writer's imagination as well as his intelligence and compassion.
Leaving aside, for the moment, the question of Capote's *arrangement*
of the facts, and other matters of style and technique, it would perhaps
be well to have a look at those facts which seemed to offer such instant
symbolism for the writer.

The victims, first of all: we know the Clutter family already—
immortalized as they have been in Norman Rockwell illustrations,
Coca-Cola advertisements, and as "the folks next door" in countless
Hollywood movies. Herbert William Clutter was the embodiment of
the self-made man, as well as an exemplar of the White Anglo-Saxon
Protestant values with which that favorite of all American myths is
conventionally associated—a leading member of the local Methodist
church, a joiner and organizer, a dedicated husband and father, a
teetotaler, a generous but strong-willed man who had achieved his
patrician standing in nearby Garden City through diligence, integrity,
and good works. On the last day of his life he addressed the Garden
City 4-H Club ("Head, Heart, Hands, Health"), and, with the future
security of his family in mind, signed a $40,000 life insurance policy.
The family was in a particularly happy mood on that final Saturday,
for on the previous evening they had watched Nancy, the one daughter who remained at home, play the role of Becky Thatcher, "a real
Southern belle," in a student production of *Tom Sawyer.* The final day
in Nancy's life emphasized that scope of ladylike and generous talents
which gave her family such pride: she spent the morning baking
cherry pies with a nine-year-old neighbor, then supervised another
young neighbor in rehearsing the trumpet solo she was to play at a
school concert, ran errands for her mother, made lunch, worked on the
bridesmaids' dresses she had designed for the forthcoming wedding of
her sister Beverly, and spent the evening entertaining her beau.
Kenyon, the Clutters' fifteen-year-old son, devoted part of this final
day to giving a coat of varnish to the mahogany hope chest which he

intended to give Beverly on her wedding day; in the "den" which he
and Nancy had decorated together, he was surrounded by numerous
examples of his handiwork—including his newest "invention," an
electric deep-dish frying pan.

To this point, at least, the Clutters remind us of the reinforcing reality which rests behind America's dreams of herself—an intelligent,
public-spirited family, who lead a simple, unpretentious life. If at moments they remind us of the opening lines of a song from *South Pacific,*
"I'm as corny as Kansas in August, / I'm as common as blueberry pie,"
there is a more appropriate phrase later in the song: "a cliché coming
true." For however much like cliché these Bible Belt aristocrats may
seem, they are nonetheless real and believable people: the life which
they led is, to be sure, an uncommon one in America, it does not make
good newspaper copy, and it has no place in a Muggeridge-eye view
of America. In some respects the Clutters' way of life was an anachro-
nism, but a genial and alluring one—the small but influential seed of
reality at the heart of the American Dream.

What we see, finally, in their murder is not just the horrifyingly
brutal death of four individuals but the murder of a part of America
which has not only fattened the songwriter, the movie producer, and
the fancies of advertising men, but has repeatedly proved a vital factor
in America's political stability and economic prosperity. Add to this the
fact that the Clutter farm was located at almost the exact geographical
center of America, and one has a sense of the "instant symbolism" on
which the imagination of a sensitive novelist would have seized.

But however admirable their history may seem (and *was,* no
doubt, in its essentials), admiration does not go unqualified: there is
something almost compulsive about the Clutters' good works, their
cherry-pie public spirit and unimpeachable respectability; even Capote's gently accommodating picture of the self-reliant life at River
Valley Farm is tinged with occasional irony—not that the Clutters
seem too good to be true, but that their own standards seem to place
such ferocious demands on the individual, and to ask him to perform
in an uncompromisingly public arena. Not only the doors· of the
Clutter house remained unlocked, but the windows of their private
lives as well, and at least one member of the family found it impossible
to meet the public gaze. Mrs. Clutter suffered from "nerves" and for six
years had been a part-time psychiatric patient; she was not a "joiner,"
she was uneasy in the world of conquests and public example which
her husband occupied; most of her days, including the last one of her
life, were spent in the austere bedroom where she slept apart from her
husband—the windows always closed against the world outside, even
in the most sweltering Kansas summers. Everything the Clutters did
was on a vast scale—the farm they ran, the house Mr. Clutter had
designed for them, the public duties they assumed. Mrs. Clutter's
prized possessions were, significantly, a collection of miniature baubles

—scissors, thimbles, crystal flower baskets, toy figurines, forks and knives, teacups, and a tiny paper fan. As she lay in her bed on the afternoon of November 14th, she was troubled by thoughts of the twenty house guests who would soon arrive for the Thanksgiving holidays (the remainder of the guests would stay elsewhere), and of preparations for Beverly's wedding. There is something about the scale, the scope, and the entirely *public* nature of the Clutters' lives which strikes a disquieting note. And the note becomes bizarre, even macabre, when Beverly Clutter, one of the two surviving daughters, is married in the same Garden City church where, three days before, the Clutters' mass funeral had been held. Dressed in white and surrounded by her bridesmaids, Beverly was married in a full-scale wedding; as the Garden City *Telegram* reported: "Vere and Beverly had planned to be married at Christmastime. The invitations were printed and her father had reserved the church for that date. Due to the unexpected tragedy and because of the many relatives being here from distant places, the young couple decided to have their wedding Saturday." In reporting such facts as these, Capote must inevitably resort to irony, but it is never permitted to blur the essential outlines of the story he has to tell. Whatever disturbing shadows there are on this portrait of the ideal American family, the faults seem finally the excess of their virtues, and much of what is most admirable about the American spirit was unquestionably embodied in the victims of this savage murder.

When we turn to the killers themselves, the sense of a "national" drama assumes even wider proportions: as Perry Smith, who was to fire the four shotgun blasts, stationed himself before a drugstore on Saturday morning to await his confederate, Richard Hickock, his mind was filled with advertising slogans: "FORTUNES IN DIVING! Train at Home in Your Spare Time. Make Big Money Fast in Skin and Lung Diving. FREE BOOKLETS . . ." Answering such advertisements had long been one of Perry's favorite preoccupations; the prospect of easy money and exotic adventure they provoked had only one rival in his daydreams—the picture of himself before an elegant Las Vegas audience, a sensational new star warbling "I'll Be Seeing You" to an elaborate violin accompaniment. Perry Smith had fed his intensely active imagination, as well as a remarkable but untrained intelligence, on the fruits of American advertising, on its reiterated images of the easy life bought now and paid for later, the life to which all Americans are entitled. And that afternoon the killers drove four hundred miles to the Clutter farm, carrying with them Perry's old Gibson guitar and a twelve-gauge pump-action shotgun bought on the installment plan.

The killers themselves, as Capote frequently points out, had little in common outside of police records, their desire for easy money, and the belief that, by killing all witnesses (they were prepared for an even dozen), they could escape undetected. But two further, and far more suggestive, factors linked the two murderers: both were among the "cheated" in whom Nathanael West saw America's greatest single threat. For the Hickock family there was never the deprivation of real poverty, but a life lived remorselessly near the subsistence level, a level below which they might fall at any moment (and did once when Mr. Hickock became ill and unable to work). Life for the Smiths was more erratic and more sordid: poverty, alcoholism, prostitution, and violence formed the background in which Perry Smith grew up. He passed through a series of orphanages, child welfare agencies, and reformatories, before beginning a life of vagabondage with his father. Of the two killers Smith interests the reader most not simply because he was the man to fire the shotgun, but because from an early age he demonstrated a keen intelligence, musical talent, artistic ability, and an almost passionate interest in words; his formal education ended with the third grade. As a half-breed child, Perry Smith faced not only the usual terrors of poverty, but a great deal of prejudice as well. One of the most vivid memories he carried with him was of the beatings he used to receive in the California orphanage where he was kept for a time—in particular, of a nun who beat him for wetting his bed: "She woke me up. She had a flashlight, and she hit me with it. Hit me and hit me. And when the flashlight broke, she went on hitting me in the dark." There were many memories of this sort, and however much they may have been embroidered by Smith's active imagination, there is no reason to question their essential validity; two of the four Smith children committed suicide in their twenties, but by then Perry's sister Flo had changed her name to "Joy."

And there was a further link between these two young men: Hickock was disfigured in an automobile accident and Smith maimed in a motor-cycle wreck; Smith's legs, broken in five places, pained him so continuously that he became addicted to aspirin. Both were, in a sense, victims of the "open road" which has been such a familiar component of American romance—from Cooper through Twain, Whitman, Hemingway, and Kerouac. But the myth has been inverted: speed, recklessness, unchecked mobility were the cheap narcotic in which Hickock and Smith (whose length of siphon hose was his prized "credit card") sought adventure and escape—from a society which had cheated them, from the crimes they committed, and finally from themselves. No aspect of *In Cold Blood* is quite so absorbing or, in a strange way, so unnerving, as Capote's detailed description of the erratic 10,000 mile odyssey which Hickock and Smith made after the Clutter murder—moving restlessly south into Mexico, then crisscrossing America—with an occasional stop for petty thievery, to siphon gas, steal a car, or visit the launderette. Nothing else in the book symbolizes so well the frantic, directionless course of these men's lives. There was a time in America's development when the open road was not only a theme for romance, but a vital factor in economic expansion and political continuity. If for many it was merely the chance to opt out, for others it represented the possibility of making a new beginning. But not only is the open road in America rapidly becoming "unsafe at any speed," it has also become a relentless common denominator—linking islands of filling stations and hot-dog stands and motels—interchangeable units connected by ribbons of concrete, and uniformly *Sanitized for Your Protection*, as George Crowther has recently suggested in his parody of the mobile society. It is not the sense of a "new" place in which they might make a new start that emerges from the scores of towns and cities which Hickock and Smith visit, but of their deadening sameness—which for them could only have meant the same temptations, the same frustrations.

And the killers themselves finally cease to seem unique. After Dr. Joseph Satten of the Menninger Clinic had examined them, he felt that both—but in particular Perry Smith—conformed to the conclusions of a study he had written in collaboration with three of his colleagues on the phenomenon of "Murder Without Apparent Motive": "When such senseless murders occur, they are seen to be an end result of a period of increasing tension and disorganization in the murderer starting before the contact with the victim who, by fitting into the unconscious conflicts of the murderer, unwittingly serves to set into motion his homocidal potential." Perry Smith's "real and only friend," a fellow convict, had made a similar appraisal in a farewell letter written when Perry won a parole from the Kansas State Penitentiary (where he met Hickock) four months before the Clutter murder: "You are a man of extreme passion, a hungry man striving to project his individuality against a backdrop of rigid conformity. You exist in a half-world suspended between two super-structures, one self-expression and the other self-destruction. You are strong, but there is a flaw in your strength, and unless you learn to control it the flaw will prove stronger than your strength and defeat you. The flaw? *Explosive emotional reaction out of all proportion to the occasion.*" But Perry Smith's own explanation of his crime is perhaps the most persuasive of all: ". . . it wasn't because of anything the Clutters did. They never hurt me. Like other people. Like people have all my life. Maybe it's just that the Clutters were the ones who had to pay for it."

And thus, finally, we realize that what took place in Holcomb, Kansas, early on a Sunday morning in 1959, was not so much murder as suicide: in a real sense America was both killer and victim, turning the deferred-payment shotgun against herself. The terrible ritual was re-enacted almost exactly four years later, when Lee Harvey Oswald aimed a rifle from a warehouse window in Dallas, Texas. For Oswald as for Hickock and Smith, the open road had become a shabby travesty; one of the most recurrent features of his childhood, as well as his adult life, was the frequency with which he moved on whenever trouble, or authority, or responsibility seemed to threaten him. And given this extraordinary mobility, perhaps the most salient index of Oswald's maladjustment was the fact that he never learned to drive an automobile.

Much of the violence in America—that which has erupted in Watts, California, for example—is relatively simple to diagnose, if difficult to treat. But there is a great deal of apparently capricious violence, stemming from unlikely sources and spending itself on unlikely victims. When Eugene Hickock and Perry Smith entered Death Row at the Kansas State Penitentiary for Men, following their conviction for murder, there were three other inmates. One had kidnapped, raped, and tortured a young woman; another had murdered his elderly landlady, and, while in prison, stabbed another prisoner to death; the third, Lowell Lee Andrews, had been an honors student at the University of Kansas, a quiet, "sweet-natured" boy, who celebrated his Thanksgiving vacation from the university by murdering his sister, his mother, and his father; on autopsy the latter's body was discovered to contain seventeen bullets. Later the condemned men were joined in "The Corner" by a pair of teenagers, George Ronald York and James Douglas Latham; convinced that because "It's a rotten world," to kill a man was to render him a supreme favor, the two whipped and garrotted a pair of Georgia housewives, shot a travelling salesman in Tennessee, two more men in Illinois, a sixty-two-year-old "Good Samaritan" who stopped to help them repair their car in Kansas, and finally a girl of eighteen, employed as a maid in a Colorado motel. When asked by a television interviewer why they had committed the crimes, York replied with a schoolboy grin, "We hate the world."

In a work at once compelling and frightening, Capote has attempted to analyze that hatred, and the book which grows from years of painstaking research is a social document of undeniable significance. It is also a major work of literature in its own right, for only a writer of exceptional talent could so skillfully have directed our attention to the larger issues which rest behind the "facts" of this case. In an article of this length it is impossible to do more than suggest the major outlines of the themes which emerge from this story, or of the techniques which Capote has used in constructing *In Cold Blood*. As the story cuts from victims, to killers, to pursuers, as Capote piles image upon image (in a manner reminiscent of Dreiser), he reconstructs not just the lives of six people, but a microcosm of the world in which we all live, and he populates it with a cast of characters who emanate the sense of life which only a major novelist could have given them. Like all great works of literature, the implications of *In Cold Blood*, and the richness of its narrative technique, defy any simple reduction into categories, but one unifying theme—the metamorphosis of dream into nightmare—returns again and again to haunt the reader's imagination. So, too, does Perry Smith's own diagnosis of the crime: "Maybe it's just that the Clutters were the ones who had to pay for it."

Towards an Aesthetic:
Truman Capote's Other Voices

MELVIN J. FRIEDMAN

NOVEMBER 14, 1959, IS LIKELY TO BECOME AS IMPORTANT A LITERARY date as June 16, 1904. This is the day when Perry Smith and Dick Hickock murdered the Clutter family of Holcomb, Kansas, "in cold blood." Capote, in late 1965 (when *In Cold Blood* appeared in four issues of *The New Yorker*), as indelibly marked our literary calendars as Joyce did in 1922. Just as Joycians hold an annual reunion in Joyce country (visiting the many familiar landmarks including the Martello Tower and 7 Eccles Street) on this sacred day in June, so may Capotians eventually gather, with some misgivings, on November 14 in and around River Valley Farm, Holcomb, Kansas. Joyce intended Bloomsday to be an affirmative and epiphanic day; Capote characterized his day as having "blood on the walls."

These two days, as Joyce and Capote presented them, yield paradoxically different impressions: Joyce's seems quite the more real, Capote's the more fictional. Joyce invented his day so thoroughly and convincingly that our disbelief is almost completely suspended. Capote gave his day such elaborate literary trappings that it is difficult to believe he has scrupulously stayed within the bounds of strict reportage. It were almost as if Joyce had written the "nonfiction novel" instead of Capote.

It might be said about Truman Capote that everything he touches turns to literature. He is what the French have fondly referred to as an *écrivain de race*. He is sensitively attuned to what he calls "interior temperatures" (*Paris Review* interview) and "scenery of the mind" (*The Muses Are Heard*). He cannot be anything but "literary" even when he is merely reporting on the capricious tour of a *Porgy and Bess* troupe about to perform in Russia, interviewing Marlon Brando for *The New Yorker*, recording some moment of frozen time in the life of a

This is the first publication of Melvin J. Friedman's article. All rights reserved. Permission to reprint must be obtained from the author.

resident of Brooklyn, New Orleans, Hollywood, or even Haiti. Capote
has himself indicated in his *Paris Review* interview that there should
be no intrinsic stylistic difference between fiction and reportage: ". . .
one of the reasons I've wanted to do reportage was to prove that I
could apply my style to the realities of journalism."[1] Thus his entire
oeuvre seems to form a coherent, textural whole—from the early
stories like "Miriam" through the recent *In Cold Blood*. Stanley
Kauffmann recognized several years ago in his "An Author in Search of
a Character" (*The New Republic*, February 23, 1963) that Capote's
means of characterization remains the same from the fiction to the
reportage: "The characters of Holly Golightly and of Mrs. Gershwin in
The Muses Are Heard are depicted by, essentially, the same method"
(p. 22). *In Cold Blood* reinforces Kauffmann's position—and even
extends it.

The unity of Capote's work has had even another dimension. He
has achieved a contemporary realization of Horace's celebrated dictum
ut pictura poesis, with the aid of a kind of pictorial alter ego, Richard
Avedon. Avedon's photographs and Capote's inspired captions produced a unique blend of poetry and picture—which would have
waylaid the suspicions of even a Lessing or an Irving Babbitt—in their
work-of-collaboration, *Observations* (1959). Capote, for example,
underscored Avedon's Isak Dinesen: "Imposing creation come forward
from one of her own Gothic tales"; and spoke of Avedon's rather
bizarre Chaplin as "a horned Pan sprite." Avedon was called upon
once again to offer a photographic backdrop for *In Cold Blood* and the
result appeared in a seventeen-page spread in *Life* (January 7, 1966)
to celebrate the publication of Capote's latest book. This time Capote's
words were absent (they were replaced by a canned bit of *Life*
"coverage in depth" and a rather corny bit of literary reporting by Jane
Howard), but the photographs would do well as an interlinear commentary for a new edition of *In Cold Blood*.

Photographs were used to illuminate Capote's text on still another
occasion, in his series of "travelogues," *Local Color* (1950). This is
more the standard fare and lacks the unique cooperation which produced the later *Observations*—perhaps because Avedon was not involved in this collaborative venture. Still it is evident even here that
Capote's prose has a pictorial equivalent and that the lushness of his
style is somehow toned down by the sobering quality of the photographs. Capote's love of the near-clichéd image, like "bridge of childhood" and "imagination's earliest landscapes," is redeemed by realistic
pictures of existing scenes.[2]

[1] *Writers at Work: The "Paris Review" Interviews*, ed. Malcolm Cowley
(New York: Viking, 1959), p. 291. All references will be to this edition.
[2] We might mention also the slick photograph-caption piece Capote col-
laborated in: "The Sylvia Odyssey—Photographs with (Handwritten) Comment,
Vogue, January 15, 1966.

Photography has gained respectability as an art form in the past few years, as has cinema. Capote has also lent his talents to film-making. The script he wrote for *Beat the Devil* is probably better than anything Faulkner or Fitzgerald did during their Hollywood periods. And one should not forget the screenplay he co-authored with William Archibald for *The Innocents* (based on James's *Turn of the Screw*)—with its intriguing angles of cinematic vision—which seems so closely allied to his early stories and to *Other Voices, Other Rooms*. Several reviewers of *In Cold Blood* believe that he learned something from these experiences as they point to the cinematic shape of the book. Dwight Macdonald, writing his monthly film critique in *Esquire* (April 1966), speaks of "the Griffith cross-cutting in the first chapter," "the 'establishing' long shots of the Kansas milieu" (p. 44). Stanley Kauffman, long-time film critic, remarked that "Capote's structural method can be called cinematic: he uses intercutting of different story strands, intense closeups, flashbacks, traveling shots, background de-tail, all as if he were fleshing out a scenario" (*The New Republic*, January 22, 1966, p. 19). Capote admits much of this himself when he remarks in his *Paris Review* interview: "I think most of the younger writers have learned and borrowed from the visual, structural side of movie technique. I have" (p. 293).

Several of the more inspired reviewers of *In Cold Blood* realized something else about Capote—that he was now entering a more authentically American tradition of story-telling than any revealed in his earlier work. Malcolm Muggeridge came closest to explaining this: "From Huck to Dick and Perry is quite a span; from Twain to Capote, too, for that matter. If Huck was the beginning of the American Dream, Dick and Perry are perhaps its end" (*Esquire,* April 1966, p. 84). We can now begin using such literary catchphrases as "Adamic myth" to explain Capote, just as we've used them up to now to explain the "great tradition" in American fiction from Cooper to Hawthorne through William Styron.

This brings us face to face with the central ambiguity in Capote's career: his successes and failures rarely seem to have much to do with his intentions. He has always been interested in the untried and the unprecedented both in his life and his work. Thus he told a number of attentive interviewers, following the publication of *In Cold Blood,* that he had invented a new genre to be known henceforth as the "nonfic-tion novel." He admitted a certain priority in Lillian Ross' *Picture* ("a nonfiction novella") and in his own *The Muses Are Heard* ("which uses the techniques of the comic short novel") but stood firm on the essential lines of his discovery. This has had an adverse effect on several reviewers of the book who viewed rather mockingly the asser-tion that a new literary genre had been uncovered. A sober critic like F. W. Dupee (writing in the February 3, 1966 *New York Review of Books*) was able to see beyond Capote's claim and feel that "whatever its 'genre,' *In Cold Blood* is admirable" (p. 3). But the general feeling was that the author's own view of his accomplishments—as expressed by him too often and at too great length—was seriously out of line with what *In Cold Blood* delivered.[3] It would probably have served Capote's purposes better if he had not insisted so much on the uniqueness of his undertaking and allowed the merits of his book to speak for themselves. In a sense the "public Capote," which has come out repeatedly for originality in his work as well as in his behavior and in his dress, has proved unworthy of the more private Capote who has sustained an impressive body of work over a twenty-year period.

Which brings me to the point of this essay—to prove that Capote is a very traditional writer who has managed admirably in a fictional mode expected of his generation. Like his contemporaries in the South, he has profited a great deal from reading William Faulkner. F. W. Dupee has pointed out how similar the portrait of Perry Smith as a boy ("half-breed child living in a California orphanage") is to Joe Christmas in *Light in August*. We can add to this the photograph of the African wood carving of Holly Golightly's head which opens *Breakfast at Tiffany's* and its uncanny resemblance to the photograph of Caddy Compson which the librarian uncovers in the appendix which precedes Faulkner's *The Sound and the Fury;* in each case the photograph points to a period later than the events of the novel proper and is a revelation of a woman who had passed out of sight several years before. In a more basic way, the division of the characters into tree-dwellers (eccentrics) and ordinary townspeople in *The Grass Harp* is a Faulknerian device: Faulkner used it in *As I Lay Dying* when he distinguished between the eccentric Bundrens, bent upon the burial of Addie, and the townspeople who act as a kind of chorus of "respectability"; we find the same sharp division in "A Rose for Emily" and

[3] One of the interesting footnotes to the reception of *In Cold Blood* is the uncanny way literary history has a way of repeating itself. Walter Allen suggested the connection in his "London Letter" (*New York Times Book Review,* April 10, 1966): "It [*In Cold Blood*] reached us with the biggest fanfare of publicity that has accompanied any American book since 'By Love Possessed.'" *By Love Possessed* was faring remarkably well with the literary press in America until Dwight Macdonald took to dissecting Cozzens' style in the January 1958 *Commentary* and Irving Howe proceeded to close the lid on Cozzens' coffin in a now-famous review in the January 20, 1958 *New Republic;* Howe started out with his usual directness: "*By Love Possessed* is a mediocre and pretentious novel written by an experienced craftsman." Eight years later an inflatedly advertised *In Cold Blood* received a similar fate at the hands of *The New Republic,* whose reviewer, this time Stanley Kauffmann, took delight in deflating the Capote myth: "Are we so bankrupt, so avid for novelty that, merely because a famous writer produces an amplified magazine crime-feature, the result is automatically elevated to serious literature . . . ?" His proved not to be a lonely voice, as Macdonald's and Howe's were in 1958, and he was promptly joined by Sol Yurick (*The Nation,* February 7, 1966), Edward Weeks (*The Atlantic,* March 1966), William Phillips (*Commentary,* May 1966), Dwight Macdonald (*Esquire,* April 1966).

even, to a lesser extent, in *Light in August* and *Absalom, Absalom!*
Irony invariably accompanies the situation, as the author clearly
prefers the eccentrics to the *consensus gentium* in each instance. (If
Capote had more willingly taken sides in *In Cold Blood* the position
might have been the same.[4] Still one feels a sympathy for Perry Smith
which one does not feel for Alvin Dewey, even though Dewey's voice
of respectability is the last one heard—much like the final pronounce-
ment of the Greek chorus.)

The echoes of Carson McCullers and Eudora Welty have been
amply pointed out already.[5] And Capote has been grouped on several
occasions with Frederick Buechner and William Goyen.[6] A few words
might be said about the links with Flannery O'Connor and William
Styron. A story like "Jug of Silver" is very close to the tone of false
evangelism and prophecy which runs through the novels and stories of
Miss O'Connor. There is a clear connection, for example, between
Appleseed's claim, in the Capote story, that he was "born with a caul
on my head" and Enoch Emery's belief, in Flannery O'Connor's *Wise
Blood,* that he came into the world with "wise blood." Willie-Jay, in *In
Cold Blood* (whose name Capote admits he has invented), resembles
in many ways the "Bible Belt" preachers of Flannery O'Connor, both
in name (think of Onnie Jay Holy in *Wise Blood*), and in evangelical
manner. And Truman Capote is careful to identify the region about
which he is writing: "A hundred miles west and one would be out of
the 'Bible Belt,' that gospel-haunted strip of American territory in
which a man must, if only for business reasons, take his religion with
the straightest of faces, but in Finney County one is still within the
Bible Belt borders."[7] Despite the differences in geographical locale—
most of Capote's fiction occurs in the South or involves displaced

[4] Capote insisted in every interview on a Flaubertian detachment. Thus he
told George Plimpton: ". . . for the nonfiction-novel form to be entirely successful, the author should not appear in the work" (*New York Times Book Review,*
January 16, 1966, p. 38).

[5] See especially Mark Schorer, "McCullers and Capote: Basic Patterns," in
The Creative Present: Notes on Contemporary American Fiction, ed. Nona Balak-
ian and Charles Simmons (Garden City, N.Y.: Doubleday, 1963); see also Frank
Baldanza, "Plato in Dixie," *Georgia Review,* XII (Summer 1958). Paul Levine,
in his excellent "Truman Capote: The Revelation of the Broken Image," *Virginia
Quarterly Review,* XXXIV (Autumn 1958), points out the similarity between
Eudora Welty's "Why I Live at the P.O." and Capote's "My Side of the Matter."

[6] John W. Aldridge has a fine chapter, "Capote and Buechner: The Escape
into Otherness," in his *After The Lost Generation* (New York: Noonday Press,
1958). Chester E. Eisinger likens Capote to Goyen in his *Fiction of the Forties*
(Chicago: University of Chicago Press, 1963). Michel Mohrt places Capote and
Goyen in a similar literary climate in his *Nouveau Roman Américain* (Paris:
Gallimard, 1955). Finally, Ihab Hassan's *Radical Innocence* (Princeton, N.J.:
Princeton University Press, 1961) is indispensable in this area.

[7] *In Cold Blood* (New York: New American Library, 1967), p. 46. All
references will be to this edition.

Southerners living in New York City—the Kansas Capote writes about
is not significantly different from Flannery O'Connor country. Another
O'Connor reminder in *In Cold Blood* is when we are told (p. 212) that
Perry Smith's sister Fern changed her name to Joy when she turned
fourteen: several of Miss O'Connor's characters undergo name
changes, including Joy with the Ph.D. ("Good Country People") who
perversely changes her name to Hulga.

It should be made clear before we continue that the connections
which involve *In Cold Blood* are largely fortuitous. Truman Capote
was very insistent in his *New York Times* interview with George
Plimpton on his "factual accuracy" and on his refusal to "give way to
minor distortions." Despite the convincing claims of unreliability put
forth by Phillip K. Tompkins in his "In Cold Fact" (*Esquire,* June
1966), we must still believe in the essential authenticity and integrity
of Capote's account. Yet even a "reporter"—especially one of Capote's
temperament—will usually compromise his "reportorial distance" in
favor of elements borrowed from his own reading and culture. Hence
Faulkner and Flannery O'Connor have found their way through the
back door of *In Cold Blood.*

The connections between Styron and Capote are less exact than
those we have been looking at. They have in common a sense of the
inviolability of style, and their metaphors have a way of straining
towards eloquence. One has a Gallic sense of *de trop* when faced with
their more extended imagery. Thus a sentence of Styron like "In the
morbid, comfortless light they were like classical Greek masks, made
of chrome or tin, reflecting an almost theatrical disharmony"[8] could
easily have been written by Capote. On the very first page of *In Cold
Blood* he speaks of "a white cluster of grain elevators rising as gracefully as Greek temples." Styron's image, in reference to marines on a
forced march, seems as inappropriate, at first glance, as Capote's view
of the western Kansas countryside; but the suggestive power of the
figures has a way of dilating the experience into myth.

We notice from various interviews with Styron and Capote that
they have marked similarities in reading tastes and habits. Their sense
of craft, for example, makes *Madame Bovary* an essential book. Thus
Styron writes in his *Paris Review* interview: "*Madame Bovary* is one of
the few novels that moves me in every way, not only in its style, but in
its total communicability, like the effect of good poetry" (*Writers at
Work,* p. 274). Capote is less poetical on the subject; he told Jeanine
Delpech, ". . . je relis tous les ans *Madame Bovary.*" (*Nouvelles Lit-
téraires,* April 12, 1962, p. 10).

It should be no surprise that these *bovaryistes* are well received in
France. Almost all of their work is available in French translation.
Capote has had the benefit (like Styron with *Set This House on Fire*)
of M. E. Coindreau's always sensitive renderings of his prose. Capote

8 *The Long March* (New York: Random House, 1952), p. 29.

joins Faulkner, Flannery O'Connor, and other American novelists who have profited from Coindreau's inspired translations and commentary.

We can then begin to speak of a Franco-American Capote in a double sense. His reputation is at least as assured in France as it is in America, and he has himself been responsive to the French tradition in the novel from Flaubert on. In fact, it seems to me that any discussion of his work from *Other Voices, Other Rooms* through *In Cold Blood* would profit from a consideration of the French novel from Alain-Fournier's *Le Grand Meaulnes* (1913) through the *nouveau roman*. This tradition in French fiction should serve as an apt metaphor for Capote's entire career. The Italian novelist Alberto Moravia[9] and the French critic and translator Michel Mohrt[10] have already suggested a kinship between Alain-Fournier's novel and the early Capote. Fournier and Capote both partake of a Proustian magic-lantern-of-childhood atmosphere. (Jeanine Delpech quotes Capote as saying "je plonge voluptueusement dans Proust" and speaks of "le fantôme de Proust" hovering over him.)

Le Grand Meaulnes and *Other Voices* are examples of a genre which Fournier's close friend and brother-in-law, Jacques Rivière, has christened *roman d'aventure*. Both novels involve elaborate itineraries into the unknown. Augustin Meaulnes, Fournier's seventeen-year-old hero, has spent a miraculous evening at a palatial manor in the company of a certain Yvonne de Galais. He subsequently devotes all his attentions to recapturing this experience, but in spite of his un-covering of most of the mystery he never manages to recreate the "moment of being" he has irreparably lost. Meaulnes asks the question of the narrator, Seurel, "But how could a man, who had once leapt at one bound into Paradise, get used to living like everybody else?" He says a page later: "I was at the height of what stands for perfection and pure motive in anyone's heart, a height I shall never reach again."[11] There is only a thin line separating the world of Sainte-Agathe School, which offers the hero a here-and-now *point de repère*, and the world of Meaulnes' "Lost Land."

Joel Knox of *Other Voices, Other Rooms* is a somewhat younger and more effeminate Augustin Meaulnes. His "Lost Land" is Skully's Landing. He voyages there to find his father, but finds instead the wreck of a man whose only occupation is bouncing red tennis balls down the stairs. Like Meaulnes, Joel uncovers the mystery of his "Lost Land" but must settle for a reality in every way inferior to his

[9] "Two American Writers," *Sewanee Review*, LXVIII (Summer 1960), pp. 480–481.

[10] *Le Nouveau Roman Américain* (Paris: Gallimard, 1955), pp. 232–233. All references will be to this edition.

[11] *The Wanderer*, tr. from the French *Le Grand Meaulnes* by Françoise Delisle (New York: New Directions, 1928), pp. 211, 212.

dream. Joel has a caricatured Yvonne de Galais in the tomboy Idabel Thompkins—whom he finally loses to the dwarf Miss Wisteria. Consumed finally by "a sleepwalker's pattern of jigsaw incidents," Joel must settle for the transvestite Cousin Randolph and accept his world and "the zero of his nothingness" (a phrase from *Other Voices* which could easily have been written by Samuel Beckett or Roland Barthes). Joel's *roman d'aventure* ends on the same note of resigned despair as Augustin Meaulnes'.

Other Voices, Other Rooms must have seemed very old-fashioned when it appeared in 1948, especially in the manner of its telling. Many of the experiments with point of view and displacement of chronology had already been tried and Capote seems to have completely ignored them. He stays with the standard omniscient author of nineteenth-century fiction and tells a story which naively conforms to clock time. *Other Voices, Other Rooms* could easily have been published in 1913 (the year of *Le Grand Meaulnes*), but even then it would have been declared old-fashioned next to Proust's *Du côté de chez Swann* which appeared the same year.

Capote's next novel, *The Grass Harp* (1951), shows no advance in technique. There is, however, an important change in narrative: the story is told by one of the active participants, Collin Fenwick, another of Capote's adolescents. His is also a *roman d'aventure* which wavers uncomfortably between reality and the dreamworld. The temporary inhabitants of the tree house defy reality in much the same way that Joel Knox and Augustin Meaulnes did. The symbolism is not really so different: Collin and his companions look to the tree house as Joel did the Cloud Hotel and Meaulnes the lost manor house. The first-person telling, however, gives *The Grass Harp* an immediacy and colloquial nearness which *Other Voices* and *Le Grand Meaulnes* do not have.

Capote's third novel, *Breakfast at Tiffany's* (1958), is perhaps his most Jamesian work. The narrator, again a participant in the story although this time more a detached onlooker, has early counterparts in James's garrulous "posts of observation" and Fitzgerald's Nick Carraway. Once more we are faced with the old-fashioned story-teller in Capote, this time with some mild tampering with chronology—at least to the extent that we first hear of Holly Golightly, the main character, at a period later than the events of the narrative. *Breakfast at Tiffany's* has virtually nothing of the *roman d'aventure* of the two earlier novels but has much of the urban chic of a later tradition of French fiction which would include the Paris-centered novels of Gide (especially *Les Faux-Monnayeurs*), Roger Martin du Gard, Georges Duhamel, and perhaps Jean Cocteau. Françoise Sagan is probably at the end of this line and indeed Holly Golightly could easily be a Sagan heroine. The French have always been fond of the "up from the provinces" motif from *Le Rouge et le noir* on; and Capote has offered us, in *Breakfast at Tiffany's*, a female counterpart of Julien Sorel, Frédéric Moreau, and others, in the sense that Holly Golightly has confronted the urban scene with a vengeance and turned her back on her own provincial and backwoods origins. She has mastered the vocabulary of her new setting, with its many gallicisms. Yet there is something authentic about her language (which is the reverse of what René Etiemble has recently called *franglais*) and her modish behavior; this quality is captured in a remark of one of the other characters: "She isn't a phony because she's a *real* phony."

The short stories which Capote has been turning out since the early 1940's are thematically very close to the novels. The narrative devices are traditional. Most of them resemble in compactness and tightness of style the stories of Flannery O'Connor, Eudora Welty, and Katherine Anne Porter. The settings, as in the novels, are Southern or involve displaced persons living in New York City—all part of that diaspora which has experienced the bitter-sweet taste of exile. There is as much in the stories of what Irving Malin has aptly called "new American gothic" as in the novels. Chance meetings in a train ("A Tree of Night"), at a cemetery ("Among the Paths to Eden"), in a painting gallery ("The Headless Hawk"), in a neighborhood moviehouse ("Miriam") produce dire psychological consequences for the unsuspecting and innocent. The invasion of experience upon innocence (as in James's *Turn of the Screw*) is one of the central themes of the stories—with the ironical twist that children are often the experienced, adults the innocent.

These stories may have no precise equivalents in France, the way the novels clearly do. Capote's intermittent attempts at reportage, however, fit the French tradition I have been talking about. Most French novelists regard it as their solemn obligation to contribute to the day-to-day workings of the world by sounding a journalistic note. It is not surprising to pick up an issue of *Le Figaro* or *Le Monde* or any of the French weeklies and monthlies and find an editorial by an established writer. Sartre, for example, has his own journalistic and critical voice listened to regularly and attentively in the pages of *Les Temps Modernes*. Camus used the clandestine newspaper *Combat* for the same editorial purposes. There is no precise counterpart now in this country. In fact, most writers shy away from this kind of commitment. Capote is one of the rare American authors who believes in the value of reportage and remains convinced of its artistic possibilities.

The New Yorker has offered him the same literary haven as Sartre finds in *Les Temps Modernes*. He published his Marlon Brando "profile" ("The Duke in His Domain") and *The Muses Are Heard* in its pages. Michel Mohrt, who has elsewhere in *Le Nouveau Roman Américain* written perceptively about Capote, says about *The New Yorker*: "Ils se contentent d'en souligner les ridicules" (p. 255). Capote's portraits of Mrs. Ira Gershwin, Leonard Lyons, and the Ira Wolferts in *The Muses Are Heard* and the sustained "profile" of

Brando ("just a young man sitting on a pile of candy") offer a system-
atic underplaying, in a very low key, of emotional frailty. Capote
follows the formula for the "nonfiction novel," which he suggested to
George Plimpton, that "the author should not appear in the work."
Thus the Brando portrait, particularly, reminds one of the method of
another of *The New Yorker's* faithful, Lillian Ross; we are especially
reminded of her famous Hemingway "profile" with its subtle ambiguities. Capote and Lillian Ross have virtually invented in the pages of
The New Yorker a new "school" of reportage built on a sensitive ear
for the incongruous and depending on the correct measure of attentive
eavesdropping.

The other kind of reporting Capote has done has acknowledged
his "sense of place" (an expression Frederick J. Hoffman has accu-
rately used in reference to recent Southern writing).[12] Most of his
pieces in this genre, which read like tone poems, have been collected in
Local Color (1950). They are brief sketches of places like Hollywood,
Brooklyn, New Orleans, Haiti, and Tangier. The manner is not far
from the Baudelaire of *Les Petits poèmes en prose*. Mark Schorer's
expression "people in places" (in his introduction to the Modern
Library *Selected Writings of Truman Capote*) explains how Capote's
descriptions of landscapes are continually crowded by his "profiles" of
anonymous people.

Capote has been mixing his reportage with his fiction through
most of his career. Many of the reviewers noticed the two converging
in *In Cold Blood*. Jack Kroll, writing in the January 24, 1966, *Newsweek*, saw something timely in the method: "In its refusal to analyze,
to make judgments, 'In Cold Blood' is supercontemporary. This is the
attitude of the new international avant-garde—of the French 'anti-
novelists' who with bland obsessiveness describe only the surface of
reality." (p. 60). Indeed the *nouveau roman* has many techniques in
common with *In Cold Blood*. Just as *Other Voices, Other Rooms* had
an uncanny resemblance to *Le Grand Meaulnes* and *Breakfast at
Tiffany's* had much in common with the French city novel written
between the two world wars, so does Capote's book of 1966 seem more
than passingly related to the post-war novels of Alain Robbe-Grillet,
Nathalie Sarraute, Michel Butor, and Samuel Beckett.

The first point of comparison is the use of the mock-detective
motif. Sartre has already defined this genre, in his famous preface to
Nathalie Sarraute's *Portrait d'un inconnu*, as "an anti-novel that reads
like a detective story." He further elaborated on this by saying; ". . . it
is a parody on the novel of 'quest' into which the author has introduced a sort of impassioned amateur detective who becomes fascinated . . . by virtue of a sort of thought transference, without ever

[12] See his "The Sense of Place," in *South: Modern Southern Literature in Its
Cultural Setting*, ed. Louis D. Rubin, Jr. and Robert D. Jacobs (Garden City,
N.Y.: Doubleday, 1961).

knowing very well either what he is after or what they are." Thus we find Robbe-Grillet's Wallas (*Les Gommes*) and Mathias (*Le Voyeur*) turning into implausible murderers. Nathalie Sarraute's "detectives" pursue clueless paths in her novels, and the accustomed detective motif always falls gracefully to pieces. The most revealing instance of all is probably Michel Butor's *L'Emploi du temps* in which the protagonist becomes obsessed with a murder novel he has just read about the English city which he has been inhabiting for a year. He manages to piece together an elaborate crime story, based ingeniously but inaccurately on details from the murder novel and incidents from his own experience. But his theories prove as ineffectual as those of Sarraute's heroes. Each of Beckett's novels is in one way or another "a parody on the novel of 'quest' " and his "detectives" always fail to solve crimes which have not been committed.

Even though *In Cold Blood* bears as its subtitle "A True Account of a Multiple Murder and Its Consequences," it is not automatically exempt from Sartre's fictional category. There are a variety of false leads and clueless paths exploited by Capote with particular relish. Thus he shows a peculiar interest in a certain Jonathan Daniel Adrian who turns out to have nothing to do with the Clutter murders; he dotes on Adrian more as a novelist than as a reporter of a crime would do. Capote goes out of his way to pursue a jagged course rather than the rectilinear one of a Georges Simenon or an Agatha Christie (both of whose serious detective novels have been linked to the mock-detective writings of the *nouveau roman*).

The method of uncovering the murderers in *In Cold Blood* also smacks of the mock-detective. Although Capote seems to have enormous respect for Alvin Dewey and his men, he is still not above suggesting that their methods were unavailing in capturing Smith and Hickock; he gives them credit for a variety of false leads and repeated, if honest, blunders. If Floyd Wells, an inmate of the Kansas State Penitentiary, had not revealed what he knew, the solving of the murder might have been delayed indefinitely. This is perfect *nouveau roman*: the detective is the last one to solve the crime and needs the help of a criminal in doing so.

The question of the imaginary Clutter safe with the imaginary money is vintage mock-detective. This touch is worthy of the "new novelists" who generally use the criminal investigation as a flimsy substitute for plot and action.

But probably nothing is quite so revealing as Capote's portrait of Perry Smith. He is clearly not the stock figure of crime fiction—Dick Hickock is closer to that. Several reviewers have even pointed out Perry's proximity to the *poète maudit*, almost as if Capote reinvented him to make him the implausible murderer that he is. Certain things about him, as Jack Kroll remarked in *Newsweek*, "fit uncannily into the pattern of Capote's previous fiction." Thus his collection of souvenirs

and trinkets reminds us of Joel Knox's obsession "to keep and catalogue trifles." Perry's dream of "the yellow bird, huge and parrot-
faced" is not unlike the bluejay Joel sees, after he arrives at the
Landing, which seems almost to be "a curious fragment of his dream."
Perry's urgency about correcting people's grammar also has an echo in
Joel: ". . . he took odd pleasure in bringing to attention a slip of
grammar on anyone's part."[13] Perry's devotion to his guitar reminds us
of Tico Feo in Capote's short story "A Diamond Guitar."

All of these concerns of Perry Smith, beyond recalling earlier
Capote works, succeed in making him an unlikely candidate for
murder and eventual hanging, at least in the conventional detective-
story sense. Although Capote is giving us a "true account" in *In Cold
Blood,* he is still using his material in a very special way, in a way—as
I suggested—to recall the devices of the *nouveau roman.* Just as
Robbe-Grillet, Butor, Nathalie Sarraute, and Beckett are preoccupied
with certain objects which keep recurring in their fiction, so does
Capote keep reintroducing certain things. The Chinese elms which line
the Clutters' driveway is such an example. The references to snow
perhaps offer an even more poignant example. We are told, periodi-
cally, through the first three sections of *In Cold Blood* that the snow
was late in coming that year to Kansas. The suggestion is that it was
awaiting the capture of the criminals for, Capote tells us, it began to
fall almost immediately following the arraignment of Smith and
Hickock. The author dramatically saves this mention until the final
words of Part 3: ". . . the miraculous autumn departed too; the year's
first snow began to fall" (p. 280). Snow is everywhere in Capote's
work, as most of his critics have already reminded us; a good example
would be *Other Voices,* in which Zoo flees north to Washington, D.C.,
to find it; another is the lyrics to the song "I Never Has Seen Snow"
which Capote wrote for the Broadway musical version of *House of
Flowers* (based on one of his short stories).

The references to the Chinese elms and snow in *In Cold Blood*
serve much the same purpose as the repeated references to the
centipede (*La Jalousie*), the figure eight (*Le Voyeur*), the eraser (*Les
Gommes*) in Robbe-Grillet. They serve as almost musical reminders
and help to enrich the texture of the prose. Like Robbe-Grillet, Capote
has worked in art forms other than literature. His cinematic experiences, for example, are quite like Robbe-Grillet's, although his work on
Beat the Devil and *The Innocents* is scarcely comparable to Robbe-
Grillet's vitally experimental *L'Année dernière à Marienbad* and *L'Immortelle.* Robbe-Grillet called his films *ciné-romans,* and indeed we are
supposed to get a sense of the convergence of cinema and novel when
we view them. *Marienbad* and *L'Immortelle* are clearly expansions on
his career as a novelist and use many of the same devices. We shall

[13] *Other Voices, Other Rooms* (New York: New American Library, 1960),
pp. 27, 26, 9.

recall now how Stanley Kauffmann and Dwight Macdonald found unmistakable cinematic signs in *In Cold Blood*. One has a strong sense of unreeling film as one reads the book; it seems in many ways the literary equivalent of montage just as so many of Robbe-Grillet's novels do.

Robbe-Grillet has spoken out, on several occasions, for the need of a new sense of space in fiction. He has dwelt on surface effects in his own novels and has come out strongly in an early essay for ". . . the complete rejection of the old myths of *profondeur*, or depth of meaning in objects." He has been intent on destroying the image of the novel as a "time-art" and reestablishing it spatially.[14] Capote does not go as far as Robbe-Grillet, but he does seem interested in exploiting the reality of surfaces and fragmenting time in *In Cold Blood*. Some of the breathlessness of the book is doubtless due to Capote's concern with juxtaposing the parts of his narrative to give the illusion of simultaneity. Thus we have the sense of many things going on at the same time, in a kind of continuing present. The Clutter murder hovers over the narrative just as vividly and immediately at the time of Hickock and Smith's execution in April 1965 as it did in November 1959. *In Cold Blood* seems to be without a past tense, as do most of the novels of Robbe-Grillet and Butor.

One of Capote's procedures for gaining this effect is in his skilled manipulation of point of view. He tries to present the events through as many eyes as possible. He sets up, as James said in his Preface to *The Wings of the Dove*, "successive centres" who manipulate the point of view. Capote allows us to see Hickock and Smith (again quoting from James's Preface) "through the successive windows of other people's interest." Thus the final point of view of *In Cold Blood* is that of Alvin Dewey, who wanders through the cemetery which houses the graves of the Clutters. Capote has turned over the final pages of his book to Dewey because he is probably in the best position to cast the final symbolical note. The scene described is not unlike that which ends Turgenev's *Fathers and Sons* (Capote lists Turgenev among his "enthusiasms that remain constant" in his *Paris Review* interview) when the old parents, in a most pastoral and elegiac sequence, visit the grave of their nihilist son, Bazarov. The alliterative final words of *In Cold Blood* permanently freeze the experience: ". . . the whisper of wind voices in the wind-bent wheat." (There are reminders also of Joyce's "The Dead" in this final scene and especially in its alliterative ending.)

The view of Capote which I have expressed here—partly using as

---

[14] The best book on Robbe-Grillet is Bruce Morrissette's *Les Romans de Robbe-Grillet* (Paris: Les Editions de Minuit, 1963). See also his very useful booklet, *Alain Robbe-Grillet* (1965), in the Columbia Essays on Modern Writers. I am personally indebted to Professor Morrissette for certain ideas in this essay connecting Truman Capote with Alain Robbe-Grillet.

a metaphor the French convention in the novel from *Le Grand Meaulnes* through the *nouveau roman*—is of a writer who is very tradition-bound. His claim to having invented a new literary form, "the nonfiction novel," matters less than what he has accomplished in the last twenty years when he has consistently turned base metal into literature. He has brought the various art forms together harmoniously in his own work, using some of the devices of cinema, photography, and reportage to great advantage. His own writing gently holds up the mirror to what is being accomplished artistically around him. Capote likes to think of himself as being in advance of his contemporaries; it is probably more accurate to say that he is wonderfully in step with them.

Capote's Imagery

ROBERT K. MORRIS

ONCE SET OUT ON THE WAY TO FAME, EVEN THE SO-CALLED "SERIOUS" writer will find it a "broad and ample road, whose dust is gold." A little under twenty years ago, a slim volume called *Other Voices, Other Rooms* marked the first stage in a young Southerner's trek to success. Fame, of course, has a mythical quality all its own, which explains why the myth of Truman Capote seemed more substantial than the fact of his writing. While novelists like Wright Morris and John Hawkes might languish in academia, Capote languished gracefully, melancholically (but most intensely) on rococo settees, peering out from dust jackets at mesmerized readers. Somehow, by some magic, he had materialized the *Zeitgeist*, which is the way one becomes famous.

Magic, plus a brain trust. Ironically, Capote, who in his writing has dwelled continually on the victimization of the innocent, himself became the happy victim of Madison Avenue, press agents, book clubs, best-seller lists, Broadway, and Hollywood. He has had luck, an inordinate amount of it. He has seen the airy *Grass Harp* and *House of Flowers* blown into spectaculars for the theater, seen the shapely Holly Golightly emerge from a shapeless chrysalid novella and turn into the splendid butterfly Audrey Hepburn, Hollywood box-office and almost a White Goddess on the Great White Way. Without a jot of envy, but clearly with some dismay, we saw it, too: saw his success grow wilder, and his reputation zoom disproportionately; saw what began as a trek become a lark, and the gold come down not as dust, but as nuggets.

But to be sure, Capote stirred up the dust to begin with, for he is a writer of prodigious talent, fame notwithstanding. Contemporaries more prolific, more involved, more intellectual or poetic, funnier, have rarely sounded so deeply the darker reaches of the heart, or soared to the soul's brighter heights. More than any other contemporary, Capote charts the sensitive shiftings between the conscious and subconscious, reveals that our natures are neither altogether black nor white but both—often simultaneously both. More than any other contemporary, he gives us characters who are cold, yet who burn within, seared by their own spiritual frigidity. More than any other contemporary, he has been able to transmute the screaming horror of the nightmare into the "strange" (a favorite word of his) quiet horror of reality. This kind of ability is worth, perhaps, many nuggets. Certainly, *In Cold Blood,* his biggest seller to date, reflects all these aspects of his talent. It is a book that many contemporaries might have written, but that logically, artistically, only Truman Capote could have.

As of now, *In Cold Blood* marks the apex of Capote's career, fulfilling, in a rather ironic way, a recent critical prophecy:

Given our burden of bitter and inexhaustible illusions, our hopeless nostalgias and secret regressions, it is no wonder that romancers of Capote's gifts should speak keenly to our condition. But the growth of his vision and the evolution of his more dramatic style also promise, without foregoing the advantages of romance, to discover a form commensurate with the maturity to which we have so long aspired. Ihab Hassan, *Radical Innocence: Studies in the Contemporary American Novel* (Princeton, 1961), p. 258.

Like all sound, sympathetic critics, Hassan has anticipated Capote's writing a quintessential work which would be both distinctive and important. And he has written one. But the plea for "form" could scarcely have anticipated the "non-fiction novel" (a conceit which, if not a shallow joke, is an excruciatingly profound paradox), nor could the quest for "maturity" (the author's, his characters', ours!) have anticipated Perry Smith and Richard Hickock's insanely dispassionate murder of the Clutters and their subsequent ten thousand mile hegira.

Yet *In Cold Blood* seems to me to be the perfect metaphor for Capote's work to date. He has not really made it new, but he has made the old better. In the remoteness of Holcomb, Kansas, the simple lives of the Clutters, the act of terror, he has found theme and object for expressing the things he can express best: the strange isolation of human beings who become victims of an impersonal, often fearful agency. And in Perry Smith he has found a person at once filled with the dark confusion of a madman and with the weakness and solitary despair of a child. Like all Capote's darker works, *In Cold Blood* is an elegy for the death of innocence, with the exception that here what prompts evil is innocence itself.

Perry Smith is at the center of *In Cold Blood,* the empathetic concern for his madness almost obscuring, in a way indefensible and unpalatable to some, the enormity of his crime. He is less the subject of a grim biography than the protagonist of a psychological thriller, a Raskolnikov *manqué,* lacking drive and philosophic motivation, but equally as haunted and demoniac. He is less the mere result of the author's "own observations . . . official records . . . or interviews with persons" than a composite of artistic pruning, sifting, pressing, molding: at no point a journalist's re-creation, everywhere a novelist's.

In Cold Blood has a unity all its own, but it is also importantly continuous with Capote's earlier fiction. Smith, for example, is bound to the Capote gallery as securely as the family who became his victims, and as he himself is at the end. Such links may not be immediately discernible, for a Capote protagonist does not necessarily evolve directly from his predecessor. (As, say, Mann's Adrian Leverkühn is the direct heir of Hans Castorp, who succeeds from Tonio Kroeger, the sequel to Hanno Buddenbrook.) Rather, informed by Capote's steady sensibility, his characters share similar patterns of behavior, their acts differing perceptibly in kind but carried on with a like intensity. Few would admit that Joel Knox, Collin Fenwick, Holly Golightly, or even Perry Smith are complex characters, *per se;* they may be, for that matter, transparent. But they gain a profundity and urgency from their situation and the settings into which they are thrust. And this, perhaps, is the better place to start.

Setting is a novelistic exigency, but with Capote it is image as well. Just as surely as there exists a Graham Greeneland of spiritual vacillation between good and evil, or a Faulknerian universe of guilt and expiation, or a Genet underworld of thieves and "queens," there is a Capote ethos of startling originality. Whether it be the emptiness and difficulty of the road leading to Skully's Landing, the darkness of River Woods, the "gloom" of "Fred's" studio apartment, the mystery of Holly's Africa, or the town of Holcomb, Kansas, pinpointed among the singing wheat or battered by the cruel wind, it is still the "lonesome area" of "out there," where people are isolated, muted, rarely able to vent their cry of loneliness or anger or impotence or fear, and perhaps never heard when they do.

For all his subtlety of language and deftness, Capote appears self-conscious in placing the initial metaphors of loneliness and isolation before the reader. Here are selections from the openings of the four principal novels.[1] (In all cases italics are mine.) From *Other Voices, Other Rooms:*

---

[1] I have not thought it worthwhile to argue in this particular essay the pros and cons of the "non-fiction novel" but have taken the easy way out and assumed that a novel is a novel, whether it be fiction or non-fiction. In any event, the effects Capote gains in his fiction novels are present in the non-fiction one. Also,

It's a rough trip (to Noon City) no matter how you come, for these wash-board roads will loosen up even brandnew cars pretty fast and hitchhikers always find the going bad. Also, *this is lonesome country;* and here in the *swamplike hollows* where tiger lilies bloom the size of a man's head, there are *luminous green logs that shine under the dark marsh water like drowned corpses;* often *the only movement on the landscape* is winter smoke winding out the chimney of *some sorry-looking farmhouse,* or a wing-stiffened bird, silent and arrow-eyed, circling over the *black deserted pinewoods.*

From *The Grass Harp:*

If on leaving town you take the church road you soon will pass *a glaring hill of bonewhite slabs and brown burnt flowers:* this is the Baptist cemetery. . . . Below the hill grows a field of high Indian grass that changes color with the seasons: go see it in the fall, late September, when it has gone red as sunset, when *scarlet shadows like firelight* breeze over it and the autumn winds strum on its dry leaves sighing human music, a harp of voices.

From *Breakfast at Tiffany's:*

It was one room crowded with attic furniture, a sofa and fat chairs up-holstered in that *itchy, particular red velvet* that one associates with hot days on a train. *The walls were stucco, and a color rather like tobacco-spit.* Everywhere, in the bathroom too, there were prints of *Roman ruins* freckled brown with age. The *single window* looked out on a fire escape.

And from *In Cold Blood:*

The village of Holcomb stands on the high wheat plains of western Kansas, *a lonesome area that other Kansans call "out there. . . ."* After rain, or when snowfalls thaw, the streets, unnamed, unshaded, unpaved, turn from the thickest dust into the direst mud. At one end of the town stands *a stark old stucco structure,* the roof of which supports an electric sign—DANCE—but the dancing has ceased and *the advertisement has been dark for several years.*

The formality by which Capote establishes imagery within each paragraph might be almost formulaic. Immediacy, gained through the simple present—or, barely an exception, through the passive voice in the simple past—provokes a sense of uneasiness, anticipation, or ap-prehension. Further, a stasis, evoked by select images, suggests silent suspension in space and time: the winding smoke and circling bird, the play of shadows, the picture of the ruins, the obsolete sign. The "mood" is heightened by Capote's disturbing and "poetic" use of color

---

I have had, because of space limitations, to pass over the excellent openings of such stories as "A Tree of Night" and "The Headless Hawk." Both stories are remarkable for many things, but they are particularly relevant as examples of Capote's formulaic openings.

that makes the scene psychologically rather than physically vivid and keys it to the feelings of isolation implied by the narrator or his persona. What Capote is doing throughout, of course, is overlaying realistic setting with surrealistic properties that foreshadow his subsequent dream sequences.

All this is perhaps obvious. Capote's images deservedly have a life all their own, leaping from his prose with unashamed nakedness. They are, as Irving Malin points out in New American Gothic,[2] "'objective correlatives' of the psyche." But they have an added (I hesitate to say more important) function when subsumed in the function of these opening paragraphs themselves, no mere pillows for imagistic padding.

What, in effect, do they do? Objectively, they are of a piece, the movement in each being congruent. At the opening there is a vista (or expanse) narrowing in the course of commentary to a point of focus, which then widens out toward a new vista. Each paragraph describes an hourglass shape. Subjectively, what one sees here depends, of course, on what one believes Capote is about. Even a common denominator can prove an uncommon one given the chance.

Capote is about several things. The image (or images) he isolates at the beginning of a novel takes on, after the necessary transformation, a broader structural, even crucial significance by the end. Thus the "swamplike hollows" in Other Voices, Other Rooms are twice recalled during Joel's quest for the Cloud Hotel: once when he and Idabel fail at finding it, again when he and Randolph succeed. Collin Fenwick's own quest for manhood terminates at the Baptist cemetery where the past has become entombed but still remains viable, soughing its ghostly music across the strings of "the grass harp." "Fred's" window, the perfect touch of anonymity, becomes by the last page of Breakfast at Tiffany's the warm, wide frame for Holly's abandoned cat who, like Holly or "Fred" himself, no longer anonymous, has "arrived somewhere he belonged." And, in its own grim way, the "stark old stucco structure" of In Cold Blood anticipates the "bleakly lighted cavern cluttered with lumber and other debris," the dance sign the arrival of Hickock and Smith, who will do their jig of death on the gallows.

The final point to be made about the openings relates to the books as a whole, and here it becomes necessary to return to one image by way of going on to another. The hourglass shape of Capote's paragraphs, showing novelistic, even slick novelistic control, is not decorative only. It is metaphysical. For while his characters all begin with great expectations of finding something—Joel, a father; Collin, love; "Fred," success as a writer; Holly the "correlative" for her primal yearnings (does she become, perhaps, another Henderson or Ayesha!);

[2] Carbondale: Southern Illinois University Press, 1962.

Perry and Hickock a southern paradise—they experience a partial or total sense of entrapment before realizing their expectations. At a point, Capote traps them in the narrow neck of the glass. The sand sifting about them, they are caught (like Vincent in "The Headless Hawk") in a "paralysis of time and identity"; Joel in the green, ghostly life of the swamp near Skully's Landing; "Fred" in his room; Collin in atavistic uncertainty (is he realist or idealist?); Hickock and Perry on the endless road they travel. Capote traps his characters, but he does not drive them into cul-de-sacs. They can view, from under their "cone of glass," the ways out: but not everyone does, or can, break away to take them.

Some, of course, do break away. Escape (not as evasion, but as a positive thing) stamps Capote's so-called "daylight" works, while paralysis marks his "nocturnal" ones. Looking at the central "daylight" paragraphs under discussion, one can see even here that "Fred" does "escape" through the open window, and Collin northward over the wheat field. But in the "nocturnal" series, Joel, though the outcome remains ambiguous, is drawn toward the house by the beckoning fair one, the eonistic Randolph; and Perry and Hickock live the complete symbols of entrapment: the "corner," the gallows, and, ultimately, the tomb.

I have worried these four paragraphs at some length not to be merely exhausting or ingenious, but to emphasize the symbiosis between the "nocturnal" and "daylight" novels, and to persuade the reader that a Capote image—coming from either of the two styles—may function structurally as well as thematically. Since a writer can hardly escape being influenced by himself, this may not be saying much at all. But in one respect such an observation may shed some new light on *In Cold Blood*, depriving it, to be sure, of its uniqueness as a (perhaps!) prototypical genre, but advancing it considerably otherwise.

Fictionally, of course. The lean writing in *In Cold Blood*, the flat narratorial style, might suggest that Capote has given over the tricks of the novelist and kept to the trade only. But, on the contrary, the technique is all there; it is simply less obtrusive. Just as the language has become sparer, just as the narration has become less poetically oblique, so the imagery has become less obsessive. For "obsessive" is the word defining Capote's earlier use of images: those that recur with such alarming frequency that they can no longer be called *leitmotivs*. They are, even in so professional and conscientious a writer as Capote, "tics." Words like "mirror," "green," "dark," "night," "eyes," "hands," often seem brought in for no other reason but romance with favorites. *In Cold Blood* eschews the gratuitous. Here, the images have been refined, worked into the structure with a telling effect. They are Capote's handmaidens, but no longer his slaves. But to backtrack for a moment.

The "window" is one such substantial image that has played an important yet generally unobtrusive part in Capote's work. Unobtrusive, that is, compared to its counterpart, the "mirror," obsessive with Capote since Randolph's monologue in *Other Voices, Other Rooms:*

They can romanticize us so, mirrors, and that is their secret: what a subtle torture it would be to destroy all the mirrors in the world: where then could we look for reassurance of our identities? I tell you, my dear, Narcissus was no egoist . . . he was merely another of us who, in our unshatterable isolation, recognized, on seeing his reflection, the one beautiful comrade, the only inseparable love . . . poor Narcissus, possibly the only human who was ever honest on this point.

The "mirror" image calls attention to itself, screamingly. We are to guard against mirrors from now on, knowing they will get equated, in one way or another, with loneliness, alienation, inversion (sexual and social), *amour-propre,* the artist. Capote is keying us in to ultimate profundities, but often at the expense of symbolic labor.

With the continuing motif of the "window" he labors less, perhaps because it is free of mythic associations, perhaps because it makes a direct appeal to the human predicament, perhaps because it is a more rational—as opposed to romantic—image. Windows are one's outlook on the immediate world, the mediary between the extroversion of free, open spaces and the introversion of the mirror, offering escape for those who are trapped, penetration for those excluded, the possibility of distance for those living in the frustration of proximity.[3]

Joel Harrison Knox experiences the force of all three possibilities. At Skully's Landing the window at first represents Joel's longing (a sick desire, really), to project his imagination into the "far-away room"—the "other" room, of course—where, his soul no longer dark, his heart no longer confused, love might bid him welcome. Later, in his father's eyes, which, like "windows in summer, were seldom shut," he penetrates the mystery of death. Only Idabel's sunglasses, like Dr. Miracle's spectacles in *The Tales of Hoffmann,* can momentarily suspend the reality; but then they are shattered in Joel's abortive scuffle for sexual supremacy. But most significant, perhaps, is the allusion to the game of "Blackmail" Joel had played in New Orleans. The puerile fascination of those peeping-tom days, during which he "would ap-

---

[3] Elizabeth Bowen, in her excellent novel of initiation, *Death of the Heart,* has the following interesting corollary: "[Anna] knew how foolish a person looking out of a window appears from the outside of a house—as though waiting for something that does not happen, as though wanting something from the outside world. A face at a window for no reason is a face that should have a thumb in its mouth: there is something only-childish about it. Or, if the face is not foolish it is threatening—blotted white by the darkness inside the room it suggests a malignant indoor power." A trifle lower-keyed than Capote but relevant nonetheless!

proach a strange house and peer invisibly through its windows" into a kaleidoscope of anonymous lives, yields to the ambiguous commitment at the end of the novel. Drawn in a kind of tropistic trance to Randolph's window, he goes to encounter the glory or shame of a new-found manhood.

There is less ambiguity in a story like "Jug of Silver," where the image is now transmuted into a wine jug ("crammed to the brim with nickels and dimes that shone dully through the thick glass") which becomes an object of quest for the ageless, patient, prescient Apple-seed, intent upon beautifying his toothless sister. In a fascinating way it is central to *Breakfast at Tiffany's* (as we have seen); but perhaps the most touching and sensitive use of the image occurs in another "daylight" work, *The Grass Harp*. Here, in the tree-house knowing no physical barriers, yet raised by the most impenetrable of spiritual ones, a purer, powerful, almost supernatural love frees and transfigures Dolly. The scene, with its surrogate "window" image, goes beyond vision and becomes, nearly, a beatitude:

The rain, adding its voice to Verena's, was between them, Dolly and the Judge, a transparent wall through which he could watch her losing substance, recede before him as earlier she had seemed to recede before me. More than that, it was as if the tree-house were dissolving.

This is dissolution in its happier guise. A more somber sense of it occurs in two "nocturnal" stories, making their "point" by direct allusion to window imagery. In "Master Misery," the "dream" and "real" worlds—the worlds between which Sylvia moves in her quest for liberation and identity—fuse in the window displays she passes on her visits to Mr. Revercomb. Window shopping for dreams brings her up against symbols of her own isolation: the "evil . . . life-sized, mechanical Santa Claus" who discharges commercial joy in a joyless world feeding on myth and dreams; and, later, the "plaster girl with intense eyes . . . astride a bicycle pedaling at the maddest pace" who enforces Sylvia's own fearful nihilism. Yet both these grotesque, hypnotic symbols of paralysis are equally symbols of escape. Penetrating beyond them, Sylvia penetrates beyond dreams, and by the end of the story is "not afraid." Fear—the touchstone of action in Capote—haunts Kay in "A Tree of Night," save she cannot penetrate beyond the memory of her childhood, when she would imagine the "wizard man . . . tapping at the window." Kay retreats into a warm dream and is lost.

And so, finally, is Perry Smith: really! Eloquent in its empathy for a life "suspended between . . . self-expression and self-destruction," *In Cold Blood* charts the voyage of a manacled mind yearning for simple freedom, the progress of a pitiful soul making "an ugly and lonely progress toward one mirage and then another." Up to the act of terror, through the act—committed, like countless other of Capote's "acts of fear," in "a dreamlike dissociative trance"—and even after it, Smith seeks the ultimate, indefinable act that will release him from his continuing nightmare. Significantly, his greatest insight into freedom comes during the brief imprisonment in the Finney County Courthouse: an interlude that bears comparison with Meursault's period of incarceration in *The Stranger*. For, like Camus's hero, Smith tries to salvage pieces of his existence by imagining himself beyond the prison walls. The window in the courthouse becomes Smith's life, opening onto his communion with the squirrel, the "phantoms" who will aid him in a jailbreak, and finally—as he grows more and more suicidal in his desire for escape—the most fantastic vision of all:

I felt all breath and life leaving me . . . The walls of the cell fell away, the sky came down, I saw the big yellow bird. . . . She lifted me . . . we went up, up . . . I was free, I was flying, I was better than any of *them*.

The integration of Smith's vision of flight-freedom-distance into the novel may be the high watermark of Capote's ability to control theme through functional imagery. Escape, for Smith, is more than a metaphorical matter of life-and-death. It is a very real one. For Smith himself is very real, although *In Cold Blood* often seems less realistic than symbolic: especially in its preoccupation with the recurring Capotean themes of perversion, madness, violence, and death. Smith, even more than Hickock, is an instance of truth astounding us more than fiction. Part quester, part bum, part *âme damnée*, he is the synthesis of two types for which Capote has shown no bankruptcy of invention: the child and the grotesque.

The image of the grotesque and the deformed generally symbolizes a life cut off from love, hope, joy, or, simply, human contact. There is, again, something of the obsessive in the pile-up of "grotesques" in *Other Voices, Other Rooms,* something crowding a landscape already over-populated with Gothic effects. The fact that Jesus Fever happens to be a "pygmy figure . . . a gnomish little Negro," that his daughter, Missouri, is, because of her long neck, almost a "freak," that the only doctor Amy could find after Randolph had shot Sansom was a Negro dwarf, seem to me examples of symbolic padding. However, with Miss Wisteria, the side-show midget who weeps "because little boys must grow tall," becomes the structural counterpart to a stated theme. Her loveless, joyless itinerancy best exemplifies, in all its pathos, Randolph's prophecy of one-night, nightmare-like hotels, where, "with the garbage of loneliness stuffed down us . . . we go screaming round the world, dying in our rented rooms . . . eternal homes of the transient heart." In "Shut a Final Door," Walter's own worst fantasies and betrayals are realized in the disembodied, "sexless" voice coming over the telephone—the symbol of a vacuous and lonely world—but not before he has forced, in his own deformity, an unquiet peace in the arms of a crippled domestic.

Akin to Walter Ranney is Vincent of "The Headless Hawk."

Vincent, of course, *is* the headless hawk, "(curtaining) the back-ground" of his dark life, seeking out those who are (in a sense) freaks, those about whom there is "a little something wrong, broken." In D.J. he finds such a broken one, but comes up against, for the first time in his adventures of narcissistic exploitation, a deep and primitive mad-ness—the madness, perhaps, of the artist—that his sensitive, but weak, soulless, parasitic self cannot fathom. Stimulated in all ways by D.J.'s freakish nature, and by his own predacious drive to feed (hawklike) on the weaknesses of others, Vincent commits the one crime which for Capote is almost as venal as murder: the exploitation of love and violations against it.

The pathos of Miss Wisteria, Walter, and Vincent becomes the tragedy of Perry Smith, their loveless acts become his cold-blooded ones. Deformity is not peripheral to the action but at the center of it, for Smith is Capote's first "grotesque" protagonist. Even those who regard psychoanalysis most obliquely may concede that Smith's physi-cal infirmity is partially responsible for his repressions, latent homo-sexuality, and "insanity." Certainly, not all stunted men turn homi-cidal. But then they are not Perry Smith, a twisted lock turned in the horror of coincidence by the twisted key of Richard Hickock. Hickock's is the supreme madness. His insistence on being a "normal" defines normality for Smith, mainly because he has never before been ac-cepted by anyone. But his security, propped by the same parasitism one saw in Vincent, is a false one. Shamed, self-conscious, somnambu-listic at times, Smith continues to live isolated, a grotesque unable to fit in with the normal world, a child who never quite grows into the adult one.

It is, finally, the childlike qualities of Smith that further link *In Cold Blood* to the earlier fiction. Children have been with Capote a most complex motif. To say what they are is far more difficult than to say what they are not. They are not sentimentalized little men and women, on the one hand, or Hobbesian archetypes of inherent evil (*à la* March and Golding) on the other. Capote's children fall somewhere between extremes. Truly, he has never given us the same child twice, but he has always found the right one for what he has been about.

In Capote's finest novel of initiation, the Lilliputian Miss Wisteria weeps over the changes that make boys become men; the sensual, but pre-pubescently pure Miss Bobbitt of the fey "Children on Their Birthdays," and the supernaturally endowed Appleseed awaken people to the palpable and beautiful in life; Dolly (a child more in the manner of Rousseau than Capote) brings to Verbena and Collin the fullness of a sustaining, transfiguring love; while the notorious Miriam acts as the psycho-symbolic extension of Mrs. Miller, the widow who feeds on fear and wants love, and is one of the best studies of incipient schizophrenia in contemporary literature.

If there is a common accounting in all this, it is the child's ability to see into the heart of things, his ability to strip away deception and reveal, however stark and cruel, the truth beneath. To make this tentative conclusion, even to say with Oreilly that "[children] know mostly everything," is not to suggest that any one of Capote's *enfants terribles* could (or should) pass muster as a Wordsworthian "best philosopher." Where Wordsworth worked on a single ontological and philosophical plane—"the child is father of the man"—Capote works on a shifting symbolic one. Wordsworth's child is not beyond good and evil; Capote's may be. He embraces both qualities without accepting either, singing the songs of innocence and experience that have become stock in American fiction, intimating nothing so abstract as man's immortality, but struggling with the problem of his mortality.

In an unpleasant way, *In Cold Blood* focuses acutely on this problem. More than an eloquent account of murder, guilt, reprisal, justice, it is throughout an attempt to uncover the rationale for so cold-blooded an act: an act that knocks with the authority of fate to inform us how tenuously we live, how mortal we are. Why a "child," even an "innocent" like Smith, should prove the direct agent for the terrifying crime—why, that is, Capote takes pains to establish Smith *as* a "child" —is explicable, but no less frightening because it is. Murder of this sort, by its very nature seemingly irrational and amoral, needs an irrational and amoral correlative, an image to support it. This is the child—beyond legality, beyond morality, beyond rationality, beyond good and evil. And whereas neither judge nor psychologist need bother himself with evaluating an act of murder, the novelist must be able to evaluate any action, even one so incredible as Smith and Hickock's.

The irony of *In Cold Blood* (in which irony generally pales before compassion and tragedy) is that an irrational murder outside the law and rational justice within both demonstrate the potency of individual and collective fear. That a "child" pays for the crime should in no way reduce its enormity, nor even plead against capital punishment—an irrelevant point in any discussion of the book. But it should force the recognition that for some the world is lonely, suffocating, fearful, and loveless; and in a world like this such things as the Clutter murder will happen again and again. The case of Smith and Hickock unfolds the human condition; and Smith himself does seem, by example if not otherwise, to see into the heart of things. He becomes, in light of Capote's earlier work, the total symbol for the exile, the alienated human being, the grotesque, the outsider, the quester after love, the sometimes sapient, sometimes innocent, sometimes evil child. And in the same way *In Cold Blood* becomes the *recueillement* of earlier themes and images, not least of which is our ambiguous hopes and fears in the face of mortality. One must come away from *In Cold Blood* with the realization that the fragility of man is subject to a hardier fatalism; that the human condition is as fragile and eternal as the wheat bending on the immense Kansas plains, and fate as inexorable as the wind that blows it.

4. MURDER IN AMERICA: FACT AND FICTION

The Tell-Tale Heart

EDGAR ALLAN POE

TRUE!—NERVOUS—VERY, VERY DREADFULLY NERVOUS I HAD BEEN AND AM; but why *will* you say that I am mad? The disease had sharpened my senses—not destroyed—not dulled them. Above all was the sense of hearing acute. I heard all things in the heaven and in the earth. I heard many things in hell. How, then, am I mad? Hearken! and observe how healthily—how calmly I can tell you the whole story.

It is impossible to say how first the idea entered my brain; but once conceived, it haunted me day and night. Object there was none. Passion there was none. I loved the old man. He had never wronged me. He had never given me insult. For his gold I had no desire. I think it was his eye! yes, it was this! He had the eye of a vulture—a pale blue eye, with a film over it. Whenever it fell upon me, my blood ran cold; and so by degrees—very gradually—I made up my mind to take the life of the old man, and thus rid myself of the eye forever.

Now this is the point. You fancy me mad. Madmen know nothing. But you should have seen *me*. You should have seen how wisely I proceeded—with what caution—with what foresight—with what dissimulation I went to work! I was never kinder to the old man than during the whole week before I killed him. And every night, about midnight, I turned the latch of his door and opened it—oh so gently! And then, when I had made an opening sufficient for my head, I put in a dark lantern, all closed, closed, so that no light shone out, and then I thrust in my head. Oh, you would have laughed to see how cunningly I thrust it in! I moved it slowly—very, very slowly, so that I might not disturb the old man's sleep. It took me an hour to place my whole head within the opening so far that I could see him as he lay upon his bed. Ha!—would a madman have been so wise as this? And then, when my head was well in the room, I undid the lantern cautiously—oh, so cautiously—cautiously (for the hinges creaked)—I undid it just so much that a single thin ray fell upon the vulture eye. And this I did for

This story first appeared in Lowell's *Pioneers*, January 1843; the final text in *Broadway Journal*, August, 1845.

188

seven long nights—every night just at midnight—but I found the eye always closed; and so it was impossible to do the work; for it was not the old man who vexed me, but his Evil Eye. And every morning, when the day broke, I went boldly into the chamber, and spoke courageously to him, calling him by name in a hearty tone, and inquiring how he had passed the night. So you see he would have been a very profound old man, indeed, to suspect that every night, just at twelve, I looked in upon him while he slept.

Upon the eighth night I was more than usually cautious in opening the door. A watch's minute hand moves more quickly than did mine. Never before that night, had I *felt* the extent of my own powers—of my sagacity. I could scarcely contain my feelings of triumph. To think that there I was, opening the door, little by little, and he not even to dream of my secret deeds or thoughts. I fairly chuckled at the idea; and perhaps he heard me; for he moved on the bed suddenly, as if startled. Now you may think that I drew back—but no. His room was as black as pitch with the thick darkness, (for the shutters were close fastened, through fear of robbers,) and so I knew that he could not see the opening of the door, and I kept pushing it on steadily, steadily.

I had my head in, and was about to open the lantern, when my thumb slipped upon the tin fastening, and the old man sprang up in bed, crying out—"Who's there?"

I kept quite still and said nothing. For a whole hour I did not move a muscle, and in the meantime I did not hear him lie down. He was still sitting up in the bed listening;—just as I have done, night after night, hearkening to the death watches in the wall.

Presently I heard a slight groan, and I knew it was the groan of mortal terror. It was not a groan of pain or of grief—oh, no!—it was the low stifled sound that arises from the bottom of the soul when overcharged with awe. I knew the sound well. Many a night, just at midnight, when all the world slept, it has welled up from my own bosom, deepening, with its dreadful echo, the terrors that distracted me. I say I knew it well. I knew what the old man felt, and pitied him, although I chuckled at heart. I knew that he had been lying awake ever since the first slight noise, when he had turned in the bed. His fears had been ever since growing upon him. He had been trying to fancy them causeless, but could not. He had been saying to himself— "It is nothing but the wind in the chimney—it is only a mouse crossing the floor," or "it is merely a cricket which has made a single chirp." Yes, he had been trying to comfort himself with these suppositions: but he had found all in vain. *All in vain;* because Death, in approaching him had stalked with his black shadow before him, and enveloped the victim. And it was the mournful influence of the unperceived shadow that caused him to feel—although he neither saw nor heard—to *feel* the presence of my head within the room.

When I had waited a long time, very patiently, without hearing him lie down, I resolved to open a little—a very, very little crevice in the lantern. So I opened it—you cannot imagine how stealthily, stealthily—until, at length, a simple dim ray, like the thread of the spider, shot from out the crevice and fell full upon the vulture eye.

It was open—wide, wide open—and I grew furious as I gazed upon it. I saw it with perfect distinctness—all a dull blue, with a hideous veil over it that chilled the very marrow in my bones; but I could see nothing else of the old man's face or person: for I had directed the ray as if by instinct, precisely upon the damned spot.

And have I not told you that what you mistake for madness is but over acuteness of the senses?—now, I say, there came to my ears a low, dull, quick sound, such as a watch makes when enveloped in cotton. I knew *that* sound well, too. It was the beating of the old man's heart. It increased my fury, as the beating of a drum stimulates the soldier into courage.

But even yet I refrained and kept still. I scarcely breathed. I held the lantern motionless. I tried how steadily I could maintain the ray upon the eye. Meantime the hellish tattoo of the heart increased. It grew quicker and quicker, and louder and louder every instant. The old man's terror *must* have been extreme! It grew louder, I say, louder every moment!—do you mark me well? I have told you that I am nervous: so I am. And now at the dead hour of the night, amid the dreadful silence of that old house, so strange a noise as this excited me to uncontrollable terror. Yet, for some minutes longer I refrained and stood still. But the beating grew louder, louder! I thought the heart must burst. And now a new anxiety seized me—the sound would be heard by a neighbour! The old man's hour had come! With a loud yell, I threw open the lantern and leaped into the room. He shrieked once— once only. In an instant I dragged him to the floor, and pulled the heavy bed over him. I then smiled gaily, to find the deed so far done. But, for many minutes, the heart beat on with a muffled sound. This, however, did not vex me; it would not be heard through the wall. At length it ceased. The old man was dead. I removed the bed and examined the corpse. Yes, he was stone, stone dead. I placed my hand upon the heart and held it there for many minutes. There was no pulsation. He was stone dead. His eye would trouble me no more.

If still you think me mad, you will think so no longer when I describe the wise precautions I took for the concealment of the body. The night waned, and I worked hastily, but in silence. First of all I dismembered the corpse. I cut off the head and the arms and the legs.

I then took up three planks from the flooring of the chamber, and deposited all between the scantlings. I then replaced the boards so cleverly, so cunningly, that no human eye—not even *his*—could have detected any thing wrong. There was nothing to wash out—no stain of any kind—no blood-spot whatever. I had been too wary for that. A tub had caught all—ha! ha!

When I had made an end of these labors, it was four o'clock—still dark as midnight. As the bell sounded the hour, there came a knocking at the street door. I went down to open it with a light heart,—for what had I *now* to fear? There entered three men, who introduced them-selves with perfect suavity, as officers of the police. A shriek had been heard by a neighbour during the night; suspicion of foul play had been aroused; information had been lodged at the police office, and they (the officers) had been deputed to search the premises.

I smiled,—for *what* had I to fear? I bade the gentlemen welcome. The shriek, I said, was my own in a dream. The old man, I mentioned, was absent in the country. I took my visitors all over the house. I bade them search—search *well*. I led them, at length, to *his* chamber. I showed them his treasures, secure, undisturbed. In the enthusiasm of my confidence, I brought chairs into the room, and desired them *here* to rest from their fatigues, while I myself, in the wild audacity of my perfect triumph, placed my own seat upon the very spot beneath which reposed the corpse of the victim.

The officers were satisfied. My *manner* had convinced them. I was singularly at ease. They sat, and while I answered cheerily, they chatted of familiar things. But, ere long, I felt myself getting pale and wished them gone. My head ached, and I fancied a ringing in my ears: but still they sat and still chatted. The ringing became more distinct:—it continued and became more distinct: I talked more freely to get rid of the feeling: but it continued and gained definiteness—until, at length, I found that the noise was *not* within my ears.

No doubt I now grew *very* pale;—but I talked more fluently, and with a heightened voice. Yet the sound increased—and what could I do, It was *a low, dull, quick sound—much such a sound as a watch makes when enveloped in cotton.* I gasped for breath—and yet the officers heard it not. I talked more quickly—more vehemently; but the noise steadily increased. I arose and argued about trifles, in a high key and with violent gesticulations; but the noise steadily increased. Why *would* they not be gone? I paced the floor to and fro with heavy strides, as if excited to fury by the observations of the men—but the noise steadily increased. Oh God! what *could* I do? I foamed—I raved—I swore! I swung the chair upon which I had been sitting, and grated it upon the boards, but the noise arose over all and continually increased. It grew louder—louder—*louder!* And still the men chatted pleasantly, and smiled. Was it possible they heard not? Almighty God!—no, no! They heard!—they suspected!—they *knew!*—they were making a mockery of my horror—this I thought, and this I think. But anything was better than this agony! Anything was more tolerable than this derision! I could bear those hypocritical smiles no longer! I felt that I must scream or die! and now—again!—hark! louder! louder! louder! *louder!*

"Villains!" I shrieked, "dissemble no more! I admit the deed!—tear up the planks! here, here!—it is the beating of his hideous heart!"

A Good Man Is Hard to Find

FLANNERY O'CONNOR

THE GRANDMOTHER DIDN'T WANT TO GO TO FLORIDA. SHE WANTED TO VISIT some of her connections in east Tennessee and she was seizing at every chance to change Bailey's mind. Bailey was the son she lived with, her only boy. He was sitting on the edge of his chair at the table, bent over the orange sports section of the *Journal*. "Now look here, Bailey," she said, "see here, read this," and she stood with one hand on her thin hip and the other rattling the newspaper at his bald head. "Here this fellow that calls himself The Misfit is aloose from the Federal Pen and headed toward Florida and you read here what it says he did to these people. Just you read it. I wouldn't take my children in any direction with a criminal like that aloose in it. I couldn't answer to my conscience if I did."

Bailey didn't look up from his reading so she wheeled around then and faced the children's mother, a young woman in slacks, whose face was as broad and innocent as a cabbage and was tied around with a green head-kerchief that had two points on the top like rabbit's ears. She was sitting on the sofa, feeding the baby his apricots out of a jar. "The children have been to Florida before," the old lady said. "You all ought to take them somewhere else for a change so they would see different parts of the world and be broad. They never have been to east Tennessee."

The children's mother didn't seem to hear her but the eight-year-old boy, John Wesley, a stocky child with glasses, said, "If you don't want to go to Florida, why dontcha stay at home?" He and the little girl, June Star, were reading the funny papers on the floor.

"She wouldn't stay at home to be queen for a day," June Star said without raising her yellow head.

"Yes and what would you do if this fellow, The Misfit, caught you?" the grandmother asked.

"I'd smack his face," John Wesley said.

"She wouldn't stay at home for a million bucks," June Star said. "Afraid she'd miss something. She has to go everywhere we go."

"All right, Miss," the grandmother said. "Just remember that the next time you want me to curl your hair."

June Star said her hair was naturally curly.

The next morning the grandmother was the first one in the car, ready to go. She had her big black valise that looked like the head of a hippopotamus in one corner, and underneath it she was hiding a basket with Pitty Sing, the cat, in it. She didn't intend for the cat to be left alone in the house for three days because he would miss her too much and she was afraid he might brush against one of the gas burners and accidentally asphyxiate himself. Her son, Bailey, didn't like to arrive at a motel with a cat.

She sat in the middle of the back seat with John Wesley and June Star on either side of her. Bailey and the children's mother and the baby sat in front and they left Atlanta at eight forty-five with the mileage on the car at 55890. The grandmother wrote this down because she thought it would be interesting to say how many miles they had been when they got back. It took them twenty minutes to reach the outskirts of the city.

The old lady settled herself comfortably, removing her white cotton gloves and putting them up with her purse on the shelf in front of the back window. The children's mother still had on slacks and still had her head tied up in a green kerchief, but the grandmother had on a navy blue straw sailor hat with a bunch of white violets on the brim and a navy blue dress with a small white dot in the print. Her collars and cuffs were white organdy trimmed with lace and at her neckline she had pinned a purple spray of cloth violets containing a sachet. In case of an accident, anyone seeing her dead on the highway would know at once that she was a lady.

She said she thought it was going to be a good day for driving, neither too hot nor too cold, and she cautioned Bailey that the speed limit was fifty-five miles an hour and that the patrolmen hid themselves behind billboards and small clumps of trees and sped out after you before you had a chance to slow down. She pointed out interesting details of the scenery: Stone Mountain; the blue granite that in some places came up to both sides of the highway; the brilliant red clay banks slightly streaked with purple; and the various crops that made rows of green lace-work on the ground. The trees were full of silver-white sunlight and the meanest of them sparkled. The children were reading comic magazines and their mother had gone back to sleep.

"Let's go through Georgia fast so we won't have to look at it much," John Wesley said.

"If I were a little boy," said the grandmother, "I wouldn't talk about my native state that way. Tennessee has the mountains and Georgia has the hills."

"Tennessee is just a hillbilly dumping ground," John Wesley said, "and Georgia is a lousy state too."

"You said it," June Star said.

"In my time," said the grandmother, folding her thin veined fingers, "children were more respectful of their native states and their parents and everything else. People did right then. Oh look at the cute little pickaninny!" she said and pointed to a Negro child standing in the door of a shack. "Wouldn't that make a picture, now?" she asked and they all turned and looked at the little Negro out of the back window. He waved.

"He didn't have any britches on," June Star said.

"He probably didn't have any," the grandmother explained. "Little niggers in the country don't have things like we do. If I could paint, I'd paint that picture," she said.

The children exchanged comic books.

The grandmother offered to hold the baby and the children's mother passed him over the front seat to her. She set him on her knee and bounced him and told him about the things they were passing. She rolled her eyes and screwed up her mouth and stuck her leathery thin face into his smooth bland one. Occasionally he gave her a far-away smile. They passed a large cotton field with five or six graves fenced in the middle of it, like a small island. "Look at the graveyard!" the grandmother said, pointing it out. "That was the old family burying ground. That belonged to the plantation."

"Where's the plantation?" John Wesley asked.

"Gone With the Wind," said the grandmother. "Ha. Ha."

When the children finished all the comic books they had brought, they opened the lunch and ate it. The grandmother ate a peanut butter sandwich and an olive and would not let the children throw the box and the paper napkins out the window. When there was nothing else to do they played a game by choosing a cloud and making the other two guess what shape it suggested. John Wesley took one the shape of a cow and June Star guessed a cow and John Wesley said, no, an automobile, and June Star said he didn't play fair, and they began to slap each other over the grandmother.

The grandmother said she would tell them a story if they would keep quiet. When she told a story, she rolled her eyes and waved her head and was very dramatic. She said once when she was a maiden lady she had been courted by a Mr. Edgar Atkins Teagarden from Jasper, Georgia. She said he was a very good-looking man and a gentleman and that he brought her a watermelon every Saturday afternoon with his initials cut in it, E. A. T. Well, one Saturday, she said, Mr. Teagarden brought the watermelon and there was nobody at

home and he left it on the front porch and returned to his buggy to
Jasper, but she never got the watermelon, she said, because a nigger
boy ate it when he saw the initials, E. A. T.! This story tickled John
Wesley's funny bone and he giggled and giggled but June Star didn't
think it was any good. She said she wouldn't marry a man that just
brought her a watermelon on Saturday. The grandmother said she
would have done well to marry Mr. Teagarden because he was a
gentleman and had bought Coca-Cola stock when it first came out and
that he had died only a few years ago, a very wealthy man.

They stopped at The Tower for barbecued sandwiches. The
Tower was a part stucco and part wood filling station and dance hall
set in a clearing outside of Timothy. A fat man named Red Sammy
Butts ran it and there were signs stuck here and there on the building
and for miles up and down the highway saying, TRY RED SAMMY'S
FAMOUS BARBECUE. NONE LIKE FAMOUS RED SAMMY'S!
RED SAM! THE FAT BOY WITH THE HAPPY LAUGH. A
VETERAN! RED SAMMY'S YOUR MAN!

Red Sammy was lying on the bare ground outside The Tower
with his head under a truck while a gray monkey about a foot high,
chained to a small chinaberry tree, chattered nearby. The monkey
sprang back into the tree and got on the highest limb as soon as he saw
the children jump out of the car and run toward him.

Inside, The Tower was a long dark room with a counter at one
end and tables at the other and dancing space in the middle. They all
sat down at a board table next to the nickelodeon and Red Sam's wife,
a tall burnt-brown woman with hair and eyes lighter than her skin,
came and took their order. The children's mother put a dime in the
machine and played "The Tennessee Waltz," and the grandmother
said that tune always made her want to dance. She asked Bailey if he
would like to dance but he only glared at her. He didn't have a
naturally sunny disposition like she did and trips made him nervous.
The grandmother's brown eyes were very bright. She swayed her head
from side to side and pretended she was dancing in her chair. June
Star said play something she could tap to so the children's mother put
in another dime and played a fast number and June Star stepped out
onto the dance floor and did her tap routine.

"Ain't she cute?" Red Sam's wife said, leaning over the counter.
"Would you like to come be my little girl?"

"No I certainly wouldn't," June Star said. "I wouldn't live in a
broken-down place like this for a million bucks!" and she ran back to
the table.

"Ain't she cute?" the woman repeated, stretching her mouth
politely.

"Aren't you ashamed?" hissed the grandmother.

Red Sam came in and told his wife to quit lounging on the
counter and hurry up with these people's order. His khaki trousers

reached just to his hip bones and his stomach hung over them like a
sack of meal swaying under his shirt. He came over and sat down at a
table nearby and let out a combination sigh and yodel. "You can't
win," he said. "You can't win," and he wiped his sweating red face off
with a gray handkerchief. "These days you don't know who to trust,"
he said. "Ain't that the truth?"

"People are certainly not nice like they used to be," said the
grandmother.

"Two fellers come in here last week," Red Sammy said, "driving a
Chrysler. It was a old beat-up car but it was a good one and these
boys looked all right to me. Said they worked at the mill and you know
I let them fellers charge the gas they bought? Now why did I do
that?"

"Because you're a good man!" the grandmother said at once.

"Yes'm, I suppose so," Red Sam said as if he were struck with this
answer.

His wife brought the orders, carrying the five plates all at once
without a tray, two in each hand and one balanced on her arm. "It isn't
a soul in this green world of God's that you can trust," she said. "And I
don't count nobody out of that, not nobody," she repeated, looking at
Red Sammy.

"Did you read about that criminal, The Misfit, that's escaped?"
asked the grandmother.

"I wouldn't be a bit surprised if he didn't attact this place right
here," said the woman. "If he hears about it being here, I wouldn't be
none surprised to see him. If he hears it's two cent in the cash register,
I wouldn't be a tall surprised if he . . ."

"That'll do," Red Sam said. "Go bring these people their Co'-
Colas," and the woman went off to get the rest of the order.

"A good man is hard to find," Red Sammy said. "Everything is
getting terrible. I remember the day you could go off and leave your
screen door unlatched. Not no more."

He and the grandmother discussed better times. The old lady said
that in her opinion Europe was entirely to blame for the way things
were now. She said the way Europe acted you would think we were
made of money and Red Sam said it was no use talking about it, she
was exactly right. The children ran outside into the white sunlight and
looked at the monkey in the lacy chinaberry tree. He was busy
catching fleas on himself and biting each one carefully between his
teeth as if it were a delicacy.

They drove off again into the hot afternoon. The grandmother
took cat naps and woke up every few minutes with her own snoring.
Outside of Toombsboro she woke up and recalled an old plantation
that she had visited in this neighborhood once when she was a young
lady. She said the house had six white columns across the front and
that there was an avenue of oaks leading up to it and two little

wooden trellis arbors on either side in front where you sat down with your suitor after a stroll in the garden. She recalled exactly which road to turn off to get to it. She knew that Bailey would not be willing to lose any time looking at an old house, but the more she talked about it, the more she wanted to see it once again and find out if the little twin arbors were still standing. "There was a secret panel in this house," she said craftily, not telling the truth but wishing that she were, "and the story went that all the family silver was hidden in it when Sherman came through but it was never found . . ."

"Hey!" John Wesley said. "Let's go see it! We'll find it! We'll poke all the woodwork and find it! Who lives there? Where do you turn off at? Hey Pop, can't we turn off there?"

"We never have seen a house with a secret panel!" June Star shrieked. "Let's go to the house with the secret panel! Hey Pop, can't we go see the house with the secret panel!"

"It's not far from here, I know," the grandmother said. "It wouldn't take over twenty minutes."

Bailey was looking straight ahead. His jaw was as rigid as a horseshoe. "No," he said.

The children began to yell and scream that they wanted to see the house with the secret panel. John Wesley kicked the back of the front seat and June Star hung over her mother's shoulder and whined desperately into her ear that they never had any fun even on their vacation, that they could never do what THEY wanted to do. The baby began to scream and John Wesley kicked the back of the seat so hard that his father could feel the blows in his kidney.

"All right!" he shouted and drew the car to a stop at the side of the road. "Will you all shut up? Will you all just shut up for one second? If you don't shut up, we won't go anywhere."

"It would be very educational for them," the grandmother murmured.

"All right," Bailey said, "but get this: this is the only time we're going to stop for anything like this. This is the one and only time."

"The dirt road that you have to turn down is about a mile back," the grandmother directed. "I marked it when we passed."

"A dirt road," Bailey groaned.

After they had turned around and were headed toward the dirt road, the grandmother recalled other points about the house, the beautiful glass over the front doorway and the candle-lamp in the hall. John Wesley said that the secret panel was probably in the fireplace.

"You can't go inside this house," Bailey said. "You don't know who lives there."

"While you all talk to the people in front, I'll run around behind and get in a window," John Wesley suggested.

"We'll all stay in the car," his mother said.

They turned onto the dirt road and the car raced roughly along in a swirl of pink dust. The grandmother recalled the times when there were no paved roads and thirty miles was a day's journey. The dirt road was hilly and there were sudden washes in it and sharp curves on dangerous embankments. All at once they would be on a hill, looking down over the blue tops of trees for miles around, then the next minute, they would be in a red depression with the dust-coated trees looking down on them.

"This place had better turn up in a minute," Bailey said, "or I'm going to turn around."

The road looked as if no one had traveled on it in months.

"It's not much farther," the grandmother said and just as she said it, a horrible thought came to her. The thought was so embarrassing that she turned red in the face and her eyes dilated and her feet jumped up, upsetting her valise in the corner. The instant the valise moved, the newspaper top she had over the basket under it rose with a snarl and Pitty Sing, the cat, sprang onto Bailey's shoulder.

The children were thrown to the floor and their mother, clutching the baby, was thrown out the door onto the ground; the old lady was thrown into the front seat. The car turned over once and landed right-side-up in a gulch off the side of the road. Bailey remained in the driver's seat with the cat—gray-striped with a broad white face and an orange nose—clinging to his neck like a caterpillar.

As soon as the children saw they could move their arms and legs, they scrambled out of the car, shouting, "We've had an ACCIDENT!" The grandmother was curled up under the dashboard, hoping she was injured so that Bailey's wrath would not come down on her all at once. The horrible thought she had had before the accident was that the house she had remembered so vividly was not in Georgia but in Tennessee.

Bailey removed the cat from his neck with both hands and flung it out the window against the side of a pine tree. Then he got out of the car and started looking for the children's mother. She was sitting against the side of the red gutted ditch, holding the screaming baby, but she only had a cut down her face and a broken shoulder. "We've had an ACCIDENT!" the children screamed in a frenzy of delight.

"But nobody's killed," June Star said with disappointment as the grandmother limped out of the car, her hat still pinned to her head but the broken front brim standing up at a jaunty angle and the violet spray hanging off the side. They all sat down in the ditch, except the children, to recover from the shock. They were all shaking.

"Maybe a car will come along," said the children's mother hoarsely.

"I believe I have injured an organ," said the grandmother, pressing her side, but no one answered her. Bailey's teeth were clattering. He had on a yellow sport shirt with bright blue parrots designed in it and his face was as yellow as the shirt. The grandmother decided that she would not mention that the house was in Tennessee.

The road was about ten feet above and they could see only the tops of the trees on the other side of it. Behind the ditch they were sitting in there were more woods, tall and dark and deep. In a few minutes they saw a car some distance away on top of a hill, coming slowly as if the occupants were watching them. The grandmother stood up and waved both arms dramatically to attract their attention. The car continued to come on slowly, disappeared around a bend and appeared again, moving even slower, on top of the hill they had gone over. It was a big black battered hearse-like automobile. There were three men in it.

It came to a stop just over them and for some minutes, the driver looked down with a steady expressionless gaze to where they were sitting, and didn't speak. Then he turned his head and muttered something to the other two and they got out. One was a fat boy in black trousers and a red sweat shirt with a silver stallion embossed on the front of it. He moved around on the right side of them and stood staring, his mouth partly open in a kind of loose grin. The other had on khaki pants and a blue striped coat and a gray hat pulled down very low, hiding most of his face. He came around slowly on the left side. Neither spoke.

The driver got out of the car and stood by the side of it, looking down at them. He was an older man than the other two. His hair was just beginning to gray and he wore silver-rimmed spectacles that gave him a scholarly look. He had a long creased face and didn't have on any shirt or undershirt. He had on blue jeans that were too tight for him and was holding a black hat and a gun. The two boys also had guns.

"We've had an ACCIDENT!" the children screamed.

The grandmother had the peculiar feeling that the bespectacled man was someone she knew. His face was as familiar to her as if she had known him all her life but she could not recall who he was. He moved away from the car and began to come down the embankment, placing his feet carefully so that he wouldn't slip. He had on tan and white shoes and no socks, and his ankles were red and thin. "Good afternoon," he said. "I see you all had you a little spill."

"We turned over twice!" said the grandmother.

"Oncet," he corrected. "We seen it happen. Try their car and see will it run, Hiram," he said quietly to the boy with the gray hat.

"What you got that gun for?" John Wesley asked. "Whatcha gonna do with that gun?"

"Lady," the man said to the children's mother, "would you mind calling them children to sit down by you? Children make me nervous. I want all you all to sit down right together there where you're at."

"What are you telling US what to do for?" June Star asked.

Behind them the line of woods gaped like a dark open mouth. "Come here," said their mother.

"Look here now," Bailey began suddenly, "we're in a predicament! We're in . . ."

The grandmother shrieked. She scrambled to her feet and stood staring. "You're The Misfit!" she said. "I recognized you at once!"

"Yes'm," the man said, smiling slightly as if he were pleased in spite of himself to be known, "but it would have been better for all of you, lady, if you hadn't of reckernized me."

Bailey turned his head sharply and said something to his mother that shocked even the children. The old lady began to cry and The Misfit reddened.

"Lady," he said, "don't you get upset. Sometimes a man says things he don't mean. I don't reckon he meant to talk to you that-away."

"You wouldn't shoot a lady, would you?" the grandmother said and removed a clean handkerchief from her cuff and began to slap at her eyes with it.

The Misfit pointed the toe of his shoe into the ground and made a little hole and then covered it up again. "I would hate to have to," he said.

"Listen," the grandmother almost screamed, "I know you're a good man. You don't look a bit like you have common blood. I know you must come from nice people!"

"Yes mam," he said, "finest people in the world." When he smiled he showed a row of strong white teeth. "God never made a finer woman than my mother and my daddy's heart was pure gold," he said. The boy with the red sweat shirt had come around behind them and was standing with his gun at his hip. The Misfit squatted down on the ground. "Watch them children, Bobby Lee," he said. "You know they make me nervous." He looked at the six of them huddled together in front of him and he seemed to be embarrassed as if he couldn't think of anything to say. "Ain't a cloud in the sky," he remarked, looking up at it. "Don't see no sun but don't see no cloud neither."

"Yes, it's a beautiful day," said the grandmother. "Listen," she said, "you shouldn't call yourself The Misfit because I know you're a good man at heart. I can just look at you and tell."

"Hush!" Bailey yelled. "Hush! Everybody shut up and let me handle this!" He was squatting in the position of a runner about to sprint forward but he didn't move.

"I pre-chate that, lady," The Misfit said and drew a little circle in the ground with the butt of his gun.

"It'll take a half a hour to fix this here car," Hiram called, looking over the raised hood of it.

"Well, first you and Bobby Lee get him and that little boy to step over yonder with you," The Misfit said, pointing to Bailey and John Wesley. "The boys want to ast you something," he said to Bailey. "Would you mind stepping back in them woods there with them?"

"Listen," Bailey began, "we're in a terrible predicament! Nobody realizes what this is," and his voice cracked. His eyes were as blue and intense as the parrots in his shirt and he remained perfectly still.

The grandmother reached up to adjust her hat brim as if she were going to the woods with him but it came off in her hand. She stood staring at it and after a second she let it fall on the ground. Hiram pulled Bailey up by the arm as if he were assisting an old man. John Wesley caught hold of his father's hand and Bobby Lee followed. They went off toward the woods and just as they reached the dark edge, Bailey turned and supporting himself against a gray naked pine trunk, he shouted, "I'll be back in a minute, Mamma, wait on me!"

"Come back this instant!" his mother shrilled but they all disappeared into the woods.

"Bailey Boy!" the grandmother called in a tragic voice but she found she was looking at The Misfit squatting on the ground in front of her. "I just know you're a good man," she said desperately. "You're not a bit common!"

"Nome, I ain't a good man," The Misfit said after a second as if he had considered her statement carefully, "but I ain't the worst in the world neither. My daddy said I was a different breed of dog from my brothers and sisters. 'You know,' Daddy said, 'it's some that can live their whole life out without asking about it and it's others has to know why it is, and this boy is one of the latters. He's going to be into everything!'" He put on his black hat and looked up suddenly and then away deep into the woods as if he were embarrassed again. "I'm sorry I don't have on a shirt before you ladies," he said, hunching his shoulders slightly. "We buried our clothes that we had on when we escaped and we're just making do until we can get better. We borrowed these from some folks we met," he explained.

"That's perfectly all right," the grandmother said. "Maybe Bailey has an extra shirt in his suitcase."

"I'll look and see terrectly," The Misfit said.

"Where are they taking him?" the children's mother screamed.

"Daddy was a card himself," The Misfit said. "You couldn't put anything over on him. He never got in trouble with the Authorities though. Just had the knack of handling them."

"You could be honest too if you'd only try," said the grandmother. "Think how wonderful it would be to settle down and live a comfortable life and not have to think about somebody chasing you all the time."

The Misfit kept scratching in the ground with the butt of his gun as if he were thinking about it. "Yes'm, somebody is always after you," he murmured.

The grandmother noticed how thin his shoulder blades were just behind his hat because she was standing up looking down on him. "Do you ever pray?" she asked.

He shook his head. All she saw was the black hat wiggle between his shoulder blades. "Nome," he said.

There was a pistol shot from the woods, followed closely by another. Then silence. The old lady's head jerked around. She could hear the wind move through the tree tops like a long satisfied insuck of breath. "Bailey Boy!" she called.

"I was a gospel singer for a while," The Misfit said. "I been most everything. Been in the arm service, both land and sea, at home and abroad, been twict married, been an undertaker, been with the railroads, plowed Mother Earth, been in a tornado, seen a man burnt alive oncet," and he looked up at the children's mother and the little girl who were sitting close together, their faces white and their eyes glassy; "I even seen a woman flogged," he said.

"Pray, pray," the grandmother began, "pray, pray . . ."

"I never was a bad boy that I remember of," The Misfit said in an almost dreamy voice, "but somewheres along the line I done something wrong and got sent to the penitentiary. I was buried alive," and he looked up and held her attention to him by a steady stare.

"That's when you should have started to pray," she said. "What did you do to get sent to the penitentiary that first time?"

"Turn to the right, it was a wall," The Misfit said, looking up again at the cloudless sky. "Turn to the left, it was a wall. Look up it was a ceiling, look down it was a floor. I forget what I done, lady. I set there and set there, trying to remember what it was I done and I ain't recalled it to this day. Oncet in a while, I would think it was coming to me, but it never come."

"Maybe they put you in by mistake," the old lady said vaguely.

"Nome," he said. "It wasn't no mistake. They had the papers on me."

"You must have stolen something," she said.

The Misfit sneered slightly. "Nobody had nothing I wanted," he said. "It was a head-doctor at the penitentiary said what I had done was kill my daddy but I known that for a lie. My daddy died in nineteen ought nineteen of the epidemic flu and I never had a thing to do with it. He was buried in the Mount Hopewell Baptist churchyard and you can go there and see for yourself."

"If you would pray," the old lady said, "Jesus would help you."

"That's right," The Misfit said.

"Well then, why don't you pray?" she asked trembling with delight suddenly.

"I don't want no hep," he said. "I'm doing all right by myself."

Bobby Lee and Hiram came ambling back from the woods. Bobby Lee was dragging a yellow shirt with bright blue parrots in it.

"Thow me that shirt, Bobby Lee," The Misfit said. The shirt came flying at him and landed on his shoulder and he put it on. The grandmother couldn't name what the shirt reminded her of. "No, lady," The Misfit said while he was buttoning it up, "I found out the crime don't matter. You can do one thing or you can do another, kill a man or take a tire off his car, because sooner or later you're going to forget what it was you done and just be punished for it."

The children's mother had begun to make heaving noises as if she couldn't get her breath. "Lady," he asked, "would you and that little girl like to step off yonder with Bobby Lee and Hiram and join your husband?"

"Yes, thank you," the mother said faintly. Her left arm dangled helplessly and she was holding the baby, who had gone to sleep, in the other. "Hep that lady up, Hiram," The Misfit said as she struggled to climb out of the ditch, "and Bobby Lee, you hold onto that little girl's hand."

"I don't want to hold hands with him," June Star said. "He reminds me of a pig."

The fat boy blushed and laughed and caught her by the arm and pulled her off into the woods after Hiram and her mother.

Alone with The Misfit, the grandmother found that she had lost her voice. There was not a cloud in the sky nor any sun. There was nothing around her but woods. She wanted to tell him that he must pray. She opened and closed her mouth several times before anything came out. Finally she found herself saying, "Jesus. Jesus," meaning, Jesus will help you, but the way she was saying it, it sounded as if she might be cursing.

"Yes'm," The Misfit said as if he agreed. "Jesus thrown everything off balance. It was the same case with Him as with me except He hadn't committed any crime and they could prove I had committed one because they had the papers on me. Of course," he said, "they never shown me my papers. That's why I sign myself now. I said long ago, you get you a signature and sign everything you do and keep a copy of it. Then you'll know what you done and you can hold up the crime to the punishment and see do they match and in the end you'll have something to prove you ain't been treated right. I call myself The Misfit," he said, "because I can't make what all I done wrong fit what all I gone through in punishment."

There was a piercing scream from the woods, followed closely by a pistol report. "Does it seem right to you, lady, that one is punished a heap and another ain't punished at all?"

"Jesus!" the old lady cried. "You've got good blood! I know you wouldn't shoot a lady! I know you come from nice people! Pray! Jesus, you ought not to shoot a lady. I'll give you all the money I've got!"

"Lady," The Misfit said, looking beyond her far into the woods, "there never was a body that give the undertaker a tip."

There were two more pistol reports and the grandmother raised her head like a parched old turkey hen crying for water and called, "Bailey Boy, Bailey Boy!" as if her heart would break.

"Jesus was the only One that ever raised the dead," The Misfit continued, "and He shouldn't have done it. He thown everything off balance. If He did what He said, then it's nothing for you to do but thow away everything and follow Him, and if He didn't, then it's nothing for you to do but enjoy the few minutes you got left the best way you can—by killing somebody or burning down his house or doing some other meanness to him. No pleasure but meanness," he said and his voice had become almost a snarl.

"Maybe He didn't raise the dead," the old lady mumbled, not knowing what she was saying and feeling so dizzy that she sank down in the ditch with her legs twisted under her.

"I wasn't there so I can't say He didn't," The Misfit said. "I wisht I had of been there," he said, hitting the ground with his fist. "It ain't right I wasn't there because if I had of been there I would of known. Listen lady," he said in a high voice, "if I had of been there I would of known and I wouldn't be like I am now." His voice seemed about to crack and the grandmother's head cleared for an instant. She saw the man's face twisted close to her own as if he were going to cry and she murmured, "Why you're one of my babies. You're one of my own children!" She reached out and touched him on the shoulder. The Misfit sprang back as if a snake had bitten him and shot her three times through the chest. Then he put his gun down on the ground and took off his glasses and began to clean them.

Hiram and Bobby Lee returned from the woods and stood over the ditch, looking down at the grandmother who half sat and half lay in a puddle of blood with her legs crossed under her like a child's and her face smiling up at the cloudless sky.

Without his glasses, The Misfit's eyes were red-rimmed and pale and defenseless-looking. "Take her off and thow her where you thown the others," he said, picking up the cat that was rubbing itself against his leg.

"She was a talker, wasn't she?" Bobby Lee said, sliding down the ditch with a yodel.

"She would of been a good woman," The Misfit said, "if it had been somebody there to shoot her every minute of her life."

"Some fun!" Bobby Lee said.

"Shut up, Bobby Lee," The Misfit said. "It's no real pleasure in life."

The Madman in the Tower

IN THE FORENOON OF A BLAZING AUGUST DAY, A BLOND, HUSKY YOUNG MAN strolled into a hardware store in Austin, Texas, and asked for several boxes of rifle ammunition. As he calmly wrote a check in payment, the clerk inquired with friendly curiosity what all the ammunition was for. "To shoot some pigs," he replied. At the time, the answer seemed innocent enough, for wild pigs still abound not far from the capital. The horror of its intent only became obvious a few hours later, when the customer, Charles Joseph Whitman, 25, a student of architectural engineering at the University of Texas, seized his grisly fame as the perpetrator of the worst mass murder in recent U.S. history.

That morning, Charles Whitman entered two more stores to buy guns before ascending, with a veritable arsenal, to the observation deck of the limestone tower that soars 307 feet above the University of Texas campus. There, from Austin's tallest edifice, the visitor commands an extraordinary view of the 232-acre campus, with its green mall and red tile roofs, of the capital, ringed by lush farm lands, and, off to the west, of the mist-mantled hills whose purple hue prompted Storyteller O. Henry to christen Austin the "City of a Violet Crown." Whitman had visited the tower ten days before in the company of a brother, and had taken it all in. Today, though, he had no time for the view; he was too intent upon his deadly work.

Methodically, he began shooting everyone in sight. Ranging around the tower's walk at will, he sent his bullets burning and rasping through the flesh and bone of those on the campus below, then of those who walked or stood or rode as far as three blocks away. Somewhat like the travelers in Thornton Wilder's *The Bridge of San Luis Rey,* who were drawn by an inexorable fate to their crucial place in time and space, his victims fell as they went about their various tasks and pleasures. By lingering perhaps a moment too long in a classroom or leaving a moment too soon for lunch, they had unwittingly placed themselves within Whitman's lethal reach. Before he was himself perforated by police bullets, Charles Whitman killed 13 people and wounded 31—a staggering total of 44 casualties. As a prelude to his senseless rampage, it was later discovered, he had also slain his wife and mother, bringing the total dead to 15.

From *Time,* LXXXVIII (August 12, 1966), 14–19. Reprinted by permission from *Time,* The Weekly Newsmagazine; © Time Inc., 1966.

In a nation that opened its frontiers by violence and the gun, Whitman's sanguinary spree had an unsettling number of precedents, both in fiction and in fact. The imaginary parallels are grisly—and suggestive—enough: from *The Sniper,* a 1952 movie about a youth who shoots blondes, to *The Open Square,* a 1962 novel by Ford Clarke, whose protagonist climbs a tower on a Midwestern campus and begins picking people off. (So far as police know, Whitman had neither seen the movie nor read the book.) Even the fiction, however, pales before the fact. There was Scripture-reading Howard Unruh's 20-minute orgy that brought death to 13 people in Camden, N.J., in 1949, and bandy-legged Charles Starkweather's slaying of ten during a three-day odyssey through Nebraska and Wyoming in 1958. There were the two murderers of the Clutter family, Richard Hickock and Perry Smith, now enshrined in Truman Capote's *In Cold Blood,* the year's most talked-about bestseller. Only last month, when eight student nurses were slain in a Chicago town house, and Richard Speck was charged with the crime, an official there called the murders "the crime of the century." Sadly, Austin Police Chief Robert A. Miles observed last week: "It isn't any more."

Like many mass murderers, Charles Whitman had been an exemplary boy, the kind that neighborhood mothers hold up as a model to their own recalcitrant youngsters. He was a Roman Catholic altar boy and a newspaper delivery boy, a pitcher on his parochial school's baseball team and manager of its football team. At twelve years and three months, he became an Eagle Scout, one of the youngest on record. To all outward appearances, the family in which he grew up in Lake Worth, Fla.—including two younger brothers besides his mother and father, a moderately successful plumbing contractor—was a typical American family. Charlie joined the Marines in [14/15] 1959 when he was 18, later signed up at the University of Texas, where he was a B student.

Yet beneath the easy, tranquil surface of both family and boy there flowed some unusual undercurrents. Charlie was trained to use guns as soon as he was old enough to hold them—and so were his brothers. "I'm a fanatic about guns," says his father, Charles A., 47. "I raised my boys to know how to handle guns." Charlie could plug a squirrel in the eye by the time he was 16, and in the Marine Corps he scored 215 points out of a possible 250, winning a rating as a sharpshooter, second only to expert. In the Marines, though, he also got busted from corporal to private and sentenced to 30 days' hard labor for illegal possession of a pistol, was reprimanded for telling a fellow Marine that he was going "to knock your teeth out." He rated his favorite sports as hunting, scuba diving and karate.

A tense situation also prevailed behind the family façade. His father was—and is—an authoritarian, a perfectionist and an unyielding disciplinarian who demanded much of his sons and admitted last week that he was accustomed to beating his wife. In March, Margaret Whitman walked out on him, summoning Charlie from Austin to help her make the break. While his mother was packing her belongings, a Lake Worth police car sat outside the house, called by Charlie presumably because he feared that his father would resort to violence. To be near Charlie, Mrs. Whitman moved to Austin. The youngest son, John, 17, left home last spring. When he was arrested for pitching a rock through a storefront glass, the judge gave him a choice of a $25 fine or moving back in with his father; he paid the fine. Patrick, 21, who works for his father, is the only son who lives with him.

His parents' separation troubled Charlie deeply, and last March 29, he finally went to Dr. Maurice Heatly, the University of Texas' staff psychiatrist. In a two-hour interview, he told Heatly that, like his father, he had beaten his wife a few times. He was making "intense efforts" to control his temper, he said, but he was worried that he might explode. In notes jotted down at the time, Heatly described Whitman as a "massive, muscular youth" who "seemed to be oozing with hostility." Heatly took down only one direct quote of Whitman's —that he was "thinking about going up on the tower with a deer rifle and start shooting people." That did not particularly upset Heatly; it was, he said, "a common experience for students who came to the clinic to think of the tower as the site for some desperate action."[1] Nonetheless, Heatly urged Whitman to return the next week to talk some more. Charlie Whitman never [15/16] went back. Instead, some time in the next few months, he decided to act.

The evening before his trip to the tower, Whitman sat at a battered portable in his modest brick cottage. Kathy, his wife of four years (they had no children), was at work. "I don't quite understand what is compelling me to type this note," he began. "I've been having fears and violent impulses. I've had some tremendous headaches. I am prepared to die. After my death, I wish an autopsy on me to be performed to see if there's any mental disorders." He also wrote: "I intend to kill my wife after I pick her up from work. I don't want her to have to face the embarrassment that my actions will surely cause her."

At one point he had to break off when a fellow architecture student, Larry Fuess, and his wife dropped by to chat. Fuess found him looking "particularly relieved about something—you know, as if he had solved a problem." After the couple left, Whitman drove off in his black '66 Chevrolet to pick up Kathy at her summer job as a telephone information operator. He apparently decided not to kill her immediately, instead dropped her off at their house and sped across the Colorado River to his mother's fifth-floor flat in Austin's Penthouse

[1] Three persons have jumped from the tower to their deaths since its completion in 1937. Two others have died in accidental falls.

Apartments. There he stabbed Margaret Whitman in the chest and shot her in the back of the head, somehow also breaking several bones in her left hand with such force that the band of her diamond engagement ring was driven into her finger and the stone broken loose. "I have just killed my mother." Charlie wrote in a hand-printed note addressed "to whom it may concern." "If there's a heaven, she is going there. If there is not a heaven, she is out of her pain and misery. I love my mother with all my heart."

Back home—it was now after midnight—Whitman stabbed his wife three times in the chest, apparently as she lay sleeping, and drew the bed sheet over her nude body. Then he returned to the note— partially typewritten, partially handwritten, partially printed—that was to be his valedictory. Included was a tragic timetable: "12:30 A.M.—Mother already dead. 3 o'clock—both dead." He hated his father "with a mortal passion," he wrote, and regretted that his mother had given "the best 25 years of her life to that man." Clearly, the erratic orbit of his mind had already carried him off to some remote aphelion of despair. "Life is not worth living," he wrote. He had apparently concluded that if it were not worth living for him, it need not be for the others, either. With the special lucidity of the mad, Whitman meticulously prepared to take as many people with him to the grave as he possibly could.

Into a green duffel bag and a green foot locker that bore the stenciled words, "Lance Cpl. C. J. Whitman," he stuffed provisions to sustain him during a long siege and to cover every contingency: Spam, Planters peanuts, fruit cocktail, sandwiches and boxes of raisins, jerricans containing water and gasoline, rope, binoculars, canteens, transistor radio, toilet paper, and, in a bizarre allegiance to the cult of cleanliness, a plastic bottle of Mennen spray deodorant. He also stowed away a private armory that seemed sufficient to hold off an army: machete, Bowie knife, hatchet, a 6-mm. Remington bolt-action rifle with a 4-power Leupold telescopic sight (with which, experts say, a halfway decent shot can consistently hit a 6½-in. circle from 300 yds.), a 35-mm. Remington rifle, a 9-mm. Luger pistol, a Galesi-Brescia pistol and a .357 Smith & Wesson Magnum revolver. At home, he left three more rifles, two derringers.

Whether Whitman slept at all during the following few hours is not known. He was next seen at 7:15 A.M. when he rented a mover's dolly from an Austin firm. Then, deciding that he needed even more firepower, he went to Sears, Roebuck and bought a 12-gauge shotgun on credit, sawed off both barrel and stock. He visited Davis Hardware to buy a .30-cal. carbine. And at Chuck's Gun Shop, he bought some 30-shot magazines for the new carbine. All told, he had perhaps 700 rounds.

Around 11 A.M., Whitman boldly breezed into a parking spot reserved for university officials, near the main administration and

THE MADMAN IN THE TOWER

library building at the base of the tower. Dressed in tennis sneakers, blue jeans and a pale polo shirt, he wheeled the loaded dolly toward an elevator, gave passersby the impression that he was a maintenance man. The elevator stops at the 27th floor; Whitman lugged his bizarre cargo up three flights of steps to the 30th floor. There, at a desk next to the glass-paneled door that opens onto the observation deck, he encountered Receptionsist Edna Townsley, 47, a spirited divorcee and mother of two young sons. Whitman bashed her head in, probably with a rifle butt, with such force that part of her skull was torn away, also shot her in the head. Then he left her behind a sofa to die.

As Whitman began assembling his equipment on the deck, six sightseers arrived, led by Mark and Mike Gabour, the 16- and 19-year-old sons of M. J. Gabour, a service-station owner in Texarkana, Texas. "Mark opened the door to the observation deck and a gun went off," said Gabour. "Mike screamed." Then his sons, his wife and his sister, Mrs. Marguerite Lamport, "came rolling down the stairs. Whoever did the shooting slammed the door." Gabour turned his younger son over, saw he had been shot in the head. He was dead. So was Gabour's sister. Critically injured, his wife and his older son were bleeding profusely. Gabour and his brother-in-law dragged their dead and wounded to the 27th floor, sought help but could find none.

Outside, on the six-foot-wide walkway that runs around all four sides of the tower, Whitman positioned himself under the "VI" of the gold-edged clock's south face. Looking toward the mall, a large paved rectangle, he could see scores of students below him. Had Mrs. Townsley and the Gabours not held him up, he might have had another thousand students as targets when classes changed at 11:30 A.M. Now, at 11:48 A.M., Charles Whitman opened fire. The 17-chime carillon above him was to ring the quarter-hour six times before his guns were silenced.

For a moment, nobody could make out what the odd explosions from atop the tower meant. Then men and women began crumpling to the ground, and [16/17] others ran for cover. On the fourth floor of the tower building, Ph.D. Candidate Norma Barger, 23, heard the noises, looked out and saw six bodies sprawled grotesquely on the mall. At first she thought it was just a tasteless joke. "I expected the six to get up and walk away laughing." Then she saw the pavement splashed with blood, and more people falling. In the first 20 minutes, relying chiefly on the 6-mm. rifle with the scope but switching occasionally to the carbine and the .357 revolver, Whitman picked off most of his victims.

On the sun-dappled mall, Mrs. Claire Wilson, 18, eight months pregnant, was walking from an anthropology class when a bullet crashed into her abdomen; she survived, but later gave birth to a stillborn child whose skull had been crushed by the shot. A horrified classmate, Freshman Thomas Eckman, 19, knelt beside her to help, was shot dead himself. Mathematician Robert Boyer, 33, en route to a teaching job in Liverpool, England, where his pregnant wife and two children were awaiting him, stepped out onto the mall to head for lunch, was shot fatally in the back. More fortunate was Secretary Charlotte Darehshori, who rushed out to help when the first victims dropped, suddenly realized she was under fire and spent the next hour-and-a-half crouched behind the concrete base of a flagpole—one of the few persons to venture onto the mall and survive the siege uninjured.

At the south end of the mall, Austin Patrolman Billy Speed, 23, one of the first policemen on the scene, took cover behind the heavy, columnar stone railing, but a bullet zinged between the columns and killed him. Still farther south, 500 yds. from the tower, Electrical Repairman Roy Dell Schmidt, 29, walked toward his truck after making a call, was killed by a bullet in the stomach. To the east, Iran-bound Peace Corps Trainee Thomas Ashton, 22, was strolling on the roof of the Computation Center when Whitman shot him dead.

Directing his fire west, Whitman found shop-lined Guadalupe Street, the main thoroughfare off campus—known locally as "The Drag"—astir with shoppers and strollers. Paul Sonntag, 18, lifeguard at an Austin pool and grandson of Paul Bolton, longtime friend of Lyndon Johnson and news editor of the Johnsons' Austin television station, was accompanying Claudia Rutt, 18, for a polio shot she needed before entering Texas Christian University. Claudia suddenly sank to the ground. Paul bent over her, then pitched to the sidewalk himself. Both were dead. A block north, Political Scientist Harry Walchuk, 39, a father of six and a teacher at Michigan's Alpena Community College, browsed in the doorway of a newsstand after working all morning in the college library. He was shot dead on the spot. A few steps farther up the street, Senior Thomas Karr, 24, was walking sleepily toward his apartment after staying up almost all night for a 10 A.M. exam when he dropped to the pavement, dying.

Four minutes after Whitman opened fire, Austin police received a report about "some shooting at the University Tower." In seconds, a "10-50" trouble signal went out, directing all units in the vicinity to head for the university. In a din of wailing sirens, more than 100 city cops, reinforced by some 30 highway patrolmen, Texas Rangers and U.S. Secret Service men from Lyndon Johnson's Austin office, converged on the campus.

The lawmen sent hundreds of rounds of small-arms fire crackling toward the tower deck. A few smashed into the faces on the clocks above Whitman, and most pinked ineffectually into the four-foot high wall in front of him, kicking up puffs of dust. Ducking below the wall, Whitman began using narrow drainage slits in the wall as gunports. He proved almost impossible to hit, but he kept finding targets—to the north, where he wounded two students on their way to the Biology Building; to the east, where he nicked a girl sitting at a window in the

Business Economics Building; but particularly to the south, where the mall looked like a no man's land strewn with bodies that could not safely be recovered, and to the west, where The Drag was littered with four dead, eleven wounded.

Riding along The Drag, Newsboy Aleck Hernandez was practically catapulted off his bicycle when a bullet slammed into its seat— and his, inflicting a painful wound. Three blocks up The Drag, Basketball Coach Billy Snowden of the Texas School for the Deaf stepped into the doorway of the barbershop where he was having his [17/18] hair cut and was wounded in the shoulder. Outside the Rae Ann dress shop on The Drag, Iraqi Chemistry Student Abdul Khashab, 26, his fiancée Janet Paulos, 20, whom he was to have married next week, and Student-Store Clerk Lana Phillips, 21, fell wounded within seconds of each other. At Sheftall's jewelers, Manager Homer Kelley saw three youths fall wounded outside, was helping to haul them inside when Whitman zeroed in on the shop. Fragments from two bullets tore into Kelley's leg. Windows shattered. Bullets tore huge gashes in the carpeting inside. North of the tower, Associated Press Reporter Robert Heard, 36, was hit in the shoulder while he was running full tilt. "What a shot!" he marveled through his pain.

Unable to get at Whitman from the ground, the police chartered a light plane, sent sharpshooting Lieut. Marion Lee aloft in it. The sniper's fire drove it away. Finally four men, who had made their way separately to the tower building through subterranean passages or by zigzagging from building to building, decided to storm the observation deck. Three were Austin partolmen who had never been in a gunfight: Houston McCoy, Jerry Day and Ramiro Martinez, who was off duty when he heard of the sniper, got into uniform and rushed to the campus. The fourth was Civilian Allen Crum, 804, a retired Air Force tailgunner, who had "never fired a shot" in combat.

The four rode to the 27th floor, headed single file up the last three flights, carefully removed a barricade of furniture that Whitman had set at the top of the stairs. While cops on the ground intensified their fire to divert Whitman's attention, Martinez slowly pushed away the dolly propped against the door leading to the walkway around the tower, crawled out onto its south side and began moving stealthily to the east. Crum followed through the door and turned toward the west. Hearing footsteps, Crum fired into the southwest corner to keep Whitman from bursting around the corner and shooting him. Martinez, meanwhile, rounded one corner, then, more slowly, turned onto the north side of the walkway.

Fifty feet away from him, in the northwest corner, crouched Whitman, his eyes riveted on the corner that Crum was about to turn. Martinez poured six pistol shots into Whitman's left·side, arms and legs. McCoy moved up, blasted Whitman with a shotgun. Martinez, noting that the sniper's gun "was still flopping," grabbed the shotgun and blasted Whitman again. As an autopsy showed, the shotgun pellets did it: one pierced Whitman's heart, another his brain. Crum grabbed a green towel from Whitman's foot locker, waved it above the railing to signal cease-fire. At 1:24 P.M., 96 murderous minutes after his first fusillade from the tower, Charlie Whitman was dead.

Whitman's bloody stand profoundly shocked a nation [18/19] not yet recovered from the Chicago nurses' murders. One effect was to prompt a re-examination of U.S. arms laws and methods of handling suspected psychotics. There was a spate of ideas, some hasty and ill conceived. Texas Governor John Connally, who broke off a Latin American tour and hurried home after the shootings, demanded legislation requiring that any individual freed on the ground of insanity in murder and kidnaping cases be institutionalized for life. New York's Senator Robert Kennedy proposed that persons acquitted of all federal crimes on the ground of insanity be committed for psychiatric treatment. Had Whitman lived to face trial, said Kennedy, he would "undoubtedly" have been acquitted because "he was so clearly insane."

An autopsy showed that Whitman had a pecan-size brain tumor, or astrocytoma, in the hypothalamus region, but Pathologist Coleman de Chenar said that it was "certainly not the cause of the headaches" and "could not have had any influence on his psychic behavior." A number of Dexedrine tablets—stimulants known as "goofballs"—were found in Whitman's possession, but physicians were not able to detect signs that he had taken any before he died.

Precisely what triggered Whitman's outburst is a mystery. And it is likely to remain so, though psychiatrists will undoubtedly debate the causes for years. The role of Whitman's father in shaping—or misshaping—his son's personality has already come under intense scrutiny, but other psychiatrists feel that the cause of his illness must be sought in his relationship with his mother. Whatever its cause, Charlie Whitman's psychosis was poured out in detail in his farewell notes, which, a grand jury said, will be released only to "authorized investigating agencies, since they contain unverified statements of an insane killer concerning an innocent individual."

In the end, Charlie Whitman and his mother returned together to Florida, he in a grey metal casket, she in a green-and-white one. With hundreds of curiosity seekers gawking and jostling in a rolling, palm-fringed cemetery in West Palm Beach, mother and son were buried with Catholic rites. Charlie had obviously been deranged, said the Whitmans' priest, and was not responsible for the sin of murder and therefore eligible for burial in hallowed ground.

In Austin, where two of those wounded by Whitman remain in critical condition and three in serious condition, most flags flew at half-staff through the week. This week the flags go back to full staff as the university and the capital attempt to return to normal. That may take a while. The 17 chimes in the tower from which Charlie Whitman shot peal each quarter-hour, resounding over the tree-shaded campus and the mist-mantled hills beyond. [19]

A Violent Country

EDGAR Z. FRIEDENBERG

A Sign for Cain IS INDEED, AS ITS DUST-JACKET CLAIMS, A PROVOCATIVE book, though not so good a one as its wealth of material and the frequently stimulating insights of its author lead one to expect. It is certainly enormously concrete. Dr. Wertham's catalogue is long, through every passion ranging; he seems to have total recall for every foul deed of this century, from highschool initiations to Guernica, and many earlier. He provides an annotated list of the concentration camps of Greater Germany in 1945—there were twenty-three, many with specialized functions—and his topics extend from comic books to the McNaughton—to use his spelling—rule for legal insanity. His writing is erudite but cranky, with occasional lapses like his reference to ".024 per cent per 100,000" persons who died in automobile accidents in 1952. But nothing seems to have been omitted. In spite of its very considerable redeeming social significance, if violence turns you on you'll enjoy *A Sign for Cain* thoroughly.

The book's most serious defect is that it *is* an exploration. It has no organizing principle; and the whole is less than the sum of its parts. There is wisdom in it, like Wertham's observation that "The greatest achievement of the civil-rights movement is that it has restored the dignity of indignation," and his reference to it as "an underground of decency." But he has neither an ideology nor a coherent social theory by which his detailed observations could be related to one another. His analysis of the role of violence in contemporary life is greatly hampered by his lack of interest in and limited understanding of how people are involved in society.

This is a pity, because his subject has become supremely important, and he avoids the most serious trap into which an indignant old

From *The New York Review of Books,* VII (October 14, 1966), 3–4. Copyright © 1966, The New York Review. Reprinted by permission of *The New York Review of Books* and Edgar Z. Friedenberg.

psychiatrist might easily have fallen. He does not try to treat the widespread violence in our world as the collective expression of defective personality or emotional disorder. He is far too canny for that; but the absence of a theoretical framework tempts him constantly to go off the track to sniff among the flowers of evil.

Rather than try to follow him into these tangled thickets, it seems to me that it may be more illuminating, both to the book's subject and to the problems it presents to the reader, to take one specific instance of such derailment, and do what seems necessary to get the discussion back on the tracks again, as an illustration of the kind of intellectual effort involved. I have chosen Wertham's comment on the failure of the courts to punish two high-school boys who had seriously injured a young friend by rough hazing. In this connection, he quotes approvingly *The New York Times*'s sad observation that, "Young, unsophisticated minds may readily conclude that sadism and barbarism . . . are not really punishable," and observes: "This is precisely what happens. The Goddess of Violence usurps the place of Themis, the Goddess of Law."

"The Goddess of Violence" is the title of the first chapter of *A Sign for Cain,* and we become very familiar with her features in the course of it. But are there really *two* Goddesses? Laying aside for the moment the question whether fraternity hazing among adolescents is the same kind of phenomenon as the others Wertham also includes in his chapter on juvenile violence—for example, kick-killings and " 'rooftop murders' in which boys of fifteen or sixteen throw younger girls from the roofs of tall buildings"—let us look more sharply at the Goddess of Law. As she goes about her business, she is often very hard to distinguish from her sister. In the modern world, nearly all the violence that occurs is lawful violence; while a large proportion of that which is not is nevertheless committed by the civil, penal, or military authorities in the course of duty. The German concentration camps were lawful. Our own authorities maintain that the American intervention in Vietnam is lawful. Executions are lawful. Much of Dr. Wertham's book is taken up with atrocities of unquestionable legality in the jurisdictions in which they occurred; while the most disgusting examples he cites are proposals for legalizing new punishments for juvenile delinquents. One of these, taken from a letter to a "metropolitan newspaper" advises:

Take the ten worst juvenile delinquents arrested during the week and over a national television hookup tie them to posts, pull down their pants and beat their bare behinds until they scream for mercy.

To an Eastern reader this may seem the product of a somewhat fevered imagination in which hostile impulses have been permitted to displace devotion to due process; but any Californian would instantly recognize in this suggestion the tone of a defender of law and order.

Most Americans would say that they disapproved of violence. But what they really mean is that they believe it should be a monopoly of the state. What we fear is not violence itself so much as "taking the law into your own hands"; and we generally call people who have resisted the legitimate agents of coercion violent even when the agents have been violent and they have not. In spite of the monotonous consistency of the press reports that denigrate their protest, no Berkeley students have ever rioted, but quite a few have been manhandled by the police in the course of demonstrations; while non-violent civil-rights workers all over the country have grown quite accustomed to learning, on recovering consciousness, that X-rays reveal them to have been resisting arrest. Within the past week I have gotten into a public argument with a distinguished editor of a highly respected monthly who heatedly told me that Berkeley students had been behaving "just the way you object to our people acting in Vietnam!" Even if—as is certainly possible— this man had confused LSD with napalm, they don't drop tons of the stuff on small children in the Bay Area; and even if they had the napalm, they wouldn't drop it on anyone under thirty. It wouldn't turn them on.

On the other hand, the headquarters of the Vietnam Day Committee in Berkeley really was bombed with genuine dynamite several months ago and destroyed; and this demonstration of devotion to the new conservatism aroused no visible emotion stronger than embarrassment in the citizens who indignantly perceive the VDC's protests as riots. The crime remains unsolved; but the supporters of Mr. Reagan who scream that the dissident students are a filthy menace are not at all disturbed by the incontrovertible fact that there is a dynamiter loose among them, and not at all curious to learn who he is.

This, then, is a further complication in the social psychology of violence. Not only do most people accept violence if it is perpetrated by legitimate authority, they also regard violence against certain kinds of people as inherently legitimate, no matter who commits it. When one of these is the victim, his attackers are regarded as more legitimate than the law. The guardians of the law, for their part, seem often to concur in this judgment, and either join the attackers or slink away and leave the victim in their hands. White policemen who are ordered to protect little Negro girls from being beaten by white mobs on their way to school tend to shuffle about their task shamefacedly.

At a still deeper psychological level, there appears to be a strong though mute tendency among us to accept violence as legitimate—or at least, not to mind it very much—if it is manifested by individuals who come on with a gung-ho swagger in real or imaginary green berets. Compare the hatred and resentment aroused by draft-card burners, whose aggression is wholly symbolic and non-violent, with the rapid cooling off of public interest in Mr. Whitman after his apotheosis on the Texas Tower. His credentials were so impeccable that they almost served to license his deed. A former marine whose father had reared him with exemplary firmness, he was clearly one of our boys and not a guitar-playing Vietnik, even if he did murder seventeen people. There was nothing long-haired or queer about him: he even beat his wife and tried to sell girlie postcards. As the late Flannery O'Connor observed in her best known short story, which recounts a rather similar episode, a good man is hard to find.

Themis is no goddess in her own right; she is the paler *alter ego* of her brutal sister: violence in a respectable mask. The mask saves her a lot of embarrassment. While she is wearing it she can preside over police stations whose interrogation rooms are often the most dangerous place in town; and prisons—her grim shrines in which violence has become the ritual by which order is maintained. She can delight respectable citizens, who would be horrified by bare-faced obscenity, with the spectacular asphyxiation of the infamous kidnapper Caryl Chessman. The Goddess of Law has never been non-violent; and has usually been the enemy of those who are.

But whether as Goddess of Law or Goddess of Violence she has certainly, as Dr. Wertham notes, become more conspicuous lately, and has begun to arouse rather unfavorable comment. Her trouble is that when she has on her Themis mask she cannot keep her mouth shut. When she comes on in the role of upholder of the law she utters streams of the most appalling, unconvincing cant; but her voice is the voice of Violence, her deeds are deeds of Violence, and the disagreeable consequence is to create a crisis of legitimacy which evokes violence from others. Some imitate her, like the Hell's Angels, who volunteer to help the police by conducting mop-up operations on Vietniks whom the Constitution—never a popular document—keeps the police from touching, yet. Some newcomers and strangers in the *polis*, like the emptier sort of juvenile delinquent or aimless slum looters and stompers don't know what the hell she is talking about and don't care; but will be damned if they're going to be told what to do by a goddess who sounds to them like a crazy woman. But some, potentially the most responsible citizens of their generation, do understand her: and are so infuriated by her hypocrisy [3/4] and the keening note of hatred underlying her pomposity that they finally lose their tempers and hurl a rock or a bottle at her, or, more tragically, set fire to themselves. Altogether, they make quite a scene; but personally, I take Mr. Carmichael for a very patient man and wish him many, many more kilowatts in any color he chooses.

Dr. Wertham deals with the violence of several decades, and these phenomena cannot, therefore, be explained in terms of contemporary events. But the increased sense of urgency with which we respond to the issues he raises is, I think, largely a consequence of contemporary developments. The most obvious of these, of course, is the scope which modern technology gives to violent action. We are not, on the basis of the total historical record, an unusually brutal people; but we are the first whose military leaders and technicians have prattled of megatons and megadeaths in the interests of a free society.

But I would also attach great importance to the crisis of legitimacy to which I referred two paragraphs back, which leaves all of us edgier and more trigger-happy than we used to be. The public mood is uglier, a basic element of trust is gone, and with good reason. The war in Vietnam, undeclared, continually escalated by the adoption of military techniques and initiatives which the administration had previously undertaken not to use, and devastating the homeland of a poor and gallant people on the shabbiest of political pretexts, is generating a vast contempt for legitimate authority. The Chief Justice of the United States and his Commission appear to have made no serious effort to determine what relationships, if any, the murders of President Kennedy and Lee Harvey Oswald may have had to the political tensions and power-strivings of the time; though the assassination of course determined the succession of legitimate executive authority in this country. The unnerving fact is that we do not know which of us are murderers; though, in view of the war, we have all become so implicated in killing that we ought not, perhaps, to worry overmuch about the personal daintiness of our neighbors.

Even such melodramatic events as these, however, are but surface manifestations of the fundamental need for violence that our society—and perhaps every society—shows. Dr. Wertham does not reveal to us the source of that need—perhaps it is, as the ethologists maintain, a fundamental instinct of man which reflects his basic impotence. But he does call our attention to a relationship that consistently recurs in our culture, though the patterns of violence vary greatly through time and place. Wertham is not the first to note the importance of this relationship. Gershon Legman[1], Leslie Fiedler, and Norman O. Brown, among others, have done much more with it than he does. But he does bring it up and remind us again of its importance.

This is the curious preference we so consistently show for violence over sex. Wertham, who has been crusading against comic books for a decade or so, is particularly appalled by the way in which obviously lewd encounters are resolved by revealing that the motives of the male are destructive rather than erotic, and hence not offensive after all—an explanation that society accepts as perfectly satisfactory. "A producer of horror films said with pride over the radio," Dr. Wertham notes, "'Our pictures are absolutely clean. The monster might abduct the young bride, but only to kill her.'"

Now it is impossible to disagree with Dr. Wertham's conclusion that this is the sentiment of a very sick society, though I wish he could

[1] G. Legman, *Love and Death*, New York, Hacker, 1949.

also see how funny it is. But I think he seriously misunderstands the situation, which is even worse than he thinks.

Wertham sees the mass media and especially gory comic books as breeding and catering to sadism. But—as the producer's comment makes clear—what they are catering to is alienation, not sadism. A sadist has a real, albeit distorted sexual relationship to his partner; we may not approve of his methods, but his purpose is to make love, not war. The comic books are a lot more modern than the Marquis; their message is that their characters *get* no satisfaction, that violence must be its own reward. This is far more dehumanizing than sadism, and, for that very reason, far more functional to a mass society which fears nothing so much as real personal commitment, whatever its basis may be. A real sadist would make a very poor Eichmann; his personal tastes would constantly obtrude upon his official duties, leading him to spare some victims through ennui and others because of need.

At this point it may be illuminating to raise again the question I deferred in order to pursue the problem of Themis's identity. Wertham's perception of fraternity hazing as functionally equivalent to throwing girls off tall buildings obscures an important point. What is basically horrifying about all the forms of juvenile violence Wertham deplores is not just their violence, but the fact that they involve attacking people contemptuously and breaking them up as if they were things of no value. No sexual act has this inhuman quality, and it is precisely sexuality that prevents it; one suspects that a boy who would hurl a girl to her death would be incapable even of rape. Hazing may become comparably vicious if the boys who are inflicting it are subject to homosexual panic; and this may, of course, have been the case in the incident Dr. Wertham cites. But the contrary may also be true. Hazing may be both violent and obscene without being dangerous, if the group in which it occurs is linked by real affection and is enough at ease with its own animal nature to enjoy an honest dirty joke. It becomes dangerous as it becomes depersonalized under the influence of precisely the same social forces that moved the producer of horror films. The encounter is reduced to sniggering hostility in the interests of keeping the show clean; and the erotic empathy that might have kept it human instead—the built-in safety factor—is repressed as thoroughly as possible.

Since the world is now very much less personal indeed than it was a generation ago, hazing would undoubtedly be more likely to take an ugly turn; and since the present generation tends to approach all forms of sexuality less obliquely than its elders did, they would probably find the fraternity life that we enjoyed both archaic and grotesque. They can protect their precious polymorphous perversity from social strangulation without so often having to proceed, as we did, on the assumption that the longest way round may well be the shortest way home. Times change; hazing—and, in large measure, fraternity life itself—have become dysfunctional in a society in every way more open. In this small area of life, then, there is less violence because young people find it less necessary to use a paddle in order to keep from touching one another.

This is great; but what is great about it is not that they are less violent, but that they are more loving. There is no consistent connection between the two. Violence may be loving, or hostile, or alienated; hostility may be violent; but the worst is passive and cold. Dr. Wertham notes this; his comments on the cool technicians who ran the concentration camps show that he understands that Iago is more dangerous than Othello. But I am less sure that he realizes that what made Othello dangerous is also what made him lovable and brave. And there is nothing in his work to suggest how infinitely more horrible Emilia's life must have been than Desdemona's.

Despite his detailed attention to the concentration camps, Wertham continually gives the impression that violence is essentially disorderly, and that the more orderly life is the more humane it is likely to be. If this were true, the world would be a far less dangerous place. But it is not true; it is false—and this is more than a psychological axiom. It is a political principle of the greatest relevance and urgency. Violence is, indeed, the hallmark of our age and perhaps its most serious social problem. But one cannot hope to intervene in the processes of violence without making things much worse, unless one is careful always to distinguish the violence of a lover in his passion, or a man revolting against an unbearable reality by whatever means may be at hand, from that violence which expresses what E. M. Forster called "panic and emptiness." Panic and emptiness are the distinguishing characteristics of our time; and panicky, empty people are usually very fond of order, though the converse need not be true.

Captain Vere, beneath his devotion to discipline, was a panicky man; and it is he, as the story ends, who commits the most violent and destructive action in it; and the only one which is obscene. He and Claggart together constitute the public menace—not Billy Budd. Billy was not wholly innocent, for there are occasions when each of us is obligated to speak plainly, and this he failed to do. But a man like Vere, who feels *safer* after he had Billy hanged, must cause consternation even in Hell; he would be so boring to torment. The devil, surely, must prefer more imaginative victims; but he must put up with the clients he gets. It hardly behooves us to try to solve his personnel problems. As Dr. Wertham reminds us, we have plenty of our own.
[4]

What Comes Next

JONATHAN BAUMBACH

July 24

His wife answered. I asked if I could speak to her husband. Please. Very polite. Using my hand to disguise my voice. *Put your mister on, missus.*

She said he wasn't there, didn't know when he would be back, breathing like a whisper.

I didn't say anything, didn't want to talk to her.

"Is this Christopher? Curt's student, Christopher?"

It was getting dark. I said I would call back later, wanting to get back to my place before night.

"Why won't you identify yourself?"

"You know who it is."

"Why do you act as if you don't know me?" Her voice like splinters of glass on linoleum. "Did you find another place to stay? Is that what happened? Curt and I were under the illusion, mistakenly obviously, that you were staying with us. We kept expecting you to come back."

"Can I come back?"

She was slow to answer. Too slow. "I'll have to think about it." She laughed.

I said goodbye.

"If you have no other plans"—her voice sweet—"why don't you come to dinner tomorrow night?"

"Do you know where I can find Parks now?"

"Christopher, I really don't give a good damn. Where he is is his business, isn't it?"

Where he is is my business.

July 25

I couldn't sleep. Too heavy. The bed, triple-sized, like a field—too many possibilities of place. No spot precisely mine, belonging to me. I spread my arms out, brought them to my sides. Held myself. No spot mine. Moved from back to side to back. Holding on to myself, afraid of falling. (Have fallen, have fallen, have fallen.) I lay on my back in the middle of the bed, my arms out.

In the dark, my mother coming into my room, saying not to worry about anything, not to worry. "I don't want to die," I said. "I'm afraid of dying." *I won't let you,* she whispers. "Do you think if it's in my power, your mother will let you die?" My father calling her. "Are you all right now, my big boy? Don't worry so much. Smile." Tucking me in. I said yes. "How can you keep me from dying?" I asked her when she was gone and could no longer hear. In the night I died.

I spread myself out under the sanctifying canopy, father and mother. Myself, father and mother. I give it to her, bear my seed, give birth, am born.

I can no longer remember what I've done. What do they want me for (whoever it is that follows), what does the law want? I have not done half of what they think. What haven't I done?

Not sleeping, I dream Winnifred coming down from Chico's building. I am a block away. She runs after me. Slowly.

"Where did you go, Curt—I mean, Chris?" Touching my arm. Confident that she would get what she wanted.

"Go to hell," I said, moving out of range of her knee.

She smiled queerly. "What did you think Chico and I were doing up there?"

Chico was holding her from behind. "Hit her in the face," he said.

I pulled her away from him, knocking her into a wall, went for him, Chico stumbling back, scared of me. I pointed a finger at him and he disappeared.

"Are you all right?" I said to her. She was sitting at the base of the wall, her eyes blank like torn petals, without centers. "He won't bother you again." She made no sound. I shook her. "Are you all right?" I was shaking her. Her head rolled from her shoulders, cracking open on the sidewalk. Her body limp like cloth, her flesh surgical rubber. I held her against me, held her.

A woman, heavyset, middle-aged, was shaking me.

"Are you one of my son's friends?" she asked, "Did he tell you you could stay here?"

"Who's your son?" I said, not awake enough to lie.

"You'll have to go now," she said in a high pitched brittle voice as if she were brushing off an insect or a piece of dust.

"I'm sorry, whoever you are, you'll have to go. Who told you you could stay here? You're not a friend of Kenneth's?"

I said I wasn't anyone's friend, but enjoyed widening my circle of acquaintance, enjoyed meeting mothers so long as they weren't my own.

"I'd like to know, it's an object of much curiosity to me, how you got in here." Standing imperiously in the doorway, pushing at her hair, prodding it uselessly into place.

I made up some story about how I happened to be there, not bothering to make sense since she wasn't really listening. My right arm had been cramped under me, the circulation dead. I shook it and she winced as if I were doing it to her. This soft look on her face.

"I told Kenneth expressly that he wasn't to use the house for entertaining in our absence," she was saying. "I didn't know what to think when I saw you lying in bed that way. Do you make a habit of sleeping in other people's houses?"

By this time I had my shoes on. It was morning, I discovered—my eyes fully opened—and I wanted to get out without having to hurt her. She kept on talking about how on top of everything I didn't even know her son, and what a shock it gave her to find me there.

It worried me that she would threaten to call the police and I would have to do something to her.

I apologized in my politest voice, said I would pack my briefcase and go.

"Tell me what you were thinking of," she said, her voice so brittle the words seemed to snap like figurines as they fell. "What possessed you to spend the night in a place you didn't belong. Did you have no other place to stay?"

"There were other places I could have stayed."

"I suppose then we should be honored that you chose our apartment over all the others, though I think it's an honor we wouldn't have minded doing without."

Someone, her husband it turned out, let himself into the apartment, called *Helen*. My hostess, taking her time, going out to meet him.

"We have a guest, Ken," I heard her announce. "I found some strange boy sleeping in our bed."

"A friend of Kenneth's?"

"No."

"Then who the hell is he?"

"I haven't the foggiest. What do you intend to do about it?"

"Do you think he's . . . ?"

My briefcase bulging, I came into the livingroom, feeling, though innocent, like a thief.

"Who have we here?" he said, blustering, holding out his hand.

I said my name was Curtis Parks. We shook hands. His palm damp.

"It's a pleasure to meet you," he said, our eyes not meeting, glancing at his wife who was tapping her foot. "I guess we came home a little earlier than you expected, is that right?" He faked a laugh. Ha Ha.

"Aren't you going to ask him what he was doing in your bed? Doesn't that concern you?"

"I don't see that there's any harm done, Helen," he said in a deep voice, smiling at us both.

"You can't have any idea whether there's been any harm done," she said. "You've just this minute walked in, and I know you haven't looked around." Her chalky face as if someone had beaten it with a rock. "Why should we be subjected to this kind of treatment? He could have robbed us blind for all you know or care."

He glanced at my swollen briefcase, his eyes in flight, nervous at what he had seen.

I said I didn't take anything of theirs.

"Would you mind very much, Cliff, showing us what's in you case," he said, looking at her, "so that there'll be no false suspicions afterwards."

"How mealymouthed you are, Ken. Just tell him that he's to empty his case. Whether he minds or not is of no concern to me." Her lips in contortion as if there was something painfully sour in her mouth. "Please empty your case, young man."

"I don't think I will."

"What do you have to say to that, Ken. If my son were here, he wouldn't let me be treated this way. I can tell you that."

His eyes flew back and forth between us. He took a step toward his wife, who had her arms crossed in front of her, and shook her vigorously, unsettling her wig. "If you ever try to order me around again in front of someone . . ."

"Coward." She showed him her teeth, bellowing some awful sound. They blasted each other without moving—I stood between them, though it made no difference. "Leave her alone," I said.

"You're beneath contempt," she said softly and went into the bedroom and slammed the door.

"I'm going to have some eggs and coffee," he said. "You're welcome to join me."

I said I had to go somewhere.

"She'll be all right," he said. "She's been asking for something like that for a long time."

His face was flushed. "If you see Kenneth, don't mention this to him, huh? I trust your discretion." He held out his hand, one gentleman to another, his wife bawling, calling to him.

I took his hand, squeezed it, increasing the pressure, wanting to pay him back. Grunting, his teeth smiling, he squeezed back. His hand hard to grip, slippery. We struggled, twisting and pressing, nothing happening. "Kenneth and I used to hand wrestle this way all the time," he said. "You have a good grip, Cliff."

I let go, my shirt stained with his sweat. My hands. There was nothing to do but get away.

I called Parks but when Carolyn answered I hung up, slammed the phone on its hook. Running from the booth.

There was no place in the city to go. There is no place.

My father rushing through the house with a carving knife. My mother holding the door against him, leaning her weight against it. Phyllis and I were hiding behind the sofa. We didn't know who he was after. Phyllis crying. I had my knife in my pocket. My mother telling him to go away. *Go Away.* He forced his way in, knocking the door against her, knocking her down. "You're crazy," Phyllis said. "You're crazy," I said, pulling away from her, yelling at him. He dropped the knife at our mother's feet, staring at us as if he had been woken from a dream. How gentle he looked!

On Riverside drive, wearing Parks's shirt and pants—the clothes Carolyn had given me—looking at the shiny river, as I walked to the bridge. I was going to hitch a ride somewhere out of the city. A pair of sunglasses on a bench stopped me, the small wire rimmed kind, the glass hardly bigger than the eye. Really nice. I put them on, the wire pinching my ears. In my hurry, wanting to keep the glasses, I left my briefcase—everything I owned in it—behind. When I came back there was a young Negro sitting on the bench, a cool looking guy with a beard, puffing on a cigar.

I asked if he had seen a black briefcase.

He didn't answer, puffed contemplatively on his cigar. "Where did you get those tiny shades, Jack?" he said, not looking at me, watching his smoke ascend.

"You can have the glasses if you let me know where the case is."

"Jack, are you intimating that I took your case? Is that what you're trying to tell me? What every black man wants is a white man's black briefcase in his black hand. Is that what you think?"

"If you say so. You know better than I what I think."

"What?"

"I think you're the kind of guy that probably knows everything. Is that what you think?"

"What?"

Somebody I didn't see grabbed my arms from behind. Taking his time, the fellow on the bench got up, the teeth of his smile like flames. "It's not polite to accuse someone you don't know of taking from you, Jack. Your black briefcase—you think I need that to be human. I don't even want your gangrenous gray skin. Even if you were willing to give it up, to cut it off and hand it over, I wouldn't take a suit of it." Like a surgeon, he removed my glasses.

"Don't hurt him," the guy holding my arms said. "Just take the glasses and let him go, Omar."

"Do you think it would give me any pleasure to hurt you?" he said, his face very close. The heat of his stump of cigar palsying the air. "It wouldn't give me the slightest bit of pleasure. Not the slightest." He held the glasses as if he were going to smash them into my eyes.

"It wasn't very propitious to get him mad," the guy behind me said. "A bad mistake of strategy."

There were some people watching, white and Negro, but no one made a move to interfere. I thought I saw Rosemary among them, standing between a man and a woman I'd never seen before.

"What I want is to dismember you," he said in a soft drawl. "To take you apart piece by piece, limb by limb, skin by skin, to make a white briefcase out of you to keep my important black papers in. Remember that, though I'm a non-violent man, I want to kill you." Languorously, he went back to the bench and, putting the glasses on, sat down.

My arms were freed. I turned to see who was behind me. A bald light skinned Negro, older looking than the other, my briefcase between his legs. He dusted it off with his hand and, laughing, handed it to me as if it were fragile, as if it might blow up if it were dropped. "No hard feelings," he said.

I smiled back, put my knee in his balls, his face turning white. Ran. Hiding out in the men's room in the basement of Philosophy Hall at Columbia. Sitting in a booth, the door latched. Voices, people, going in and out, washing hands, looking for something. Washing hands. I stayed put. My black case between my legs.

July 26

I feel like a bomb set to go off at some approaching point of time, set for infinity which comes and goes, which has already been. *You bitch, Rosemary, you nun.* All day I stay away from contact. My fuse between heart and mouth, burning like a cigarette. Very short. The hands on my watch hold their position like the Queen's guards. My fuse the corded nerve of an eye. To see is to lose control, to explode.

Go, I tell myself. Now. *Now.* It takes a moment to get going (I am nine and have short legs for my age). I sense as I run, head down—the traffic heavy—that I'm not going fast enough. A steel pulley between my legs weighing me down. I anticipate the impact, a slow motion runner (again and again I watch myself cover the same few feet of ground), my nerves, somnambulists, but nothing happens. The street is deserted. I am where I begin. The rain continues.

At night, feeling better, I went to Parks's for dinner wanting to ask him something. I had a drink, a gin and tonic in a metal glass, and some cheese and salami on wheat thins. (My briefcase on the couch next to me.) Sweat like acid in the raw lines of my hands. I didn't ask where Parks was. Where wasn't he?

Not listening to Carolyn, looking at her voice, I felt better than I had for a long time—the drink maybe, the gin—felt for moments on end out of danger.

I sat on the red and gray horse, tried weight on it, rode back and forth. Gently. Pressing my knees to its sides.

"Curt built that," she said. "It's one of the few things he's ever finished. Except . . . I won't say it. I'll be kind."

His name in the room like a presence. I looked around, expecting to see him somewhere, sucking on his pipe, angry at him for not helping me.

Her anger, like the sudden touch of something cold, rode past me. "Have you seen him recently?" she said, her eyes behind me. The horse's tail flying.

"Have I seen who?"

She gave me a cunning look. "It doesn't become you to play dumb, Christopher. You're going to break that horse if you keep riding it that way."

She wanted it broken. "I haven't seen him recently," I said.

"Would you tell me if you had? Your activity on the horse is making me nervous. I don't know whether to believe you or not."

I looked around the room again, the tilt of instinct—the furniture precarious, hostile.

Carolyn was laughing.

"Why didn't you tell me he was gone? I came here to see him." I got off the horse, her tension pricking me.

Like a sleepwalker, her face clouded over, she walked away. Deserted me. The horse rocking, riderless, dying to a stop.

Unable to sit, needing to move, I walked around the room. There was a letter left out on top of the desk (a paperweight with two fishes head to head inside on the paper) from some historical magazine. Full of praise for some essay he had written, "The Murders of Lincoln and Kennedy—The Assassins in Our Mirror"—but saying it wasn't for them because they only published articles dealing with 19th Century history. From what they said, I had the feeling that it was my paper they were talking about—the one I had written for his class. I called Carolyn and got no answer, called again. Went through the drawers of the desk, which was full of useless things—souvenirs, photos, blank paper. A picture of Carolyn, much younger, in a bathing suit standing between two men, neither of which was Parks.

I found her lying across the width of their double bed, her head in her arms, as if she were holding something breakable, the room without light.

As I approached, Carolyn lifted her head to see who was there, her hand shading her eyes to no purpose. "Sometimes I need to withdraw," she said.

"Why didn't you answer when I called?"

"Why don't you go home, Christopher? I think I want to be alone now." Her hips squirming.

I wondered what it would be like to be against her body, to feel the heat between her legs. "I'm waiting for your husband," I said.

She raised herself on an arm. "If that's why you're here, you'd better go. He's not coming back."

"I didn't know that you weren't living together. It's not my fault." I closed my eyes not to look at her, but they flicked open, staring irresistibly.

She put on the lamp next to her bed, trembled at something. At seeing the way I was looking at her. The eyes of my voice. The light made her squint. "You didn't know that Curt had moved out? I don't know whether to believe you or not, Christopher—it's possible that you didn't know. If you hadn't spoken to Curt as you say, though I imagine you have other sources. Have you spoken to his girl?" Something broken in her face gleamed.

I felt the knife in my pocket, got out of the bedroom—the rest of the house in a fever of heat.

"Chris, don't go," Carolyn said, coming after me. My back to her. Not knowing where to go. "It's not you I'm angry at. I'm sorry." Her hand on my arm, rubbing, patting it, as if it belonged to her. "I'm not always this way, am I?"

"You don't know what you're sorry for." I was suffocating, pulled her arm away so I could breathe, though it made no difference. My chest heavy.

"You hurt me," she said, her head hung like a child's.

I stood facing the wall, then I sat down on the couch, then I got up. "I can't stay here."

"I'll fix you another drink. Dinner should be ready in at most five minutes. I promise. I left Jacqueline at my mother's so we could talk without interruptions."

"I don't want any dinner," I said. "I'm not hungry." Something in my stomach ticking.

"I'll have to throw it out if you don't eat it."

My mother used to say that and he would get very angry, banging his fist on the table, but then he would eat everything. Phyllis used to leave food on her plate.

"Why should it bother me whether you throw it out? I'd like to see you throw it out."

She was grinning, her mouth twisted. "It does bother you though, doesn't it? You're like my husband—you can't bear to see anything wasted."

"You threaten to throw things out but you never do it. You're like my mother—you're a fake."

I went into the kitchen after her. She was tilting a yellow enamel

pot over the garbage pail, brown stuff clinging to the sides. I took it
away from her, twisting her arm to get it away.

Sitting in his seat, I ate his dinner.

"Was Curt really a good teacher?" she asked.

"Better than most."

"Not great enough? Just better than most. Perhaps better than you
were able to recognize. Isn't that possible? You're not very generous,
Christopher."

She had no use for him, she said, neither hate nor love, just
moribund feelings and a terrible sense of waste. She was still shaky,
on tranquilizers most of the time, but feeling like a person for the first
time in years.

Her food, most of it, still on her plate. Not hungry, I finished
everything, hungrier now than I was done. Words buzzed through,
sticking to the skin like flies on a damp day. The wine had no effect.
My senses like pins. I couldn't shut her out though she didn't care
whether I listened or not, looked at me without sight. (I could have
died in the middle of her story and she wouldn't have stopped.) Too
many voices ticking in my head, women's voices—the words senseless—
the sound like being kissed to sleep.

(Wherever we lived, I always had the smallest room.)

"Nothing he does satisfies him," she was saying. "He sits around
looking miserable, suffering, blaming it on us. He's incapable of any
kind of real pleasure."

My foot itched so I removed my shoe to get at where it was.

"He may be happier with her for awhile but his unhappiness has
nothing to do with who he's with, and eventually he'll blame her for
his discontent and tell her he wants his freedom and take off and
leave her."

She's mad, I kept thinking, doesn't know who she's talking to,
who's drinking her red wine (corkscrew on the table leering at her).
Her breasts like soap bubbles.

"One of the difficulties of our marriage from the start—I say this
as a fact, you understand—is that I'm smarter than Curt . . .

"My husband has some illusion of himself as a great man. How
boring he can be. Oh God, how dull he is."

My mother was telling us how my father was the most exciting
man she knew—everything he said was original and brilliant—that's
why she married him, difficult as he is. "If you think he's so brilliant,"
Phyllis said, "why is it you never listen to him when he talks?" She said
how cute we were, her eyes floating out of her head, hugging Phyllis,
hugging us both. *How cute.*

"I don't think he's dull," I said.

She looked at me nervously, her tongue moving between her lips.
"He has a solemn manner, which I'm sure you've noticed, which passes,
I imagine, for brilliance among his students. He can be very impres-

sive, very high-serious if you don't listen too carefully to what he's saying."

I couldn't stand to listen. Some untouched terror—a vulture's dense need—creasing the walls with its shadow.

"When he finished describing what I had done to mar his potentially beautiful life, his packed suitcase was at the door waiting for him. So: out." She pointed to the door. "So clear the hell out if you're not happy here. I don't want it any more."

I thought of going but there was no place, the streets dark. Carolyn on the couch, musing, bitter. (If they found her dead, would they blame me for it? The evidence—my fingerprints too many places to be undone—would point to me, though I would be innocent. Who else would kill her?)

"Don't go yet," she said.

I sat down on a chair close to the couch, my chest heavy, burning. "Would you take him back?"

"If you had understood what I was saying," she said coldly, "you wouldn't have asked that." A suspicious look on her face, nodding to herself as if she had discovered something.

"Do you think I didn't understand you?"

She laughed like glass breaking. "I don't think anyone understands me." Getting up. "You can tell my husband if you see him, though of course you won't, that he's made his choice and he's going to have to take responsibility for it. Tell him that please." She went to the bathroom and returned with new makeup on, her hair combed, looking softer and more tired. Wearing perfume.

"Are you still here?"

If I had some place to go, I would have left.

"Do you know where he is, your husband?" I would stay with him, I decided.

"Don't you?" She smiled conspiratorially—a sad irony in the lifting of her eyebrows. Her eyes trying to get out of her skull. She gnawed on her lip, her head tilted as if she were listening to something she couldn't quite hear. "He's always been a self-concerned bastard." Covering her face with her hands. "Why are we all so miserable? Why is it nothing we do gives us satisfaction?"

I went to the bathroom, my face out of focus in the mirror, my eyes bloodshot. The place had an overripe smell, a heavy female smell. A black bra and a pair of flowered panties hung on the towel rack, a red towel between them, a pinkish rabbit slightly mutilated on the floor next to the john. A knuckle on my left hand was bleeding, the skin scraped off, without any sense of when or how it had happened. There were no band-aids in the medicine cabinet, mostly bottles of things—pills, medicines, a brownstained bottle of iodine, the applicator broken. Trying to get it out, I spilled some iodine, the stuff heavy and old, into the bowl of the sink. I scrubbed at the stain, used soap and hot water, the water scalding my hands. The stain remained, dots of red around it. My life trickling into her sink.

It struck me that the blood on my hands was from Carolyn—that I had hurt her in some way I couldn't remember, but when I got back, she was all right. My knuckle still bleeding, I asked for a band-aid.

"Let me see your hand."

"It's nothing," I said, holding it out for her to examine.

She made a face of mock-horror. "Come on in the bathroom. I'll do it for you. Come on."

She stopped the bleeding, washed the cut and bandaged it. I let her do it, pretended helplessness, my hand in her hands. Something about her doing it, the kind of pleasure it gave me, made me nervous.

"You said before that you thought I knew the girl Parks was seeing. Do you have the idea he's with Rosemary?"

"If that's her name." She looked frightened, her eyes large.

"You don't know her name?"

"I don't choose to know. I told you before I don't know where he is or who he's with. I assume that he's with this girl."

"He's not with Rosemary."

Carolyn, in the middle of the room, a statue of wearying patience. "That's your concern, not mine." She wet her lips with her tongue, her eyes cold as death. "I'd like you to go now," she said softly. "I'm very tired."

"Can I stay on the couch? I'll leave in the morning. I promise I'll leave as soon as it's light."

"I'm afraid you'll have to go, Chris. It's not so hard—just tell yourself to get up and before you know it you'll be on your feet."

I wasn't going. "Are you afraid of me?" I asked her.

"Why should I be afraid of you?" Her motor quivering. "I just want you to leave."

"I'd like a cup of coffee first. Something. You go to bed if you're tired. I'll let myself out."

"Now," she whispered, standing over me like a grade school principal, hands clenched.

I shook my head.

"Christopher, I want you to go." She extended her arm, pointed to the door.

Without reason I started to laugh.

She slapped me in the face, my eyes burning. I got up, burning. She screamed (though I hadn't touched her) and kicked me twice in the leg. "You bastard. You idiot bastard." Running from me.

I heard her barricading the door to her room, but made no attempt to get in. I took the phone in the kitchen off the hook so she couldn't call the police, and feeling safe, lay down on the couch, the air clearer, a breeze in the room.

Two police cars drove up—I watched them from the window. A

cordon of men surrounding the building. Curtis Parks with them, pointing his finger at the window. Someone had his gun drawn. I ducked back out of sight. Under the couch, pressed flat. Pretending to be unconscious, I waited, the gun in my hand under me. When they turned me over to see my face, I would start firing. The voices came and went. They looked everywhere but didn't find me. When they lifted the couch I wasn't there.

I put a light on and leafed through an old *New Yorker* left on the coffee table, turned to a smirking woman peering out from behind giant feathers—*Ambush perfume*. Was that what Carolyn was wearing? Walked around, my leg stiff where she had kicked me. Three twenty on the kitchen clock.

Carolyn wandered in as if she were lost. "What's the matter?" she said, a thin bathrobe over her nightgown, her eyes barely open. "Can't you sleep?"

"It's okay," I said.

"Would you like a sleeping pill?"

"No."

"I'm a light sleeper. Please try not to make so much noise." And she went back to her room.

I put out the light and lay down stiffly on the sofa, a flame between my legs, a secret light. *You cutter, Carolyn.* (Would I find Parks hiding between her legs?) I was laughing, listening to her listening to my laugh. My chest stretched on its bones beyond endurance. I went to the window to breathe. A light going on in the hallway.

"Once I wake up during the night I can't get back to sleep," she whispered as if there were others in the apartment who might be disturbed by a normal voice. "I thought I might take some pills—something—though I feel sleep-proof at this point."

I said I was sorry I had woken her, reading the outline of her soap bubble breasts under her bathrobe, unable not to. Carolyn seeing me look, smiling queerly. "Are you a good pill?" she asked.

"A bad pill." I grabbed her, kissed her neck.

"You have to learn to be gentle," she said, holding me away, her breath heavy.

I followed her, our hands touching, into the bedroom—cold, sweating. It seemed to me I was looking on, an eavesdropper on myself. Watching the kid Christopher follow Parks' wife, his eyes on her ass, following her to her marital bed. He is mad though she doesn't know—doesn't *choose* to know—her own madness, vengeance, all.

Her tongue fills his mouth, plays like a fish between his teeth. She gives instructions.

Lie down. Lie down next to me. Up. Down.

(I think of putting my fist against the side of her face, her mouth like a piece of fruit gone bad.)

He bites his tongue which is salty and raw, a slab of gristle. The blood fills his mouth. The pain. His eyes are closed. He tastes himself, his pain, which is sweet and like a dream.

"I'm waiting for you, Christopher," she says in a murderous voice.

(I pumped my fist into her mouth. Boom. Boom. Boom. Pumped it in. Until the wound in her face shuts.)

It is like a dream. It is like other things, other pains, but it is most like a dream.

5. QUESTIONS AND BIBLIOGRAPHY

Questions for Study and Discussion

Although the questions below force the student to think about the psychology of murder and the nonfiction novel, he should turn to outside sources for longer papers.

For the subject of murder he can read *Dark Legend* by Fredric Wertham (Duell, Sloan & Pearce, 1941); *The Mind of the Murderer* by M. S. Guttmacher (Farrar, Straus & Cudahy, 1960); *The Show of Violence* by Fredric Wertham (Doubleday, 1949); *Encyclopedia of Murder*, edited by Colin Wilson and Pat Pitman (Putnam, 1962); *The Psychology of Murder* by Stuart Hunter Palmer (Crowell, 1962); *Murder, Madness and the Law* by Louis H. Cohen (World, 1952); *Murder Followed by Suicide* by Donald James West (Harvard, 1965). *A Sign for Cain* by Fredric Wertham (Macmillan, 1966) contains an extensive bibliography on violence.

For American novels and short stories dealing with murder and its consequences, the student can read, among other modern works, *An American Tragedy* by Theodore Dreiser; *Compulsion* by Meyer Levin; *One Day* by Wright Morris; *The Violent Bear It Away* by Flannery O'Connor; *Reflections in a Golden Eye* by Carson McCullers; and *63:Dream Palace* by James Purdy. He will then be able to compare these not only with each other but with the "theoretical" and "factual" studies listed above. How do the various characterizations of the murderer differ? Why are American novelists drawn to murder as a theme? What audience reactions to murder do fiction and sociology inspire? Such questions can be answered in research papers.

The student who wants to trace the relation of specific "documentary" accounts of murder to works of the imagination can contrast the real background used by Dreiser with *An American Tragedy* itself, or the Leopold and Loeb case (the literature here is extensive) with Meyer Levin's fictional presentation in *Compulsion*.

The broad areas for research are, therefore, the psychology and sociology of murder, the novelistic treatments of murder, and the subtle interactions of "art" and "life."

Background of *In Cold Blood*

1. Palmer: *A Farmer Looks at Farming 1954*. Discuss the characterization of Herbert Clutter. Does it differ in any ways from the one presented by Capote? Does this article, written five years before the murder and eleven years before *In Cold Blood*, help us understand the differences between journalism and the nonfiction novel?

2. *Wealthy Farmer, Three of Family Slain.* This news item inspired Capote to travel to Holcomb. What details do you think "moved" him? Is Earl Robinson's comment at all prophetic? Does the description of Clutter convey any of his "essential" qualities?

3. Hickock and Nations: *America's Worst Crime.* Contrast the characterizations of Hickock and Smith as presented here with Capote's. Why is this account "journalistic" or "fictional"? For what audience does Hickock write?

4. Plimpton: *The Story Behind a Nonfiction Novel.* Discuss the reasons for Capote's desire to write "the nonfiction novel." (Consider the various criticisms of the "form" by Diana Trilling, Kauffmann, Phillips, *et al.*) Why did Capote choose the Clutter murders as the subject? Does he omit some deeper reasons for this choice—reasons suggested by Levine and Langbaum, among others? What kinds of material do you think Capote used to learn about the criminal mentality? Trace Capote's use of "select" and "manipulate" in the interview. Discuss the irony of Smith's statement: "An incredible situation where I kill four people and *you're* going to produce a work of art." Contrast the views of Capote and his critics on "invention" and "involvement."

5. Tompkins: *In Cold Fact.* How does Tompkins establish his credentials as a reporter? Discuss in detail the reliability and validity of two of his examples. Why is this essay important in any discussion of the "nonfiction novel"? Explain the reasons for the Auden quotation in the last paragraph.

Reviews of *In Cold Blood*

1. Kauffmann: *Capote in Kansas.* Discuss the "virtues" and "vices" of the cinematic method used by Capote. Why does Kauffmann call one quotation unforgettable? Do you agree with his cutting remarks about Capote's style? Are the portraits of Smith and Hickock really shallow? Comment on this statement: "Any one of the pictures is worth several thousand of his words."

2. Kramer: *Real Gardens with Real Toads.* What does Kramer mean by his title? Does Kramer agree with Levine or Garrett about Capote's early fiction? How does Capote use "counterpoint"? Why does Kramer believe that *The New Yorker* has had a "beneficient influence" on Capote's style? How is fiction the "refraction of a serious moral imagination"? Explain the last sentence of this essay.

3. Dupee: *Truman Capote's Score.* Explore the implications of this statement: "Overnight, as it were, Holcomb had joined the mid-twentieth century." Do "our celebrated delinquents" really become a "part of the national heritage"? Can Smith and Hickock? Can Whitman? Relate "parajournalism"—say as practiced by Tom Wolfe—to *In Cold Blood.* (See Plimpton interview.) Do the scene endings violate Dupee's acceptance of the *factual* quality of Capote's book? Which other critics attack these endings?

4. Yurick: *Sob-Sister Gothic.* Explain the title. What is the meaning of the statement that "Capote's choice of detail is more influenced by *The Folk-Motif Index,* or amateur readings in Jung's moonshine of the racial

unconscious, than by any disinterested resolution of social forces"? Does
Yurick agree with Kauffmann about Capote's style? Why does *In Cold Blood*
as a title anger Yurick? Is he misreading it? Does he use his review to write
a sermon against the middle class? Do any of the other critics sermonize at
length?

5. Garrett: *Crime and Punishment in Kansas*. Does Garrett distinguish
between the "classic" and "nonclassic" qualities of *In Cold Blood?* Is Capote
at all allegorical? Why can Garrett call Perry Smith "a kind of inverted, mid-
century Billy Budd"? How does Garrett defend Capote's objectivity or
understatement? Would Mrs. Trilling agree with such a defense? Should
Capote have included himself in the book? Would his own story lend itself
to objectivity? Why does Garrett claim that the "final effect" of Capote's
book is "one of 'nocturnal' romance"?

6. West: *A Grave and Reverend Book*. Does Capote make "the victims
of the murder . . . brilliant, powerful, and important in their goodness"?
Would Diana Trilling agree? How were the Clutters a "natural feature" of
the Kansas landscape? Explore Smith as "guilty of a sin which is the spiritual
equivalent of usury." How is he a "holier-than-thou" moralist? Why are
some elements in the tragedy "beyond our control"? Can we *ever* control
such elements? Explain the choice of Dame West's adjectives—"grave" and
"reverend"—to characterize *In Cold Blood*.

7. Tanner: *Death in Kansas*. Explore the allusions to Emerson, Mailer,
Goethe, and Conrad. Does Tanner agree with Galloway about the American
Dream? Explain the meaningful contrast in the last two sentences. This
essay appeared in a British periodical. Is it different in tone and vision from
the American essays reprinted here?

8. Phillips: *But Is It Good for Literature?* Explain the following statement: "*In Cold Blood* reads like high-class journalism, the kind of journalism
one expects of a novelist." Compare the views of Dupee and Diana Trilling
on such "high-class journalism." Why does "serious" modern literature have
to free itself of the "clichés of naturalism"? Do you agree that "sometimes it
almost seems as though Capote identifies himself with the killers, particularly
when he makes their most perverse desires look plausible and ordinary, the
way we like to think of our own desires"? Cite instances. Do we identify
with the killers presented by Baumbach, *Time*, and Flannery O'Connor?
Can *In Cold Blood* have "very little appeal for younger people"?

9. Trilling: *Capote's Crime and Punishment*. Is the novel the only
literary form "in which the writer is free to make any use he wishes of
material drawn from real life"? How does Capote's "neutrality" defeat his
purposes? How does it help him accomplish his intentions? Does Mrs.
Trilling define the personality of Herbert Clutter? What does he represent
to her?

10. Langbaum: *Capote's Nonfiction Novel*. Do you agree that Capote
wanted "to tell us that the book is no digression from his career as a fiction
writer, but a 'culmination'—that all his experience writing stories went into
it"? Do the various interviews reprinted here support this contention? What
are the implications of the De Quincey statement? Discuss the role of *fate*
in Capote's book. How is the "process of selection" a "creative act"? Contrast Langbaum's allusion to Oswald with those of Friedenberg, Tanner, and

Galloway. How does Capote "blur the distinction between sanity and insanity"? Why does Langbaum finally condemn *In Cold Blood* as a "lightweight"?

The Worlds of Truman Capote

1. Capote: *A Tree of Night*. Discuss the relationship of Kay and the couple. Does it resemble the one of the Clutters and Smith and Hickock? Interpret the symbols of the guitar, the shroud, the deformity, and the "wizard man." Do these reappear in *In Cold Blood*? Can you agree with the comment of Paul Levine that there is a "religious" message in this story? Is there one in *In Cold Blood*?

2. Hill: *Truman Capote Interview*. Discuss Capote's definition of "control." Explore the meaning of this sentence: "However, one of the reasons I've wanted to do reportage was to prove that I could apply my style to the realities of journalism." What, exactly, are the "realities of journalism"? How does Capote define style? Do you think Capote saw *In Cold Blood* "in one flash" or was he moved by "infinite surprises"? Contrast the style of this interview with the one from the *New York Times*.

3. Levine: *Truman Capote: The Revelation of the Broken Image*. What is the basic distinction that Levine explores? Is the "central focus" in *In Cold Blood*, as well as in the early fiction, the "moment of initiation"? Explore the figure of the "precocious child" in "early" and "late" Capote. Levine notes the "tension between the individual and society." Trace this tension in Capote's work. How does it culminate in *In Cold Blood*? Is "man's innate guilt" one theme of *In Cold Blood*?

4. Galloway: *Why the Chickens Came Home to Roost in Holcomb, Kansas*. Explore the implications of the Nathanael West paragraph. Is this paragraph applicable to the Whitman murders? Why does Galloway separate "peripheral" biographical matters from *In Cold Blood* itself? Should he? Define the "instant symbolism" of facts Capote used. Why does Galloway claim that Smith and Hickock are victims of the "open road"? What is his purpose in quoting Smith's statement as the final sentence?

5. Friedman: *Towards an Aesthetic*. Does connecting Capote with the Southern writers, his immediate contemporaries, and with the French tradition in the novel in any way detract from his own skill as a writer? Does Capote's work show increasing maturity? What would you expect to be the future course of his work?

6. Morris: *Capote's Imagery*. Does our *concern* for Perry Smith "obscure our understanding of the enormity of his crime? Are Capote's characters always "transparent"? How does Morris use his analysis of imagery to define "nocturnal" and "daylight" fiction? Trace the window image in all of Capote's fiction.

Murder in America: Fact and Fiction

1. Poe: *The Tell-Tale Heart*. Discuss the motivation of the narrator. Is he insane? What is the significance of the eye? How does Poe convey the tensions of the narrator? Explore the implications of the title.

2. O'Connor: *A Good Man Is Hard to Find.* In what ways do the contrasts between the grandmother and the Misfit remind you of *In Cold Blood?* Does the Misfit's "religiosity" resemble that of Whitman or Smith? Explore his desire to rebel against "authorities." What causes it? How does Miss O'Connor use irony to convey her vision of evil? Does Capote use irony in the "nonfiction novel"?

3. *The Madman in the Tower.* Does *Time* offer any real clues into Whitman's motivation? Discuss Whitman in relation to Smith and the Misfit. Compare and contrast their education, parents, and sexual orientations. Is the title of the essay correct? How does the essay approach "fiction"?

4. Friedenberg: *A Violent Country.* Why does Friedenberg claim that the two Goddesses are similar? Is it possible to relate Lee Harvey Oswald (at least from the facts we have about him) to Smith and Hickock? How does Friedenberg distinguish between alienation and sadism? Should this distinction be applied to the Clutter murder? Is the world now "very much less personal" than it was a generation ago? Does this impersonality influence fiction or "nonfiction novels"? Compare the uses of *Billy Budd* by Friedenberg and Garrett.

5. Baumbach: *What Comes Next.* Although this is a chapter from a novel, it is possible to read it as one study of the murderer's mind. How does Baumbach convey the meetings of dream and reality? In what ways is Chris "normal"? Does his growing "madness" generate fear and/or pity in the reader? Is Baumbach at all concerned with "public" violence?

Truman Capote: A Bibliography

JACKSON R. BRYER

THIS BIBLIOGRAPHY ATTEMPTS TO LIST VIRTUALLY ALL OF TRUMAN CAPOTE'S published work in English and a representative sampling of material about the author and his writings. It is divided into two basic sections—works by Capote and works about him. Within the first, no attempt has been made to include either foreign translations of Capote's works or reprintings of his books in English. Rather, only the first appearances of each book in this country and in Great Britain is listed. This has been done because the reviews of Capote's books in Section II, C of the bibliography refer only to these editions. In Sections I, B and I, C, reprintings of shorter fiction and nonfiction are listed, although, undoubtedly, this compilation must be considered as only partially complete.

In Section II, A, virtually every mention of Capote in books has been included, due, primarily, to the dearth of such material. Also included here are reprintings of reviews and essays which have previously appeared in periodicals. Annotations usually indicate the original source of the material. In Section II, B, again, very little selectivity has been exercised in listing periodical references. Here, too, brief annotations often indicate the scope and nature of the items.

Because most of the significant critical comment on Capote has appeared in reviews of his work, particular effort has been expended in locating as many of these as possible. Despite this effort, however, the listing in Section II, C must be regarded as merely a representative selection, due to the unavailability of publishers' files. Nonetheless, Section II, C would not have been nearly as complete as it is without the cooperation of Hamish Hamilton, Ltd. and William Heinemann, Ltd. and the tireless research assistance of Mrs. Mary Galli. I would also like to acknowledge the support of a grant from the General Research Board of the University of Maryland. Reviews of more than ordinary scope and interest are marked with an asterisk.

The use of abbreviations has been avoided in all but two cases: Capote's name has been abbreviated to TC in annotations, and New York (both city and state) has been shortened to NY. Where only a few pages of an essay or a review refer specifically to Capote, the page numbers of the entire reference are listed first, followed by the pages on Capote in parentheses.

I. Works by Capote

A. BOOKS

Other Voices, Other Rooms. NY: Random House, 1948; London: William Heinemann, 1948.

A Tree of Night and Other Stories. NY: Random House, 1949; London: William Heinemann, 1950. Contents: "Master Misery," "Children on Their Birthdays," "Shut a Final Door," "Jug of Silver," "Miriam," "The Headless Hawk," "My Side of the Matter," "A Tree of Night."

Local Color. NY: Random House, 1950; London: William Heinemann, 1955. Contents: "New Orleans," "New York," "Brooklyn," "Hollywood," "Haiti," "To Europe," "Ischia," "Tangier," "A Ride through Spain."

The Grass Harp. NY: Random House, 1951; London: William Heinemann, 1952.

The Grass Harp [A Play]. NY: Random House, 1952.

The Muses Are Heard. NY: Random House, 1956; London: William Heinemann, 1957.

Breakfast at Tiffany's: A Short Novel and Three Stories. NY: Random House, 1958; London: Hamish Hamilton, 1958. Contents: "Breakfast at Tiffany's," "A Diamond Guitar," "The House of Flowers," "A Christmas Memory."

Observations [Photographs by Richard Avedon, comments by Truman Capote]. NY: Simon and Schuster, 1959; London: George Weidenfeld & Nicolson, 1959.

The Selected Writings of Truman Capote. NY: Random House, 1963; London: Hamish Hamilton, 1963. Contents: "A Tree of Night," "Miriam," "The Headless Hawk," "Shut a Final Door," "Children on Their Birthdays," "Master Misery," "A Diamond Guitar," "House of Flowers," "A Christmas Memory," "Breakfast at Tiffany's," "Among the Paths to Eden," "New Orleans," "Ischia," "A Ride through Spain," *The Muses Are Heard*, "The Duke in His Domain," "A House on the Heights."

In Cold Blood. NY: Random House, 1966; London: Hamish Hamilton, 1966.

A Christmas Memory. NY: Random House, 1966.

B. SHORT STORIES

"The Walls Are Cold," *Decade of Short Stories*, IV (Fourth Quarter 1943), 27–30.

"A Mink of One's Own," *Decade of Short Stories*, VI (Third Quarter 1944), 1–4.

"The Shape of Things," *Decade of Short Stories*, VI (Fourth Quarter 1944), 21–23.

"My Side of the Matter," *Story*, XXVI (May–June 1945), 34–40. Collected in *A Tree of Night*.
 Reprinted: *"Story": The Fiction of the Forties*, Whit and Hallie Burnett, eds. NY: E. P. Dutton, 1949. Pp. 218–228.
 Reprinted: *The Modern Short Story in the Making*, Whit and Hallie Burnett, eds. NY: Hawthorn Books, 1964. Pp. 195–204.

"Miriam," *Mademoiselle*, XXI (June 1945), 114–115, 184, 186–190. Collected in *A Tree of Night* and *Selected Writings*.
> Reprinted: *O. Henry Memorial Award Prize Stories of 1946*, Herschel Brickell, ed. Garden City, NY: Doubleday, 1946. Pp. 103–114.
> Reprinted: *Short Stories in Context*, Woodburn O. Ross and A. Dayle Wallace, eds. NY: American Book Co., 1953. Pp. 170–181.
> Reprinted: *40 Best Stories from "Mademoiselle," 1935–1960*, Cyrilly Abels and Margarita G. Smith, eds. NY: Harper, 1960. Pp. 371–382.

"A Tree of Night," *Harper's Bazaar*, LXXIX (October 1945), 110, 176, 178, 180, 182, 184, 187–188. Collected in *A Tree of Night* and *Selected Writings*.
> Reprinted: *Modern Short Stories—The Fiction of Experience*, M. X. Lesser and John N. Morris, eds. NY: McGraw-Hill, 1962. Pp. 413–423.
> Reprinted: *Two and Twenty—A Collection of Short Stories*, Ralph H. Singleton, ed. NY: St. Martin's Press, 1962. Pp. 421–434.
> Reprinted: *Identity—Stories for This Generation*, Katherine Hondius, ed. Chicago: Scott, Foresman, 1966. Pp. 33–43.

"Jug of Silver," *Mademoiselle*, XXII (December 1945), 142–143,, 238–247. Collected in *A Tree of Night*.
> Reprinted: *American Short Stories—1820 to the Present*, rev. ed., Eugene Current-García and Walton R. Patrick, eds. Chicago: Scott, Foresman, 1964. Pp. 586–599.

"Preacher's Legend," *Prairie Schooner*, XIX (Winter 1945), 265–274.

"The Headless Hawk," *Harper's Bazaar*, LXXX (November 1946), 254–255, 330, 334, 336, 343–344, 346, 348, 350, 352, 358. Collected in *A Tree of Night and Selected Writings*.
> Reprinted: *The Best American Short Stories—1947*, Martha Foley, ed. Boston: Houghton Mifflin, 1947. Pp. 31–55.
> Reprinted: *The House of Fiction*, 2nd ed., Caroline Gordon and Allen Tate, eds. NY: Charles Scribner's, 1960. Pp. 353–369.

"Shut a Final Door," *Atlantic Monthly*, CLXXX (August 1947), 49–55. Collected in *A Tree of Night* and *Selected Writings*.
> Reprinted: *Prize Stories of 1948—The O. Henry Awards*, Herschel Brickell, ed. Garden City, NY: Doubleday, 1948. Pp. 1–14.
> Reprinted: *Contemporary Short Stories—Representative Selections*, Maurice Baudin, Jr., ed. NY: Liberal Arts Press, 1954. Vol. III, pp. 196–213.
> Reprinted: *First-Prize Stories 1919–1963—From the O. Henry Memorial Awards*. Garden City, NY: Doubleday, 1963. Pp. 427–439.

"Master Misery," *Horizon*, XIX (January 1949), 19–37. Collected in *A Tree of Night* and *Selected Writings*.
> Reprinted: *Harper's Magazine*, CXCVIII (February 1949), 38–48.

"Children on Their Birthdays," *Mademoiselle*, XXVI (January 1949), 88–90, 146–151. Collected in *A Tree of Night* and *Selected Writings*.
> Reprinted: *The Short Story*, James B. Hall and Joseph Langland, eds. NY: Macmillan, 1956. Pp. 219–235.

"The House of Flowers," *Botteghe Oscure*, VI (1950), 414–429. Collected in *Breakfast at Tiffany's* and *Selected Writings*.

Reprinted: *Mademoiselle,* XXXII (April 1951), 140–141, 152–159.

Reprinted: *Prize Stories of 1951–The O. Henry Awards,* Herschel Brickell, ed. Garden City, NY: Doubleday, 1951. Pp. 32–45.

Reprinted: *Stories of Sudden Truth,* Joseph Greene and Elizabeth Abell, eds. NY: Ballantine Books, 1953. Pp. 43–55.

Reprinted: *Bennett Cerf's Take Along Treasury,* Leonora Hornblow and Bennett Cerf, eds. Garden City, NY: Doubleday, 1963. Pp. 236–247.

"A Diamond Guitar," *Harper's Bazaar,* LXXXIV (November 1950), 164, 170, 172, 175–176, 178, 188. Collected in *Breakfast at Tiffany's* and *Selected Writings.*

Reprinted: *The Modern Talent–An Anthology of Short Stories,* John Edward Hardy, ed. NY: Holt, Rinehart and Winston, 1964. Pp. 238–248.

"The Grass Harp," *Botteghe Oscure,* VII (1951), 246–265 [First chapter of novel in progress]. Incorporated into *The Grass Harp.*

Reprinted: *Harper's Bazaar,* LXXXV (July 1951), 42–43, 106–108.

"A Christmas Memory," *Mademoiselle,* XLIV (December 1956), 70–71, 125–131. Collected in *Breakfast at Tiffany's, Selected Writings,* and *A Christmas Memory.*

Reprinted: *30 Stories to Remember,* Thomas B. Costain and John Beecroft, eds. Garden City, NY: Doubleday, 1962, Pp. 569–577.

Reprinted: *The Short Story–Classics & Contemporary,* R. W. Lid, ed. Philadelphia: Lippincott, 1966. Pp. 476–488.

Reprinted: *Look,* XXX (November 29, 1966), 79–83, 85–86 [Excerpts from story, illustrated by stills from TV production].

Reprinted: *Ladies Home Journal,* LXXXIII (December 1966), 86–87, 133–138.

"Breakfast at Tiffany's," *Esquire,* L (November 1958), 134–146, 148, 150, 152–153, 156–162. Collected in *Breakfast at Tiffany's* and *Selected Writings.*

"Among the Paths to Eden," *Esquire,* LIV (July 1960), 53–57. Collected in *Selected Writings.*

C. NONFICTION

"Notes on N. O.," *Harper's Bazaar,* LXXX (October 1946), 269–271, 361–362. Collected in *Local Color* and *Selected Writings.*

"Brooklyn Notes," *Junior Bazaar,* III (September 1947), 104–105, 125–126, 128. Collected in *Local Color.*

Reprinted: *The Empire City–A Treasury of New York,* Alexander Klein, ed. NY: Rinehart, 1955. P. 155 [Brief excerpt entitled "In Defense and Praise of Brooklyn"].

"This Winter's Mask," *Harper's Bazaar,* LXXXI (December 1947), 100–105, 195–196 [Review of theatre season to date].

"Call It New York," *Vogue,* CXI (February 1, 1948), 193, 258–259. Collected in *Local Color.*

Reprinted: *The Empire City–A Treasury of New York,* Alexander Klein, ed. NY: Rinehart, 1955. Pp. 461–464 [Excerpt entitled "The Diamond Iceberg"].

"Haitian Notes," *Harper's Bazaar*, LXXXII (December 1948), 120, 165, 167–168, 173. Collected in *Local Color*.

"Faulkner Dances," *Theatre Arts*, XXXIII (April 1949), 49 [Concerns dance adaptation of *As I Lay Dying*].

"The Bridge of Childhood," *Mademoiselle*, XXIX (May 1949), 91, 144–146. Collected in *Local Color*.

"Tangier," *Vogue*, CXV (April 1, 1950), 120–121, 166–167. Collected in *Local Color*.

"Isola d'Ischia," *Mademoiselle*, XXXI (May 1950), 110–111, 166–168. Collected in *Local Color* and *Selected Writings*.

"Our Far-Flung Correspondents—A Ride through Spain," *New Yorker*, XXVI (September 2, 1950), 42–45. Collected in *Local Color* and *Selected Writings*.

"A House in Sicily," *Harper's Bazaar*, LXXXV (January 1951), 116–117, 153–155.

"La Divine," *Harper's Bazaar*, LXXXV (April 1952), 148–149 [Appreciation of Greta Garbo].

"Onward and Upward with the Arts—Porgy and Bess in Russia," *New Yorker*, XXXII (October 20, 1956), 38–40, 42, 44, 47–49, 52, 54, 56, 58, 60–62, 65–66, 69–70, 72, 74, 76, 78–80, 83–100, 105; XXXII (October 27, 1956), 41–42, 44, 46, 48–52, 57–59, 62–64, 67–69, 71–72, 74, 76–80, 83–84, 86, 88–92, 94, 96–98, 101–104, 106–114. Collected as *The Muses Are Heard* and in *Selected Writings*.
   Reprinted: *The Open Form: Essays for Our Time*, Alfred Kazin, ed. NY: Harcourt, Brace & World, 1961. Pp. 214–219 [Brief excerpt entitled "In Leningrad"].

"Profiles—The Duke in His Domain," *New Yorker*, XXXIII (November 9, 1957), 53–54, 56, 59–61, 64–66, 68, 70, 72–74, 77–80, 82, 84, 87–88, 90, 92–100. Collected in *Selected Writings*.

"Brooklyn Heights: A Personal Memoir," *Holiday*, XXV (February 1959), 64–68, 112–115. Collected in *Selected Writings*.

"Maya Plisetskaya," *Harper's Bazaar*, XCIII (September 1959), 182–183 [Photography by Richard Avedon and text by TC]. Collected in *Observations*.

"A Gathering of Swans," *Harper's Bazaar*, XCIII (October 1959), 122–125 [Photography by Richard Avedon and text by TC]. Collected in *Observations*.

"New Focus on Familiar Faces," *Life*, XLVII (October 12, 1959), 136–143 [Photography by Richard Avedon and text by TC]. Collected in *Observations*.

"The $6 Misunderstanding," *NY Review of Books*, I (No. 2, 1963), 14 [Review of *Mobile* by Michel Butor].

"Plisetskaya: 'A Two-Headed Calf,' " *Vogue*, CXLIII (April 1, 1964), 169.

"A Curious Gift," *Redbook*, CXXV (June 1965), 52–53, 92–94 [Reminiscence of raven given to TC as Christmas gift in Sicily in 1952].

"Annals of Crime—In Cold Blood," *New Yorker*, XLI (September 25, 1965), 57–60, 62, 65–66, 68, 70, 72, 75–76, 78, 80, 82, 85–86, 88, 90, 92, 97–98, 100, 102, 104, 107–108, 110–111, 114, 116, 118, 121–122, 124, 126, 128,

133–134, 136, 138, 140, 143–144, 146, 148, 150, 153–154, 156, 158, 160,
163–164, 166; XLI (October 2, 1965), 57–60, 62, 65–66, 68, 71–72, 74,
77–78, 80, 83, 85–86, 88, 90, 95, 97–98, 100–101, 105–106, 108, 110–
112, 117–118, 120, 122, 124, 127–128, 130, 132–134, 139–140, 142, 144,
146, 149–150, 152, 155–156, 158, 161–162, 164, 167–168, 170, 172,
174–175; XLI (October 9, 1965), 58–62, 64, 67–68, 70, 72, 74, 79–80,
82, 84, 86, 91–92, 94, 96–98, 103–104, 106, 108–110, 115–117, 120, 122,
127–128, 130, 132–134, 139–140, 142, 144–146, 151–152, 154–158,
163–170, 173–183; XLI (October 16, 1965), 62–64, 66, 69–70, 72, 74, 76,
81–82, 84, 86, 88, 91, 93–94, 96–98, 103–104, 106, 108, 110, 113–114,
116, 118, 120, 125–126, 128, 130, 132, 135–136, 138, 140, 142, 147–148,
150, 152–154, 157–158, 160–162, 164, 169–170, 172, 174–176, 179–180,
182–193. Collected as *In Cold Blood*.

"The 'Sylvia' Odyssey," *Vogue*, CXLVII (January 15, 1966), 68–75 [Photo-
graphs and text on sailing trip among Greek islands].

"Two Faces and . . . a Landscape . . . ," *Vogue*, CXLVII (February 1,
1966), 144–149 [TC on Smith and Hickock and *In Cold Blood*].

"Truman Capote Introduces Jane Bowles," *Mademoiselle*, LXIV (December
1966), 114–116. Also printed as Introduction to *The Collected Works of
Jane Bowles*. NY: Farrar, Straus & Giroux, 1966. Pp. v–ix.

"Oliver Smith." In Roddy McDowell. *Double Exposure*. NY: Delacorte
Press, 1966. Pp. 152–153.

" 'Extreme Magic'—An Awake-Dream, Cruising up the Yugoslavian Coast,"
Vogue, CXLIX (April 15, 1967), 84–89, 146–147.

D. MISCELLANEOUS

"*The Grass Harp*," *Theatre Arts*, XXXVI (September 1952), 34–64 [Com-
plete text of play].

"Protest Answered," NY *Times*, February 13, 1955, Sec. II, p. 3 [Letter to
the Drama Editor replying to letter of protest about theme of *House of
Flowers* from Friday Drama Group of Montclair (N.J.) Women's Club].

"The Guts of a Butterfly," London *Observer*, March 27, 1966, p. 21 [Reply
to Kenneth Tynan's review of *In Cold Blood*].

II.   Works about Capote

A. BOOKS

Aldridge, John W. "Capote and Buechner—The Escape into Otherness."
In his *After the Lost Generation—A Critical Study of the Writers of Two
Wars*. NY: Noonday Press, 1958. Pp. 194–230; see also pp. 104–105
[Emphasis on *Other Voices*].

Allen, Walter. *The Modern Novel in Britain and the United States*. NY:
E. P. Dutton, 1964. Pp. 301–303 [Emphasis on *Other Voices*].

Beaton, Cecil, and Kenneth Tynan. *Persona Grata*. London: Allan Wingate,
1953. Pp. 25, 28–29 [Photograph of TC by Beaton and brief appreciation
of TC by Tynan].

Bentley, Eric. "Pity His Simplicity." In his *The Dramatic Event—An American Chronicle*. NY: Horizon Press, 1954. Pp. 20–24 [Reprinted review of
The Grass Harp].

[Biographical sketch]. In Anna Rothe, ed. *Current Biography*. NY: H. W. Wilson, 1952. Pp. 92–93.

Bradbury, John M. *Renaissance in the South—A Critical History of the Literature, 1920–1960*. Chapel Hill: University of North Carolina Press, 1963. P. 132.

Breit, Harvey. "Truman Capote." In his *The Writer Observed*. Cleveland: World, 1956. Pp. 235–237 [Reprinted interview].

Brickell, Herschel. "Introduction." In his ed. *O. Henry Memorial Award Prize Stories of 1946*. Garden City, NY: Doubleday, 1946. Pp. vii–xxi (xiv: brief comments on "A Tree of Night," "Miriam," and "Preacher's Legend").

———. "Introduction." In his ed. *Prize Stories of 1948—The O. Henry Awards*. Garden City, NY: Doubleday, 1948. Pp. ix–xx (x–xi: comment on "Shut a Final Door").

———. "Introduction." In his ed. *Prize Stories of 1951—The O. Henry Awards*. Garden City, NY: Doubleday, 1951. Pp. vii–xxvi (viii–ix, xii, xx, xxi: brief comments on TC and on "The House of Flowers").

"Capote, Truman." In Stanley J. Kunitz, ed. *Twentieth Century Authors—First Supplement*. NY: H. W. Wilson, 1955. Pp. 167–169 [Includes autobiographical statement by TC and résumé of his career].

Cowley, Malcolm. *The Literary Situation*. NY: Viking Press, 1954. Pp. 43, 45, 47, 61, 67, 68.

Current-García, Eugene, and Walton R. Patrick [Note on TC and "Jug of Silver"]. In their ed. *American Short Stories—1820 to the Present*, rev. ed. Chicago: Scott, Foresman, 1964. Pp. 585–586.

Eisinger, Chester E. "Truman Capote and the Twisted Self." In his *Fiction of the Forties*. Chicago: University of Chicago Press, 1963. Pp. 237–242; see also *passim* [Emphasis on Gothic elements in TC's work, with brief discussions of *Other Voices, Tree of Night*, and *The Grass Harp*].

Gassner, John. "*The Grass Harp*: Capote versus Saroyan." In his *Theatre at the Crossroads—Plays and Playwrights of the Mid-Century American Stage*. NY: Holt, Rinehart and Winston, 1960. Pp. 149–151 [Reprinted review].

Gordon, Caroline, and Allen Tate. "Commentary on Capote and O'Connor." In their ed. *The House of Fiction*, 2nd ed. NY: Charles Scribner's, 1960. Pp. 382–386 [Comparison based primarily on "The Headless Hawk" and "A Good Man Is Hard to Find"].

Gossett, Louise Y. "Violence in a Private World: Truman Capote." In her *Violence in Recent Southern Fiction*. Durham, N.C.: Duke University Press, 1965. Pp. 145–158.

Hall, James B., and Joseph Langland. "Comment" [on "Children on Their Birthdays"]. In their ed. *The Short Story*. NY: Macmillan, 1956. Pp. 235–236.

Hardy, John Edward. "Truman Capote's 'A Diamond Guitar.'" In his ed. *The Modern Talent—An Anthology of Short Stories*. NY: Holt, Rinehart and Winston, 1964. Pp. 248–251.

246   QUESTIONS AND BIBLIOGRAPHY

Hassan, Ihab. "Truman Capote." In his *Radical Innocence—The Contemporary American Novel.* Princeton, N.J.: Princeton University Press, 1961. Pp. 230–258 [Basically, reprinted essay from *Wisconsin Studies in Contemporary Literature*].

Hill, Pati. "Truman Capote." In Malcolm Cowley, ed. *Writers at Work— The "Paris Review" Interviews.* NY: Viking Press, 1959. Pp. 283–299 [Reprinted interview].

Kazin, Alfred. [Prefatory note on TC]. In his ed. *The Open Form: Essays For Our Time.* NY: Harcourt, Brace & World, 1961. Pp. 213–214 [Emphasis on *The Muses Are Heard*].

————. "Truman Capote and 'The Army of Wrongness.'" In his *Contemporaries.* Boston: Little, Brown, 1962. Pp. 250–254 [Reprinted review of *Breakfast at Tiffany's*].

Klein, Marcus J. *After Alienation—American Novels in Mid-Century.* Cleveland: World, 1962. Pp. 23–24.

Lesser, M. X., and John N. Morris [Prefatory note on TC and "A Tree of Night"]. In their ed. *Modern Short Stories—The Fiction of Experience.* NY: McGraw-Hill, 1962. P. 412.

Ludwig, Jack. *Recent American Novelists,* University of Minnesota Pamphlets on American Writers, No. 22. Minneapolis: University of Minnesota Press, 1962. Pp. 33–36 [Emphasis on *Breakfast at Tiffany's*, with briefer discussions of *Other Voices* and *The Grass Harp*].

Malin, Irving. *New American Gothic.* Carbondale: Southern Illinois University Press, 1962. Pp. 14–19, 50–54, 79–83, 107–111, 127–133, 156–157, and *passim* [Emphasis on *Other Voices*, "Miriam," "The Headless Hawk," "Master Misery," and "Shut a Final Door"].

Meeker, Richard K. "The Youngest Generation of Southern Fiction Writers." In R. C. Simonini, Jr., ed. *Southern Writers—Appraisals in Our Time.* Charlottesville: University Press of Virginia, 1964. Pp. 162–191 (181–183).

Nathan, George Jean. "Truman Capote." In his *The Theatre in the Fifties.* NY: Knopf, 1953. Pp. 84–88 [Reprinted review of *The Grass Harp*].

Newquist, Roy. "Truman Capote." In his *Counterpoint.* Chicago: Rand McNally, 1964. Pp. 75–83 [Interview].

Prescott, Orville. "The Young Decadents: Capote, Bowles, Buechner, Goyen, Williams, Yorke." In his *In My Opinion—An Inquiry into the Contemporary Novel.* Indianapolis: Bobbs-Merrill, 1952. Pp. 110–121 (113–116: *Other Voices* and *The Grass Harp*).

Schorer, Mark. "Introduction." In Truman Capote. *Selected Writings.* NY: Random House, 1963. Pp. vii-xii.

————. "McCullers and Capote: Basic Patterns." In Nona Balakian and Charles Simmons, eds. *The Creative Present: Notes on Contemporary American Fiction.* Garden City, NY: Doubleday, 1936. Pp. 83–107 (94–107).

Singleton, Ralph H. [Biographical note on TC]. In his ed. *Two and Twenty —A Collection of Short Stories.* NY: St. Martin's Press, 1962. Pp. 418–420.

Sullivan, Walter. "The Continuing Renascence: Southern Fiction in the Fifties." In Louis D. Rubin, Jr. and Robert D. Jacobs, eds. *South: Modern Southern Literature in Its Cultural Setting.* Garden City, NY: Doubleday, 1961. Pp. 376–391 (385–386).

Warfel, Harry R. "Truman Capote." In his *American Novelists of Today.* NY: American Book Co., 1951. P. 81 [Brief biographical sketch].

West, Paul. *The Modern Novel.* London: Hutchinson, 1963. Pp. 300–301.

B. PERIODICALS

Aldridge, John W. "America's Young Novelists—Uneasy Inheritors of a Revolution," *Saturday Review of Literature,* XXXII (February 12, 1949), 6–8, 36–37, 42 (42: *Other Voices*).

————. "The Metaphorical World of Truman Capote," *Western Review,* XV (Summer 1951), 247–260. Incorporated into his *After the Lost Generation.*

————. "What Became of Our Postwar Hopes?" *NY Times Book Review,* July 29, 1962, pp. 1, 24. Reprinted in his *A Time to Murder and Create.* NY: McKay, 1966.

Alexander, Shana. "A Nonfictional Visit with Truman Capote," *Life,* LX (February 18, 1966), 22.

Austin, H. Russell. "The Reading Glass," Milwaukee *Journal,* February 27, 1949, Sec. V. p. 4 [Brief biography and personality sketch on TC].

Balakian, Nona. "The Prophetic Vogue of the Anti-heroine," *Southwest Review,* XLVII (Spring 1962), 134–141 (137–138: emphasis on Holly Golightly).

Baldanza, Frank. "Plato in Dixie," *Georgia Review,* XII (Summer 1958), 151–167 (TC and Carson McCullers; see esp. pp. 162–167).

Beaton, Cecil. " 'Grass Harp' Dressed Up in Colors of Nostalgia," NY *Herald Tribune,* March 23, 1952, Sec. 4, pp. 1, 2 [Play's designer discusses his designs and justifies them].

Breit, Harvey. "Talk with Truman Capote," *NY Times Book Review,* February 24, 1952, p. 29. Reprinted in his *The Writer Observed.*

Breslin, Jimmy. *"In Cold Blood,"* NY *Herald Tribune,* January 19, 1966, p. 21.

Bucco, Martin. "Truman Capote and the Country below the Surface," *Four Quarters,* VII (November 1957), 22–25.

"Capote Prefers Books to Play," Indianapolis *News,* November 29, 1958, p. 2 [Brief syndicated news item in which TC is quoted as saying that he'd rather write books than plays].

"Capote Sued for One-Tenth of 'Cold Blood' Royalties," *Publishers' Weekly,* CLXXXIX (May 30, 1966), 60 [Suit being brought by former newspaper reporter who claims he helped in writing book].

Chamberlain, John. "Critic Finds New Authors Work Things Out in Their Own Ways," *Life,* XXII (June 2, 1947), 81–82 [See also photograph of TC, with caption, p. 75].

"Cold-Blooded Crossfire," *Time,* LXVII (April 15, 1966), 48 [TC vs. Tynan on *In Cold Blood*].

Collins, Carvel. "Other Voices," *American Scholar*, XXV (Winter 1955–56), 108, 110, 112–116 (113–116: *Other Voices*).

Connolly, Cyril. "Introduction," *Horizon*, No. 93–4 (October 1947), 1–11 (5: Connolly's famous brief reference to vogue of TC in U.S.).

"Correspondence—In Hot Blood," *New Republic*, CLIV (February 5, 1966), 35–37 [Letters to the Editor about *In Cold Blood*].

Delaney, [William E.] "A New Art Form? No, New Depth in Reporting," Charlotte *Observer*, January 16, 1966, p. 6F [About *In Cold Blood*].

Durgin, Cyrus. "A Ribbon of Memory—Reading by Truman Capote," Boston *Daily Globe*, December 15, 1958, p. 14 [Account of TC's reading at Boston's Sanders Theater].

"The Fabulist," *Newsweek*, LXIV (December 28, 1964), 58 [Account of reading by TC in which latter previewed sections of *In Cold Blood*].

Foster, William. "Murder, Capote, and a Myth," *The Scotsman* (Edinburgh), March 12, 1966, Week-end Magazine, p. 5 [Background on TC and *In Cold Blood*].

Frankel, Haskel. "The Author," *Saturday Review*, XLIX (January 22, 1966), 36–37 [Interview].

Fremont-Smith, Eliot. "Capote Book's Reception Stirs Doubts," Hartford *Times*, January 29, 1966, p. 22 [Syndicated column on reviews of *In Cold Blood*].

Gehman, Richard B. "Where Are the Postwar Novels?" *Esquire*, XXXI (March 1949), 74, 91 (91: *Other Voices*).

Geismar, Maxwell. "The Postwar Generation in Arts & Letters—1. Fiction," *Saturday Review*, XXXVI (March 14, 1953), 11–12, 60 (11).

Gilroy, Harry. "A Book in a New Form Earns $2-million for Truman Capote," NY *Times*, December 31, 1965, p. 23 [TC interviewed about *In Cold Blood*].

Girson, Rochelle. " '48's Nine," *Saturday Review of Literature*, XXXII (February 12, 1949), 12–14 (13–14: interview).

"Golightly at Law," *Time*, LXXIII (February 9, 1959), 90 [Girl intends to sue TC, claiming she is real-life original of Holly Golightly].

Hassan, Ihab H. "Birth of a Heroine," *Prairie Schooner*, XXXIV (Spring 1960), 78–83 [About *Breakfast at Tiffany's*].

———. "The Character of Post-War Fiction in America," *English Journal*, LI (January 1962), 1–8 (6 and *passim*). Reprinted in Joseph J. Waldmeir, ed. *Recent American Fiction—Some Critical Views*. Boston: Houghton Mifflin, 1963.

———. "The Daydream and the Nightmare of Narcissus," *Wisconsin Studies in Contemporary Literature*, I (Spring–Summer 1960), 5–21. Reprinted in his *Radical Innocence: Studies in the Contemporary American Novel*.

———. "Love in the Modern American Novel: Expense of Spirit and Waste of Shame," *Western Humanities Review*, XIV (Spring 1961), 149–161 (159). Incorporated into his *Radical Innocence: Studies in the Contemporary American Novel*.

Hewes, Henry. "Broadway Postscript—Rebels in the Wings," *Saturday Review*, XXXV (April 19, 1952), 45 [TC interviewed on stage production of *The Grass Harp*].

Hill, Pati. "Truman Capote," *Paris Review*, No. 16 (Spring–Summer 1957), 34–51 [Interview]. Reprinted in Malcolm Cowley, ed. *Writers at Work—The "Paris Review" Interviews*.

"Horror Spawns a Masterpiece," *Life*, LX (January 7, 1966), 58–69 [On *In Cold Blood*].

Howard, Jane. "A Six-Year Literary Vigil," *Life*, LX (January 7, 1966), 70–72, 75–76 [Background on *In Cold Blood* and interview with TC].

Hyman, Stanley Edgar. "Some Trends in the Novel," *College English*, XX (October 1958), 1–9 (3).

"'In Cold Blood' Target of Threatened Law Suit," *Publishers' Weekly*, CLXXXIX (April 25, 1966), 81 [Suit threatened by Mrs. Eunice Hickock, mother of one of murderers].

"In a Novel Way," *Time*, LXXXVI (October 8, 1965), 74, 76 [On *In Cold Blood*].

Kahn, E. J., Jr. "Author! Author! Where's the Author?" *New Yorker*, XXVIII (April 19, 1952), 100, 102–104 [Satiric sketch which concerns TC spending opening night of *The Grass Harp* at home of David Lilienthal].

Levidova, I. "Lost Souls," *Voprosi Literaturi* (Problems of Literature), No. 10 (October 1960), 108–131.

Levine, Paul. "Truman Capote: The Revelation of the Broken Image," *Virginia Quarterly Review*, XXXIV (Autumn 1958), 600–617. Reprinted in Joseph J. Waldmeir, ed. *Recent American Fiction—Some Critical Views*. Boston: Houghton Mifflin, 1963.

Long, Barbara. "In Cold Comfort," *Esquire*, LXV (June 1966), 124, 126, 128, 171–173, 175–176 [Interview with TC and estimate of his pre-publication royalties from *In Cold Blood*].

Mengeling, Marvin E. "*Other Voices, Other Rooms:* Oedipus between the Covers," *American Imago*, XIX (Winter 1962), 361–374.

Moravia, Alberto. "Two American Writers (1949)," *Sewanee Review*, LXVIII (Summer 1960), 473–481 [see esp. pp. 477–481: "Truman Capote and the New Baroque].

Norton, Elliot. "Fable Drawn from Life—Capote's 'The Grass Harp' Deals with Characters He Knew as a Child," *NY Times*, March 23, 1952, Sec. 2, pp. 1, 3 [Interview and biographical sketch].

"Objection," *NY Times*, February 6, 1955, Sec. II, p. 3 [Letter to the Drama Editor from the Drama Study Group of the Montclair (N.J.) Women's Club protesting theme of *House of Flowers*]; Truman Capote. "Protest Answered," *NY Times*, February 13, 1955, Sec. II, p. 3 [TC's reply].

"Objectivized Subjective." In Whit and Hallie Burnett, eds. *The Modern Short Story in the Making*. NY: Hawthorn Books, 1964. Pp. 204–206 [Biographical sketch and brief interview which focuses on "My Side of the Matter"].

O'Connor, William Van. "The Grotesque in Modern American Fiction," *College English*, XX (April 1959), 342–346 (344). Reprinted in his *The*

Grotesque: An American Genre. Carbondale: Southern Illinois University Press, 1962.

"Other People's Mail," *Esquire,* LXIV (December 1965), 149–152, 264, 266, 270, 274, 276, 280, 282, 284, 286 (150, 264, 266: James Michener on TC).

"Other Voices, Other Rooms," *Newsweek,* LXVIII (August 1, 1966), 26–27 [TC testifies before Senate Judiciary Subcommittee].

Pearman, Robert. " 'In Cold Blood'—The People in Capote's Book: What They Say about Him," Detroit *Free Press,* January 30, 1966, p. 5–B [Syndicated article which includes comments on TC and *In Cold Blood* by persons who are mentioned in the latter book].

"People Are Talking about . . . Truman Capote," *Vogue,* CXLVI (October 15, 1965), 94–95.

Plimpton, George. "The Story behind a Nonfiction Novel," *NY Times Book Review,* January 16, 1966, pp. 2–3, 38–43 [Extensive interview which focuses on *In Cold Blood*].

Robinson, Selma. "The Legend of 'Little T,' " *PM* (NY), March 14, 1948, pp. m6–m8 [Extended and detailed biographical sketch and interview].

Rolo, Charles J. "The New Bohemia," *Flair,* I (February 1950), 27–29, 116–118 (118).

Rosenfeld, Arnold. " 'In Cold Blood': Capote's Killers," Houston *Post,* October 24, 1965, *Spotlight* Magazine, p. 8 [Appraisal of book based on *New Yorker* installments].

Rosenthal, M. L. "New York Letter—Capote's Happenings," *The Spectator,* No. 7181 (February 11, 1966), 172 [On *In Cold Blood*].

Saint-Subber. " 'I'd Do It Again,' " *Theatre Arts,* XXXVI (September 1952), 32–33 [Producer of *The Grass Harp* comments on play and production].

Smith, Harrison. "Sizing Up the Comers," *Saturday Review of Literature,* XXXII (February 12, 1949), 9–11 (10: *Other Voices*).

"Talent up a Tree," *Life,* XXXII (April 14, 1952), 142, 145 [Picture-story on *The Grass Harp*].

Tallmer, Jerry. "Truman Capote, Crime Reporter," NY *Post,* January 16, 1966, p. 22 [Biographical sketch and comments on TC by his friends].

"The Theatre—Truman Capote," Boston *Herald,* December 15, 1958, p. 23 [Account of TC's reading at Boston's Sanders Theater].

Tompkins, Phillip K. "In Cold Fact," *Esquire,* LXV (June 1966), 125, 127, 166–168 [Criticism of accuracy of *In Cold Blood*].

Trilling, Diana. "What about Writers under Twenty-Five?" *Junior Bazaar,* IV (April 1948), 91, 104–106 (104).

"Truman Capote and the Country Studio He Designed for Work," *Vogue,* CXLVI (November 1, 1965), 208–211 [Picture-story].

Tynan, Kenneth. "Tynan Replies," London *Observer,* April 3, 1966, p. 31 [Tynan's response to TC's critique of Tynan's review of *In Cold Blood*].

"Voices of Authors," *Life,* XXXV (October 12, 1953), 129–130, 132, 134 (132: TC records reading from his work).

Wall, Richard J., and Carl L. Craycraft. "A Checklist of Works about

Truman Capote," *Bulletin of the NY Public Library,* LXXI (March 1967), 165–172.

Walter, Eugene. "A Rainy Afternoon with Truman Capote," *Intro Bulletin,* II (December 1957), 1–2 [Interview].

Warren, Virginia Lee. "New Home for Capote: 'Very Cozy,' " NY *Times,* October 22, 1965, p. 38 [Description of TC's new NY apartment and his own comments about it].

Wilson, John S. "Building a House of Flowers," *Theatre Arts,* XXXIX (January 1955), 30–31, 91 [TC interviewed regarding genesis of show].

Winn, Janet. "Capote, Mailer and Miss Parker," *New Republic,* CXL (February 9, 1959), 27–28 [Account of TV program which featured discussion between TC, Mailer, and Dorothy Parker].

"Work in Progress: Romance with Reality," *Newsweek,* LIX (February 5, 1962), 85 [TC interviewed about *In Cold Blood*].

C. REVIEWS OF BOOKS BY CAPOTE

Other Voices, Other Rooms

Allen, Walter. "New Novels," *New Statesman and Nations,* n.s. XXXVI (November 20, 1948), 444–446 (445).

Baker, Carlos. "Deep-South Guignol," *NY Times Book Review,* January 18, 1948, p. 5.

Barzun, Jacques. "Delicate and Doomed," *Harper's,* CXCVI (April 1948), unpaged.

Best Sellers, VII (March 1, 1948), 245.

Boulton, Richard N. "Lavender Pastiche," Hartford *Daily Courant,* February 15, 1948, Magazine Section, p. 12.

Brady, Charles A. "Idyllic, Realistic Balance in 'Other Voices,' " Buffalo *Evening News,* January 17, 1948, Magazine Section, p. 5.

Brighouse, Harold. "New Novels," Manchester *Guardian,* October 29, 1948, p. 3.

Carousso, Georges. "Characters on Parade," Brooklyn *Eagle,* February 1, 1948, p. 13.

Cross, Jesse E. *Library Journal,* LXXII (December 1, 1947), 1685.

D., R. J. Boston *Daily Globe,* January 21, 1948, p. 15.

Elie, Rudolph, Jr. " 'Other Voices' a Very Fine First Novel," Boston *Herald,* February 25, 1948, p. 15.

Farrelly, John. "Fiction Parade—Maturation," *New Republic,* CXVIII (January 26, 1948), 31–32.

Fiedler, Leslie A. "The Fate of the Novel," *Kenyon Review,* X (Summer 1948), 519–527 (522–523).

Fineman, Morton. "Heir to Terror and Love," Philadelphia *Inquirer,* January 18, 1948, Book Section, p. 5.

Follows, Arthur J. "A Strange First Novel," Milwaukee *Journal,* January 25, 1948, Editorial Section, p. 5.

Gannett, Lewis. "Books and Things," NY *Herald Tribune,* January 21, 1948, p. 23.

Gray, James. "A Story of Decadence," Chicago *Daily News*, January 21, 1948, p. 24.

[Gross, John B.] "Able Young Writer Tells Unique Story," Hartford *Times*, February 7, 1948, p. 12.

Guilfoil, Kelsey. "Exotic Tale of Youth in Odd Setting," *Chicago Sunday Tribune Magazine of Books*, January 18, 1948, p. 5.

Habas, Ralph. "First Novel of 23-Year-Old Displays Brilliant Talents," Chicago *Sun and Times*, February 1, 1948, p. 7X.

Hansen, Harry. "The First Reader—Unfolding Talent," NY *World-Telegram*, January 19, 1948, p. 15.

Hardwick, Elizabeth. "Much Outcry, Little Outcome," *Partisan Review*, XV (March 1948), 374–377 (376–377).

Harriss, W. E. *Commonweal*, XLVII (February 27, 1948), 500.

Jackson, Joseph Henry. "A Bookman's Notebook—A Boy Grows Up," San Francisco *Chronicle*, January 27, 1948, p. 12.

K., H. T. "Part Mystery, Horror," New Orleans *Times-Picayune*, February 15, 1948, Sec. 2, p. 15.

Kee, Robert. "Fiction," *The Spectator*, No. 6282 (November 19, 1948), 674, 676.

Kuehn, Susan. "Talent Vivid but Tale Is Swampy," Minneapolis *Sunday Tribune*, March 7, 1948, p. 16W.

Leonard, George. "First Novel Is Sinister Tale Set in South," Nashville *Banner*, February 20, 1948, p. 26.

McGrory, Mary. "Lonely People Gain Sympathy in Two Novels," Washington (D.C.) *Sunday Star*, January 18, 1948, p. C–3.

McLaughlin, Richard. "A Dixieland Stew," *Saturday Review of Literature*, XXXI (February 14, 1948), 12–13.

Morris, Lloyd. "A Vivid, Inner, Secret World," NY *Herald Tribune Weekly Book Review*, January 18, 1948, p. 2.

Murphy, Ethel Allen. "'On Verge of a Fourth Dimension,'" Louisville *Courier-Journal*, February 1, 1948, Sec. 3, p. 11.

New Yorker, XXIII (January 24, 1948), 74.

Newsweek, XXXI (January 26, 1948), 91.

N[orth], S[terling]. "Hunted, Haunted Characters in Brilliant Book," Richmond (Va.) *Times-Dispatch*, January 25, 1948, p. 8–D. See also Washington *Post*, January 18, 1948, p. 7B; Indianapolis *News*, January 24, 1948, p. 7; Philadelphia *Sunday Bulletin*, January 18, 1948, Book Review Section, p. 2.

Pippett, Roger. "A Boy's Thoughts Are Long Thoughts," *PM* (NY), January 25, 1948, p. m13.

Prescott, Orville. "Books of the Times," NY *Times*, January 21, 1948, p. 23.

———. *Yale Review*, XXXVII (Spring 1948), 575.

Rago, Henry. "The Discomforts of Storytelling," *Sewanee Review*, LVI (Summer 1948), 514–521 (519).

Rogers, W. G. "First Novel Reveals How Heart of Boy Is Shaped," Charlotte *Observer*, January 25, 1948, p. 5–D. See also Atlanta *Constitution*, February 1, 1948, p. 15–C.

Rolo, Charles J. *Atlantic*, CLXXXI (March 1948), 109.

S[cott], W[infield] T. Providence *Sunday Journal*, January 18, 1948, Sec. VI, p. 2.

Sherman, Thomas B. "Reading and Writing—In the Shadows of the Mind," St. Louis *Post-Dispatch*, February 1, 1948, p. 4B.

*Shrike, J. S. "Recent Phenomena," *Hudson Review*, I (Spring 1948), 136–138, 140, 142, 144.

"Spare the Laurels," *Time*, LI (January 26, 1948), 102.

Tinkle, Lon. "Just off the Press: New Young Novelist Makes Brilliant Debut," Dallas *Morning News*, January 18, 1948, Sec. III, p. 17.

*Trilling, Diana. "Fiction in Review," *Nation*, CLXVI (January 31, 1948), 133–134.

"Unhappy Families," *Times Literary Supplement*, October 30, 1948, p. 609.

*Young, Marguerite. "Tiger Lilies," *Kenyon Review*, X (Summer 1948), 516–518.

"Youth Shows Promise in First Novel," Miami *Herald*, January 25, 1948, p. 4–5.

A Tree of Night and Other Stories

Allen, Morse. "No More Pig Than We Had," Hartford *Courant*, April 10, 1949, Magazine Section, p. 15.

"Anguish of Mind," *Times Literary Supplement*, April 14, 1950, p. 225.

Baker, Carlos. "Nursery-Tales from Jitter Manor," *NY Times Book Review*, February 27, 1949, pp. 7, 33.

Barry, Iris. "Short Stories of Truman Capote," *NY Herald Tribune Weekly Book Review*, February 27, 1949, p. 2.

Beck, Cameron. "Truman Capote's Book of Shorter Fiction," Dallas *Morning News*, February 27, 1949, Sec. II, p. 6.

Bennett, Virginia. *Commonweal*, L (April 29, 1949), 77.

B[ole], A[llen]. "Capote Rings Gong with Three Stories," Hartford *Times*, March 5, 1949, p. 14.

Booklist, XLV (March 15, 1949), 241.

Brady, Charles A. Buffalo *Evening News*, February 26, 1949, Editorial Section, p. 5.

———. *Catholic World*, CLXIX (May 1949), 156–157.

C., B. C. "Stories by Truman Capote," Providence *Sunday Journal*, February 27, 1949, Sec. VI, p. 8.

Crane, Milton. "Parade of Horribles," *Saturday Review of Literature*, XXXII (February 26, 1949), 12.

*Fiedler, Leslie A. "Capote's Tales," *Nation*, CLXVIII (April 2, 1949), 395–396.

Fineman, Morton. "Capote's Tales of Terror," Philadelphia *Inquirer*, March 20, 1949, Books Section, p. 2.

G., L. "8 Short Stories Far Superior to Capote's Novel," Washington *Post*, March 6, 1949, p. 7B.

Guilfoil, Kelsey. "Capote Bids for Fame in Short Tales," *Chicago Sunday Tribune Magazine of Books*, February 27, 1949, p. 3.

Hutchens, John K. "Books and Things," NY *Herald Tribune*, March 1, 1949, p. 15.

Kennedy, John S. "Fiction in Focus," *The Sign*, XXVIII (April 1949), 69.

Kiessling, E. C. "Eight Dreamlike Truman Capote Short Stories," Milwaukee *Journal*, February 27, 1949, Sec. V, p. 4.

Kirkus, XVII (January 15, 1949), 34.

Klein, Alexander. "Nothing Ordinary," *New Republic*, CXXI (July 4, 1949), 17–18.

McG[rory], M[ary]. "Truman Capote, 1948 Literary Find, Reveals Mastery of Mood in These Tales," Washington (D.C.) *Sunday Star*, February 27, 1949, p. C–3.

New Yorker, XXV (March 19, 1949), 98–99.

"Private Light," *Time*, LIII (March 14, 1949), 110, 113.

R., H. "Good Short Stories by Truman Capote," Kansas City *Star*, March 12, 1949, p. 14.

Richardson, John. "New Novels," *New Statesman and Nation*, n.s. XXXIX (April 29, 1950), 492, 494 (492).

Rivette, Marc. "Strange and Short Stories," San Francisco *Chronicle*, March 6, 1949, *This World* Magazine, p. 13.

*Rogers, W. G. "Capote Is Individualist," Richmond (Va.) *Times-Dispatch*, February 27, 1949, p. 9–D. See also Minneapolis *Sunday Tribune*, February 27, 1949, Sec. C, p. 19; Los Angeles *Times*, February 27, 1949, Part IV, p. 6.

Rolo, Charles J. *Atlantic*, CLXXXIII (April 1949), 87–88.

Rosenfeld, Isaac. "Twenty-Seven Stories," *Partisan Review*, XVI (July 1949), 753–755 (755).

"Short Story Writers Show Top Technique," Miami *Herald*, March 20, 1949, p. 4–F.

Terral, Rufus. "Same Voices, Same Rooms," St. Louis *Post-Dispatch*, February 27, 1949, p. 4C.

United States Quarterly Book List, V (June 1949), 161.

Local Color

B., E. H. "Capote Sketches," New Orleans *Times-Picayune*, September 17, 1950, Sec. 2, p. 9.

Barkham, John. "People and Places," Washington *Post*, October 1, 1950, p. 5B.

B[radley], V[an] A[llen]. Chicago *Daily News*, September 20, 1950, p. 38.

Brady, Charles A. Buffalo *Evening News*, September 16, 1950, p. 8.

Cleveland *Plain Dealer*, September 17, 1950, p. 38–D.

Cogley, John. *Commonweal*, LII (September 29, 1950), 610.

D., E. V. "Capote Travel Tales Explicit, Perceptive," Hartford *Times*, September 16, 1950, p. 14.

E., R. "Some Fine Photos in 'Local Color,'" Boston *Sunday Herald*, October 1, 1950, Sec. 2, p. 2.

Engle, Paul. "Sansom Goes Traveling; So Does Capote," *Chicago Sunday Tribune Magazine of Books*, September 17, 1950, p. 4.

F[ineman], M[orton]. "Capote the Traveler," Philadelphia *Inquirer*, September 17, 1950, Magazine Section, p. 44.

Hilton, James. "Travels of Truman Capote," *NY Herald Tribune Book Review*, October 15, 1950, p. 16.

Kirkus, XVIII (July 15, 1950), 405–406.

McGrory, Mary. "Truman Capote, Still the Boy Wonder, Takes a Flight into Non-Fiction," Washington (D.C.) *Sunday Star*, September 17, 1950, p. C–3.

Morris, Alice S. "Pieces for Patchwork," *NY Times Book Review*, September 17, 1950, p. 7.

New Yorker, XXVI (September 23, 1950), 123.

Paris, Rosemary. *Furioso*, VI (Winter 1951), 69–70.

Parone, Edward. "Truman in Wonderland," Hartford *Courant*, December 10, 1950, Magazine Section, p. 14.

Paulding, Gouverneur. "Capote and Places," *Saturday Review of Literature*, XXXIII (October 14, 1950), 28–29.

R., W. San Francisco *Chronicle*, December 3, 1950, *This World* Magazine, p. 28.

S[cott], W[infield] T. "Abroad with Capote," Providence *Sunday Journal*, September 24, 1950, Sec. VI, p. 8.

Sherman, John K. "A Dead Cat for Capote; Gifted Author Goes Doodling," Minneapolis *Sunday Tribune*, September 17, 1950, Sec. F, p. 12.

Sherman, Thomas B. "Reading and Writing—Truman Capote at Home and Abroad," St. Louis *Post-Dispatch*, September 24, 1950, p. 4B.

Sivia, Harry. "Capote's Curious Fillip," Houston *Post*, September 17, 1950, Sec. 5, p. 5.

Stover, Frances. "Mr. Capote Sees the World," Milwaukee *Journal*, September 17, 1950, Sec. V, p. 4.

"Travel, Sort Of," Cincinnati *Enquirer*, September 23, 1950, p. 5.

"Young Writer Sketches Oddities in Travels," Los Angeles *Times*, September 24, 1950, Part IV, p. 7.

The Grass Harp

Allen, Morse. "Youth's Freshness," Hartford *Courant*, October 21, 1951, Magazine Section, p. 18.

Barensfeld, Thomas. "Maturer Capote Emerges in Young Man's New Novel," Cleveland *Plain Dealer*, September 30, 1951, p. 32–D.

Barkham, John. "Capote's New Novel Has Imprint of South," Chicago *Sun-Times*, October 7, 1951, Sec. 2, p. 7. See also New Orleans *Times-Picayune*, September 30, 1951, Sec. 2, p. 8; Buffalo *Evening News*,

September 29, 1951, Magazine Section, p. 7; St. Louis *Post-Dispatch*, October 12, 1951, p. 2C.

Baro, Gene. "Truman Capote Matures and Mellows," *NY Herald Tribune Book Review*, September 30, 1951, p. 4.

Booklist, XLVIII (November 1, 1951), 85.

Bradley, Van Allen. "Slapstick and Fancy in Two Light Novels by Cary and Capote," Chicago *Daily News*, October 10, 1951, p. 44.

Broadwater, Bowden. Providence *Sunday Journal*, September 30, 1951, Sec. VI, p. 8.

"Capote Can Be Funny," *Newsweek*, XXXVIII (October 15, 1951), 101.

Curtis, Anthony. "New Novels," *New Statesman and Nation*, n.s. XLIV (November 29, 1952), 656, 658 (658).

Engle, Paul. "New Capote Novel Sharp and Diverting," *Chicago Sunday Tribune Magazine of Books*, October 14, 1951, p. 3.

Fairall, Helen K. "The Ability to Evoke a Mood, a Sound, a Picture: Capote Has It," Des Moines *Sunday Register*, November 18, 1951, p. 5–A.

"Fantasy from the South—Completely Crazy, but It Has Its Points," Miami *Herald*, October 7, 1951, p. 4–F.

Gannett, Lewis. "Books and Things," NY *Herald Tribune*, October 2, 1951, p. 17.

Goyen, William. "Exquisite, Bizarre, Controlled—New Capote Fantasy Has Message, Charm," Houston *Post*, October 7, 1951, Sec. 4, p. 14.

"*Grass Harp* Lovely Miniature," Hartford *Times*, September 29, 1951, p. 14.

Hayes, Richard. *Commonweal*, LV (October 26, 1951), 73–74.

Heth, Edward Harris. "Witchfire and Old Lace," Milwaukee *Journal*, September 30, 1951, Sec. V, p. 4.

Hicks, Granville. "A World of Innocence," *NY Times Book Review*, September 30, 1951, p. 4.

Jackson, Joseph Henry. "Bookman's Notebook—The Maturing Capote," San Francisco *Chronicle*, November 6, 1951, p. 16. See also Los Angeles *Times*, November 7, 1951, Part II, p. 5.

Jackson, Katherine Gauss. *Harper's*, CCIII (November 1951), 121–122.

John, K. "Fiction of the Week," *Illustrated London News*, CCXXI (December 27, 1952), 1090.

Kingery, Robert E. *Library Journal*, LXXVI (October 1, 1951), 1563.

Kirby, John Pendy. "Fashions in Sinning," *Virginia Quarterly Review*, XXVIII (Winter 1952), 126–130 (130).

Kirkus, XIX (August 1, 1951), 407.

La Farge, Oliver. "Sunlit Gothic," *Saturday Review of Literature*, XXXIV (October 20, 1951), 19–20.

Laski, Marghanita. "Fiction," *The Spectator*, No. 6491 (November 21, 1952), 710, 712 (710).

L[aycock], E[dward] A. "Innocence up a Tree," Boston *Sunday Globe*, October 7, 1951, p. A–23.

Lazarus, H. P. " 'A Blizzard of Butterflies,' " *Nation*, CLXXIII (December 1, 1951), 482.

McGehee, Charles White. "Always Telling Stories," Birmingham (Ala.) *News,* September 30, 1951, Sec. E, p. 6.

Neville, Margaret. "Five Individuals in a Tree House," *Books on Trial,* X (December 1951), 156.

"New Fiction—Natural Rebels," London *Times,* November 8, 1952, p. 8.

New Yorker, XXVII (October 27, 1951), 126.

North, Sterling. NY *World-Telegram and Sun,* October 2, 1951, p. 22.

O'Leary, Theodore M. "Capote's Rebels Live in a Tree," Kansas City *Star,* November 3, 1951, p. 16.

"On the Tree Top," *Times Literary Supplement,* November 7, 1952, p. 721.

O'Neill, Lois Decker. "Looks at Books," Louisville *Courier-Journal,* October 14, 1951, Sec. 3, p. 9.

Paul, David. "New Novels—Childhood Spells," London *Observer,* November 9, 1952, p. 9.

Prescott, Orville. "Books of the Times," NY *Times,* October 2, 1951, p. 25.

Price, R. G. G. "Assorted Fancies," *Punch,* CCXXIII (November 12, 1952), 609.

The Queen, CC (December 3, 1952), 57.

Rolo, Charles J. *Atlantic,* CLXXXVIII (November 1951), 89–90.

Sherman, John K. "Capote Shows Growth in Fable of Tree House," Minneapolis *Sunday Tribune,* October 21, 1951, Sec. F, p. 8.

Shrapnel, Norman. "New Novels," Manchester *Guardian,* November 7, 1952, p. 4.

Spearman, Walter. "Literary Lantern," Charlotte *Observer,* October 7, 1951, p. 16-C.

Thompson, J. M. "Theme and Variations," *Time and Tide,* XXXIII (November 8, 1952), 1308–1309 (1309).

W., B. "Recent Novels," *Irish Times* (Dublin), November 8, 1952, p. 6.

W., S. T. "One-Sentence Review," Columbus (Ohio) *Dispatch,* September 30, 1951, p. F–23.

W[eissblatt], H[arry] A. "Escape from Reality," Trenton (N.J.) *Sunday Times-Advertiser,* November 25, 1951, Part 4, p. 12.

Yaffe, James. *Yale Review,* XLI (Winter 1952), x, xii.

Yeiser, Frederick. Cincinnati *Enquirer,* September 30, 1951, Sec. 4, p. 14.

The Grass Harp (Play)

Booklist, XLVIII (July 1, 1952), 356.

Freedley, George. *Library Journal,* LXXVII (August 1952), 1307.

The Muses Are Heard

"Behind the Curtain with Porgy, Bess," New Orleans *Times-Picayune,* December 9, 1956, Sec. 2, p. 14.

Bess, Donovan. "Capote Rode away from His World of Imagination on the Blue Express," San Francisco *Chronicle,* November 18, 1956, *This World* Magazine, p. 25.

Best Sellers, XVI (December 15, 1956), 326.

Bingham, Mary. "Masterful Reporting of the 'Porgy' Venture in Russia," Louisville *Courier-Journal,* December 2, 1956, Sec. 4, p. 6.

Booklist and Subscription Books Bulletin, LIII (December 15, 1956), 193.

[Brady, Charles A.] "Capote in Russia Proves Good Reporter," Buffalo *Evening News,* November 10, 1956, Magazine Section, p. 8.

Duffy, Joseph M., Jr. "Travels in Russia," *Commonweal,* LXV (December 21, 1956), 318–319.

Feld, Rose. "Porgy, Bess and Mr. Capote on a Junket to the U.S.S.R.," *NY Herald Tribune Book Review,* December 9, 1956, p. 15.

Freedley, George. *Library Journal,* LXXXI (December 1, 1956), 2868.

"Gershwin in Russia," *Times Literary Supplement,* July 5, 1957, p. 408.

Hanlon, John. "Porgy and Bess in Russia," Providence *Sunday Journal,* November 18, 1956, Sec. VI, p. 8.

Holland, E. L., Jr. " 'Porgy and Bess' in Russia Makes Delightful Reading," Birmingham (Ala.) *News,* December 2, 1956, Sec. E, p. 7.

"Home for Dead Cats," *Time,* LXVIII (November 19, 1956), 112.

Hutchens, John K. "Book Review," NY *Herald Tribune,* November 8, 1956, p. 25.

Kirsch, Robert R. "The Book Report," Los Angeles *Times,* December 24, 1956, Part III, p. 5.

Kloss, Gerald. "Porgy Goes to Russia," Milwaukee *Journal,* November 25, 1956, Christmas Books Section, p. 16.

Nordell, Rod. "Russia, Capote, and 'Porgy and Bess,' " *Christian Science Monitor,* November 8, 1956, p. 9.

North, Sterling. "Truman Capote in Darkest Russia," NY *World-Telegram and Sun,* November 9, 1956, p. 27.

Rolo, Charles J. "Capote in Russia," *Atlantic,* CXCIX (January 1957), 86.

Sherman, Thomas B. "Reading and Writing—The 'Porgy and Bess' Company's Visit to Russia," St. Louis *Sunday Post-Dispatch,* December 23, 1956, p. 4B.

Slonim, Marc. "Ivan and Porgy," *NY Times Book Review,* December 2, 1956, p. 20.

Sutton, Horace. "Capote in Muscovy," *Saturday Review,* XXXIX (December 8, 1956), 16.

"Truman Capote on Tour," *Newsweek,* XLVIII (November 12, 1956), 140.

Wilson, Samuel T. Columbus (Ohio) *Dispatch,* November 18, 1956, TAB Section, p. 10.

"With *Porgy and Bess* in Russia," Miami *Herald,* December 9, 1956, p. 4–G.

Wright, Elizabeth Anne. "Invading Red Russia with Truman Capote," Dallas *Morning News,* November 11, 1956, Part 5, p. 15.

Breakfast at Tiffany's: A Short Novel and Three Stories

Allen, Walter. "New Short Stories," *New Statesman,* n.s. LVI (December 20, 1958), 888–890 (889).

"Bad Little Good Girl," *Time,* LXXII (November 3, 1958), 96.

Barensfeld, Thomas. "Truman Capote Offers Long Story, 3 Shorter," Cleveland *Plain Dealer*, November 23, 1958, p. 8–F.

Boles, Paul Darcy. "Legend of Holiday and the Lost," *Saturday Review*, XLI (November 1, 1958), 20.

Booklist and Subscription Books Bulletin, LV (December 1, 1958), 183.

Boyd, John D. *America*, C (January 10, 1959), 434–435.

Culligan, Glendy. "Just Browsing—Innocents but Quite Offbeat," Washington *Post and Times Herald*, November 2, 1958, p. E6.

Curley, Thomas F. "The Quarrel with Time in American Fiction," *American Scholar*, XXIX (Autumn 1960), 552, 554, 556, 558, 560, (556).

D., E. Charleston (S.C.) *News and Courier*, November 23, 1958, p. 13–C.

D., K. *Wisconsin Library Bulletin*, LIV (November–December 1958), 520.

Engle, Paul. "Truman Capote: Lively and Lifelike," *Chicago Sunday Tribune Magazine of Books*, November 2, 1958, p. 3.

"Fuss and Feathers," *Newsweek*, LII (November 3, 1958), 108–109.

Goyen, William. "That Old Valentine Maker," *NY Times Book Review*, November 2, 1958, pp. 5, 38.

Hanscom, Leslie. "Other Stories, Other Qualities: Capote's Continued Brilliance," NY *World-Telegram and Sun*, October 30, 1958, p. 27.

Hogan, William. "A Bookman's Notebook—The Silver-Polished Mr. Capote at Work," San Francisco *Chronicle*, November 4, 1958, p. 27.

Howe, Irving. "Realities and Fictions," *Partisan Review*, XXVI (Winter 1959), 130–136 (131–132).

Hutchens, John K. " 'Breakfast at Tiffany's,' " NY *Herald Tribune*, November 4, 1958, p. 17.

*Kazin, Alfred. "Truman Capote and 'the Army of Wrongness,' " *The Reporter*, XIX (November 13, 1958), 40–41.

Kirkus, XXVI (September 1, 1958), 675.

Kirsch, Robert R. "The Book Report," Los Angeles *Times*, November 10, 1958, Part III, p. 5.

*Levine, Paul. *Georgia Review*, XIII (Fall 1959), 350–352.

Levy, Evelyn. "4 Stories by Capote," Baltimore *Sun*, November 23, 1958, Sec. A, p. 12.

McSherry, Elizabeth A. "Lonely Search," Hartford *Courant*, November 16, 1958, Magazine Section, p. 13.

Maner, William. "Outrageous Story Told Very Well," Richmond (Va.) *Times-Dispatch*, November 23, 1958, Christmas Book Section, p. 16.

*Mayhew, Alice Ellen. "Familiar Phantoms in the Country of Capote," *Commonweal*, LXIX (November 28, 1958), 236–237.

Mercier, Jeanne. "A Lass Named Holly," Milwaukee *Journal*, November 23, 1958, Part 5, p. 4.

*Merrick, Gordon. "How to Write Lying Down," *New Republic*, CXXXIX (December 8, 1958), 23–24.

Moore, Harry T. "Lively Portrait," Boston *Sunday Herald*, November 16, 1958, Sec. V, p. 8.

"New Fiction—Crises and Solutions," *The Scotsman* (Edinburgh), December 13, 1958, Week-end Magazine, p. 11.

New Yorker, XXXIV (November 15, 1958), 241–242.

Nicholson, Geoffrey. "Goodbye to New York," *The Spectator,* No. 6805 (November 28, 1958), 787.

Novak, Rosanna. "New Capote Tone Poem Rings with Artistry," Washington (D.C.) *Sunday Star,* October 26, 1958, p. C–14.

O'Gorman, F. E. *Best Sellers,* XVIII (November 1, 1958), 296.

Peden, William. "On the Short Story Scene," *Virginia Quarterly Review,* XXXV (Winter 1959), 153–160 (157–158).

Robb, Mary. "After Seven Years—Capote Welcome but Not Earthshaking," Pittsburgh *Press,* November 2, 1958, Sec. 5, p. 10.

Roberts, Edwin A., Jr. "Reading for Pleasure—Study in Melancholy," *Wall Street Journal,* October 20, 1958, p. 14.

Rolo, Charles J. *Atlantic,* CCII (November 1958), 171–172.

Rosenberger, Coleman. "Truman Capote: One Long, Three Short," NY *Herald Tribune Book Review,* November 2, 1958, Part I, p. 3.

Rutherford, Marjory. "Capote Scores Again in 'Breakfast' Novel," Atlanta *Journal* & Atlanta *Constitution,* November 9, 1958, p. 2–E.

Schickel, Richard. *The Progressive,* XXII (December 1958), 49.

Schott, Webster. "Exotic Plots by Dinesen, and Characters by Capote," Kansas City *Star,* November 1, 1958, p. 8.

Shapiro, Charles. "Truman Capote at His Best," Louisville *Courier-Journal,* November 23, 1958, Sec. 4, p. 7.

Shaw, J. "In Big City—Complex Picture of Trollop," Birmingham (Ala.) *News,* November 30, 1958, Sec. E, p. 6.

Shrapnel, Norman. "The World of Mr. Capote," Manchester *Guardian,* December 2, 1958, p. 4.

"Uprooted Blooms," *Times Literary Supplement,* December 19, 1958, p. 733.

W[eissblatt], H[arry] A. "Hill-Billy Zombie," Trenton (N.J.) *Sunday Times-Advertiser,* November 2, 1958, Part 4, p. 16.

Zarem, Jack Daniel. "Impressionistic Pieces Set in Off Beat Tempos," Savannah *Morning News,* November 16, 1958, Magazine Section, p. 12.

Observations

B[alish], J[acquelyn]. *Modern Photography,* XXIV (June 1960), 33.

Enequist, Robert L. *Library Journal,* LXXXIV (November 1, 1959), 3464.

"An Eye for a Face," *Times Literary Supplement,* November 20, 1959, p. 678.

Gottlieb, Gerald. "Celebrities in Conventional and Unconventional Poses," *NY Herald Tribune Book Review,* December 13, 1959, p. 8.

Gravett, Guy. "Gimmick and Reality," *New Statesman,* n.s. LIX (January 16, 1960), 80–81 (80).

"Images with a Glow," *Newsweek,* LIV (October 12, 1959), 122, 124.

Jackson, Katherine Gauss. *Harper's,* CCXX (January 1960), 96.

Kirstein, Lincoln. *Nation,* CLXXXIX (December 12, 1959), 447.

"Peeping Tome," *Time,* LXXIV (October 12, 1959), 120.

Popular Photography, XLVI (February 1960), 116.

Preston, Stuart. "Face to Face," *NY Times Book Review,* October 11, 1959, p. 7.

San Francisco *Sunday Chronicle,* November 22, 1959, Christmas Books Section, p. 6.

*Waugh, Evelyn. "The Book Unbeautiful," *The Spectator,* No. 6856 (November 20, 1959), 728–729.

Selected Writings

Boston *Sunday Globe,* February 24, 1963, p. A–57.

Brooke, Jocelyn. "New Fiction," *The Listener,* LXX (July 18, 1963), 103.

Brown, Irby B. "Capote's Works," Richmond (Va.) *Times-Dispatch,* March 17, 1963, p. 6–L.

Griffin, Lloyd W. *Library Journal,* LXXXVIII (January 15, 1963), 222.

*Hicks, Granville. "Literary Horizons—Beware the Wizard Man," *Saturday Review,* XLVI (February 16, 1963), 27.

Hogan, William. "A Bookman's Notebook—An Introduction to Truman Capote," San Francisco *Chronicle,* February 18, 1963, p. 39.

*Hyman, Stanley E. "Fruitcake at Tiffany's," *New Leader,* XLVI (April 15, 1963), 24–25.

"Involved Innocent," *Times Literary Supplement,* July 12, 1963, p. 505.

*Kauffmann, Stanley. "An Author in Search of a Character," *New Republic,* CXLVIII (February 23, 1963), 21–22, 24.

Littlejohn, David. "A Premature Presentation—Capote Collected," *Commonweal,* LXXVIII (May 10, 1963), 187–188.

Malin, Irving. "From Gothic to Camp," *Ramparts,* III (November 1964), 60, 62.

Mayne, Richard. "Supper at Lindy's," *New Statesman,* n.s. LXVI (August 30, 1963), 258–259.

In Cold Blood

Anderson, L. T. "A Classical Non-fiction Novel," Charleston (W. Va.) *Sunday Gazette-Mail,* January 30, 1966, p. 18m.

Appel, David. "Turning a New Leaf—Capote's 'Cold Blood' a Classic of Crime," Philadelphia *Inquirer,* January 16, 1966, Sec. 7, p. 7.

Attaway, Roy. "Capote's New Book Called 'Masterpiece,'" Charleston (S.C.) *News and Courier,* January 16, 1966, p. 5–B.

Bannerman, James. "Capote's Unanswered Questions," *Maclean's,* LXXIX (March 5, 1966), 42.

Barkham, John. "The Bookshelf—True Murder Tale Horrifies and Chills," NY *World-Telegram and Sun,* January 12, 1966, p. 23. See also Rochester (NY) *Democrat and Chronicle,* January 16, 1966, p. 11W; Toledo *Blade,* January 16, 1966, Sec. B, p. 5; San Diego *Union,* January 16, 1966, p. E6; Tucson *Daily Citizen,* January 15, 1966, Magazine Section, p. 27.

Barley, Rex. "Hailed as Masterpiece in Reporting—Truman Capote's 'In Cold Blood,'" *Arizona Republic* (Phoenix), January 23, 1966, p. C–19.

Barnabas. "Looks at New Books," *Together*, X (May 1966), 62–65 (62–63).

Booklist and Subscription Books Bulletin, LXII (February 1, 1966), 505.

Bradford, Nancy. "What Price a Gallows?" Nashville *Tennessean*, January 23, 1966, p. 8–D.

Bunke, Joan. "Capote Work a Triumph of Reporting," Des Moines *Sunday Register*, January 16, 1966, p. 19–G.

"Capote's Dissection of Murder Brilliant New Literary Form," Miami *Herald*, January 16, 1966, p. 7–K.

Carpenter, Don. *Ramparts*, IV (April 1966), 51–52.

*Chester, Alfred. "American Gothic," *Book Week*, January 16, 1966, pp. 1, 19.

Choice, III (April 1966), 111.

Clowes, Molly. "Moving and Unforgettable," Louisville *Courier-Journal*, January 23, 1966, p. D5.

Comans, Grace P. "Tour de Force," Hartford *Courant*, February 6, 1966, Magazine Section, p. 13.

Conaway, James. "Capote Uses New 'Non-Fiction' Form," New Orleans *Times-Picayune*, January 23, 1966, Sec. 2, p. 6.

*Connell, Evan S., Jr. " 'In Cold Blood': A Dissenting Voice," San Francisco *Sunday Examiner & Chronicle*, January 16, 1966, *This World* Magazine, pp. 32, 34.

Cook, Bruce. "A Tragedy Inspires a New Literary Form," *Extension*, LX (March 1966), 45.

Cooke, Robert J. *Social Education*, XXX (April 1966), 307.

Cooley, Franklin D. "Factual Presentation of Brutal Murders," Richmond (Va.) *Times-Dispatch*, January 30, 1966, p. L–7.

Cooley, Margaret. *Library Journal*, XCI (January 1, 1966), 123.

"The Country below the Surface," *Time*, LXXXVII (January 21, 1966), 83.

Cross, Leślie. "Four Murders that Stunned a Town Stir New Horror in an Epic Retelling," Milwaukee *Journal*, January 16, 1966, Part 5, p. 4.

Curtis, Anthony. "Killers on the Farm," London *Sunday Telegraph*, March 13, 1966, p. 22.

Delaney, William E. " 'Terrible and Poignant'—Murder in Cold Blood," Charlotte *Observer*, January 16, 1966, p. 6F.

Derrickson, Howard. "Kansas Family Slaying; Capote Tells All—New Type 'Novel'—It's True," St. Louis *Globe Democrat*, January 8–9, 1966, p. 4F.

Dolbier, Maurice. "In-Depth Report on Brutal Crime in Rural Setting," NY *Herald Tribune*, January 14, 1966, p. 29. See also Buffalo *Evening News*, January 22, 1966, p. B–12.

Doolittle, William. "Murder Needn't Make Sense," Newark (N.J.) *Sunday News*, January 30, 1966, Sec. 7, p. B5.

Dunne, John Gregory. "Fictitious Novel," *National Review*, XVIII (March 8, 1966), 226–229.

*Dupee, F. W. "Truman Capote's Score," NY *Review of Books*, February 3, 1966, pp. 3–5.

Eckstein, George. "Apropos *In Cold Blood*," *Dissent*, XIII (July–August 1966), 433–435.

Enright, D. J. "A Few Dollars and a Radio," *New Statesman*, n.s. LXXI (March 18, 1966), 377–378.

Flanigan, Marion. " 'Non-Fiction' and Fiction Novels," Providence *Sunday Journal*, January 16, 1966, p. N–38.

Floyd, Mary Emma. "Capote's 'In Cold Blood'—New Non-Fiction Novel Probes Killers' Minds," Birmingham (Ala.) *News*, January 30, 1966, p. E–7.

Fournier, Norman. "Book Beat," Portland (Me.) *Sunday Telegram*, January 23, 1966, p. 4C.

Frater, Alexander. "Horror into Art," *Punch*, CCL (March 23, 1966), 436–437.

Fremont-Smith, Eliot. "Books of the Times—The Killed, the Killers," NY *Times*, January 10, 1966, p. 23. See also Indianapolis *News*, January 15, 1966, p. 6; Los Angeles *Herald-Examiner*, January 16, 1966, p. C–6; Omaha *Sunday World-Herald*, January 23, 1966, Magazine Section, p. 24; Wilmington (Del.) *Evening Journal*, January 12, 1966, p. 27; Indianapolis *Star*, January 30, 1966, Sec. 9, p. 5.

Galbraith, John Kenneth. "That Book," *The Reporter*, XXXIV (March 10, 1966), 58.

*Garrett, George. "Crime and Punishment in Kansas: Truman Capote's *In Cold Blood*," *Hollins Critic*, III (February 1966), 1–12.

Gavin, John A. "Crime of Horror," Boston *Sunday Herald*, February 13, 1966, *Show Guide* Section, p. 21.

Godfrey, Dave. "A Member of the Stock Exchange," *Tamarack Review*, No. 39 (Spring 1966), 91–92, 94.

Govan, Christine Noble. "A Serious Study of Two Criminals," Chattanooga *Times*, January 23, 1966, p. 12.

Grady, R. F., S.J. *Best Sellers*, XXV (February 1, 1966), 409–410.

Greene, Tom. *"In Cold Blood*," *America*, CXIV (January 22, 1966), 142, 144.

[Grosvenor, Peter]. "Probing the Minds of Two Killers," London *Daily Express*, March 17, 1966, p. 18.

H., R. "Capote Book Weds Fact with Fiction," Salt Lake *Tribune*, January 9, 1966, p. W 15.

Hamilton, Ian. "Mr. Capote's Varnished Truth," *Illustrated London News*, CCXLVIII (March 26, 1966), 36–37.

Herr, Dan. *Catholic Market*, V (March–April 1966), 34.

*Hicks, Granville. "Literary Horizons—The Story of an American Tragedy," *Saturday Review*, XLIX (January 22, 1966), 35–36.

Hodor, Mary Jean. *"In Cold Blood*," *Ave Maria*, CIII (April 2, 1966), 30.

Holloway, David. "Experiment with a Case of Murder," London *Daily Telegraph*, March 17, 1966, p. 20.

Holmesly, Sterlin. "Capote's 'In Cold Blood'—Sensitive Analysis of Murder, Killers," San Antonio *Express and News*, January 16, 1966, p. 5–H.

H[unter], A[nna] C. "Brilliant Recapitulation of a Tragedy," Savannah *Morning News*, January 9, 1966, Magazine Section, p. 8.

*" 'In Cold Blood' . . . An American Tragedy," *Newsweek*, LXVII (January 24, 1966), 59–63.

Johnson, Pamela Hansford. "An Unbridgeable Gap," *The Scotsman* (Edinburgh), March 12, 1966, Week-end Magazine, p. 5.

*Kauffmann, Stanley. "Capote in Kansas," *New Republic*, CLIV (January 22, 1966), 19–21, 23.

Kennedy, Gerald. "Browsing in Fiction," *Together*, X (September 1966), 53.

King, James. "Turning New Leaves," *Canadian Forum*, XLV (March 1966), 281–282.

Kirsch, Robert R. "Forget Publicity—Read Capote's Non-Fiction Novel," St. Paul *Sunday Pioneer Press*, January 23, 1966, Lively Arts Section, p. 10.

Kirvan, John J., C.S.P. *Catholic World*, CCIII (April 1966), 55–56.

Klauser, Alfred P. "Kansas Tragedy," *Christian Century*, LXXXIII (February 23, 1966), 237–238.

Knickerbocker, Conrad. "One Night on a Kansas Farm," *NY Times Book Review*, January 16, 1966, pp. 1, 37.

Knight, Al. "Killers, Victims Share Death in Cold Blood," Norfolk *Virginian-Pilot*, January 9, 1966, p. B–6.

*Kramer, Hilton. "Real Gardens with Real Toads," *New Leader*, XLIX (January 31, 1966), 18–19.

Kuehn, Robert E. "The Novel Now: Some Anxieties and Prescriptions," *Wisconsin Studies in Contemporary Literature*, VII (Winter-Spring 1966), 125–129 (126–127).

La Fleche, D. "Capote Book Is Touching . . . and Chilling," Albany (NY) *Knickerbocker News*, January 15, 1966, p. B2.

*Langbaum, Robert. "Capote's Nonfiction Novel," *American Scholar*, XXXV (Summer 1966), 570, 572–580.

Laycock, Edward A. "Book of the Day—Capote Rediscovers Four Kansas Murders," Boston *Globe*, January 20, 1966, p. 14.

Leone, Arthur T. "Death Dealing," *The Tablet*, CCXX (March 19, 1966), 332.

*Levine, Paul. "Reality and Fiction," *Hudson Review*, XIX (Spring 1966), 135–138.

Library Journal, XCI (March 15, 1966), 1726.

Lloyd, Eric. "The Bookshelf—Capote's Dissection of a Multiple Murder," *Wall Street Journal*, January 21, 1966, p. 12.

Lowery, Raymond. "Capote on Murder—Such a Thing Did Happen," Raleigh *News and Observer*, January 23, 1966, Sec. III, p. 3.

Lundegaard, Bob. "Kansas Murders in 'Novel' Form," Minneapolis *Tribune*, January 16, 1966, Entertainment Section, p. 6.

McCabe, Bernard. "Elementary, My Dear Man," *Commonweal*, LXXXIII (February 11, 1966), 561–562.

McCormick, Jonathan. "The Non-novel Fiction," *Yale Literary Magazine*, CXXXIV (May 1966), 22.

McNally, Arthur, C.P. "A Time to Die," *The Sign*, XLV (March 1966), 51–52.

Maddocks, Melvin. " 'Dragnet for the Highbrows?' " *Christian Science Monitor*, January 20, 1966, p. 11.

Malin, Irving. "Murder in Kansas," *The Progressive*, XXX (March 1966), 42.

Martz, Russell. "Blood Bath in Kansas," Pittsburgh *Press*, January 16, 1966, Sec. 8, p. 5.

Meacham, William Shands. "A Non-Fiction Study in Scarlet," *Virginia Quarterly Review*, XLII (Spring 1966), 316–319.

Menn, Thorpe. "Most Chilling Is Murder without Apparent Motive," Kansas City *Star*, January 9, 1966, p. 1D.

Miller, Jonathan. "In Cold Print," *The Listener*, LXXV (March 17, 1966), 395.

Moon, Barbara. "Wolfe's New Journalism: Capote's Old Tricks," *Saturday Night*, LXXXI (March 1966), 42, 44–45 (42, 44).

Mortimer, Raymond. "Death on the Plains," London *Sunday Times*, March 13, 1966, p. 33.

von Moschzisker, Felix. "Death, Death, Death, Death—The Killers, Minute by Minute," Philadelphia *Sunday Bulletin*, January 16, 1966, News and Views Section, p. 3.

Muggeridge, Malcolm. *Esquire*, LXV (April 1966), 82, 84.

Nettell, Stephanie. "Reportage," *Books and Bookmen*, XI (April 1966), 24.

Newquist, Roy. NY *Post*, January 16, 1966, p. 43. See also Chicago *Sunday American*, January 16, 1966, Sec. 4, p. 10.

Newton, Virgil Miller, Jr. "Capital Punishment—A Case History," Tampa *Tribune*, January 23, 1966, *Florida Accent* Section, p. 30.

Noll, Keith. *Oregon Journal* (Portland), January 15, 1966, p. 6J.

Novak, Michael. "The Nameless Evil in Strangers," *The Critic*, XXIV (April–May 1966), 64–65.

Pearre, Howell. "Will Success Spoil Truman Capote?" Nashville *Banner*, January 14, 1966, p. 24.

Peckham, Stanton. "Non-Fiction Novel Superb Reporting," Denver *Sunday Post*, January 9, 1966, *Roundup* Section, p. 39.

Perley, Maie E. "The Book Scene—Capote's Breathtaking Drama Is Solid Literary Achievement," Louisville *Times*, January 19, 1966, p. A 11.

*Phillips, William. "But Is It Good for Literature?" *Commentary*, XLI (May 1966), 77–80.

Pryce-Jones, David. "Murder Most Foul," *Financial Times* (London), March 15, 1966, p. 19.

Rose, Lloyd. "Curl Up and Read," *Seventeen*, XXV (May 1966), 190.

Rosenfeld, Arnold. "Murder," Houston *Post*, January 16, 1966, *Spotlight* Magazine, p. 8.

Ryley, Robert. "Br-r-r-r-r-," *North American Review*, n.s. III (March 1966), 32–33.

S., M. A. "Capote Turns Reporter," Trenton (N.J.) *Sunday Times-Advertiser*, January 23, 1966, *Pleasure* Magazine, p. 8.

S., W. "Sordid Murders Get Keen Literary Analysis," Columbus (Ohio) *Dispatch*, January 16, 1966, TAB Section, p. 19.

Semple, Robert B., Jr. "On a New Lit'ry Tack with Mr. Capote," *National Observer*, January 17, 1966, p. 25.

Sister M. Lucille, C.D.P. *Catholic Library World*, XXXVII (March 1966), 484.

Smith, Miles A. "Novelist Capote Turns Reporter," Baltimore *News American*, January 16, 1966, p. 7F. See also Memphis *Commercial Appeal*, January 16, 1966, Sec. 5, p. 6.

Smith, Patricia Barbara. "Books & More Books," Detroit *Free Press*, January 9, 1966, p. 5–B.

Steiner, George. "Happening at Holcomb," *Manchester Guardian Weekly*, XCIV (March 24, 1966), 10.

Stella, Charles. "Capote Holds a Literary Mirror to Our Society," Cleveland *Press*, January 21, 1966, *Showtime* Magazine, p. 15.

Stern, Richard. "Book of the Week—A Work of Art: 'In Cold Blood,'" Chicago *Daily News*, January 16, 1966, *Panorama* Section, p. 8.

"Story or Documentary?" *The Economist*, CCXVIII (March 19, 1966), 1140.

"Stranger than Fiction," *Times Literary Supplement*, March 17, 1966, p. 215.

Symons, Julian. "In Cold Print: The Anatomy of a Killing," London *Evening Standard*, March 15, 1966, p. 10.

Tanner, Tony. "Death in Kansas," *The Spectator*, No. 7186 (March 18, 1966), 331–332.

Thomas, Sidney S. *"In Cold Blood*—A Total Triumph," Atlanta *Journal and Constitution*, January 16, 1966, p. 2–B.

Thorpe, Day. "Capote's Crime Story a Brilliant Recreation," Washington (D.C.) *Sunday Star*, January 16, 1966, pp. D–1, D–3.

Tinkle, Lon. "Reading and Writing—Death in Kansas: Capote's Mosaic," Dallas *Morning News*, January 16, 1966, p. 8E.

Towne, Tony. *Motive*, XXVI (May 1966), 38–39.

Tracy, Robert. *"In Cold Blood,"* *Southern Review*, n.s. III (January 1967), 251–254.

°Trilling, Diana. "Capote's Crime and Punishment," *Partisan Review*, XXXIII (Spring 1966), 252–259.

°Tynan, Kenneth. "The Kansas Farm Murders," London *Observer*, March 13, 1966, p. 21.

Valenzuela, Elvira. "Capote Turns Reporter in Study of Murders," Wichita *Sunday Eagle* and Wichita *Beacon*, January 16, 1966, p. 2C.

°Wade, H. V. "Truman Capote: A Study in Scarlet," Detroit *News*, January 23, 1966, *Book News* Section, pp. 1, 10.

Weeks, Edward. *Atlantic*, CCXVII (March 1966), 160.

*West, Rebecca. "A Grave and Reverend Book," *Harper's*, CCXXXII (February 1966), 108, 110, 112–114.

White, Terence de Vere. "Professional Job," *Irish Times* (Dublin), March 12, 1966, p. 8.

Williams, Harold A. "Capote's Study of Murder," Baltimore *Sun*, January 16, 1966, Sec. D, p. 5.

⟨ Yarborough, Tom. "Reading & Writing—A Novelist Turns to Sensational Fact in a Masterpiece of Reporting," St. Louis *Sunday Post-Dispatch*, January 16, 1966, p. 4C.

⟨ Yurick, Sol. "Sob-Sister Gothic," *Nation*, CII (February 7, 1966), 158–160.

Zaslove, Jerald. "*In Cold Blood:* More Cultural Cool-Aid," *Paunch*, No. 27 (October 1966), 79–84.

A Christmas Memory

Barkham, John. "World of Books—A Memory of a Small Boy's Christmas Recalled by the Man He Has Become," NY *World Journal Tribune*, November 3, 1966, p. 38.

Best Sellers, XXVI (December 1, 1966), 322.

Jackson, Katherine Gauss. *Harper's*, CCXXXIII (December 1966), 132.

McKenzie, Nancy K. "End Papers," NY *Times*, November 17, 1966, p. 45.

D. REVIEWS OF STAGE PRESENTATIONS BY CAPOTE

The Grass Harp (Opened, March 27, 1952,
Martin Beck Theatre, New York City)

Atkinson, Brooks. "First Night at the Theatre," NY *Times*, March 28, 1952, p. 26.

————. " 'The Grass Harp,' " NY *Times*, April 6, 1952, Sec. 2, p. 1.

*Bentley, Eric. "On Capote's *Grass Harp*," *New Republic*, CXXVI (April 14, 1952), 22–23.

*Beyer, William H. "The State of the Theatre: The Season Climaxes," *School and Society*, LXXV (May 24, 1952), 323–327 (323–324).

Bolton, Whitney. " 'Grass Harp' Translated into Entrancing Dramatic Terms," NY *Morning Telegraph*, March 29, 1952, p. 3.

Brown, John Mason. "Seeing Things—With the Magic Gone," *Saturday Review*, XXXV (April 19, 1952), 43–44.

Chapman, John. "Capote's 'Grass Harp' Screwiest Play in Town but Excellently Staged," NY *Daily News*, March 28, 1952, p. 77.

Colby, Ethel. "On Broadway: 'Grass Harp' Is Play of Elusive Charm," *Journal of Commerce* (NY), March 31, 1952, p. 9.

Coleman, Robert. " 'The Grass Harp' Brings Theatre a New Talent," NY *Daily Mirror*, March 28, 1952, p. 40.

Dash, Thomas R. " 'The Grass Harp,' " *Women's Wear Daily*, March 28, 1952, p. 41.

Field, Rowland. " 'The Grass Harp,' " Newark (N.J.) *Evening News*, March 28, 1952, p. 56.

Gassner, John. "Broadway in Review," *Educational Theatre Journal*, IV (October 1952), 221–226 (225–226).

Gibbs, Wolcott. "The Wind in the Willow," *New Yorker*, XXVIII (April 5, 1952), 62, 64 (62).

"The Grass Harp," Newsweek, XXXIX (April 7, 1952), 94.

Hawkins, William. "'Grass Harp' Comes to Broadway," NY *World-Telegram and Sun*, March 28, 1952, p. 25.

Kerr, Walter. *"The Grass Harp," Commonweal*, LVI (April 25, 1952), 68–69.

————. "'The Grass Harp,'" NY *Herald Tribune*, March 28, 1952, p. 12.

————. "New Play with Beauty, Style, and Little Drama," NY *Herald Tribune*, April 6, 1952, Sec. 4, pp. 1, 2.

McClain, John. "'The Grass Harp': Here Grows Biggest Tree since Brooklyn," NY *Journal-American*, March 28, 1952, p. 18.

Marshall, Margaret. "Drama," *Nation*, CLXXIV (April 12, 1952), 353.

*Nathan, George Jean. "The Grass Menagerie," *Theatre Arts*, XXXVI (June 1952), 17–18.

"New Play in Manhattan," *Time*, LIX (April 7, 1952), 77.

Sheaffer, Louis. "Curtain Time—Truman Capote's 'Grass Harp' Original, Humorous, Charming," Brooklyn *Eagle*, March 28, 1952, p. 10.

Watts, Richard, Jr. "Two on the Aisle—Truman Capote's Romantic Fantasy," NY *Post*, March 28, 1952, p. 55.

Wyatt, Euphemia Van Rensselaer. *Catholic World*, CLXXV (May 1952), 147–148.

The Grass Harp (Revival opened, April 27, 1953, Circle in the Square Theatre, New York City)

Clurman, Harold. "Theater," *Nation*, CLXXVI (May 16, 1953), 421–422 (421).

Coleman, Robert. "The Theatre—Circle in the Square Offers Interesting 'Grass Harp,'" NY *Daily Mirror*, April 29, 1953, p. 38.

F., J. P. "'The Grass Harp,'" *Women's Wear Daily*, April 29, 1953, p. 61.

Hawkins, William. "Theater—'Grass Harp' Plays at Circle in Square," NY *World-Telegram and Sun*, April 28, 1953, p. 17.

Hayes, Richard. "The Stage—Modest Proposals," *Commonweal*, LVIII (May 22, 1953), 179–180 (179).

Hewes, Henry. "Broadway Postscript—The Sweetest Music the Other Side of Fourteenth Street," *Saturday Review*, XXXVI (May 16, 1953), 30–31 (30).

Hoffman, Theodore. "Broadway off Broadway," *Theatre Arts*, XXXVII (July 1953), 16.

Kerr, Walter F. "Off Broadway—The Grass Harp' Revived at Circle in the Square," NY *Herald Tribune*, April 28, 1953, p. 24.

S., J. P. "First Night at the Theatre," NY *Times*, April 28, 1953, p. 32.

Sheaffer, Louis. "Capote's 'Grass Harp' Ably Revived by Circle Players," Brooklyn *Eagle*, April 28, 1953, p. 6.

Wyatt, Euphemia Van Rensselaer. *Catholic World*, CLXXVII (June 1953), 228.

The House of Flowers (Opened, December 30, 1954, Alvin Theatre, New York City)

Atkinson, Brooks. "Theatre: Truman Capote's Musical," NY *Times*, December 31, 1954, p. 11.

Bolton, Whitney. "'House' Treasure-Filled, but Book Hurts Show," NY *Morning Telegraph*, January 1, 1955, p. 3.

Chapman, John. "'House of Flowers' Rich in Music and Exotically Set and Costumed," NY *Daily News*, January 1, 1955, p. 17.

Colby, Ethel. "Entertainment—On Broadway," *Journal of Commerce* (NY), January 3, 1955, p. 9.

Coleman, Robert. "The Theatre—'House of Flowers' Offers Sensational Sincopation," NY *Daily Mirror*, January 1, 1955, p. 14.

Cooke, Richard P. "The Theatre—The Bright and the Drab," *Wall Street Journal*, January 3, 1955, p. 10.

Dash, Thomas R. "'House of Flowers,'" *Women's Wear Daily*, January 3, 1955, p. 44. See also *Daily News Record* (NY), January 4, 1955, p. 47.

Field, Rowland. "Along Broadway—'House of Flowers' Is Sprightly Romp," Newark (N.J.) *Evening News*, December 31, 1954, p. 10.

Gibbs, Wolcott. "All Sizes and Shapes," *New Yorker*, XXX (January 8, 1955), 62, 64, 66–69 (62).

Hewes, Henry. "Broadway Postscript—Romanoff and Capote," *Saturday Review*, XXXVIII (January 15, 1955), 31.

Kerr, Walter F. "Theater—'House of Flowers,'" NY *Herald Tribune*, December 31, 1954, p. 8.

McClain, John. "'House of Flowers': Capote Play Often Vulgar," NY *Journal-American*, December 31, 1954, p. 14.

"New Musical in Manhattan," *Time*, LXV (January 10, 1955), 34.

Newsweek, XLV (January 10, 1955), 62.

Sheaffer, Louis. "'House of Flowers' Spotty Musical Set in West Indies," Brooklyn *Eagle*, December 31, 1954, p. 4.

Watts, Richard, Jr. "Two on the Aisle—Musical Tour of a Caribbean Isle," NY *Post*, December 31, 1954, p. 10.

Wyatt, Euphemia Van Rensselaer. *Catholic World*, CLXXX (March 1955), 469.

Zolotow, Maurice. "The Season on and off Broadway," *Theatre Arts*, XXXIX (March 1955), 22–23, 90–92 (90–91).